THE WAY WE WERE

The History and Genealogy *of the*
Town of Collins
Erie County, New York

BECOMING A TOWN

Volume One
Pre-Historical through 1852

Linda and Charlie Munro

HERITAGE BOOKS
2008

HERITAGE BOOKS
AN IMPRINT OF HERITAGE BOOKS, INC.

Books, CDs, and more—Worldwide

For our listing of thousands of titles see our website
at
www.HeritageBooks.com

Published 2008 by
HERITAGE BOOKS, INC.
Publishing Division
100 Railroad Ave. #104
Westminster, Maryland 21157

Copyright © 2008 Linda and Charlie Munro

All rights reserved. No part of this book may be reproduced or transmitted in any form or by any means, electronic or mechanical, including photocopying, recording or by any information storage and retrieval system without written permission from the author, except for the inclusion of brief quotations in a review.

International Standard Book Numbers
Paperbound: 978-0-7884-4759-4
Clothbound: 978-0-7884-7454-5

DEDICATION

There are no persons more fitting to dedicate this book to than the Natives who roamed free, surviving by means that their European counterpart looked upon as primitive and the Pioneers who braved the wilderness to set forth the parameters of what would become the town of Collins. Many of today's people look upon the absence of a vehicle or the lack of a home computer as a hardship. They give little consideration to the technology which is now a way of life, when just a few short years ago, that same technology was but a mere dream. Even less consideration is granted the Natives, whose land was unconscionably annexed, their ways of life obliterated by a mixture of fear and compassion. Nor is the pioneer who walked hundreds of miles with his family at his side, a musket and axe upon his back to start life in the midst of the wilderness that existed, acknowledged.

There are also four persons who have helped to shape my way of thinking, my quest for knowledge and my love of history; recognition: my Mom: Louise Nunweiler, my Pa, Lloyd Linde, my aunt, Bernice Linde and last, but by far not least Erasmus Briggs, author of the first history of the town of Collins. To my family, who's unyielding love and faith in me has led me to believe that each and every one of those who helped shape our history deserve to be memorialized for the part that they inadvertently played; and to Erasmus Briggs, a man who put his heart and soul into the preservation of our history yet died a pauper lying for years in an unmarked grave, I salute you.

It is to these people, the Native American who yielded his way of life so that our ancestors could survive by the means of which they were accustomed; to the pioneers, the persons who had the foresight of what could be and the courage and perseverance to make it happen; to my family who unwittingly led me down this path and to Erasmus Briggs, who years after his death has finally received the recognition due him, that we dedicate this book.

INTRODUCTION

    I have spent all but nine months of my fifty some years as a resident of the town of Collins. My husband, Charlie has lived in this town nearly a dozen years. Charlie realized early in our marriage that I was captivated by not only the history of the town of Collins, but also by the people who made this area into a town. Although I had never imagined that my marriage would bring a partner into my research, it has. Without the assistance he has given me, this book would still be in the research stage rather than the publication stage.

    My interest in the town's history began in the late 1970's when I picked up a copy of *The Collins Story*, an authorized history requisitioned by the town of Collins in 1962. Some years earlier, I had located an 1883 copy of the *History of the original town of Concord: being the present towns of Concord, Collins, N. Collins, and Sardinia, Erie County, New York* while traveling through the western states with my family. We had located a yard sale while in Nevada, and I spent twenty five cents on an original edition of the book. While ten of us were crowded into a nine passenger station wagon, traveling across country, I spent my time reading the book. Upon reading the 1962 history I realized that the two histories did not mesh well.

    The newer history utilized a great deal of information from the original history, but it was reported inaccurately, with both a biased and prejudiced twist unbecoming of both history and historian. I do not mean to fault Mr. Painter for his work, but rather open the eyes of my reader to the bias that appears time and again in historical renditions.

    As a means of proving the point I previously made, let us take a brief look at one of the all time great American historians, Francis Parkman. Parkman's histories are true adventures in which he partook. His financial situation allowed for him to journey westward, living the tale he would put to paper. These histories give us a first hand look into life in a past era. However, these histories have also created historical figures who suffer from similar illnesses as Parkman himself suffered. Although I am not qualified to diagnose Mr. Parkman, I lean towards the belief that the man was a manic depressive, it also appears that the great Warrior Pontiac of whom he wrote, seemed to suffer a similar illness. Despite this transference, without the chronicles of Francis Parkman, a great piece of history would be lost to us now.

Having made a study of Parkman during my college years, I realize that I need to make all possible attempts to remain unswayed by bias and/or transference. In the hopes that this document will remain a work of actuality, my husband, Charlie and I debate each issue which will be laid within the following text. Should I feel sympathy towards the Natives, Charlie will choose to sympathize with the colonist. We will debate these issues until we feel we have come to terms with a more accurate picture of what our research has taught us.

Here lies yet another issue of which the reader needs to be aware; the history is only as accurate as the research material. Here again, we can utilize Parkman as an example. After spending a great deal of time researching in Canada, Parkman would learn only after his history had gone to press, that a town had actually kept two sets of records; one set displaying actual events, the other fictionalized. Without this knowledge before hand, Parkman had utilized the fictional set of records in his research, learning of the transgression too late to alter what he had already written.

My research of Parkman has taught me a valuable lesson. Due to the period of time we are researching and thus writing in an effort to preserve an accurate history, many times we have relied on secondary sources alone. In order to avoid utilizing fictitious materials within our history, we have made every effort to locate three viable sources that agree on specific issues without using an identical source of reference. While this may sound quite easy, it is without doubt a time consuming portion of our research. It is important to point out that at times, we have been truly unable to locate information which does not utilize identical sources.

Whenever possible, we have used primary sources. However, it is advisable to our readers that they understand that even primary sources can be biased or inaccurate. In regards to census materials, those who have researched their family genealogy may be well aware that one person may appear to be missing in one Federal Census, while being listed twice in following census reports. As an example of the difficulties we have happened across, I will relay to the reader a brief story about researching my own family history.

Relying on the microfilmed sources of Church of Latter Day Saints, I have been able to locate members of my family prior to their immigration to America. Researching the Welter family, I would learn that when my rather large family of ancestors left their native country, their last name was spelled Welter, upon arrival into the United States, members of the same family became known as Welter, Welters, Walter and Walters. Misspelling of the name continued on birth, death and marriage records. In fact, my great-great grandparents are buried in a cemetery not far from where I live. My great-great grandfather's headstone reads, Johan Welter, my great- great grandmother's headstone reads: Catherine Walter wife of John. As if that was not enough to cause mass confusion during the research of my family history, I was led to the great-grandparents, the family Ales [pronounced Ellis].

I was forced to rely on my Mother's story concerning the spelling of my grandmother's maiden name. According to my mother, my grandmother's maiden name was spelled A-H-L-ES, yet every document I located spelled the name A-L-E-S. In order to research this dilemma, I began contacting every family I could locate within a fifty mile radius of my grandmother's home with the last names of Ales and Ahles, and as luck would have it, I located the answer.

Eager to assist me, a man who not only knew my grandmother, happened to know a tale concerning the family name. According to this man, while living in Germany, my great-great grandfather's name was spelled Ahles. He was a wealthy land baron and had decided to divorce his wife, leaving her and their children penniless. [Please note, my family was Catholic, therefore, I had difficulty accepting this until I researched German history.] My great-great grandfather remarried, eventually bringing his new family to America. The three children left behind set a goal to reunite with their father. My great-grandfather would be the first of the three children to arrive in America.

To separate his family from those of his step-siblings, my great-grandfather was said to have changed the spelling of his name from Ahles to Ales. [NOTE – the pronunciation of the name is Ellis.] However, the spelling alone did not hinder problems in deciphering family. He would soon learn that his family was also often becoming confused with a neighboring family named Ellis; therefore, his next act was to change the pronunciation of his last name from Ellis to Olleese. While I have yet to confirm the story in its entirety, I have since been able to locate members of my family previously concealed to me by searching census records using the later pronunciation.

I hope this little tale has provided our readers with two facts; first a family history no matter how inaccurate, is as important to the family genealogy as each individual; second and more important is that history reflects on the people as much as people reflect upon history. Therefore, both Charlie and I have made it our goal to add the family genealogies of as many of the pioneers of the town of Collins as we are able.

Returning to the issue of primary sources, imagine Fox News having been the only primary news source available for our research. Rupert Murdoch has purportedly changed the way news is reported. [Murdoch is said to willingly utilize his newspaper/news broadcast lines to pursue his own agendas, a highly documented claim for those of you who do not believe.] Claims state that not only do his journalists report every news item with a Republican twist, but they are also allowed to broadcast out and out untruths. In years to come, history may be unwittingly altered by those who, without the knowledge of Murdoch's purportedly biased news coverage, use these implied untruths as a primary source.

Although many may feel that newspaper reports from the past are more accurate, let us review a series of articles which appeared in the New York Sun beginning on August 25, 1835 and continuing through September 16, 1835 and the effects that this hoax had on America. This series of articles was reportedly reprinted from a *'nonexistent'* magazine named The Edinburgh Journal of Science. The first installment of the hoax began on page two of the New York Sun under the headline: *Celestial Discoveries.*

According to the article, astronomer Sir John Hershel had set up a *new fangled* telescope in South Africa which allowed him to not only discover new planets and new solar systems, but life on the moon! Daily articles described herds of lunar Bison, Blue Unicorns, upright beavers, crude huts and the use of fire, but it didn't stop there. Descriptions of furry winged people only four feet tall, sapphire temples with gold colored roofs and lilac pyramids caused the great author, Edgar Allen Poe to cease writing his newest novel because; *'there was no way his fiction could equal the momentous truth.'*

Even though the articles finally revealed themselves as a publicity hoax, the circulation of the New York Sun never again dwindled. What would happen if only a portion of those articles had been retained? Would we, still today be wondering about life on the moon, or would we be wondering what had occurred between 1835 and 1969 when men first walked on the moon to altar what we had believed to be true? The fact is, even primary sources need verification and we hope that our research has provided verification of every factor that appears in this history as truth.

We would like to pass on one final aspect before delving into the actual history of the town of Collins. The Seneca Tribe and the Iroquois Confederacy hold a great aspect in regards to our history. Unfortunately, we must rely on the written information passed to us by French and British explorers as well as accounts as written by the white man, for the Natives passed their history from generation to generation orally. Most realize how distorted such a history can become, with each new person in line to pass the history to the next. Therefore, although we realize that without writing the history of the Native American, we cannot truthfully tell the story of our area; we will, for the most part, be relying on a biased rendition as written by the white man. We can only hope that our own banter in regards to debating the issues that we have discovered during our research will eliminate at least a portion of the bias from the truth that we wish to tell.

We have but one further piece of information to pass on to our readers. In order to offer an accurate portrayal of the history of the town of Collins, we felt it necessary to revisit the history of our country in general. Without this knowledge, our local history would be lacking a great deal of information pertinent to the people and history of this town. Instead of reiterating what nearly every American citizen already knows, we have chosen to tell an alternate tale; a tale while indeed factual, is much less likely to be taught in our schools. While our readers may not have previously learned these historically significant specifics, those who lived during these eras more than likely held this knowledge, and with this knowledge they acted and reacted, thus leading us, our town and our people to where we are today.

              Linda & Charlie Munro
              Collins Center, NY
              Town of Collins, Erie County
              © October 2008

THE WAY WE WERE
THE HISTORY & GENEALOGY OF THE TOWN OF COLLINS, ERIE COUNTY NY
VOLUME ONE
PRE-HISTROY THROUGH 1852

The Layout

The history of the town of Collins, where does one start? There are many places one could truly begin; from the viewpoint of the first European explorer and/or missionary in the area, at a point where the area had a designated county and township, at the point of the first white settlement in the area, at a point that closest resembles what we now know of the area, being the original establishment known as the town of Concord, at the point when the town of Collins was established, at the point when the actual boundaries of the present day town of Collins existed, or at the beginning?

There exists a literal ton of documentation which both directly and indirectly affects both the area known as the town of Collins and the people who first settled the area. We have collaborated and compromised on this issue, finally deciding on a specific outline to follow. Granted, most readers are familiar with at least a portion concerning the discovery, exploration and eventual settlement of America. However, we have also concluded that many only know the briefest scenario consisting of Columbus' discovery to the arrival of John Smith and eventually the Pilgrims, to the Revolutionary War. Additionally, we have learned that fewer know the actual history of New York State or the influence of the Native American upon the European settlers. Consequently, we have decided to begin this history with first an overview of the discovery, exploration and settlement of America. From this point we will move into a more in-depth history of New York State and hopefully an accurate portrayal of the Iroquois Confederation but more specifically the Seneca Tribe. Finally, we will approach the settlement of the area now known as the town of Collins.

While we cannot promise a book that you cannot put down, we can affirm an accurate portrayal of the area and the people who made it what it is today. Due to the wealth of information we feel is required to fulfill this compact, this will be the first of four volumes which will include both historical and genealogical information regarding both the area and our forefathers. We hope you will enjoy and learn from our research.

REMEMBERING COLLINS
THE LAST ONE HALF CENTURY

I grew up in a different era, an era that probably includes you, the reader. We did not have computers as research aids or news affiliates; we watched one of three local television stations that broadcasted news twice a day, once at six PM and again at eleven PM. For more in-depth news, we relied on either the bigger city newspapers, the Courier Express or the Buffalo Evening News. For local coverage we relied on the weekly newspapers from the surrounding villages of Gowanda or Springville.

Our spare time was spent outdoors, no matter what the weather. Our games were geared by our own imagination and physical endurance. We had no video games, no VHS or DVD players by which to watch movies or record what we may not have time to watch on television. In fact, if we missed a show, we more than likely missed the show! There were live television shows which caused a great deal of inadvertent mistakes to be aired. Saturday morning lineups included not only cartoons, which by the way were truly cartoons not the strange anime of today. There were also child and family oriented shows such as My Friend Flicka, Fury and Sky King. Every Sunday evening, our entire family would gather in front of the black and white television set to watch the Ed Sullivan Show.

One of this country's greatest losses was the *Blue Laws*, laws originally enacted by seventeenth century Puritans to enforce a morality code, specifically designating what could or could not be done on the Sabbath. The Blue Laws forced families together on at least one day per week, Sunday. Families could not drive to the Mall or go shopping, instead they spent time together. For some that meant church services, for some it meant huge family gatherings, for some it meant both. As the restrictiveness of the blue laws lessened, families began to drift apart, to go their separate ways; their single day of togetherness was no longer bound by law.

I also grew up at a time when there was a single employed person, when fathers worked to support their families and mothers stayed home tending to the home and children. There was no need for babysitters or day care centers on a regular basis. For those rare families who had a single parent or both parents were employed, children would stay at the neighbor's where the parents knew they would be safe. We were not latch key kids, we were safe kids. At the age of five, a child could walk from one end of town to the other to pick up supplies at the local grocer or pick up the mail at the local post office. There was no need to worry whether or not the child would make it to their designated errand and home again, there were adults along the way who made sure the children were safe. Those days are long gone. No longer does everyone know their neighbors, no longer do people watch out for one another. People move from town to town, holding up in their apartment or home, sometimes never as much as saying hello to their neighbor.

In the tiny hamlet of Collins Center, the Collins Center School district tended to the educational needs of all of our area children. As the population grew, a second site was added in the hamlet of Collins. By the late 1950's, the school district was no more. Children, who had grown up knowing every other child who resided within the town limits, were now forced to make new friends and attend new schools. The district was divided into three districts, with a portion attending Gowanda Central School District, a portion attending North Collins School District and the remainder attending the Springville Griffith Institute School District. The school building in Collins Center became an elementary school tending to grade levels kindergarten through sixth grade, with students being bussed to Springville thereafter. The Collins School building also became an elementary school, with the older students bussed to the Gowanda School District. The loss of the Collins Center school district meant that townspeople had suddenly lost their means of contact with one another.

For a while the population of the area continued to expand, creating the necessity for two portable classrooms to be added to the Collins Center Elementary School. Alas, that growth became stifled; the extra classrooms became a hindrance rather than a necessity. Eventually Springville would bus children from sixth grade, leaving Collins Center Elementary to service only to the fifth grade. As time went by, more classes were bussed to Springville, leaving but kindergarten, first and second grade in Collins Center. Finally, as all good things come to an end, so did any schooling in the Collins Center School building, it eventually closed and the building was sold to the Collins Correctional Facility, yanking yet another source of pride from the area residents. The Collins School building would suffer the same fate, but the town residents would benefit from the sale of the building which now houses the L. K. Painter Community Center and the local Veteran's Administration Office.

Religion, another great part of the Collins Community would also change over the past fifty years. Every Friday, those of us who were of the Free Methodist or Catholic religion were bussed from our school to the local church where we would receive our weekly religious instructions. This included approximately eighty percent of all of the elementary school students, the remaining ten percent were allowed a free time on Friday afternoons. It was during one of our religious education classes where a few of us were preparing to make our First Holy Communion that I recall learning of the execution of our President.

We were reciting our prayers when the Priest entered the church from the vestibule. His head was down, his hands were clasped together and he appeared to be crying. We all quieted, waiting for the Priest to make his way to the back of the church where we sat. His voice was cracking as he said; *'Could we all bow our heads in prayer, our President has been shot.'* I will never forget that day. John Kennedy was my hero, yet I cannot tell you why. I suppose that he was by far the only President that would capture not only my head, but my heart. To me, John F Kennedy was living proof of the American Dream.

I recall listening to adults discuss Kennedy, before his death. Not once did I hear the normal arguments that politics so often brought forth amongst even the best of friends. John Kennedy, young, handsome, wealthy, well spoken, had united the country for the first and only time that I can remember during my entire life. Even during the *Cuban Missile Crises* United States residents rallied behind their President. I remember crying at the church, and later how solemn everyone was at my home. For the first time I could ever remember businesses all across the country shut down, my mother was actually home during the work week.

My mother always had things to do when she was at home, but not during the time of the Kennedy Funeral. She sat before the television, something I had never recalled her doing prior, to watch the funeral procession, just as I am positive millions of other Americans did. The assassination of John F Kennedy was a senseless tragedy; it robbed Americans of not only their President, but also a chance for Americans to continue living as *one nation under God*. Still today one image stands clear in my mind, an image that causes chills and creates tears, the image of John Kennedy Jr. saluting the casket carrying his father's remains.

As I mentioned earlier, religion was a big part of the Collins community. When I was growing up, the religious communities had grown enough to assess the need for larger churches. The Free Methodist Church, once a tiny building was replaced by a huge church allowing for ten times the original parishioners to attend. In 1955, just prior to my birth, a Catholic church was built in Collins Center, making it the second

Catholic Church within the limits of the town of Collins [the first being St. Joseph's Roman Catholic Church in the town of Collins side of the village of Gowanda]. Additionally, there existed the United Methodist Church in Collins Center proper and the Collins Friends Meeting in Collins proper, all other churches within the town of Collins existed on the Collins side of the village of Gowanda. A multidenominational church also existed on the grounds of the Gowanda Psychiatric Center. Residents of the town were allowed to attend mass at this facility as well as any of the other churches of their choice.

Today, with the exception of the Churches on the Collins side of the Village of Gowanda only two Churches exist in the town of Collins; the Collins Friends Meeting and the United Methodist Church. The more recently built Free Methodist Church is now home to Blossom Garden School, a private school for those with learning disabilities. The Catholic Church stands empty, a sad reminder of days gone by.

Collins Center was named due to its location, the hamlet, once a thriving village is located directly in the center of the town of Collins. Even in the days of my youth, Collins Center was a hustling bustling community. The Collins Co-Op, [known locally as the Milk Plant] a milk processing plant stood as long as I can remember, employing a great many local citizens. It grew and expanded, but needless to say, the Environmental Protection Agency stepped in, demanding that the plant add a million dollars worth of renovations to keep the pollution spewing from the smoke stacks and dumping into Clear Creek to a minimum. Even after all of the renovations had been made, there was still more necessary to pass the strict codes of the EPA. Eventually the plant closed, leaving an empty building and taking the only real jobs the town offered.

While Collins Center nearly always boasted hosting two general stores, by my time we had been reduced to one. Of course, you could go in to purchase anything from milk to toilet paper to the gift card and wrapping paper, things one always seemed to be in need of. There had been a store owned by the Tarbox family for generations, although the store had closed before my memory can recall it existing. I have never known the reasoning behind its closure. Today the building holds the Collins Center Post Office. The store of my youth had been Mugridge's Store, although locals simply referred to it as Charlie's. The store was owned by the third generation Mugridge child, Charlie and his wife Martha during my days. The building that housed the store was originally built by Charlie's grandfather, Joseph Mugridge an emigrant from England who settled first in Utica and then Buffalo before finally removing to Collins Center where he built his store in 1864.

Joseph and his wife Susanna Hill Mugridge operated the store, leaving it to their only son Edward. Edward continued the store's operation, finally retiring and leaving it in the capable hands of his only son, Charles. Charlie and Martha had no children, when it came time for them to retire the building was closed; Charlie's store became yet another memory in a long line of memories crowding the minds of local residents.

The hamlet of Collins also had at least one general store, during my time that store belonged to Art Herrington. I remember trudging up the steep cement steps leading into Herrington's store, going through the few aisles with the barest of necessities, the huge candy display case and the entire back section devoted to the processing of meat. Whether it was dressing deer for local hunters or cutting the choicest cut of steak, grinding the freshest hamburger or making his exclusive sausage, Herrington's was the most dependable meat market around. As time went by, thus the store business dwindled, eventually causing the closure of yet another Collins icon.

The building housing Harrington's store has been converted into a private dwelling. The building housing Mugrdige's store was remodeled. It now hosts three apartments and a single business, Cat's Corner, a family hair care boutique.

Hair care seems to have always been in the hearts of area residents. As long as I can remember, various persons have run beauty salons from their homes locally. Although we did have our own Barber shop run by Roland Smith a descendent of one of Collins forbearers, Augustus Smith. [See genealogy of Christopher Smith]. I recall the barber pole sitting outside his shop which was located next to out post office at the time. Rolly would be outside when business was dwindling, an apron covering his clothing, sweeping the sidewalk in front of the shop. As happened with most local businesses, his only son did not want to follow in his father's footsteps and when it came time to retire, the barber shop was closed. Both the barber shop and the early post office building are now private residents. I often wonder if those residing within realize the history that surrounds them.

Both Collins and Collins Center had their share of service stations. As once was the norm, these service stations hosted the auto mechanic and the gas pumps. Two such service stations existed in Collins Center, one in Collins. The Esso station was a glass block building situated on the corner of Route 39 and School Street, directly across from the intersection of

Route 75. My biggest recollection of that specific service station includes a car not stopping at the stop sign at the corner of Route 75 and 39, but rather driving directly across the street, through the garage and hanging out the back of the building. Of course, the business lost its life when the state deemed it necessary to widen route 39, taking trees, front yards and the Esso Station.

The Texaco station remained through the 70's, but eventually the new trend of traveling caught up with the local small businesses and it too closed. Eventually a small general store with self serve gas occupied the building until 1987 when necessary repairs outweighed the advantage of housing a business or renting the upstairs apartments any longer. The building was demolished and an empty lot remains as a memory of what was.

Despite rules and regulations, despite traveling well away from home to secure work, Mopert's in Collins has remained steadfast. The gas pumps are no longer a part of the business, but the auto repair portion is still booming. Hopefully, the service station will remain well into the twenty first century.

Of course, Collins Center held other businesses during my youth. The saw mill which began business during the late 1800's hung on until the early 1960's. Later a tractor dealership occupied the building, but small farms have slowly evaporated from the landscape; thus the business could not succeed. Today, the building has been converted into two apartments, but the general outlines of the original sawmill remains as a stark reminder of yesteryear.

Across the street from the sawmill was the town's hardware store. I recall cutting across lots to get to the hardware store before closing on a Saturday afternoon to purchase a pound of two penny nails for my father's newest construction project. The hardware business ended in the late 1960's. This building, as all of the others, has also been converted into an apartment building.

The only thing that has held steadfast throughout the area is that of the restaurant; although these businesses now occupy former taverns. On the site of the old VFW post just west of Jennings Road now stands Rolling Hills restaurant. Over the years, many bars have started business on the location, but it seems that the fire which consumed the original VFW post in the late 50's also cursed the property, nullifying any future attempts to build and succeed with an establishment concerned with the business of alcohol. Maybe the forbearers of the town of Collins, especially those involved with the temperance movement have somehow staked claim to the area, guaranteeing failure where alcohol is concerned.

    The Collins Center Hotel, owned by Jim and Leone Mason for many years was a focal point of Collins society. Every Friday night one found cars lining both sides of route 39 and North Division as well as a filled parking lot, as locals and outsiders came to enjoy the Collins Center Hotel's famous fish fry. On Saturday's live bands played from nine until one and the building would be filled to overflowing. Those days ended well before the Mason reign. A few establishments have since rented the property, but no one has held the success that Jim and Leone Mason held, nor has anyone offered the townsfolk a place of entertainment such as the Mason's had offered.

    During the mid 1800's, Collins Center was by far the place to live, work and play. Residents were self sufficient. Industry was plentiful. During my younger days, the old timers would often say it was the decision of the railroad to come into Collins rather than Collins Center that killed the town. Yet the town remained a bustling place for nearly a century. Things change, people die or move, we have become a mobile society hooked on modern technology, and places like the hamlets of Collins and Collins Center have suffered a slow paralyzing death similar to the small towns of Route 66.

    Yet, all that was during my youth still calls to me; memories of my own past have yet to die. They make me wonder, will we, at some time in the future regain our control or will the vast suburbs continue to spread out until they have totally devoured the small towns of America? If the forbearers of this area were able to time travel what would they feel of their hardships which created this town? What I wonder more than anything at all is why did they choose this area to begin with? Was it simply the fact that the Holland Land Company opened the area up to them, or was there more?

    Recently, my husband and I choose to make a trip *back in time*, so to speak. One of the things that we had noticed is that a great portion of those who moved to the town of Collins had moved from Danby, Rutland County, Vermont. Citizens of Danby made up a portion of the *Green Mountain Boys*, those historical fugitives who fought the system in order to reclaim land that should have already legally been theirs. It would seem that after the great battle that had been waged between New York State and the Green Mountain Boys, no one would have wanted to venture into the realm of New York, but venture they did.

They came in groves, on foot, in oxcarts, in sleighs, in any manner of transportation they could find; they came. They moved westward, across the short distance of Vermont into New York State, following old Indian trails which would become the *road of the pioneer*. They left the luxury of their frame dwellings, their finished and furnished homes. They left their family and friends, their communities which had years prior, grown from the wilderness to literally start from scratch, beginning once again.

I had an old map of Danby, which included Danby proper in 1869. The first thing I noticed was the names of that era seemed to coincide with the pioneers of Collins, what I would learn in that the 1869 map of Danby was still fairly easy to follow. The growth of Danby ceased with the westward migration, yet the town continued to thrive; maybe not as greatly as it once had, but most of what was, still remained.

I walked into the hamlet of Danby and found myself realizing that Danby had by far done more then lend its people to the town of Collins, it had lent a bit of itself. Today, technology has left Danby a dieing area, just as it has allowed Collins to die. The pioneers that had left this area had not only left a piece of themselves behind, they had taken with them the memories of Danby which would help to shape the town of Collins.

Europeans Visit America
COLUMBUS' VOYAGES

Albeit the children's poem 'In 1492', acquaints us with the epic voyage and discovery of Christopher Columbus, yet the true story behind that discovery is often neglected. Christopher Columbus, born Cristoforo Columbo in Genoa, Italy in 1451, was the son of a wool merchant and weaver. He would begin his navigational career at the age of thirteen. Historians have referred to Columbus as a great navigator, a visionary, a mystic. Whatever one chooses to believe about Columbus, all can be assured that the man, unlike the peers of his era who were certain that the world was flat, knew in his heart that such a theory was implausible, thus it was indeed possible for a ship to sail westward to reach the Spice Islands. Christopher Columbus, being a true visionary, was determined to prove his theory was correct.

Columbus had, it seems, been born by design. His foresight would have led to a severe blunder had he been born a mere century earlier. By the time Columbus had purged his theories of improprieties, the timing for adventure was ripe. The Renaissance had served to inaugurate exploration of new worlds into the minds of many Europeans. By the fifteenth century, exploration opportunities had grown scarce throughout Europe while social and economic conditions throughout the same European nations extended a felicitous need to discover new worlds.

After having approached the monarchy of many other lands, Columbus took his theory to the Catholic Monarchs King Ferdinand and Queen Isabella of Spain. His proposition was simple, if the Monarchs would finance his expedition; he would give them new lands, spice, money and most important, new people to join their Christian religion. The Spanish Monarchs agreed to finance the expedition. Columbus set forth from Palos in Southern Spain on August 3, 1492 with three ships the Santa Clara, better known by its nickname, the Nina, the Pinta and the Santa Maria, of which Columbus was Captain.

This was a time of little technology; there were no giant engines or engine rooms, no state rooms. The ships were in fact, nothing more than extremely large sail boats, their huge masts held high so that they would be powered by the wind. At the top of the mast was a large basket, called the crow's nest, in which a sailor would climb to view the ocean, in search of land or other ships. Sailors worked in shifts measured by the use of a half hour glass. Even during their allotted time to sleep, they slept on deck.

Navigational equipment included a compass, a traverse board and a log line. The traverse board was a simple board equipped with pegs and a series of holes. The upper section of the board was marked with the thirty two points of the compass. At the end of each half hour watch, the sailor would place a peg into the hole of the compass bearing which had been completed during that half hour. Each half hour would be marked by these pegs, the first pegs being inserted into the holes closest to the center of the compass markings on the board, moving outward with each progressing half hour. At the end of four hours, the placement of the pegs told the navigator the direction in which he had traveled.

The bottom portion of the traverse board told the navigator how fast the ship had traveled. Again, there were rows of holes, at the center of which were a set of eight pegs tied on strings. These holes were divided into two parts, during the first two hours the holes on the left side of the board were used; the holes on the right side were used during the second two hour period. At the end of each half hour, the sailor in charge would mark the hole which represented the knots-per-hour that the vessel had been traveling. [For example, if a ship were traveling at two knots-per-hour, the peg would be placed two holes from the center, counting from left to right.]

A log-line was used to determine the speed of travel. This instrument was comprised of a flat piece of wood known as the log, which had been weighted at the bottom edge in such a manner to allow the log to float. The log line was wound on a spool, known as a log reel, so that the log could be reeled out after it had been thrown into the water at the aft, or rear of the ship. The friction of the water would hold the log in place as the ship sailed away from it.

On the log line itself, knots were tied at a distance of seven fathoms, or six feet. As the ship sailed away from the log, the sailor would count the number of knots that passed over the rail in roughly, thirty seconds. [Most historians agree that the sailor actually used a twenty eight second glass to calculate the knots per hour that the ship traveled.] By counting the knots that had passed over the railing, the sailors were able to roughly calculate the speed of the ship. At the end of each four hour period, the officer in charge would transcribe the information from the traverse board to a slate, and the process would begin all over. At the end of the day, the navigator would use this information to chart the progress of the ship on his maps, while the ship's Captain used the same information to write his daily log, a detailed record of the voyage.

A food supply was necessary, and each ship would be loaded with barrels of both fresh water and wine to drink. Their food source would include barrels of salted fish as well as live animals and poultry which would be killed and cooked as needed.

On October 12, 1492, land was spotted from the crow's nest of the Pinta. Columbus would call this land San Salvador, today the land is known as the Bahamas. The next island to be visited by Columbus and his crew would become known as Cuba. Leaving Cuba, Columbus would loose one of his ships when on November 22, Martin Alonzo Pinzon, Captain of the Pinto sailed off on his own, in search of an island the Natives had called *Babeque* where, according to his Native guides, there was much gold. On December 5, with only the Santa Maria and the Nina, Columbus would reach what he referred to as Hispaniola, better known as the Dominican Republic and Haiti, claiming the land for Spain. Since Columbus was convinced he had landed in the Indies, he called the natives Indians. As a gesture of friendship, Columbus presented the Natives with cheap gifts such as bells.

The flag ship Santa Maria became grounded on a reef in Hispaniola on Christmas day. The remains of the ship were used to build a fort, which Columbus dubbed *La Navidad* [Christmas]. Being left with only the tiny ship Nina, Columbus was forced to leave approximately forty of his men at the fort from which he sailed away on January 2, 1493. Four days later, the Pinta would be spotted.

On January 16, Columbus with both the Nina and the Pinta left Hispaniola to return to Spain. On February 14, the ships were met by a fierce North Atlantic storm and separated. The captains of each ship thought the other lost. Columbus arrived back to his home port of Palos more than seven months later on March 15, 1493. A few hours later, the Pinta also arrived at the home port. Columbus' historic journey had come to a close, but his ideal had yet to have been met. Columbus was still in search of a western route to China.

It is important to interject a piece of prevalent information at this point. Many will be stunned by this disclosure. Others will simply sigh, with a *yeah, I heard that, so what* attitude. While the rest will simply close their eyes to another factor which lies in a long line of Papal 'over-authority' and abuse. The *Papal Bull of May 4, 1493* [a formal proclamation issued by the Pope] granted all property of the New World to be divided amongst Portugal and Spain, with the largest portion belonging to Spain. Furthermore, all inhabitants of this new land were to be subdued and brought to the Catholic Faith. This proclamation was to include not only the islands that Columbus had discovered, but also any main lands and islands yet to be discovered.

Columbus began his second voyage to the west on October 13, 1493, bringing with him horses, sheep and cattle, the first European livestock that would reach America. His second voyage took but twenty one days. The crew would travel the area for two weeks before returning to Hispaniola on November 22. During these explorative travels, Columbus would chart the present day Leeward Islands, Virgin Island and Puerto Rico. Upon his return to La Navidad, Columbus would find the fort destroyed and his men dead. Relying solely on the testimony of Chief Guacanagari, Columbus learned that his men had taken to arguing amongst themselves over women and gold. A portion of the men thus abandoned the fort; the remaining men raided an inland tribe, kidnapping women. Under retaliation, the tribesmen killed the remaining Spanish crew, burning the fort as a final reprisal.

Abandoning the area of the first fort, Columbus anchored at another location on Hispaniola. It was a swampy area with poor resources and an equally poor harbor where he created the colony of La Isabella. Continuing his exploration of the area in search of a passage to China, Columbus fell gravely ill. His health forced him back to Isabella where he took up his post as Colonial Governor. Damned by the rift of the colonist, Columbus would soon learn that his relationship with the Natives had become flawed to the extent that war loomed over the colony. The Spaniards undoubtedly held a technological advantage over the Natives, therefore once war broke out, those Natives who were not killed were taken captive and forced to work searching for gold. By the time the war had ended, supplies had dwindled to a dangerous low. On March 10, 1496, Columbus set out for Spain, arriving on June 8.

The third voyage of Columbus began on May 30, 1498 in the company of six ships. Three were to sail directly to Hispaniola with supplies for the colonist; the other three were to begin exploration. A new problem assailed Columbus on this voyage, a lack of wind. Those aboard the ships of exploration were becoming board and worried, their fresh water supply rapidly dwindling. With the return of the winds on the 22nd day of July, Columbus ordered a change of course, heading towards the island of Dominica. Shortly thereafter, another island was sighted. The devoutly Christian Columbus seeing three hills rising from the island thought of the Holy Trinity, thusly naming the island Trinidad.

Columbus' health rapidly failing, forced his return to Hispaniola where he found the colonist revolting against his rule. Although he agreed to what he felt were humiliating terms in order to quell the revolt, word of Columbus' previous abuse of power had reached Spain. Isabella and Ferdinand thusly appointed Francisco de Bobadilla royal commissioner, with powers surpassing those of Columbus. Upon de Bobadilla's arrival at the colony, Columbus was placed under arrest and in October of 1500, returned to Spain in shackles.

By 1502, Columbus, despite his health afflictions made a final attempt to locate a passage to China. On May 11, unwelcome in the colony of Hispaniola, in the company of his brother Bartholomew and his youngest son, Fernando, Columbus gathered four old ships and one hundred forty men to begin his last voyage. Arriving in Santo Domingo on June 29, 1502, on the verge of a hurricane, Columbus found himself denied shelter. Taking shelter in a nearby estuary shortly before the hurricane struck, Columbus' ships survived with only moderate damage, while twenty other ships had been sunk in the harbor. Through storms and attacks, Columbus lost ship by ship, finally becoming marooned on Jamaica, where he would remain with the survivors of the expedition until June 29, 1504, when Diego Mendez, one of Columbus' captains returned with a small ship to rescue them. His last voyage, ended with his safe return to Spain on November 7, 1504.

Columbus died in Valladolid, Spain on May 20, 1506; his eldest son Diego dying twenty years later. The two bodies were interred side by side. Diego's widow, realizing the hard fought battle of Columbus petitioned the Spanish Court to move both bodies to Santo Domingo, Hispaniola. The petition was approved and both bodies were removed from Spanish soil and re-interred at the cathedral in Santo Domingo where they would remain until 1795. After the French captured Hispaniola, the Spanish, relying on old records, removed the remains of Columbus, burying them at Havana, Cuba. Once Cuba had won her independence, the bones would again be removed, this time they would be returned to Seville, Spain and interred at a cathedral in Seville, where one can still visit the tomb of Columbus; or can they?

In 1877, while working on repairs at the cathedral in Santo Domingo, under the left side of the altar a box containing human bones was discovered. The name Christopher Columbus was engraved on the box. The question now arises, where exactly is Christopher Columbus buried? Historians have been left to ponder the true location of Columbus' body ever since the discovery was made.

Some argue that since the right and left perspective would depend upon which side of the altar one was facing; the remains moved to Havana in 1795 were the remains of Diego rather than Christopher Columbus. Some historians argue that the bones never left Valladolid in the first place; others argue that the correct body was moved from Santo Domingo to Havana, but the wrong bones left Havana, therefore Columbus is buried in Havana. No matter where the bones were or are interred, as the case may be, there is one final note of importance which should be documented. Notations have been found which indicate that a portion of the bones that were removed to Seville were given to the City of Genoa for its quadri-centennial celebration of 1892, which has led to another historical argument, just whose bones were given to Genoa? The arguments continue amongst historians even today.

Europeans on the New Continent

Henry VII, has been quoted as disclosing his regrets at having allowed a rival power to be first to discover a continent full of both advantages and resources. To this discourse, John Cabot, a Venetian residing in England suggested to the King that while lands had been discovered in the south, it was quite possible that such lands also existed in the north. With a commission of discovery, granted by Henry VII, John Cabot and son, Sebastian, on the same premise as Columbus used in seeking a shorter route to the Indies, arrived at the continent of North America in approximately 1495.

The Cabot's exploration brought them to the coast of North America, their first discovery being the islands of Newfoundland and St. John. From the borders of Labrador, Canada the duo continued southward along the coast to what would become Virginia. Father and son made a second voyage in 1498. Extreme cold hindered the idea of exploring further than the coastal lands during their second trip to America. Prior to returning to England, the Cabot's reiterated their original route going as far south as where the southern extremity of present day Maryland is located.

In 1501, Gasper Cortereal, under the auspices of Portugal made a similar voyage, the results of which were a partial survey of the southern coastline and the capture of fifty natives who would be taken to Portugal and sold as slaves.

Twenty four years later, Francis I, King of France would begin a protest against the Papal Bull which made the newly discovered territory a possession of Spain and Portugal. John De Verranzana sailed towards the new world with four ships and enough provisions to last eight months. They arrived near the present city of Willingham, North Carolina, traveling northward to the New England coast. De Verranzana made notes of the Natives who stood on the shore watching them; he also noted their kindness when the crew was forced to go ashore for water. Despite the kindness they were shown, De Verranzana and his crew noted two women, one old, one young, each burdened with three children standing near the coastline. The crew grabbed one of the children before leaving. It has been noted that they had considered taking the younger women, but feared her screams would allure to their own capture.

James Cartier sailed from France on April 20, 1534, to both explore the new world and ready it for colonization. After surveying the coast of Newfoundland, Cartier returned to France with a favorable report. In May of the following year, he again set sail for the New World, this time with two ships and one hundred and twenty men. Entering into the St. Lawrence, Cartier and his crew sailed on meeting from time to time with the natives along the way. Upon reaching the village of Hochelaga, Cartier climbed a hill overlooking the vast island. He would name this hill Mount Royal [Montreal].

From this hill he noted vast forest as well as great fields planted in corn which surround the Indian Village. It is believed that at this time, it was the Iroquois who possessed the land of Cartier's exploration. The Village itself was curious to Cartier. It was round, with three ramparts; an embankment built around a city for defensive purposes, there was a single gate which was shut with piles, stakes and bars. Cartier noted that the enclosure was approximately two rods high [thirty three feet], with ladders along the inside, and piles of stone for defense. Within the village were fifty houses, all built of wood and covered in bark. Each house was divided into many rooms. Despite all he saw, it was what the natives told him that would cause Cartier to plant a cross and shield, emblazoned with the arms of France, claiming the land for the country of France, naming this new place, New France.

The native told of three great fresh water lakes, of which no man had ever found an end. It continued with information of a great river on which one would sail for a month before arriving at a land of no ice or snow. The inhabitants of the warm area were perpetually warring and the curious dress of the people was similar to that of the French. They heard of endless supplies of apples, oranges, limes and nuts. The native also told Cartier of great stores of gold and copper. Despite this tale, Cartier's report included the absence of gold and precious stone, and a stormy landscape. French colonization was deferred.

It was during this exploration that the foundation was laid for the troubles between the French and the Iroquois, thus leading to the French and Indian Wars. Troubles were initiated when upon his return trip to England; Cartier took three Chiefs against their will. The Chiefs were of both the Algonquin and Huron Tribes.

Francis De La Roque, Seigneur de Roberval, was granted a charter by Francis I in 1540. He was told to take one of every art and every trade and set forth a colony on New France. Cartier was commissioned by the King to be chief pilot of the expedition.

Volunteers did not come to the beckoned call to settle the wilderness, and Roberval was forced to find his new settlers in France's prisons and work houses. While Roberval built a fort at Newfoundland, Cartier continued down the St. Lawrence, building a fort at Quebec. By 1543, the settlements were abandoned and the so-called settlers had returned to France.

England, although behind in exploration was not out of the race; in 1584, Queen Elizabeth I sent Sir Walter Raleigh to locate lands on which a settlement could be based. The ships anchored off the coast of North Carolina at Roanoke Bay. The following year a settlement of one hundred and eight persons would begin on Roanoke Island and start a mystery which has plagued historians for over four hundred years.

A group led by Sir Francis Drake attempted colonization of the island from 1585 through June 19, 1586. The following year, another group of one hundred seventeen settlers, led by Governor John White attempted again to colonize Roanoke. This group of settlers added to their numbers by the birth of the first white person upon American soil, Virginia Dare, granddaughter of Governor White. It is written that a portion of the problems suffered by this settlement came from arguments amongst their ranks which overtook the necessity of planting crops and building shelters before winter fell upon them. Supplies dwindled. Governor White left Roanoke Island the First English colony in America on August 27, 1588 to return to England for supplies and man power.

Deterred by obstacle after obstacle, John White was unable to return to Roanoke until the spring of 1590. Upon his arrival he found the settlement in ruins and the settlers gone leaving no trace. The only clue left were carvings on trees. The letters C-R-O was found on one tree, the word C-R-O-A-T-O-A-N was found carved into another. What had happened to the settlers? This is a mystery that has plagued historians for more than four centuries. Without graves, or corpses, the only clue that became clear was that the settlers were not annihilated by massacre or plague.

Looking at the facts, we have learned that two Native tribes resided in the area of Roanoke Island, the Roanoke's and the Croatians'. Were the settlers attacked by the Croatians' and forced to flee? Could it be that the Croatians' kidnapped the settlers? Had the settlers run out of every provision thus heading to the Croatians' for help? Was it possible that the settlers banded together heading inland in hopes of locating other settlers or explorers to help them? Over the years, no trace was ever found which indicated what had actually occurred, thus the mystery and debate.

Some historians feel that the settlers simply abandoned their settlement in search of other settlers, meeting their demise along the way. Some feel they were kidnapped and assimilated into a local tribe. One of the best theories we have located was that the group fled to their neighboring Native brethren for help, becoming assimilated into a tribe. The factors leading us to this belief are as follows; a tribe of Native Americans residing somewhat north of Roanoke held strange physical anomalies. This tribe was lighter skinned than most area natives. Members had blue or gray eyes, rather than the brown eye color prominent amongst the Native Americans. The final anomaly being this tribe spoke only English. While the mystery of the Roanoke settlers may never be solved to the satisfaction of every historian, these aforementioned facts speak multitudes in solving the mystery. ....

Although Queen Elizabeth I had fought to colonize the new world, no successful English Colonies existed at the time of her death, March 24, 1603. Ironically, exploration of the new world beginning in the year of the Queen's death would lead not only to successful English Colonization, but also to the formation of the Holland Land Company and the eventual settlement of Western New York. Bartholomew Gosnold, in 1603 would take one ship and thirty men on his quest for a closer passage to the new world. Upon his return to England, Gosnold's findings spread like wildfire. Soon, merchants of Bristol, UK, sent two ships to follow up on what Gosnold had reported.

Upon their return, King James I would succumb to petitions, granting patents to Sir Thomas Gates, George Somers, Richard Hakluyt and their associates granting all lands in the New World from the 34th degree of North latitude [area of Virginia] to the 45th degree of North Latitude, [area of Maine], which would include all islands within one hundred miles of the coast. The territory was thus divided; the northern territory became known as New England was granted to the Plymouth Land Company. The Southern territory became known as Jamestown and was granted to the London Land Company.

Samuel Champlain, mariner and partner in a company formed at Rouen for the purpose of colonization, directed an expedition which led to the colonization of Quebec in 1603. By the time Champlain sailed into the area, it is believed that the Algonquin were now its occupants.

Champlain felt the unrest created by Cartier's exploits could be used to his advantage. Knowing that the tribes were upset with the British, Champlain figured he would unite with the Canadian Natives, easily overtaking both the British and the American native. Eager to set his plan in to motion, Champlain gathered with the two tribes, and advanced southward into Iroquois territory. Meeting the Iroquois near Ticonderoga, their enemy split, allowing Champlain to stand as their leader. To witness the white man taking the position of power was indeed a shock for the Iroquois, but when shots rang out from either side of the progressing Iroquois, they were at first shocked by the sound, then stunned to see that three of their chiefs had fallen; two were dead and the third was severely injured. This would become known as the Battle of Fort Ticonderoga; the first recorded battle ever to be fought on American soil. The Iroquois may have lost the battle, but the war had just begun. Provided guns and ammunition by both the Dutch and the English, they became apt students in weaponry thusly increasing their territory by over two thousand miles.

The first unsuccessful attempt to colonize Northern Virginia dampened the spirits of the entrepreneurs for a short while. A later colonization attempt however would prove fruitful. Settlers landed on Jamestown Island on May 14, 1607, this would become the first successful English colony in the New World. When Captain Smith returned to England in 1609, he left behind two hundred fourteen settlers. Although the settlers had lived at Jamestown for nearly two years, they paid little attention to their agricultural needs, a mere thirty to forty acres of land was being used for crops. The settlers of Jamestown depended upon the natives or imports from Europe to sustain them. The winter following Smith's departure found even minimal necessities scarce, leaving one hundred and fifty four settlers to fall subject to *'starving time.'*

The first in-depth exploration of what would become New York State was accomplished by an Englishman in the employ of the Dutch East India Company. On September 30, 1609, Henry Hudson entered the waters of New York, ascending the river which would come to bear his name, traveling the length of the river all the way to the area which would become Albany. Along the way, inland explorations would be made, some as far as what would become Troy. Hudson did far more than explore and chart the area, his camaraderie with the natives not only formed a bond, but allowed for Hudson to note the condition of the Native.

Hudson noted that the Native was curious and friendly, providing that he was treated in the same manner. However, one of the youthful natives stole aboard the vessel, stealing a pillow and clothing, the strangeness alluring him. When a member of the crew saw the Native retreating, his arms filled, he shot, killing the young native. In a scuffle to retrieve the stolen items, a second native was killed. The friendly, helpful native turned on the European encroacher, ambushing them as they neared a bend in the river. It was thusly noted that the Native was a friendly lot unless the white encroacher harmed them in either reality or as an assumed harm. Unfortunately for the natives, who ambushed Hudson, they shot with bow and arrow and the white man returned fire with canon and musket, killing nine additional natives in the volley. Despite this tragedy, a tense relationship continued between Hudson, his crew and the Natives.

Hudson was the first documented European to introduce the Native to what would become the *red man's curse*, alcohol. While docked near the present city of Albany, Hudson opened his ship to the curious natives. [The location has been inferred by various historians who have studied Hudson's journal.] With knowledge of alcohol *'loosening one's lips"* Hudson offered the Native an abundance of wine and *aqua vita* [we have yet to determine exactly what type of alcohol this is]. When one of the intoxicated Native Chiefs stumbled and fell, the rest fled Hudson's ship, fearing for their lives. The following day, curious as to the condition of their brethren, the Native once again boarded Hudson's ship, only to find their Chief totally recovered. Collecting their Chief, the Natives returned to land, returning to the ship later in the day with gifts of tobacco and venison. After a celebratory meal, the Natives left, with the exception of the chief who had seemingly acquired a taste for what would later be termed, *fire water* by the Native.

In 1613, an expedition lead by Captain John Smith explored the New England area, both along the coast and the interior. When Smith returned to England, the Captain of his accompanying ship declared that he had decided to stay behind. Once Smith had sailed away, Captain Hunt enticed a number of Indians to come aboard his ship then set sail for home, his kidnapped cargo headed to the slave market. Although few Europeans knew of the kidnapping, they did realize that the northern Native was suddenly to be feared. Although the hostilities had been noted, the area was still determined to be colonized, and those fleeing England due to religious persecution were taken to New England rather than Jamestown.

The Pilgrims, who fled their Mother Land to avoid religious persecution, would be the first group to settle the New England area. Pastor John Robinson first led the Pilgrims from Scrooby, England to Leyden, Netherlands, the country from which they would sail to America. From the start, this group appeared doomed. First, the second boat that was to sail with them had problems, *the Speedwell* thus remained behind. Similar to their Jamestown counterpart, the Mayflower Pilgrims brought with them a woman close to birth. However, this child could not wait to reach land and was born at sea. Elizabeth and Stephen Hopkins set foot upon the land of the New World with a new child, Oceanus. Their journey took over one month [from November 9 to December 11, 1620] and their ship landed them far north of the Jamestown settlement they had anticipated joining. [Note, it has been written that although the pilgrims thought they were heading to Jamestown, their Captain was actually sailing towards the mouth of the Hudson River and missed by one degree, thus landing in Plymouth.] The Pilgrims landed in a strange land in the winter, too late to plant crops and desperately in need of shelter. The Natives to the north appeared to regard them as encroachers rather than friends.

When the Pilgrims set foot upon American soil, they could not imagine the hardships that they would endure. Within three months of landing at Plymouth Rock, one half of the colonist had died. One of the most famous deaths would be that of the wife of William Bradford who drowned at what would become Provincetown. Both colonist of the time and many historians feel that the drowning was more a suicide than accident. Speculation of suicide includes the desolation the young woman felt in the new country. Their food supply was scarce. The neighboring Nauset Tribe kept the community under close scrutiny, at one time leaving a group of arrows at the settlement as a warning of their unfriendly nature. The colonist had arrived too late in the season to plant crops. Shelter was inadequate at best. Others believe that the woman had had an affair soon after her arrival to the new world, leaving her plagued by guilt. Accident or suicide, we will probably never know for certain.

Despite the unfriendly attitude of the neighboring tribe, the pilgrims were welcomed by one native brave, Samoset. His assistance kept many alive, yet the Pilgrims felt leery having the man in their camp so frequently, especially when they were making plans for their own future. Despite being repeatedly sent away by the Pilgrims, Samoset would return. One day, Samoset brought with him a young, English speaking brave named Squanto who told a remarkable tale. When Captain Hunt explored the area, he took more than information back to Europe. Hunt had kidnapped Squanto and several of his tribesmen, selling them at a European slave market. Squanto had worked his way through Europe to London, finally retuning on one of the many ships that made their way across the Atlantic, finally returning home. A vague understanding of the underlying dissention was finally realized by the Pilgrims; yet nothing would be done to hinder subsequent attacks on any American colonists.

It is important to understand that the American aborigine tribes assimilated prisoners into their culture. Some feel that the assimilation was meant to assist the grieving family in the loss of their loved one by presenting the family with a new member. Others feel that the assimilation made for a stronger, more vital tribe. Either way, it has been noted throughout the history of the United States that prisoners of the aborigine were much better off than the prisoner of the white man. While some prisoners were killed by their Native captor, most it appears became assimilated into the tribe, such as the case of Mary Jemison. At the same time, the native prisoners of the white man were tortured, killed or sold into slavery in far off nations. With this in mind, we shall travel to the Jamestown settlement.

A portion, but not all, of those within the Jamestown settlement had created a fund to educate the Indian children. The education was meant as a twofold project, to both civilize and Christianize the native. Entire native families had been brought into the settlement and given homes. Most of the white settlers however, despised the native, verbally abusing them, accepting their silence as subservience, while anticipating that the entire native tribe would accept this *cultural suicide*.

Robert Beverly in his *The history and present state of Virginia* tells us that the white man became lulled into a false sense of security, while the native learned every detail of the settlement's condition, including; when and where they traveled, their use of arms, their strengths and weaknesses. So secure was the white man that he loaned his boats to the native, not realizing that visits to other tribes meant consultation on a planned attack.

It was the morning of Good Friday, March 22, 1622. The native moved freely through the settlement, bringing gifts of wild deer, turkey, fish and fruit, feasting before their attack. Not one white man was aware of the plan, nor were they prepared to be slaughtered by their own tools. This massacre left one third of the population or 347 settlers dead. The question that has never been answered concerning *the*

Good Friday Massacre is; was this a cold hearted maneuver on the part of the Native American, or were they simply retrieving the members of their own community; members that they felt had been assimilated into the white man's culture?

While the Pilgrims were the first noted Puritan sect to colonize America, other groups would soon follow. Having fled England due to religious persecution, one would not suspect the Puritan a persecutor, yet they were. The Puritans held very little tolerance to persons of other religions; especially those who held views opposing their own. Roger Williams, founder of Providence, Rhode Island and the first Baptist Church in America was banished from the Boston colony. Anne Hutchinson, an outspoken wife and mother who had immigrated to America with her family, held great influence over men and women alike, but when she openly denounced the church, she too was banished. Banishment was a mild punishment compared to what the Puritans dealt those of the Quaker Religion, who were fined whipped, imprisoned and hanged.

Lawrence and Cassandra Southwick and their children were repeatedly punished by authorities for their religious beliefs and for harboring Quakers. Their eldest son Josiah was *'sentenced to be whipt at a cart's tail, ten stripes in Boston, the same in Roxbury and the same in Dedham.'* This means of flogging was an atrocious punishment. The wounds, especially in the winter months, would become cold between the times of punishment. Sometimes, the wounds would actually freeze, resulting in intolerable agony.

Although Lawrence and Cassandra Southwick were an elderly couple and members of the Salem Church, they were arrested in 1657 for merely harboring two Quakers. Lawrence was released a few days after his arrest; Cassandra was sentenced to seven weeks in prison and fined forty shillings for being found with a Quaker pamphlet on her person. Shortly after Cassandra's release, the couple along with their eldest son were arrested once again, this time for being absent from worship for six consecutive Sundays. Punishment was without trial. The trio was taken to Boston where they were publicly whipped and imprisoned for eleven days each. All of their cattle was seized and sold to pay their fine of four pounds, thirteen shillings. Finally the couple was banished and rearrested for not leaving town quickly enough.

While in prison they were starved and tortured. Upon being released they were told to make haste in leaving. When the elderly couple pleaded that they had no place else to go, they were threatened with death. They fled without their younger children who had been taken by the state to be sold into slavery to pay the accumulated fines for their parent's repeatedly missing Sunday worship as well as for being vagabonds. [Salem authorities applied strict penalties to anyone who offered refuge to the young Southwick children. People refused to purchase the Southwick children as slaves and they were eventually freed.] The couple found refuge on Shelter Island, but years of torture, flogging, starvation and worry for the welfare of their children had taken its toll on them, they died within days of one another.

American poet, John Greenleaf Whittier immortalized the plight of the Southwick Family in his poem *Cassandra Southwick* penned in 1658. Southwick descendants would become faithful Quakers, moving westward, first into the Danby, Vermont area and finally into several areas of Western New York, including the town of Collins. [The Southwick genealogy is included in this volume of *The Way We Were: The History and Genealogy of the town of Collins.*]

After the exploration of Hudson, several Dutch explorers traversed the Hudson River. Although the English had attempted a settlement upon the banks of the river, they failed. The Dutch however, found their niche, and by 1623 the colony of New Netherlands had been created.

One truth remains evident, the European held little tolerance for the native. In 1634, a series of what the colonist would consider *Pequet outrages* began. In reality, the problems began between the English and the Dutch, the Pequet rebellion seemed a means by which they withheld the honor of their word. Jacob Van Cutler, an agent for the Dutch East India Company, purchased land from the Pequet Tribe in 1632, building an outpost for trade. The English cut off access to the trading post when they claimed prior rights to similar lands. These rights of a dubious nature came from a supposed deed they had purchased from an expelled sachem of the Pequet tribe. Taking offense to the English's unauthorized advances upon the land, the Pequet retaliated. Their first act was to murder a Narragansett trading party; their second offense was the murder of John Stone. The final straw, as conceived by the English, was the 1636 murder of John Oldham and eight of his companions as they slept on a docked ship.

In retaliation, John Endicott of Massachusetts led a raid against the Black Island tribe, with explicit order to kill every male member. Despite the successful massacre led by Endicott, he had yet to become satisfied with his retaliation. He continuously inflicted casualties upon the members of the Pequet Tribe. In retaliation, the Pequet wrote their own demise by raiding the settlement of Wethersfield, Connecticut, killing and kidnapping settlers, including two young girls who were later tortured by the tribe.

In May of 1636, Captain John Mason of Connecticut, with more than ninety men joined forces with Endicott and his men. In a pre-dawn raid, the settlers lay fire to the huts of the sleeping Pequet Tribe, firing upon them as they fled their burning huts. Of nearly seven hundred tribesmen, only seven survived. This would become the English's first act of genocide against the Native American.

As had become the custom of Europeans, Captain Mason declared the annihilation as acceptable in the eyes of God: *"..this did the Lord judge among the heathen, filling the place with dead bodies."* Soon after the genocidal massacre, the General Court of Massachusetts tolerated the act by decreeing that June 13, 1636 should be a Day of Thanksgiving. Those who fled persecution had become the persecutor, giving thanks for their act of genocidal violence, which resulted in the opening of the Connecticut River Valley for settlement.

Another famous documented massacre from the spring of 1763, has become know as *Pontiac's War* [some referred to it as *Guyasutha's War*] named for a well known, distinguished Seneca. This well planned attack involved the Shawnee, Delaware and the Ohio Indians playing a major role. French outposts including: Le Boeuf, Venango, Presqu'ile, all on or near Lake Erie; La Bay on Lake Michigan, St. Joseph's on the Michigan River; Miami's on the Miami River; as well as Ouochtanon, Sandusky and Makina. Only two outposts escaped the massacre, Fort Pitt in Detroit which fought a rigorous, victorious battle and Niagara due to the knowledge of its heightened strength it was not attacked. Peace did not reign throughout the land until November 28, 1763.

Despite loses from the massacres; the Europeans continued their encroachment upon Indian lands. To make matters worse, where the native was concerned, Governor John Penn of Pennsylvania issued a proclamation in 1764, enacting bounties upon the native as it would later enact bounties on wild animals. For the scalp or capture of an Indian, the following bounty would be paid; $150.00 for a captured male over ten years of age, $134.00 for the scalp of same; $130.00 for every female or male under ten years of age captured, or $50.00 for the scalp of same.

In an effort to halt encroachments and needless deaths, a *Congress* was held at Fort Stanwix [New York] on October 24, 1768. In attendance were; Sir William Johnson, Superintendent of Indian Affairs, the Governor of New Jersey, a Commissioner from Virginia, Richard Peters and James Tilghman of Pennsylvania, Tyanhasare [Abraham] sachem of the Mohawk Tribe, Senaghsis representing the Oneida, Chenughiata representing the Onondaga, Gaustrax representing the Seneca, Sequarisera representing the Tuscarora, and Tagaaia representing the Cayuga. In consideration for $10,000.00, the native representatives sold to Thomas and Richard Penn of Pennsylvania all of the land from the east side of the east branch of the River Susquehannah at a place called Owegy, running down until it comes opposite the mouth of a creek called Awandac, then across the creek and up on the south side along a range of hills called Burnett's Hills by the English. Although the description continued on, a general confusion was apparent when at subsequent treaty held in 1784 the native was intensely questioned concerning the whereabouts of these locations. The fact remains, that despite the confusion, the native sold the entire lands which now constitute the State of Pennsylvania for a mere $10,000.00.

Despite the urgency with which the Dutch, the English and the Spanish moved towards colonization of the New World, actual progress was slow. Although a common consent regarding discovery and claims existed, this did little to ward off conflicting claims to specific territory.

The Ancient Occupants of our Area

It has been written, that after the pillage of the native of this land, once their warriors had acquiesced to the white man's ways that men of history sat with the elders questioning them of their own annals, their own antiquity, that the elders could recite but one century of history before proceeding into lore. Despite the lack of written documentation and the inability to proclaim a detailed account of their history, evidence existed of an ancient, highly sophisticated human population in the New York State area of the country. Ancient ruins and archeological digs would determine a numerous population that resided in the area.

In the mid 1800's, it was believed that an ancient European man had first lived in the area populated by the Iroquois. At the turn of the twentieth century, after researching both geology and ethnological history [a branch of anthropology that analyzes culture], many believed that the Autochthonic theory was most accurate in determining the origin of the Native American. The Autochthonic theory indicated simply that the Native originated where they had been found. Technology and research in the twenty first century tells a different story.

According to archeologists and other men of knowledge, an interglacial period lowered sea levels between Siberia and Alaska which became known as Beringia. Approximately 20,000 BCE man began departing Asia, crossing the land mass and beginning their long trek southward. These men, who traveled and settled the western coast of North America, would become the first inhabitants of the New World. While there are only assumptions as to when the migration of man inland began, researchers now estimate that at approximately 1000 CE, a nomadic people known as Algonquin were inhabiting the Niagara Frontier. It is believed that the Iroquois replaced the Algonquin about 1300 CE.

The Iroquois, made up of several tribes including the Seneca, Cayuga, Onondaga, Oneida and Mohawk who shared a similar culture and language, occupied the region of the lower Great Lakes and St Lawrence River Corridor. Often referred to as people of the longhouse, due to the name they took upon forming the Iroquois Confederacy; 'Konoshioni' which literally meant the cabin makers or people of the longhouse. This people had both structured villages and government well before the infusion of the European. It is estimated that the League of the Five Nations [AKA the Iroquois Confederacy] was formed about 1500 CE. In 1677, the Covenant Chain became a political rule between the European settler and the Iroquois. [The Covenant Chain was an ongoing set of councils and treaties between the Colonial-settlers/ English colonies and the Iroquois Confederacy. Treaties and councils covered proceedings including trade, settlement, and violence. The Covenant Chain began during the late seventeenth century, continuing through mid 1750s.]

To the north, a separate Confederacy ruled, the Algonquin. Their territory ranged from New Foundland to the Rocky Mountains; from the Churchill River to Pamlico Sound. We have also noted that the Algonquin have been listed as inhabitants of both the islands and mainland around New York Bay. History and historians seems to agree, that of the two Confederacies; the most organized, most civilized, best sustained in warfare and most intelligent were the Iroquois.

The placement of their villages, towns or dwelling spaces appeared to have been situated to provide the best means of defense, maintenance and immunity to both natural elements and the advance of enemies. Ruins have been located on both hill and ravine. Their villages consisted of several communal longhouses as well as a longhouse for special purposes such as Council Meetings.

The average size of the longhouse is estimated to be one hundred foot long, eighteen feet wide and eighteen feet high. Sleeping platforms were built along the sides of the longhouse. The Native would use this area during the warmer months of the year, for it provided a haven against rodents as well as a place of rest. During the colder months, mats would be spread across the floor near the many fireplaces extending down the middle of the structure. The rafters were used for storage, while dried foods were stored in in-ground bark lined pits.

Each building would contain several nuclear families. Being a matrilineal culture, upon marriage the man would move into the longhouse of his wife. His children would all belong to her clan.

Ancient burial mounds unearth a people that some felt were buried in a hurry to deflect location, while others felt that the burials held the mystery of a death ritual. As the white settler cleared the forest and plowed the ground, he would turn up mysterious implements that told a story of the forbearers of this land. The finds were rude to some, highly sophisticated to others; showing that the culture that once existed in this area was well versed in tools of domestic, farm, hunting and warring needs.

During the mid 1800's, the white man would gather the treasures turned up with the ground, taking them to the area chiefs for identification and explanation. In turn, they would be told great stories of traditional folk lore or receive a blatant truth of unknown origin. At that time, the educated white man felt that the Indian was lacking in intellect, retelling stories from long ago to amuse them in their quest for knowledge. In other words, many times what was told by the Indian neighbor was scoffed at, their tales not written down, but rather forgotten, and the Chief that articulated the tale would become known as 'stupid.' Should the white intruder have listened with both his heart and his head rather than his superiority, he would have realized that in the tales passed from generation to generation by his red brethren, lay a semblance of truth, and a clue to the past which has now been lost forever.

Despite the white man's knowledge of the ancient ruins in Central America, the treasures their plows turned up were compared only to written documents from what they felt were the worlds earliest existence. However, even the mere educated realized that Columbus did not discover a new world; he merely discovered one half of two old worlds that appeared to have at one time known of each other. Writers of the time were more apt to be scoffed at as they realized that the *'virgin soil'* of the new world was filled with antiquities, proving the existence of others before them.

Orsamus Turner asks in his "Pioneer History of the Holland Purchase..." 'Who is to say that the scholar, the antiquarian, of another far off century, may not be a Champollion deciphering the inscriptions upon our monuments, - or a Stevens, wandering among the ruins of our cities, to gather relics to identify our existence?' While we can be sure that the majority would have looked at that question as a dramatic clause, we now know that what Turner was seeing, was the acclamation of history.

In 1850, it was known that the Western New York area heaved relics of the past, far more so than any other area of the country then known to man. The question stares at us some one hundred fifty years later, did the Western New York area call to the ancient ones as it called to the pioneers of whom we write? Was there a type of inducement that attracted persons here as the Holland Land Company attracted pioneers of the nineteenth century? Or were those who originally inhabited this area driven here in desperation, was this a mere point of fleeing annihilation?

In 1811, DeWitt Clinton, while addressing the New York Historical Society, noted that prior to what the white man had found upon his arrival to the area *'it was inhabited by a race of men much more populous, and much further advanced in civilization.'* To date, the previous questions remain satisfactorily unanswered, leaving us with a void, an ache for the knowledge for truth of the original inhabitants of Western New York.

Early villages, or forts as some have referred to them, have been located across the entire area considered Western New York. They have been described as being located in the most advantageous area, with earthen walls and ditches built around the outside of the walls. Some of these *forts* showed areas of one entrance, while others showed areas of two entrances. Each *'fort'* varied in size from two to six acres. In the confines of the earthen walls would be found pieces of earthen ware and a pulverized substance that some thought to be human bone. However, the consensus of the white man remained stead fast; that the skills used to create these ancient fortresses far surpassed those of their red brethren and therefore marked the structures as having been built by those of European descent, despite the claims of the Native American that the fortresses had been created during a time some five hundred years past when the Western Indians made their way into the area to war with those who abounded here.

Whatever the origin of these forts, there is no natural explanation for their existence, as there once seemed to be for the seventy eight mile ridge which appeared a natural road between points near Rochester to Lewiston, New York. This ridge ran from east to west at an approximate elevation of thirty feet above the surrounding land and ranged from a great to a small width. On either side of that ridge was a gradual decline covered in rock and gravel, at a distance of six to ten miles from Lake Ontario. This ridge appeared to the white man to be a natural turnpike, one which would need little work for it to have been the best road in America at the time. As explanation of its existence some thought the ridge had originally been an ancient boundary of the lake itself. Later, however, it would be discovered that being a natural boundary for the lake would have caused specific deposits to have been left upon the gradual slopes; deposits that were not located anywhere near what had become known as *The Ridge Road*.

Dewitt Clinton, in a speech to the New York State Historical Society in 1811, indicated that the natural occurrence, known as Ridge Road, was once a boundary of Lake Ontario. Despite the fact that by 1850 it was known that no natural deposits existed within the slopes of the Ridge Road, the 1992 publication *Somewhere to go on Sunday* by Margaret Wooster indicated that the Ridge Road, now New York State Route 104, was actually a natural boundary created by an ancient glacial lake. Was it crafted by an ancient inhabitant, or was it indeed an ancient lake boundary? Modern technology has undoubtedly taken our means to distinguish the actual facts.

At the time that the early white encroachers set foot upon the vast wilderness of the new world, they brought one thing to the native that would quickly devastate the vast, healthy population; disease. Although the white settler had formed natural immunity to these illnesses through exposure, the disease brought to this land would begin an irrevocable destruction to the Native American, causing the loss of nearly half of their population.

[NOTE – Although we have searched for copies of the actual documents, pamphlets, books, etc which would prove what we are about to inform readers of, we were unable to locate any such documentation. We have, however, found reference amongst various authors to indicate that the following ideas of the white man are true. Since, we have located no conflicting evidence to this white man's ideal, we feel that it is important to the history of our area, and therefore we shall include it.]

When one reflects back onto the historical renderings of our youth, we think of the poor white settler, thousands of miles from their civilized homelands. A people who, forced to abscond their native countries or risk persecution, historically appear a kind, gentle, caring people, a people lost to a vast new wilderness filled with savages who threatened at every blink of an eye. Yet, when we but merely glimpse the truth of what was, we see a man so eager in his greed, that he could regard a catastrophe as a travesty of God.

Thomas Hariot, an English mathematician and astronomer, who accompanied Sir Walter Raleigh on his 1584 expedition to Virginia felt that the Indian plagues were a *"speciall worke of God for our sakes."* John Winthrop, the first Governor of Massachusetts, when asked *"What warrant have we to take that land, which is and hathe been of long tyme possessed of other soones of Adam?"* is reported to have replied: *"God hath consumed the natives with a miraculous plague; where by a great parte of the country is left voyde of inhabitants."*

After the epidemic of 1616-1618, the Mohawk Tribe set out to replenish their losses, specifically in the area of military strength. In order to accomplish this feat, they waged war on neighboring tribes, capturing and assimilating the tribesmen into the Mohawk realm, thus saving the prisoners from torture and death. It became well known to the white settler that few chose to escape their captivity by any of the Iroquois Confederacy. Those captives who were to become assimilated into the tribe did not find themselves strangers in the midst of terrorist, but rather extensions of a well founded family. Those of the Iroquois Confederacy extended to their captive a sense of belonging without coercion or torture.

It appears the main difference between the tribes of both the Algonquin and Iroquois Confederation and those of the European explorer / settler was religion. There were no native churches, no native priests, and no native ministers to spread the Christian truths to other native tribes. They believed in one *Great-Spirit* and life after death in *a happy hunting ground*. Their rites of worship were dances and feasts, each clothed about nature. European's would consider the natives as pagan.

Despite the superior means of the white encroacher, the native had indeed made great strides on his own. They constructed canoes by which to travel the rivers and streams. Bone and stone forged instruments necessary for everything from cultivation to war were creative and kept available in quantity. Their major arms, the bow and arrow far surpassed those of the European. Pottery manufactured by the native was not only useful, but indeed works of art. Despite their lack of manufacturing evolvement, they made clothing, shoes and had learned to tan hides and preserve furs well before the Europeans had set foot upon this continent.

Although they had no school or written language they passed stories from generation to generation. They were cultivated as orators. Many who ranked position within American history are noted as amongst the country's greatest orators.

HISTORY OF THE IROQUOIS
The Legend of the Iroquois Confederation

As a reminder: nearly all of the history that we have collected on the Iroquois came from Euro-American sources. It is important that when reading the following history the reader places it into perspective, that of course, being a white perspective. Portions may be biased, dramatized or even fictionalized; since the early Iroquois left no written documentation for us to follow; we cannot be positive that this information is one hundred percent accurate.

Two distinct Iroquois legends seem to exist; one concerning the origin of the Iroquois, the second concerning the creation of the Iroquois Confederation. During our research, we have located many versions of what appear to be the same story. This legend is important to our understanding of our native brethren; therefore, we have chosen the version that somewhat combines both legends to share with our readers:

For years the Iroquois, consisting of six tribes, were confined under a mountain near the great Oswego. One day the *Great Holder of the Heavens, Hi-a-wat-ha* [the very wise man] came to guide the Iroquois from their imprisonment. Leading them into the beautiful Mohawk Valley, the Great One allowed them to choose where they wished to live. Each Tribe chose a different location within and west of the Valley. Despite their new found freedom within the beautiful valley, the Iroquois were not satisfied with what the Great One had given them. Wanting more, the tribes constantly warred between one another.

Unable to handle the warring, the tribe known as the Tuscarora moved south, following the birds when they flew away in the fall. Still, the remaining tribes warred until one day when a fierce, warlike tribe came from the home of the North Wind. Falling upon the Onondagas first, the fierce tribe left the Onondagas in near ruin, close to extinction. This caused concern on the remaining tribes. They knew they would either have to overcome the northern barbarian or face certain annihilation.

In their distress, they called upon Hi-a-wat-ha for advice. Hi-a-wat-ha told his people to call a council with representatives from each tribe. The council must be held on the banks of Onondaga Lake. Following Hi-a-wat-ha's instructions, the Council was called. For three day, the great council fires burned, yet Hi-a-wat-ha had not shown himself to the tribesmen. At the close of the third day, the tribesmen saw Hi-a-wat-ha, accompanied by his young daughter coming across the lake in a beautiful white canoe.

As Hi-a-wat-ha and his daughter stepped upon the land, a bird so large it darkened the countryside swooped from the heavens, crushing Hi-a-wat-tha's daughter to death. Stricken by grief, Hi-a-wat-ha silently mourned three long days and nights without speaking. Suddenly, his face alight with wonder, Hi-a-wat-ha stood, addressing his tribesmen.

"Brothers, I have come a long way to answer your question on how you can keep yourselves and your homes safe. You cannot do this alone. You cannot do this as one individual tribe. You must unite all of the tribes as one, a band of brothers. That is the only way you can keep enemies from your land."

Pointing to the Mohawks, Hi-a-wat-ha instructed; "You who are warlike yet mighty like the great tree whose roots sink into the earth and whose branches spread vast over the country. You shall be the first nation."

Turning to the Oneidas, Hi-a-wat-ha continued: "And you, who are like the everlasting stone that cannot be moved because you give such great council; you shall be the second nation."

Slowly turning to face the Onondaga, Hi-a-wat-ha pointed: "You, who are gifted in speech, mighty in war, and make your home in the great mountain shall be the third nation."

Nodding to the Cayuga, Hi-a-wat-ha, spoke on: "You, who inhabit the dark forest, whose home is everywhere, and hold a superior cunning in hunting shall be the fourth nation."

Finally facing the Seneca, Hi-a-wat-ha smiled: "And you, who inhabit the open country and possess great wisdom, knowing better than any the art of raising corn and building cabins shall be the fifth nation."

Raising his arms, Hi-a-wat-ha's voice thundered: "You, five great and powerful nations must unite and hold but one common interest. Do this and the Great Spirit will smile upon you, allowing no foe to disturb or overpower you. Hear my words, admit no other nations, for if you do, you will sow the seeds of jealousy and discord, becoming few, feeble and enslaved. Remember these words, for the Great Master of Breath is calling me."

Hi-a-wat-ha stepped into his canoe which rose into the heavens, leaving the five nations to heed his word or forever risk annihilation.

The Iroquois Confederation

Long before the European stepped foot upon the soil of the New World, the Iroquois formed a government 'of the entire community, by the entire community, for the benefit of the entire community.'

The Euro-American has long felt that the similarities between the governmental façade of both the white man and their red brethren came from like situations and conditions. In each case, both the European and the aboriginal were forced to deal with similar issues; issues that called for creation of a governing body, thus producing the similarities.

There were however, distinct differences. No prisons existed amongst the Iroquois Confederation, nor were dungeons built. On a rare occasion that a tribesman committed murder, he was either killed immediately or banished from his community. Crime amongst the Iroquois was virtually nonexistent, so no criminal code existed. During war, their enemies were rarely tortured, they were either put to death, or more likely assimilated into the tribe that had captured him.

When a family was wronged, by the murder of one of their own at the hands of a rival tribe, there was immediate retribution on those who wronged them. Once the warriors returned with prisoners from the rival tribe, more often than not, it was the wronged family who selected the punishment they received; and more often then not, the punishment was not punishment at all. The prisoners became assimilated into the tribe, becoming a member of the family to replace the life they took.

The adoption was by ritual. Once adopted, all members of the tribe treated that person as he would one of their own. The white girl, Mary Jamison who was kidnapped by the native replaced two brothers who had been lost in battle. The native held a ceremony to adopt the white child and gave her an Indian name, De-he-wa-mis. From that point in time, she was called daughter and sister. Mary lived among the natives for eighty years, with but a single regret; that her true parents had died.

The tale she told the white man was one of love. She claimed that everyone was kind to her, and everything they did was favorable to win her love. Although she spoke only the native tongue, Mary would recite her mother's prayers when she was alone, certain that she would be able to communicate when the white man came to free her. Instead, at the age of fourteen, she was married. Her husband was handsome, kind and gentle, and from that point in time on, Mary never wanted to leave her native family.

The native held no desire to gain, for their community was one where everyone shared in common. Lacking the need for more, there was no need to steal.

In the Western most portion of New York State, originally just east of the area occupied by the Neutral Nation, the Iroquois placed the Seneca Tribe as a defense against the fiercely strong Western Tribes. On the opposite end of the spectrum, the eastern gate was protected by the Mohawk. The two strongest, ablest tribes were positioned in places of protection of the remaining tribes.

Near Lake Onondaga, where the legendary Hi-a-wat-ha appeared, was what may be construed the capital of the Confederation. Here the council fires burned. The Onondaga were charged with keeping the council fire guarded at all times.

Initial contacts between the Iroquois and the European left the distinct impressions on the white man that he recorded. According to notes of both explorers and missionaries, it appears that the Iroquois were gaining influence over neighboring tribes. Some historians have noted that if the white man would not have arrived on the American Continent when they did, that the Iroquois would have extended their reign across the entire North American Continent. As it was, their domain stretched from the St Lawrence and the Great Lakes in the north to the Carolinas in the south. The eastern boundary was the mighty Hudson River the western region extended into the Ohio region near the Mississippi River.

THE IMMEDIATE ANCESTORS OF WESTERN NEW YORK

THE SENECA TRIBE

It is well known that the Seneca Tribe was to be considered the immediate ancestors of the Western New York area. It was from the Seneca Tribe that title to the land was achieved. It is written that the Seneca were the fifth nation of an alliance. Some have written that this tribe referred to themselves as *Mingoes*, others insist that the tribe referred to themselves as *Ho-de-no-sau-nee*. English referred to them as the *Confederates*. Dutch references list them as *Maquaws*. Southern Indians referred to them as *Massowamacs*. However, it would be the French title that they would often be referred to, the *Iroquois*.

According to historians the original *Confederates* included five tribes: the Mohawk lived principally on the river. The Oneidas lived upon the shores of Oneida Lake. The Cayuga's lived near Cayuga Lake. The Seneca occupied Western New York. The Onondagas lived upon both Seneca Lake and the Genesee River. This is said to have been their principal seats, or the place where they held their council fires. The aforementioned location being relatively narrower than their actual inhabitation lands is the area perceived by the white man as being their central location, rather than their actual residing location. The actual Confederacy entailed nearly all of what would become New York State. As previously noted, there are varying dates as to the establishment of this confederacy, dating as far back as 4000 B.C.E.

With the invasion of the European settlers, one must realize that the Native American become of two minds. Some fought to keep their ways, the knowledge and traditions that white Americans did not then or will never truly understand. This is the hollowed ground sacred tradition that although practiced is not to be shared. Some fell to the vice of the white man and the evil that he brought with him. Whether they fell to temptation, or struggled to live their tradition, the Native American became crushed, sent from the land he ruled to live under the white man's rule.

Their ancient council fires have long since been extinguished by a way they did not understand. Their confederacy dwindled first to a shadow and then to a mere memory. Today, they continue to struggle; their ancient language sought by few amongst their ranks, the traditions and customs becoming more a means for tourist to gawk at, then for the ancient rite of which they served.

Although the white settlers did not capture and enslave the tribes as a whole with whips and chains, the tribes were none the less captured, shoved onto the Reservation prisons and taught to live by the white man's rule or risk annihilation. Enslaved by the traditions and values of the white man, our red brethren were, in a manner of speaking, consumed. Represented by the people we elect to govern us as a single entity, we are still empowering the white man to continuously enslave and annihilate the forbearers of the area we now call home.

Most do not consider our present government as solicitors of torment and torture, nor do we consider our politicians as chief judge and prosecutor to an ancient American civilization. We tsk when we hear of our native brethren complain, but look towards the problem as being theirs, after all, *if it does not affect us why get involved?* Those who turn a blind eye to present day struggles between the native and the government we have elected to represent us need to reexamine the issues in an historic perspective. Would a nation, so well organized, with a political system mirroring and at times outshining that of the white settler, without written guidelines to follow, ever request what was not rightfully granted them? Is it possible, that despite the decades and centuries that have passed since the initial meetings of the native with the white settler, that the mindset of the politician of today does not reflect the mindset of those of days gone by? Is the greed of government overtaking responsibility? More recently, has the New York State Government shown an excessive greed by ceding lands to the Native American for the explicit means of raising revenue?

In a 2005 report by the New York State Comptroller, it was noted that during the 2004-2005 fiscal year, the Native American Casinos generated $57.1 million to the state and local counties. More specifically, during the fiscal year ending on March 31, 2005, New York State received $44.1 million from Seneca Niagara and Seneca Allegany Casinos, while Niagara and Cattaraugus Counties received $13 million. Yet, that same state government continuously harasses the Seneca Nation while cutting services to all who reside in the Western New York area.

The aforementioned is fact, not speculation. Although we have promised to attempt to remain unbiased, this issue has us wondering; how many will turn away, how many will close their eyes, how many will remain mute and leave a legacy of greed and deceit to our heirs, as our forbearers unwittingly left us?

The French historian, Volney, was the first to indicate that those of the Iroquois Confederacy were equal to the Romans of ancient times, referring to the red man as The Romans of the West. Volney suggested that if the red man would have had the same advantages as the Greeks and Romans, they would not have been considered inferior. He considered the Iroquois to have *minds equal to any effort within their reach*. He claimed that unlike the Greeks and Romans who had ample means by which to improve, the Iroquois lacked these means. Yet the Iroquois have been said to have been distinguished by their accomplishments in policy, government, negotiations, eloquence and war. Historians have noted that the powers of the Iroquois Confederacy were apt in not only defining power, but also in relinquishing power for the greater good of all.

By 1660, when the French traveled through the area, they noted that the Iroquois occupied all of the area which would become New York State and the Upper Canada Peninsula. This proud race, according to documentation of that era, had two thousand two hundred warriors ready to defend what was theirs from any antagonist. In 1667, an English agent was sent to the area to confirm this detail, which he did. There has been no discovery on how those numbers were obtained, nor does an explanation exist as to how such a vastly organized Confederacy would include only two thousand two hundred warriors. However, important notes have been made by a variety of early historians; the Iroquois Confederacy of the New York area held strength and uniform success over their enemies, something no other tribes within the United States ever possessed. By far, all concur that the members of the Iroquois Confederacy far excelled all other aboriginal tribes in America in both physical and mental capabilities.

Champlain wrote details of his travels throughout Western New York in 1615, which would be published nearly two hundred years later. It is important here to add for the readers a portion of that report which not only describes treatment of prisoners, but also the male attitude towards women. *"Now it is noted that one of these chiefs seeing these prisoners, cut the finger off one of these poor women, as commencement of their usual torture. Whereupon, I interfered, and censured the Iroquit Captain, representing to him that a warrior, as he called himself, was not in the habit of acting cruelly towards women, who have no defense but their tears and who, by reason of their helplessness and feebleness, ought to be treated with humanity..... Whereupon he replied, that their enemies treated them in the same manner. But, since such customs displeased me, he would not act so anymore to women, but exclusively to men."*

Since the discovery of America and the subsequent explorations, the Iroquois Confederacy was a known contingency in this area. Without the written testimony of the original Natives, one must concur with the fact that their time here may have been endless. Even those within the various tribes of the Confederacy offered varying details on their holds within the area. Some claimed to have always been here, their people a part of the landscape since the beginning of time. Some indicated that it was conquest that brought their tribes to this area. Still others indicated that the move to New York was a search for better living condition. How long the Seneca and other members of the Iroquois Confederacy maintained homes within Western New York can be documented since before the first written histories of the area, as does the organization of the Confederacy itself.

Many historians feel that the Confederacy was organized as a form of government to assure offense and defense in times of war. The supreme power of the Confederacy belonged to fifty sachems [rulers]. Each tribe was designated a specific number of sachems; according to Turner *the Mohawks had nine, the Oneidas had nine, the Onondagas had fourteen, the Cayuga's had ten and the Seneca's had eight*. Their representatives were apparently similar to our present governmental structure. However, rather than electing the sachems, the power was hereditary. These fifty sachems formed a type of executive and judicial governing body and were referred to as *the Council of the League*. In turn, the sachems would become the governing bodies of the individual tribes.

In addition to the Sachems, each tribe was allotted an identical number of war chiefs, their military power. Of the military chiefs, two were *raised up* above the rest; again this was a hereditary position. These two war chiefs would always be from the Seneca Nation. They had the obligation of tending to the *Western Door* where attacks were most likely to arise prior to the influx of the European. The Seneca held the responsibility of keeping those who proposed an attack upon the confederacy from advancing past their regime.

It is written that the third tier of government, the Chiefs, an elected position amongst individual tribes did not come into being until after the influx of the European. They were to tend to the home affairs of each tribe, but as time eluded, the chiefs would gain rank with the sachems. Additionally, it is said that to make the Confederacy stronger, each individual Nation was divided into tribes, now referred to as clans. These tribes were; wolf, deer, bear, snipe, beaver, heron, turtle and hawk. This establishment would become the strongest tie between the nations, in effect creating a perfect union between their nations. For example, the wolf tribe of the Mohawk nation would look at the wolf tribe of the Seneca Nation as brothers, etc. This cross-relationship became the strongest tie amongst the Confederacy.

Accordingly, these tribes became a governing force in regards to marriage as well. For example, the wolf, bear, beaver and turtle tribes were considered brothers to each other and cousins to the remaining tribes, and therefore were not allowed to marry within any of these clans, no matter what tribe they belonged to. This restriction would relax, by the mid 1800's; the Native American would be allowed to marry into any clan of any tribe with the exception of their own clan and tribe. The children bore by these marriages would follow into the mother's clan, for even at that early age, the Native realized that a child must be the son of its mother, but not necessarily a child of the mother's husband.

While many realize the significance of the Seneca Tribe to the Western New York area, many more do not realize that the Seneca Tribe were not always the only tribe that possessed and resided within this area. Whether the Seneca abounded in this area in early years, or claimed the domain in its entirety in later years remains unclear. Documentation does exist to indicate they at least shared the area with those of the Neuter Nation, thusly named by French Missionaries for their ability to remain neutral while residing between two warring tribes, the Huron and Seneca, as well as those of the Erie or Cat Nation. The French account, a letter written by Father L'Allemant dated at St Mary's Mission, May 19, 1641, states: the Neuter Nation Village populous Tribe held approximately forty villages with about *12,000 souls of which they could produce 4,000 warriors.*

It was believed that although the food and clothing of the Neuter Nation differed from those of their brethren, that they, at one time had belonged to the larger Iroquois family. [Note, what was written at this time speaks of the existence of the Confederacy: *"there is reason to believe that not long before the Hurons, Iroquois and Neuter Nations formed one people..."*] The differences noted in dress, included the fact the men of the Neuter Nation '*are less particular than the Hurons in concealing what should not appear.*" Of the women's dress was noted, "the squaws are ordinarily clothed, at least from the waist to the knees, but are more free and shameless in their immodesty..." Accordingly, the difference in the food of the Neuters was also noted; "they have Indian Corn, beans and gourds in equal abundance..." and "..also plenty of fish, some which abound in particular places only..." Later historians would note that the Neuter Nation enjoyed enhanced prestige amongst the various tribes because *'the woman who was recognized as a lineal descendant of the first woman on earth [the direct descendant of the first Iroquoian Family] lived in a Neuter Nation Village near the Niagara..."* The following year, Charlevoix would describe the Neuter people as *'...larger, stronger and better formed.. than any savages south of Huron Country."*

At the time of the Missionary's visit, the Seneca [referred to As *Sonontonheronons*] were but a mere day's travel from the easternmost village of the Neuter Nation, located at *Onguiaahra* [Niagara]. Therefore, we can deduce that the Seneca Tribe was residing within the limits of Western New York at that time. From here, it appears that both French and English have become distorted in what had actually occurred between the Neuter Nation, the Erie's and the Seneca. historians do agree that many of those belonging to both the Neuter Nation and the Erie Tribe were both massacred and assimilated. References lead to the conclusion that most of these tribes assimilated in fear of annihilation, within a range of time between 1643 and 1655. More in-depth research leads one to believe that the 1655 date is most accurate. All accounts prove that once these tribes were extinguished, the ranks of the Iroquois, and more specifically the Seneca swelled.

Over the years, the question has arisen as to exactly how much land mass was originally ruled by the Iroquois. Dewitt Clinton, in an 1825 speech before the New York State Historical Society sustained that *'the supremacy of the Iroquois probably prevailed at one time over territory as far east as the Connecticut River.'* A written account of the French indicates that Iroquois at one time resided in what is now Montreal. Historians such as D. P. Thompson concur that the Iroquois probably held a strong hold in the area of Vermont at least one hundred years prior to the French appearance in the New World. As French influence increased through Canada, Thompson felt that the Iroquois relinquished their hold on areas around Lake Champlain and the Upper Hudson River.

While we may never know for certain, we do know that the Indian names that have been applied to lakes and rivers in Vermont are

Algonquin in character. Reference has also been made by early historians to a correspondence between then New York Governor Tryon and British Minister Lord Dartmouth in 1773. Tryon refers several times to ancient maps, one in particular which would signify an Iroquois influence on the aforementioned area.

According to the various historians who mention these correspondences, Tryon indicated that Lake Champlain was professed to be *Mere des Iroquois.'* The correspondence continues with other significant information including the Sorel River which leads from Lake Champlain to the St. Lawrence River being labeled, *'Riviere des Iroquois'* and the tract of land just east of the lake labeled, *'Irocoisa.'*

[*Note – The Caughnawaga Tribe supposed descendants of the Iroquois, attempted over an eighty year period to establish claim to this territory. Legislature repeatedly refused their claim to the land citing a 1763 Treaty between France and Great Britain and a 1783 Treaty between the colonies and Britain, both of which extinguished Indian claims to all territory within the state of Vermont. While this says little about the honor of the white man, it does speak multitudes about the extended territory having at one time belonging to the Iroquois.]

Indeed, over the next century, the Iroquois would enter into their *'Golden Age of recorded history.'* Not only did the Iroquois Confederacy dominate all native tribes of the East, but they would also become a safeguard to both Dutch and English Colonist where the French were concerned. The Iroquois would remain in command until the French were finally defeated. At this time, they would also come to a sudden, terrifying realization; their power had come to full term.

While the Indian was busy fending off French attacks, the European immigrants had been busy strengthening their rule of the new world. It became obvious to the Confederacy that their existence would soon be essentially terminated, for in order to survive, they now would become the people of which assimilation would become mandatory.

The native assimilation had previously been proven acceptable to those who had been taken captive. The captive was now an extended family member with all rights within their new tribe, which in essence, was quite similar to what the captive was all ready accustomed. The white man however, was different in every aspect then their red brethren. Their way of life, their dress, their language, their religion, their traditions were all indeed foreign to the native. Unlike the assimilation of tribe to tribe captives, the white man demanded attentiveness, and in a way, subservience from the red man. Indeed, the Iroquois must have feared *the end of the world as they knew it.'*

Archeology digs across New York State have unearthed little that would account for tribes other than the Iroquois to have been in possession of the land. However, this does not provide definitive proof that the Iroquois was the only group to have ever lived within New York State. Knowledge of assimilation tactics offers us a brief insight as to what may have occurred to any previous area inhabitants. Once a captive was to be assimilated into a tribe, their dress would be immediately exchanged for the dress of the Iroquois, destruction of the original clothing an apt part of the assimilation process. With this knowledge in hand, one can assume that the Iroquois may have assumed possession of what would be later termed *'ancient artifacts'* thus unknowingly, the archeologist may be viewing items that once belonged to a differing tribe. These digs do, however, provide adequate proof that the Iroquois were ancient tribes of New York State.

Enter the White Man

AN ERA OF CHANGE

When the white man finally entered into the realm of the Iroquois, they would find well worn paths that led from village to village, to hunting and fishing grounds, and even to the villages of other Nations. These paths became known as trails and were used first by the French Missionaries and traders, then by the Dutch, the English and even during the Revolutionary War by Butler's Rangers. These trails became well known by the pioneers of the Holland Land Purchase.

Accordingly, the trail from the east would lead the pioneer through what would become Canandaigua, West Bloomfield and Lima, crossing the Genesee River at Avon. From here the pioneer would travel north westerly through Caledonia, then westerly crossing Allen's Creek near Leroy. The trail then crossed Black Creek near Stafford, continuing on to the banks of the Tonawanda Creek just above the present town of Batavia. Following the east bank of the creek, the trail continued past what would become known as the Great Bend, past *the Arsenal* turning north-west towards Caryville, finally crossing the Tonawanda Creek at an Indian village. Here the trail branched, one part heading in a north-west direction, the other a south-west direction towards what would become Collins.

The pioneers taking the south-west trail would cross Murder Creek at Akron, then through Clarence Hollow through Williamsville, crossing Ellicott Creek to Cold Springs finally coming out at the mouth of the Buffalo Creek. From Buffalo, the pioneers would follow the lake shore to Angola, finally cutting across the Cattaraugus Reservation to Collins. Others would follow the Genesee Road to Marshfield, while still others chose to follow the lake shore to the mouth of the Cattaraugus concluding their venture along the babbling creek.

Missionaries often followed traders throughout the new areas of this vast young country. There were even times when the missionary had arrived prior to the trader. Those belonging to the order of St. Francis, known as Franciscans preceded the Jesuits in the New World, arriving about 1615. The Jesuits arrived some ten years later, around 1625. Fathers Viel and Le Caron and Brother Sagard; missionaries and members of the provincial of the Recollets of Saint-Denis left France arriving to live amongst the Herons, becoming the first Europeans to set foot in Western New York. These missionaries instructed tribes along the western banks of the Niagara. How ironic this becomes, as we realize that nearly at the same time the Catholics were reaching out to the natives of Western New York, the Pilgrims found asylum from persecution by the Catholic faith eastern shores of the same continent.

[The following is a portion of a speech given by Dr. Peter Wilson, an educated Cayuga Chief, to the New York State Historical Society. This portion of the speech not only constitutes agreement of the infrastructure of trails running throughout New York State, it also allows a glimpse into the mindset of a broken man.]

"The land of Ga-nun-no or the Empire State as you love to call it was once laced by our trails from Albany to Buffalo. Trails that we had trod for centuries, trails worn so deep by the feet of the Iroquois that they became your roads of travel as your possessions gradually eat into those of my people! Your roads still traverse those same lines of communication which bound one part of the long house to the other. Have we, the first holders of this prosperous region, no longer a share in your history? Glad were your fathers to sit down on the threshold of the long house. Rich did they hold themselves from getting the mere sweepings from its door. Had our forefathers spurned you from it when the French were thundering at the opposite side to get a passage through, and drive you into the sea, whatever has been the fate of other Indians, we might still have had a nation, and I – I, instead of pleading here for the privilege of lingering within your borders, I – I might have had a country."

A sentimental speech it very well may have been, however, archeology digs have proven Dr. Wilson's speech true. Some historians feel that the native coveted the *superior* tools of the white man, as the modern child covets the technological marvels of today. Other historians feel that the tools of the white man are simply proof of the native culture being assimilated into the white man's culture. A great percentage of historians agree that the tools of the white man were far superior to the tools of the native. By the mid-colonial period Iroquois towns would be found strewn with brass and iron. Grave sites would produce guns, scissors, copper and brass kettles and numerous glass beads. The native culture had greatly given way to the culture of the white settler. By the end of the nineteenth century, few genuine Indian articles could be found around either Indian settlements or within the borders of *modern* Reservation. Archeologist and historians alike, agree that both the white man's tools and his ways of living had all but erased the Iroquois' way. From early estimates until the 1920 Federal census, the native population had dwindled to a mere 5,503.

History of New York State

The States of Holland formed a company meant strictly for colonization in both America and Africa; the East India Company. After having made two previous journeys to the new world, Hudson offered his services to the Dutch. On April 4, 1609, Hudson, accompanied by his son and a crew of eighteen, one half being English, one half Dutch sailed towards the new world on the Dutch ship, *Half-Moon*.'

Attempting as he had during his first two voyages to the new world, Hudson sailed northward seeking again, a passage to India. As in his prior voyages, ice blocked his passage, forcing him to change course. Upon viewing Cape Cod, Hudson declared the lands beyond, *New Netherland*, giving the Dutch their first point of boundary on their new claim.

The area claimed by the Dutch extended along the Atlantic Ocean from Cape Cod to Delaware Bay and included all islands along the coast. The St Lawrence River was the Northern inland boundary and the Delaware Bay was the southern boundary. As with all land claims of the time the western boundary extended endlessly. Their claim was called, New Netherland.

Earlier, we spoke of the fact that during treaties between nations such as the Colonies, Britain and France, all Indian rights were extinguished. The Dutch, on the other hand, purchased land from the native. By 1615, they had not only purchased land on the bank of the Hudson River, but had also gained permission to build a trading house. Being guarded by a palisade fence [a fence made by securing stakes in the ground as for defense] this became known as the first Dutch Fort.

By 1615, New Amsterdam, later to become New York, had firmly taken hold as a settlement. Begun by traders, the settlement consisted of a stockade fort, a few huts for shelter and a solitary ship. Beads and shells became their money. Otter skins and green tobacco was their merchandise.

Unlike the other colonies, colonization had not been the object of the Dutch in New Amsterdam. The Pilgrims who settled Massachusetts were people of wealth and education. Equality of rights was the feature that distinguished their colony. Jamestown had been settled by those seeking a spirit of conquest and adventure. Once wealthy men, they came in search of new wealth. But the Dutch West India Company's goal was pure avariciousness; they wanted but to control and promote trade as the largest monopoly of the time.

The company had five separate stations of administration; the portion being in control of New Amsterdam being called the *College of Nineteen.*

New York & New England under Foreign Rule

To more understand the people who would eventually become the pioneers of the town of Collins, it is important for us to review those who colonized states such as Massachusetts, Connecticut, Pennsylvania and New Hampshire. Societies that evolved in other parts of the country would hold a direct impact on the persons, who would finally settle the south towns of Erie County.

Pastor Robinson's congregation which had fled to Leyden to avoid religious persecution was eager to colonize America. Although they had sought the right to settle amongst the Dutch, they were denied. Despite the fact that the Pilgrims resided in the homeland of the Dutch, having been driven from England to avoid religious persecution, the Dutch still considered them to be English. Fearing that an English settlement in the middle of a Dutch colony would serve to strengthen the English claim, the States General felt justified in denying the permission.

Obtaining a patent from the Virginia Company to settle the *northern part of Virginia*, the group sailed towards America in late 1620, their intentions to land near the coast of Delaware. Instead, those referring to themselves as Pilgrims landed at Cape Cod Bay. Although they were the first colony of immigrants to sail to America to avoid religious persecution, they would not be the last.

French Protestants known as Walloons, who had also fled their native land to avoid persecution appealed to the Plymouth Company for permission to also settle in America. When denied, they took their request to the Dutch West India Company, who saw the advantages of taking the group abroad. In May of 1623, the ship *New Netherland* landed at Manhattan, bringing thirty Walloon families, a total of one hundred and ten new citizens to New Netherland.

Unlike the Pilgrims who worked to build a single community, these colonists would separate; a few would begin a community in Esopus [Kingston]. [Note – it has been written that thirty families left Manhattan to settle near the present day Albany and a few were left to settle Esopus. We have yet to locate an actual number of families, or persons who began this settlement.] A fort would be built at the site of present day Albany, named Orange in honor of their Prince. Four families sailed with eight crewmen to a site approximately four miles south of the present day city of Philadelphia, building Fort Nassau. Two families with six seamen were sent up the Connecticut River where they would build Fort Hope, near present day Hartford. The remaining pioneers would settle an area which would become Brooklyn.

The Dutch had not only made their mark on the New World, they had virtually colonized the eastern portion of New York, Long Island, Connecticut and eastern Pennsylvania. Word of their success spread rapidly and soon more immigrants from Holland would join their ranks. To add to the ranks of Europeans, the first child of European descent, Sarah Rapelye, would be born in New Netherland in what would become Brooklyn.

Captain Cornelius Jacobsen May would become the first director of New Netherland, ruling over the settlers for one year, from 1624 to 1625. His first order of business was to send his ship back to the Netherland, laden with furs. In exchange, a few months later the ship would return to America. This time, instead of settlers it contained livestock, seeds and other necessities for farming.

May's rule would be followed by that of William Verhurst. A more specific rule would come into play in May of 1626. Peter Minuit would be commissioned director-general [governor]. To assist in the governing process, he was appointed a council of five who would become civil administrators. Also appointed was a Koop man [commissary-general] and a schout [a sheriff].

This group held legislative, judicial and executive power. However, should a capital punishment case come before the men, they were to send the suspect back to Amsterdam to be dealt with. Minuet's first true act as governor would be to satisfy the possession of Manhattan Island, presently possessed merely by default of first discovery and occupation. Calling together his council and a council of natives, Minuet made a treaty for the mutual satisfaction of the purchase of the land.

Over the years, many have immortalized this treaty in works of art, poetry and of course renderings of history. The truth of the treaty at times has been speculated. The fact of the treaty Minuet offered is simple: the natives were paid sixty guilders, an approximate twenty four dollars for twenty two thousand acres of land.

Treaties with the natives were not the only relationships Minuet attempted to broaden. Shortly after his arrival, he began writing letters to the Pilgrims in hopes of creating a trade treaty between the colonies. The Trade Treaty was made in 1627, shortly thereafter, William Bradford, the Puritan Governor, prodded by England, would warn the Dutch to *'clear their title.'* England still staked claims to New Netherlands by rights of discovery.

Refusing to heed to the Puritan threat, the Dutch continued to purchase land from the natives, this time at the mouth of the Connecticut River. The Puritans, still loyal to England threatened the new trading post. Rather than dispute, the Dutch purchased another tract of land from the natives; this time some sixty miles upstream where they would build Fort Good Hope in 1633.

Being businessmen, the Dutch knew the best way to increase their fur trade would be to populate the area. After careful consideration, they deduced the best way to encourage emigration was by means of company members. In 1629, a charter was offered to any member who purchased land from the natives and populated it with at least forty eight persons within a six year time frame. For each member who succeeded they would receive a manor on their choice of property *'six miles along the coast, or on both sides of a navigable river.'* To sweeten the deal, the member would be given the title, *patroon* which would entitle them to feudal rights over their tenants; as well as freedom to trade along the seacoast, unrestricted fishing and salt manufacture and most important, they would each receive a representative in the governor's council.

This idea brought immediate response and results. Eight members of the company became patroons. Of these eight, only one would become successful, Killian Van Rensselaer. The system that had been created became an obstruction to the prosperity of the colony. Rather than working eloquently as had been pictured, patroons argued amongst themselves, with their tenants, the governors and the company. Additionally, the patroons had worked to exclude the company from trading within the regions they ruled. Resulting from shear desperation, the company finally bought out some of the patroons, while remanding the claims of the rest.

Subsequent governors would make significant changes within the colony; some to the soul advantage of the governor. Changes that would take place around the year 1640 would mark a new era in colonization.

The most effective change was that of land ownership. No longer was land to be held merely by members of the Dutch West India Company. Anyone willing to settle in the new world would be given opportunity. Additionally, any farmer willing to move his family would be given free transportation to New Netherland. Upon his arrival, he would receive land complete with house and barn, livestock and tools in consideration of an approximate two hundred dollars per year for six years.

Patroons, although they reserved their feudal rights, were now restricted to waterfront areas stretching one mile wide and no more than two miles inland. Restrictions on manufacturing were lifted, as were monopolies in the trade industry. Those of English descent were allowed to move into the area providing they pledged allegiance to the Dutch government. The outcome appeared to prove beneficial to all.

Historically proven time and time again, with growth comes greed. The penalty of trading firearms to the native was death, but greedy traders could not be stopped. Maximizing unrest was Governor Willem Kieft's dictatorial rule of the colony as well as his policy to tax the Algonquin in return for protection. When claims were made that the Raritan [Indian Tribe] had stolen hogs and attacked a trading yacht in 1641, Kieft, driven by his dictatorial vengeance, sent fifty men to deal with the savage. Several warriors were massacred and their crops burned. In retaliation, the native stole onto Stanton Island destroying an entire plantation and killing every tenant. Kieft placed a bounty of ten fathoms of wampum [wampum was native money made out of shells, each fathom was a six foot length] for the head of every Raritan brought to him.

The attack on the native would do far more than settle Kieft's vengeance, it would start a war. Death and destruction reigned until the Treaty of Fort Amsterdam in 1645. Complaints by the citizenry of the colonies had Kieft recalled. He would never make it home; the ship he sailed on was destroyed at sea as the ship neared Wales. Kieft, along with about eighty crewmen were lost.

Although everyday life appeared choice to the Dutch, the English had not forgotten their claim to the area, based upon first discovery. In 1662, King Charles II issued a land grant to the settlers of Connecticut. This grant stretched indefinitely westward and included a large portion of New Netherland. Two years later, he would revoke that grant, offering instead a patent to his brother James, Duke of York, which included the entire land portion of New Netherland. The Duke at once sent an armed fleet to secure his patent. Although Governor Stuyvesant declared *"I would rather be carried to my grave than yield;'* the settlers, many of which were now English, urged his surrender. In September 1664, Dutch rule ended in New Netherland.

Under Dutch rule, society in New Netherland had been structured via class. The upper class consisted of both landowners and traders. The middle class consisted of independent farmers, small traders and those considered *professional men*. The lower class consisted of the common laborers and tenants. On the bottom of the social scale were the black slaves. It is written that at one time, New Netherland held more black slaves than any other colony.

The first changes instituted by the English was to make the approximate nine thousand citizens English subjects. They appointed the first English Governor, Richard Nicolls. Governing officials became known by English titles; for example koopmen became secretaries and the schouts became sheriffs. Colonial names were also changed. New Netherland now became New York; Fort Amsterdam became Fort James and Fort Orange became Albany.

After three years, Nicolls resigned his able rule, succeeded by Sir Francis Lovelace, who in a short period of time, made enemies of those under his rule. Overtaxing the citizens was not enough for Lovelace; he also withdrew all citizen liberty. When war broke out between England and Holland, Lovelace's days as ruler of New York would end. A fleet of six hundred men sailed into New York harbor and were soon joined by an additional four hundred Dutch citizens of New York. In but a few days, New York, New Jersey and Delaware were once again under Dutch rule, with Captain Anthony Colve appointed Governor. [August 1673] A treaty ended the war in 1674, returning the area to English rule.

A description of New York written by Governor Edmund Andros in 1678 noted the changes that had occurred since the initial English rule had begun. According to Andros, the colony now had twenty four towns. While most of the buildings were constructed of wood, a few were now constructed of stone and brick. The exports included sixty thousand bushels of wheat, as well as peas, beef, pork, fish, tobacco, furs, timber, horses, pitch and tar. During Andros reign as Governor, it is written that he had reorganized the militia, strengthened defenses, held the Iroquois as faithful allies, raised the condition of all of the colony's citizenship, and increased trade. However, he also made a great deal of political enemies and in 1680 was dismissed of his duties. He would be replaced by Thomas Dungan.

During Dungan's reign, a new government was instituted. A council was appointed to assist Dungan in conducting his job of governing the people. An additional seventeen representative of the land holders were elected. These men would become the first New York State Legislature. Their first meeting was held at Fort James, where they adopted fourteen acts; including the *Charter of Liberties and Privileges*.

This Charter declared that legislative authority shall forever be held between the governor, council and the people. The people would meet in general assembly. It also stated that there would be no tax imposed unless assembly approved such tax. The Charter was signed by both the governor and the Duke. However, the Duke did reserve the right to veto any laws. Two years later, the Duke would void this charter.

Other laws that were passed divided New York into ten counties to be known as: Kings, Queens, Richmond, Suffolk, Westchester, Orange, Dutchess, Ulster and Albany. [Albany County would encompassed all of Western New York.] A law requiring four distinctive courts was also passed; town courts to be held once monthly, would host the trial of small cases; County Courts would be held quarterly; a General Court would convene twice annually in each county and finally a Supreme Court which would be composed of the governor and his council. Any appeals were to be directed to the King. The next important law regarded naturalization. Foreigners were to be provided easy terms by which they could become citizens. In 1686, Dungan gave the city of New York a charter.

In February 1685, Charles II would die of complications from a stroke he had suffered, leaving the throne to his brother, the Duke of York, making New York a Crown Colony. Thus, New York became under the direct control of the crown, losing the representative government it had begun to enjoy.

Three years later, word would arrive at the New York harbor concerning the English Revolution, and would create a revolution of its own in the colonies. Headed by Jacob Leisler, German immigrant and head of the local militia; the revolt overthrew British Command in America and assumed control over local government.

Wishing to extend his power, Leister sent an armed force up river to compel the river towns to submit to his authority. However, it would not be until the French and Indian Massacre at Schenectady that Leister's power would be recognized. Leister would call together the first Continental Congress to ever be held in America.

Seven delegates of the Congress would meet in Albany in February of 1690. Leister, together with authorities of Massachusetts and Connecticut made their assault by land and sea against the French and Indians in Canada.

Leister had been viewed as a hero by the common people for his unassuming patriotism, yet the King refused to appoint him as governor to the colony. Instead, Henry Sloughter was appointed. Major Richard Ingoldesby preceded Sloughter in his arrival to America. Along with two companies of soldiers, Ingoldesby marched to Fort James demanding surrender. A scuffle ensued, and eight men died. Leister agreed to surrender only to Sloughter. Upon Sloughter's arrival, March 1691, Leister surrendered the fort to him.

Leister and his chief supporters were arrested, tried and convicted as traitors. Sloughter signed a death warrant for both Leister and Milborne. Both men were hanged in May 1691.

William Bradford was the *royal printer* for fifty years beginning in 1693, publishing all of the laws of New York. Under instructions of the King, he remained the sole printer in the colony for more than thirty years.

While we wonder these days about the truth of separation of Church and State, in the seventeenth century there was no such wonder. In 1693, assembly passed as act to *maintain* six ministers in New York, Westchester, Richmond and Queens's counties, such was the origin of the Trinity Church in the city of New York.

A Dutch Reformed, French Protestant, Dutch Lutheran and Jewish synagogue were also located within the confines of the city. Dutch Reformed churches were also located in Albany and Kingston, while Independent and Protestant meeting houses were located mainly on Long Island. Quakers were found throughout the area. However, Catholics were not welcomed by more than the Iroquois.

While the nation's history shows affects of both King William's and Queen Ann's Wars, neither was of much consequence to New York.

Bradford would be persuaded by Governor Fletcher to reprint the 'London Gazette' for colonist in 1696. Nearly thirty years later, Bradford would cease reprinting the London Gazette to start his own newspaper, the New York Gazette. Politically swayed, Bradford's paper upheld Governor Burnett and his administration.

In 1720, Fletcher was succeeded by William Burnett. Although his tenure appears to have placed significance on the citizenry, his administration was controversial. Burnett encouraged trade with the native to reduce French influence. He strengthened outposts such as Fort Oswego, in effect, strengthening the colony's position on the frontier. Without forewarning, Burnett was recalled, replaced by Colonel William Cosby.

The administration of Cosby was stormy at least, his attention geared towards quarreling with the people he ruled rather than following up on Indian affairs. While Bradford's Gazette continued to praise the government, in less than one year of Cosby's reign, Peter Zenger began a newspaper, rival to the New York Gazette; the New York Weekly Journal, the newspaper condemning Cosby and his regime.

Cosby did everything in his power to suppress coverage by the Journal, nothing worked, especially since the citizens sided with Zenger. Finally, Cosby ordered the Journal to be burned and Zenger jailed. Zenger continued to edit his newspaper even in jail and his public kept purchasing it.

The two lawyers defending Zenger contended that the court trying the case was illegal, before their claims could be heard, Cosby had them disbarred. Eager for justice, an old Quaker lawyer from Philadelphia, Andrew Hamilton took Zenger's case. It would take two years to bring Zenger to court where his eager public, realizing that Zenger had spoken the truth acquitted him. Not only was this the first great libel suit in New York, it was also a victory for what would later be known as freedom of speech. One little known fact and most famous outcropping from this trial was the formation of the Sons of Liberty.

Although most of the history of early New York State deals with the New York City area, this era remains important in the formation of what would become known as the Empire State.

Continued upheaval between the French and British, both eager to prove world supremacy spilled into the New World, involving the colonies. King George's War [AKA the War of Austrian Succession], which raged from 1744 through 1748, cost the colonist in more than monetary losses. Besides supplying money over £100,000, guns and men, sixteen hundred to the cause; during the Saratoga Massacre [November 16, 1745] twenty homes were burned, a dozen settlers were murdered and more than one hundred were taken captive. The Treaty of Aix-la-Chapelle may have ended that war, but it did not end the drive for American supremacy.

During the skirmish, Admiral George Clinton, then Governor of New York, appointed Sir William Johnson, Indian Superintendent. While some were skeptical of the appointment, Johnson proved to be perfect for the position. Johnson took his position seriously, first learning their language, then adopting their dress and customs. He became a true friend and advocate, joining them in hunting, sports and game. Eventually, his marriage to a native woman would lead to a new position, *Sole Superintendent to the Six Nations*, a position he would hold until his death in 1774.

The colonist realized that the English and the French were far from satisfied with their quest for domination in the New World. In 1754 all colonies north of the Potomac held a congress at Albany. Their plans were to form an alliance with the Iroquois against the French. Five representatives of the colonies met with one hundred fifty warriors from the Six Nations. After securing the cooperation of the natives, Benjamin Franklin prepared a plan to unite the colonies which would be rejected on both ends. The colonist rejected the union on the grounds that the proposal offered too much power to the King. The King vetoed the proposal because he felt it offered too much power to the colonies.

During this era, March 12, 1772, Tryon County, named for Governor Tryon, would be set off from Albany County. Tryon encompassed all of New York State west of historical Ulster, Albany and Charlotte Counties.

Early in 1775, General Edward Braddock arrived from England leading a full military force. Calling a convention of governors in Alexandria, Virginia, Braddock outlined his plan for three expeditions against the French. The first attack on Fort Duquesne would be led by Braddock himself. The second attack on Fort Niagara would be led by Governor Shirley of Massachusetts. The final attack would be led by Colonel William Johnson.

The first two plans met with failure and Johnsons attack seemed doomed from the start. His expedition unlike the other two included six hundred men from New York and New England, mainly farmers; plus another two hundred and fifty natives rather than trained militia. At first, it appeared all was lost when the French circled around, catching the group sent to head them off, off guard killing both leaders. The remaining men ran back to their camp, leading the exhilarated French straight to the encampment. After a bitter six hour battle the leader of the French, seriously wounded, was taken captive. Those in the French company who were busy beating their retreat were met by New York and New Hampshire Rangers. Victory belonged to the colonist.

Under English rule it was the state that oversaw schooling. Like the Dutch, the English required teachers to be licensed by either the church or the government. Education was far more liberal under English rule. Students were now taught not only the common branches of education but also catechism, as well as the use of arms, dancing, embroidery, navigation and languages. In 1772, a city tax paid the salary of the first who taught under an educational act brought about by legislation.

According to this act, the teacher still must be licensed, he also must belong to the Church of England, teach both common branches and language arts. The *Grammar Free School*, created by this act was for the *education and instruction of youth and male children* with English, French or Dutch parents.

The New York – New Hampshire Border Wars

The year 1749 marked the beginning of a battle which would stifle colonist living in what would become the State of Vermont for decades. Caught between the political ambitions of two Governors who were more concerned with fulfilling their wants than maintaining the needs of their citizens; the New York – New Hampshire Boarder Wars would become a fatal game of power, with the settler as the pawns.

It all began when New Hampshire became a royal province in the year 1741. Prior to this time, the Governor of Massachusetts was also the acting governor of the New Hampshire area. Benning Wentworth, son of John Wentworth, Lieutenant Governor of Province from 1717 until 1730 and Mary Benning became the first governor of New Hampshire. Benning literally *had it all*. He was a wealthy Harvard graduate, who became known for his story book romance and second marriage to Martha Hilton, his serving maid on his sixtieth birthday; the tale of which was celebrated by a poem written by Henry Wadsworth Longfellow: *Tales of the Wayside Inn*.

Eight years after his appointment as governor, Wentworth decided to pursue the royal policy of *subduing the wilderness*. On January 11, 1749, Wentworth made his first land grant within the present State of Vermont. The new township was named, Bennington. During a fifteen year period, he would make one hundred thirty one township grants, a portion of which he would grant to himself. At the end of fifteen years, his personal land grants totaled sixty five thousand acres.

Two factors, important both to history and the border crises should be interjected at this point. Throughout history, it can be noted that power, money and greed have been a driving force in humans. While one would think that politicians would consider the needs of their constituents over the wants of themselves, history repeatedly proves that greed and power overshadow all else. After having made the first land grant within the present State of Vermont, Wentworth not only urged New York Governor Clinton to also make land grants, but also requested information on the eastern boundary of New York Colony.

In response, Clinton reiterated the grant made to the Duke of York by his brother, indicating that the eastern boundary of New York Colony was the Connecticut River. Apparently, Wentworth, realizing early on the wealth to be his from the process of granting land noted to Governor Clinton that both Connecticut and Massachusetts had extended their boundaries westward to the Connecticut River, therefore New Hampshire should hold equal right with westward expansion. Noting that he felt it unwise to start a border war, Wentworth indicated that he would submit the matter to the King.

Settlers had made an original attempt to secure the township grants from the Colony of New York. On September 24, 1760, a meeting was held at the home of Nathan Sheppard of Nine Partners, New York. Samuel Rose was appointed as agent for the interested parties and sent to Albany to secure a grant for two townships, Danby and Pawlet. Unfortunately, Rose failed in his appointment. New York was not granting lands. On October 15, 1760, Jonathan Willard was appointed as agent for the same group of people and sent to Portsmouth, New Hampshire to secure the same. He successfully returned with grants for the townships of Danby, Pawlet and Harwick, now Mount Taber.

As the previous paragraph states, the settlers went first to New York, the colony who claimed rights to the land west of the Connecticut River, returning without a land grant. Upon returning from New Hampshire, the settlers had received their grant. Surveys of the area were made during 1762 and 1763 and a road was laid at the expense of the grantees between Bennington and Danby in the autumn of 1764. Five men from Nine Partners, New York and the New Hampshire area would settle in the Danby area the following spring.

Joseph Soper, the first settler of the town of Danby and one of the original grantees also bears the title of having made the first clearing and erecting the town's first log house. Several months would pass before another family would move into the Danby area. Soper had come to the area with his family, traveling a path through marked trees. Their entire worldly possessions had been carried on the backs of two horses. Two of his brothers had settled, at the same time, in the town of Dorset.

Being the only settler, Soper either had to pound his own grist or take it on horseback fourteen miles to the nearest mill. A few years after settling, Soper would find it necessary to make such a trip to a neighboring mill. His return trip home began later than he had originally anticipated it would be; a wild storm had begun to ravish the area. Soper's last stop before home was to visit his brother in Dorset who pleaded with him to stay until morning. Having no means by which to contact his wife, Soper refused his brother's hospitality and continued towards his home, hoping to spare his wife a night's worry. Concern led his brother's to travel to his house early the next morning, assuring themselves that Joseph had arrived safely. They would find his horses and grist and finally his body. He had frozen to death less than a mile from his home. Soper's would be the first grave in the town of Danby.

It is the contention of many Vermont historians that the New York governors, having realized the wealth that was extended to Wentworth from the grants he made, looked upon the land with greed, rather than the settlers such as Soper. One year after Wentworth made his final grant, New York Lieutenant Governor, Calwallader Colden, under the contention that the province of New York extended eastward to the Connecticut River, began making grants of the same property that Wentworth had already granted. The land consisting of twenty six thousand acres to be named Princetown, was issued to twenty six grantees in lots of one thousand acres each on May 21, 1765. Within a few weeks all but one grantee had sold or transferred their holdings to land speculators; James Duane, Attorney General John Taber Kemp and Walter Rutherford.

New York's next governor to make land grants consisting of the New Hampshire grants would be Sir Henry Moore, Governor from November 13, 1765 until his death, September 12, 1769. During Moore's reign, he confirmed six New Hampshire grants, while continuing to make grants of pre-granted lands.

Colden became acting governor upon Moore's death, immediately reenacting his program of granting lands. In October of 1770, the Earl of Dunmore became the Royal Governor of New York. He too conveyed land grants despite the claims of the settlers on the New Hampshire grants, as did his successor Governor Tryon. Tryon also confirmed and re-granted several of the original New Hampshire grants during his reign.

When Tryon was called to England, Colden was once again acting governor. Once again, he immediately began making grants against the New Hampshire claims. Tryon continued the grant program upon returning to the colonies. As a result of the New York land grants a bitter feud would encompass the area for the next twenty five years.

Early settlers, after having been turned away from New York without a grant for land had thus gone to New Hampshire, making good faith purchases. Their sole purpose had been to establish homes. Not only had they paid the fees required for the grants, they had suffered the hardships of other pioneers of the time while taming the wilderness and improving the land. Those settlers who appeared in Albany to confirm their New Hampshire Grants were told that they must now pay a fee to New York in the amount of twenty five pounds New York money, equivalent to fourteen pounds sterling per each one thousand acres of land they had been granted. In other words, they were being asked by the State of New York to buy the same land a second time.

Quarrelling between the Governors of New York and New Hampshire amounted to whining letters addressed to the King and Parliament. Each governor cited his position and in many cases dramatized their own thoughts. Out and out lies were also written to the King, each governor turning more childish as the feud heated. Colden attempted to bribe members of council to assure his case was won. He whined that despite the fact the New Hampshire claimed the land was bought and settled, that the actual land had been sold to land speculators eager to turn a dollar at the expense of the government. Wentworth effectively chose to turn the tables to the heart of the matter, stating; *'New York pretends to claim even to the banks of the Connecticut River although she never laid out and settled one town in that part of His Majesty's land since she existed as a government.'*

On July 20, 1764 an order issued by the King in Council reaffirmed New York's claim to the land in dispute. Although Colden saw fit to reiterate this as a win, he ignored the ground rules which forbad New York to issue any further grants made on the lands annexed to New York by His Majesty's determination of ownership of land between New York and New Hampshire. While New York Council indicated that the Surveyor General was not to act upon any warrants of survey against any lands lived on by the New Hampshire grantees, Colden was busy re-granting the lands. It soon became apparent that no matter who issued proclamation, no matter who had previously settled these lands, acting Governor Colden would do what he wanted, when he wanted to do it.

A letter from His Majesty, dated the eleventh of December 1767 reiterated his concern for the settlers on the New Hampshire grants, but New York governors continuously ignored the decrees. The response of Governor Moore simply reiterated his position by declaring that of the twenty one townships granted by New Hampshire, only three held any settlers, those of Bennington, Pownel and Shaftsbury. His letter continued stating that in regards to the massive grant of land he had taken upon himself was meant merely to be handed to the poor in small farm lots, the only repayment being that the settlers were to immediately set up the manufacture of pot ash and the cultivation of Hemp. Moore denied requesting money from the settlers to confirm their New Hampshire grants, calling New Hampshire's claims of more than one thousand settlers bogus. He continuously insisted that the holders of the New Hampshire grants were land speculators. Yet, even those of criminal mind such as Colden himself spoke against Moore, claiming that Moore refused to grant any lands without receiving his full fees in return.

Soon, the feud began to more closely fall upon the shoulders of the settlers as they received ejection notices from the New York grantees. Unfortunately, the ejection trials would be held in New York, the presiding judge's brother-in-law was well known as a person interested in the land. While the judge was within his right to declare the New Hampshire grants void on the sole fact that the land had been a possession of New York State, his declaration served only to enrage the settlers.

Now that it had become evident that New York meant to evict the settlers holding New Hampshire grants, the settlers formed their first militia. Whether it's a tall tale or an actual occurrence, it is been written in several Vermont histories that the New York Governor, upon learning of the formation of the militia in the areas of land dispute proclaimed: *'I will drive to the Green Mountains those who oppose my authority.'* Utilizing the threat to provoke the governor, the opposition named itself *The Green Mountain Boys*.

From this point in time until the uprise against Britain came into play, the land dispute had turned deadly. Those holding New Hampshire grants, in full knowledge of the decree issued by the King became determined to see justice. New York Governor's accepted their behavior as a means to exert power. Many on both sides of the struggle would now suffer.

A Struggle for Independence

Prelude to a War

However, English rule was soon to become history. The colonies were beginning to revolt, quietly at first, their voices growing and their fight for justice created an unexpected uniting of body, mind, and soul throughout each of the colonies.

Prior to the French and Indian Wars, England had enjoyed a good relationship with her far west colonies. Not only did the Crown trade freely but she found the trade to be exceptionally profitable. To maintain this relationship, England had to merely leave the colonies to themselves, allowing, for the most part, those across the Atlantic to their own governing, but financial troubles would force a Crown burden upon the colonists.

The French and Indian Wars had been a financial burden to the Crown. King George III felt it only fair that the colonies pay their share of that burden, thus he enacted new taxes, duties and trade restrictions. Unlike the previous laws enacted upon the colonies which were rarely enforced; harsh laws were now passed to assure the crown that the colonies would be forced, legally, to pay their share of the war burden.

Although the French and Indian Wars had been an extension of greater European Conflicts, they had turned to local conflicts, not only with the French but also their native allies, leaving the bewildered colonist looking to the Crown for protection. Colonist realized that although the British had been inept at best and the colony militia had bore the brunt of homeland warfare, the colonist still felt an allegiance to England. While many historians feel that the colonist felt disdain towards the crown for taxing the colonies in an effort to offset the war deficit; many more feel that the truth of the matter lies far beneath the apparent.

A wedge had been driven between the colonists and their homeland, but the actions of King George III would actually set the colony's rebellion into motion. While the colonists did not understand the taxation, they would have gladly paid their share with a small provision; the colonists made a simple request of Parliament, colony representation before payment of taxation. When Parliament responded that they [Parliament] represented all English subjects including those in the colonies and therefore the need for seats to be granted to the colonies was inappropriate, the avant-garde rose amongst the colonists.

Those politically inclined colonists rationalized that the distance between the mother country and her colonies acted as a barrier for effective representation. The interest of the colonies and the people of England were extraneous. With the population of the colonies growing as rapidly as they were, there was absolutely no way Parliament could afford to offer the colonies a proportionate representation. Thus, the politician born of the depravity of taxation without representation realized the facts as thus: with Parliamentary representation being virtually impossible and taxation without representation showing proof of an autocratic power, there were but two solutions to the problem; either the Crown could voluntarily grant the colonies their independence or the colonist could stage a revolution.

By 1760, legislature felt the need to appoint its own Supreme Court Judges, the popular party of the time contending that *all authority was derived from the people*. Acting Governor, Cadwallader Colden vetoed the idea. In 1762, legislature took its appeal to the King, petitioning for *the independency of so important a tribunal*. At the same time, legislature denounced *involuntary taxes and impositions* as being *contrary to a state of liberty*. Again, the appeals went unheeded.

A proposed *Stamp Act* by English Parliament as a means to raise permanent revenue from the American colonies met with condemnation in New York. This hated act was reprinted in America affixed with a death's head. It was titled *The Folly of England and the Ruin of America*. When English Officer, Major James announced '*I will cram the stamps down the throats of the people with the end of my sword,*' an angry mob destroyed all the personal possessions in his home, threatening physical violence for his part in the hated act.

New Yorkers were not the only Americans enraged by this act. Massachusetts called upon every assembly in America to meet in conference. The *Stamp Act Congress* met in New York City in October of 1765. A *Declaration of Rights and Grievances* was adopted, a copy sent to each house of Parliament.

Upon the stamps reaching New York City merchants agreed not to import any goods while the Stamp Act was in effect. Others were warned; *the first man that either distributes or makes use of stamped paper should take care of his house, person and effects.'* The colonist rose to the occasion, banding together as one against the act. Their actions brought fear upon the English, on March 13, 1766, the Stamp Act was repealed, while the right to tax the colonies stood firm. In 1767, the British, determined to raise money from the colonies placed a tax on glass, lead, paints, paper and tea.

To force the colonist to obedience, the British sent troops to America, who were in turn, denied *quarters*. As punishment, Parliament suspended legislative power of assembly, which remained in effect for two years at which time another assembly was elected. Upon realization that the new assembly was loyal to the colonist, it too was dissolved. The next assembly proved to favor the king, and thus was left intact.

The Sons of Liberty would become notorious for their acts of rebellion. One such act, not as renowned as the Boston Tea Party, followed the example however, of the Boston gentlemen. When the East India Company begged Parliament for relief on its tea that could not be sold in England, Parliament granted the request, making tea less expensive in New York than in London. The colonist declared they would still not touch the tea, and made preparations to prevent the ships from landing.

Governor Tryon, for whom the fourteenth county of New York was named, declared that the tea would be delivered, even if it were *sprinkled with blood*. The Sons of Liberty were not to be thwarted in their efforts. The first ship was forced to return to England with its cargo intact. The second ship was not quite as lucky. Taking their cue from the Boston gentlemen, the Sons of Liberty dressed as Mohawks, boarded the ship, broke open the chests of tea and poured it into the bay.

During this time of upheaval two new political parties were born; the Whigs and Tories. The Whigs platform was to oppose all British taxation by both boycott and coercion. The Tories, while also against the British taxation, believed in petitioning against the wrongs through proper governmental channels. These parties were later become known as the Revolutionist and the Loyalist.

It was not until the British closed the port at Boston that the colonist revolt became more controlled. The Sons of Liberty in New York, under Tory influence requested a Congress be held. Taking the proposal a step further, Massachusetts called the First Continental Congress which would be held in Philadelphia in September of 1774. It was here that John Jay drafted the famous declaration of rights addressed to the people of Britain, declaring; *'no power on earth has the right to take our property without our consent.'*

The British would be shocked to realize the high degree of communication which existed between the colonies. Both The *Sons of Liberty* and the *Committees of Correspondence* in each colony worked to coordinate local actions across their colony. Each event now became an item of *national* importance. Ironically, the tax programs that England had established for the colonies had served to unite into a single nation a group of colonies which prior to the taxation had been seen as a mere collection of competitive territories.

American poets have given rise to both heroes and Revolutionary War dates. Paul Revere would probably never have gained national attention if it were not for Henry Wadsworth Longfellow's epic poem; *Paul Revere's Ride*. Although he was a true patriot, he did little more than any other revolutionary rider. Had it not been for Longfellow, Revere would probably been know simply as a world class silversmith rather than an historical hero.

Officially, the Revolutionary War began on Wednesday April 19, 1775. However, that was merely for those who participated or witnessed the confrontations at Lexington and Concord. It would be four days later that the citizens of New York City would learn that shots had been fired, when Israel Bissel, an express rider rode into the city crying the news. Therefore, technically the starting date of the Revolutionary War became 4:00 PM Sunday April 23, 1775 for those residing in New York. Philadelphians would learn of the incident the following day, making their technical starting date April 24, 1775, while those in Williamsburg, Virginia would hold the starting date as April 28, 1775. Virtual weeks would pass before the citizens of Georgia would become involved in the Revolution, via either knowledge or immersion. More than one month would pass, when on May 28, 1775 King George III would finally be informed of the Revolution.

Despite the time it would take for all involved to be brought up to date on the facts of the Revolutionary War, April 19, 1775 would become the very first time throughout history that the phrase *the shot heard around the world*, would be used to describe the beginning of a major war. This was the last line in the opening stanza of Ralph Waldo Emerson's epic Revolutionary Poem *The Concord Hymn* written in 1837.

While most know the basics of the revolution, few realize the contribution Americans gave as a whole. After questioning many persons concerning the participants of the revolution, we have realized that author Thomas Fleming in his work entitled; *Everybody's Revolution* depicts not only the most accurate portrayal of American involvement, but also dispels misconceptions that a great percentage of American's hold.

First and foremost, the American Revolution was not simply former British citizens fighting the British for their freedom; the diversity of American society at the start of the revolution was startling. Those fighting for our freedom included persons of nearly every ethnic circumstance, including the African American slaves. While recruiting posters called for *brave, healthy, able bodied and well disposed young men*, neither age nor gender seemed significant during the actual conflict. Male and female teenagers participated, men and women held not only positions of authority, but acted as well maintained spies. As the revolution progressed, persons around the world joined in battle, the French becoming allies of the colonist and the Hessians being paid mercenaries of the British. In actuality, the American Revolution can be considered the *First World War*

Despite the fact that the opening volleys of war had already been played, John Dickinson drafted *the Olive Branch Petition*, basically a last ditch effort by the colonist to assert their rights while maintaining loyalty to the crown. The petition was adopted by the Second Continental Congress on July 5, 1775 and forwarded to King George III, who rejected the petition.

One year later, between June 11 and June 28, 1776, Thomas Jefferson would draft the *Declaration of Independence*, an expression of American convictions and grievances against the King. One of the grievances expressed in the original draft condemned the King for supporting slavery. This clause however, was overridden by delegates who were also southern slave holders and northern merchants who profited from the slave trade. The original intent of this document was to justify to the world the reasoning behind the colonies tie severing with the Crown. Of the fifty six delegates who signed this petition, eighteen were not of English ancestry and eight were first generation immigrants.

Of those whose names appear as members of the *Continental Army*; nearly thirty three percent were of Irish ancestry and another twenty percent were of German ancestry. By 1780, one in every seven men in the army was of African descent, each willingly joining in the service to free their new country from British tyranny and themselves from slavery. [Although it would be August before all of the signatures would be collected on the Declaration of Independence, July 4th became the accepted official anniversary of the signing of the document. The first celebration of its anniversary was celebrated the following year, 1777. By the 1800's the tradition of parades, picnics and fireworks had been firmly established.]

While northerners held little reluctance in arming their black counterparts, southern leaders feared arming the slaves, who greatly outnumbered the whites, would grant the African Americans the idea of starting their own revolution. During the 1777 Continental Congress, Washington's request that each soldier enlist for three years, passed. Additionally, each state was assigned a quota of soldiers to provide the army. In turn, each state required individual towns to provide a specific quota of men. White men, reluctant and/or unwilling to commit to a three year enlistment more often than not hired an African-American to take their place in service to the country.

Many former slaves were offered their freedom in return for service to their country, greatly increasing their ranks. There were so many black Americans serving that they formed an entire company within one regiment. In Rhode Island, the General Assembly passed a law which allowed General James Varnum to recruit a regiment of African Americans in 1778. The assembly *guaranteed* that once the war ended these men would be *absolutely free*. More than two hundred African Americans joined forming the First Rhode Island Regiment of Black Soldiers.

Black Soldiers included: Peter Salem, Pomp Blackman and Prince Estabrook of Lexington. Estabrook would become the first casualty of the Revolution. Fourteen officers sent a petition of praise concerning Salem Poor, a hero at Bunker Hill, to the Massachusetts legislature. Oliver Cromwell made the historical Delaware Crossing with General George Washington. The Carter brothers; Aaron, Jacob, Asher, Edward and Esau each enlisted in the Rhode Island Regiment. Although she was not a member of the army, *Mammy Kate* is noted for rescuing her Georgia master, Stephen Heard, from British captors in 1779. In 1781, a slave known only as *Jim*, owned by Williamsburg, Virginia patriot, William Armistead became a voluntary spy for the Continental Army. James Forten, a free fourteen year old African American would become a hero for his actions after being captured by the British while serving his new country. The British had offered to take Forten to England and pay for his education if he would give up his allegiance to the colonies. History records Forten's response as "*No, I was captured fighting for my country. I will never be a traitor to her interest.*"

While many recall that the Native American for the most part had sided with the British, few realize that several Native Americans not only fought in the Continental Army, but also won commissions for their service. In mid May of 1778, after a harrowing winter spent at Valley Forge, the soldiers would witness yet another experience which would be entered in the annals of history some two hundred years after the occurrence; forty nine Oneida Tribesmen who wanted to join the colonist in their fight for freedom had entered the fort.

Washington's recommendation would commission Oneida warrior Lewis Atayataghronghta as lieutenant colonel in the Continental Army in 1779. That same year found seven additional men of the Oneida Nation and two of the Tuscarora Nation commissioned as lieutenants and captains. Although these men were commissioned, they were by far not the only Native American volunteers. Volunteers were also sent by the Stockbridge and Mashpee Tribes of Massachusetts and the Catawba Tribe of the Carolinas.

Of all the Native American volunteers in the Continental Army, those of the Oneida Tribe would suffer most. Late in the revolution, in retaliation for loyalty to the Americans, the Mohawks and other tribes loyal to the British, attacked and killed many men and women of the Oneida Tribe, yet their loyalty to the American cause never wavered. Although the Oneida had been part of the Iroquois Confederation, most of the Confederation had backed the British. Divided loyalties would lead to Sullivan's successful raid of Iroquois lands in northwestern New York which caused many of the Iroquois to flee to Canada, abandoning their villages to destruction.

Mary Ludwig Hays McCauly, AKA Molly Pitcher, is probably the most well known female of revolutionary fame. [NOTE – some historians believe that the tale of Molly Pitcher was merely an urban legend passed along to offer respect to the women who served their country by manning cannons on the battlefield. Is this story true? We have yet to look deep enough to extract the truth of this tale, we do, however know that Fort Sill, Oklahoma carries the tale of Molly Pitcher on their website.] While serving the army by bringing refreshments to the men, Molly witnessed her husband being shot. After first rushing to attend his wounds, Molly then manned his cannon, helping to send the British into retreat. It is claimed that General Washington commissioned her *Sergeant Molly Pitcher.*

As stated earlier, there are indeed many women who manned cannons. During the Revolution many women followed their husbands during battle. One such woman was Margaret Corbin. When the *gunner* was shot and killed in battle, Margaret's husband became gunner while Margaret took over her husband's position as matross, the person who loaded the cannon. During the battle, Margaret's husband was also shot and killed. Margaret herself was shot and left for dead, as luck would have it a passing doctor found Margaret and saved her life. Her wounds left her permanently disabled, but her bravery made *Captain Molly of the Invalid Regiment* the first woman to receive a lifetime pension for wounds suffered during battle.

The biggest life line that women of the revolution could offer was their abilities as spies; the most well known of which are Lydia Darragh an undertaker, nurse and midwife from Philadelphia, as well as Long Island's Secret Service *Agent 13*.

Youngsters were also involved in the call for Independence. Fifteen year old Joseph Plumb Martin of Connecticut lied about his age as did twelve year old Ebenezer Fox of Massachusetts to enlist in the cause. Sixteen year old William Diamond of Lexington, Massachusetts signed up as a drummer boy. Young women such as sixteen year old Sybil Ludington helped spread the word amongst Connecticut Militiamen to muster on the road to Danbury. Fourteen year old Jemima Boone, daughter of famed frontiersman Daniel Boone exasperated her captors giving her father time to rescue her. Sixteen year old Elizabeth Zane rushed passed the enemy who were hesitant to shoot a female, to carry gunpowder to the American troops.

[NOTE – Joseph Plumb Martin wrote a narrative of his adventures during the Revolutionary War. Benchmark Books re-published this narrative as *The diary of Joseph Plumb Martin, a Revolutionary War soldier*, in 2001. We suggest that each of our readers read this book for a look at the Revolutionary War in a first person perspective.]

The American Revolution united this country in a way that would never again be equaled. Age, race, sex, ethnic origins no longer mattered to the colonists their only goal was winning their freedom. To successfully reach their goal, they had to work as one. Eight years after the battle had begun; the colonists successfully achieved that goal.

Although the Treaty officially ending the revolution would not be signed until 1783, the siege at Yorktown served to effectively end the war. In the eight years of fighting, it would be the last big battle of the war; *the Battle of Eutaw Springs, South Carolina,* that would cost the British the most, hosting the highest casualty rate the British had encountered throughout the eight year duration of the Revolution. Although King George III was against retreat, Parliament now pushed for peace.

Population statistics show that at the time of the Revolutionary War, there were 3.5 million people living in the United States, two hundred thousand of which joined the ranks of the newly formed Continental Army; of which 4,435 lost their lives an additional 6,188 were wounded. Costs of the War range from $13.8 to $170 million, being the worth at the time of the war; this would translate roughly at $1.2 Billion in today's dollars. These figures do not include the costs to the settlers.

Settlers faced the horrors of Indian attacks, burning of entire towns and massacre. Some families lost their means of support as the husband/father left them to defend his country, leaving them distressed and destitute. The psychological damage has never been accounted for, not has time in make-shift hospitals or for those taken prisoner who were forced onto British Prison Boats. Yet, the call of the country, the call of freedom held a much stronger calling. The persons of the Revolution were fighting not only for their freedom, but also for the freedom of every generation to come.

On September 3, 1783 the Treaty of Paris had been ratified by each government and signed. Great Britain now recognized the United States as an Independent Nation. The United States now bounded Canada to the north, the Mississippi River to the West the thirty first parallel to the south and the Atlantic Ocean to the east. Additionally, Americans were now free to fish off the banks of both Newfoundland and Nova Scotia. Legal debts would be honored by each country. No penalties would be enacted against citizens of any other country which had been involved in the revolution. Finally, all remaining British troops would evacuate the area and the Mississippi River would be opened to navigation by both Americans and the British.

With freedom came responsibility and an oppressive fiscal dilemma. The new government found itself heavily indebt and without power to levy taxes by which to alleviate at least a portion of the burden. The original constitution of the fledgling country *the Articles of Confederation* agreed to by the Continental Congress on November

15, 1777; ratified and in force on March 1, 1781, had created a weak, nearly powerless central government. The new government realized an urgent need to revise the Articles of Confederation existed. On May 17, 1787 the Federal Convention convened at the State House in Philadelphia, PA [Independence Hall] but was adjourned day to day until enough delegates [a quorum of seven states] were finally obtained on May 25. After much discussion and debate, it was realized that rather than revise the existing Articles a new frame of government was required. Scraping the Articles of Confederation, the Congress drafted the Constitution.

'To all to whom these Presents shall come, we the undersigned Delegates of the States affixed to our Names send greeting. Articles of Confederation and perpetual Union between the States of New Hampshire, Massachusetts bay, Rhode Island and Providence Plantations, Connecticut, New York, New Jersey, Pennsylvania, Delaware, Maryland, Virginia, North Carolina, South Carolina and Georgia' came : 'We the people of the United States, in order to form a more perfect union, establish justice, insure domestic tranquility, provide for the common defense, promote the general welfare, and secure the blessings of liberty to ourselves and our posterity, do ordain and establish this Constitution for the United States of America.'

1787 proved to be a busy historical year; Delaware [December 7, 1787] Pennsylvania [December 12, 1787] and New Jersey [December 18, 1787] all became states of the newly formed Union. The Constitution was drafted on September 17, 1787 and ratified on March 4, 1789, placing a strong, centralized government into position. [Originally, each state received a copy of twelve amendments, but only articles three through twelve were ratified on December 15, 1791, known to the people of the United States as our *Bill of Rights*. The original first two amendments which were not ratified concerned the number of constituents for each representative and compensation of Congressmen.]

Eight states would be admitted to the union in 1788; Georgia [January 2, 1788] Connecticut [January 9, 1788] Massachusetts [February 6, 1788] Maryland [April 28, 1788] South Carolina [May 23, 1788] New Hampshire [June 21, 1788] Virginia [June 25, 1788] and New York [July 26, 1788]. Over the next three years one state would be admitted to the union per year; 1789 North Carolina [November 21], 1790 Rhode Island [May 29] and 1791 Vermont [March 4].

Once the Constitution had been ratified, the country found itself in need of a leader. Since the amendments had yet to be passed, the election of the time was quite different from today. First and foremost, there had yet to be formed any political parties, the nomination process was not in place; the framers of the Constitution had taken for granted that Washington wanted to be President, which was untrue and he had to be coaxed into running for the position. His popularity was at an all time high, once convinced that retirement was not yet an option for him, Washington agreed to run, but no one ran against him.

The Birth of a Nation

With the Revolution behind them and a new government being formed great changes were taking place throughout the colonies, including New York. Tryon County, which had been named for English Governor William Tryon was amongst the first of the old things to give way to the new. With the victorious end of the Revolution, the young country wiped itself of horrifying reminders of the former governor by changing the name of Tryon County to Montgomery County, named in honor of General Richard Montgomery, in 1784.

Settling disputes created during British rule now became crucial. Charters granted to both New York and Massachusetts described their boundaries, using distances from coastal rivers as a baseline, as extending westward to the Pacific Ocean. This irregularity allowed both colonies to claim the same land. The exact area in dispute included all of New York west of Seneca Lake, and extending westward to the Niagara River and Lake Erie. The northern boundary was Lake Ontario and southward to Pennsylvania. New York and Massachusetts agreed to divide the rights to the lands in question, with Massachusetts obtaining preemptive rights to approximately six million acres of land. [These preemptive rights allowed for Massachusetts to have rights over any other person, company or governmental institution to purchase the lands from the native owners.] New York maintained governing rights to the same lands. This agreement between the states is known as the *Hartford Treaty of 1786*.

April 1, 1788, Massachusetts had sold the preemptive rights all six million acres of land to Oliver Phelps and Nathaniel Gorham for $1 million in specie [a Latin term meaning in the actual form] or in certain Massachusetts securities, payable in three equal annual installments. This transaction would assist Massachusetts in repaying some of her debt incurred during the Revolutionary War. By July 8, Phelps and Gorham had extinguished Indian rights to 184, 300 acres of land within their purchase. The duo paid the Iroquois $5,000 plus a $500 annuity.

While in the process of purchasing the preemptive rights and extinguishing Indian rights to the land, additional changes were taking place within New York. In 1789, all land in New York State from north to south with an eastern boarder that touched upon the western shore of

Seneca Lake and extending westward now became Ontario County and the town of Northampton covered the entire western sector of the state.

Phelps and Gorham defaulted on their 1790 installment and 3, 750,000 acres of land reverted back to Massachusetts on March 10, 1791. Two days later, Massachusetts re-sold the pre-emptive rights to the richest man in America, signer of the Declaration of Independence and financier of the Revolutionary War, Robert Morris for the sum of $333,333.33. The land conveyed was to Morris in five deeds on May 11, 1791.

The Holland Land Company, an unincorporated syndicate of thirteen Dutch investors from Amsterdam, who had placed funds in the hands of American trustees to purchase land in the central and western sectors of New York and the western sector of Pennsylvania would purchase all but 500,000 acres of land from Morris which he reserved for himself. Sales of land were made in December of 1792 and February and July of 1793, but money from those sales would not be received until Indian claims were extinguished. [American trustees were necessary because aliens were not allowed to own land in America. This action also saved time for the investors because they never found the necessity to travel to America to check on their investment.] Morris would not extinguish Indian claim to this land until 1794 at *the Treaty of Big Tree* [now Geneseo, NY]. Morris had but five years left to live at this point in time and three of them were spent in debtor's prison after the collapse of his company caused by the *Panic of 1797* [a depression of the commerce markets that held direct repercussions on financial, commercial and real estate markets along the coastal United States and the Caribbean]. While the Holland Land Company agents were busy with preparations in accordance with their purchase, two more states would be admitted to the union; Kentucky [June 1, 1792] and Tennessee [June 1, 1796].

Although the native wanted to hold onto their lands, bribery and liquor succeeded in betrayal of the Iroquois by the white man. In the end, under sanction of the United States Government, the Indian rights were extinguished with the signing of the Treaty of Big Tree on September 15, 1797. Ten Reservations comprising a total of 337 square miles were set aside as Indian lands, the largest, Buffalo Creek, being assigned to the Seneca. The remaining land title encompassing 3, 250,000 acres of land from a line approximately twelve miles west of the Genesee River to the present western border of the State of New York was purchased for $100,000, to be paid the Iroquois in installments.

With the Treaty signed, the land area now became known as the Holland Purchase. The original intentions of the Dutch investors were to rapidly sell their purchase at a great profit. However, they spent years investing more and more into their purchase to survey the land, build roads and canals, anything that would make the land more attractive to potential purchasers. By 1801 a log cabin was used as the first land office. Two years later, after the founding of the new county, the office would be moved to Batavia. The building was replaced by a frame dwelling in 1809 and a fireproof building replaced the frame building in 1815. This building still stands in downtown Batavia today, acting as the Holland Land Company Museum. Not only does the building hold history, it is a piece of history as prevalent to the town of Collins as it is to Batavia. Built after the *burning of Buffalo*, the building became a local fireproof storehouse for each of the land contracts the Holland Land Company sold.

The Holland Purchase was ready for inhabitation, allowing for even more growth within New York State. As the population of the country began moving westward, many settling within the confines of central New York, a few pushing into the western area of the state it was time once again, to split counties. On March 30, 1802 a new county was formed from Ontario County. Comprising all of the land west of the Genesee River, the new county became Genesee County. According to some, the valley along the stream was called *Zon-esche-o* by the Iroquois, some tribes actually pronouncing the name *Gen-nes-see*. The name is said to mean '*beautiful valley*' and a more fitting name for the area there could not have been. At the same time, the town of Northampton was divided into four townships. Batavia township now covered the entire Holland Land Purchase.

The Louisiana Territory, a section of land extending from the Mississippi River to the Rocky Mountains and covering 800,000 square miles of land was purchased by the United States from France on April 30, 1803. The price was $60 million francs [approximately $15 million] doubling the size of the young country and giving those with the pioneering spirit adequate land on which to settle. [Louisiana however would not be admitted to the union as a state until April 30, 1812.] 1803 also brought the seventeenth state into the union; Ohio on March 1.

In 1804, the town of Batavia was divided into four townships. The first, second and third ranges of the Holland Purchase would now be the town of Batavia; the fourth, fifth and sixth ranges of the Holland Purchase would now be the town of Willink [this included the area now known as the town of Collins]; the seventh, eighth, ninth and tenth ranges of the Holland Purchase would now become the town of Erie; and the remainder of the purchase would now become the town of Chautauqua. On March 11, 1808 [or March 11, 1807, dates are noted as such by various historians] counties within Western New York were once again split. From Genesee County was taken Niagara County, which comprised the present area of Niagara and Erie Counties. Chautauqua and Cattaraugus Counties were also taken from Genesee County at this time. [These two counties have remained within the same border context since that date.] While the area appeared in its wilderness state, the town of Willink, County of Niagara, State of New York was finally ready for the influx of permanent white settlers.

THE TREK TO COLLINS

They had no cars to drive, no maps to find a route or follow. There were no roads past the main settlements such as Albany. The mode of travel was foot, some were lucky enough to have oxen or horses and a wagon. Most were able to carry all of their earthly possessions on their backs. They came alone. Some came with friends. A few traveled with their neighbors. Some simply traveled with others they had met along the way. Few brought their families before they had an opportunity to stake their claim, clear the land and at least build a shelter. They came from Massachusetts; from towns such as Orange. They came from Rhode Island; from places like Providence. They came from Pennsylvania; from cities like Philadelphia. Most came from the small establishment of Danby, Vermont. [Mileage may have been a bit shorter utilizing a more direct route, but the average miles traveled to reach their destination was 424 miles.] They were the pioneers, the sturdy men and women who came into the wilderness that would one day become Collins.

There were no luxuries; no radios to keep one company on such a long journey, no rest stops with clean restrooms to stop by; no McDonald's where you could grab a quick burger. When the roads that the pioneer was accustomed to ran out they were faced with a vast expanse of wilderness. They traveled mainly through large forest, although they may run into an occasional clearing. If they were lucky, they would run across a small settlement along the way. Of course, even a single family settled amongst the long distance was a comfort.

They slept along their chosen path, sometimes building a small campfire to ward off the darkness or the chill. At times, the pioneer, being exceptionally weary found himself waking near a tree he had sat against to rest his weary bones. Pine branches were often used for cover, as protection from harsh weather or chill.

Utilizing the skills taught to every child of the time, the pioneer found his way west using what nature had granted him. The sun, when visible through the trees pointed direction and helped to know the time of day. When the trees were too thick, looking for moss and lichen growth on tree trunks generally told the pioneer which direction was north. The forest also provided much of the pioneer's food on his journey. Knowing which berries and roots were edible kept the pioneer nourished as he made his trek westward.

The journey to Collins may have been long and hard, but by far, it was the easiest task the pioneer would endure. Upon arrival and selection of land the work started. The land had to be cleared and a home built. During the early years, settlers were few and far between. Most men found themselves on their own, or helped only by their family if they had been lucky enough to be accompanied on the initial trip by their family. Clearing the land was a job very few of today's population could endure. There was generally but a single axe with which to work and acres of land that needed to be cleared. Many of the early pioneers who had made the trek alone had come equipped with an axe, a gun and seeds to sow. Everything that needed to be tended to had to be tended to with those simple items or whatever the pioneer could fashion from his surroundings.

Erasmus Briggs wrote word for word his interviews with those who had settled the area early and were alive to tell their tale when he was working on his history of our area in the late 1870's. The following is an exert taken from an interview with Sylvenus Bates, a pioneer who came alone to Collins in 1811, preparing the area for his family:

"...I built me a shanty about eight foot square, on a side hill near the creek, the lower side about eight feet high and the back side about two; I drove down four crotches and laid some stick across for a bedstead, and measured myself and peeled a piece of ash bark the proper length and laid it on, and that, with a blanket, composed my bed.

"That summer I chopped and cleared four acres and sowed it to winter wheat; I worked all summer, early and late; I had no meat t o eat except a hog's leg, which I bought of Samuel Cooper. I planted some potatoes in the spring, and when the new ones got to be as big as walnuts with the shucks on, I use to dig and eat them, the new and old ones together. I would eat a half a dozen for my dinner, and would take as many more out and lay them on a stump for luncheon; sometimes I became so weak that I staggered as I walked about..."

Life indeed was hard in the days of the pioneers and it was only beginning.

It was 1806 the Friends Annual Meeting of Philadelphia chose a trio, two bachelors and a bachelorette to live as a family near the Cattaraugus Indian Reservation *and instruct the untutored red-man the arts of civilization.* The missionaries were; Jacob Taylor family manager,

Stephen Twining and Hannah Jackson. Although the missionaries came in universal brotherhood, this was a mission, they were missionaries, their expectations had not been to come as permanent settlers for each of these missionaries had spent time on other such missions. Yet Jacob Taylor not only became a permanent settler to the area, his influenced on those who eventually made their way to the vast wilderness was felt long after his death.

The trio remained basically shut off from civilization for more than two years, their nearest neighbors the natives on the Reservation and forest surrounding them on all other sides. Finally in 1809 more white settlers entered the area seeking land for a new home, finally settling the area in 1810. They were; Turner Aldrich, Stephen Lapham, Joshua Palmerton, Stephen Peters, Arad Howard, and Aaron Lindsley. The third Federal census of the United States now listed our first settlers as persons living in the town of Willink, county of Niagara, and state of New York.

By 1811, despite news of another conflict between the newly formed United States and Britain looming on the horizon, word of the prime land within the Holland Purchase had traveled and more settlers streamed into the area. They were; Stephen Wilbur, Sylvenus Bates; Luke Crandall, Benjamin Albee, Warren Tanner Allen, Arnold, John and their father Nathan King.

On March 20, 1812 due to the influx of settlers into the area, Willink would be divided into four towns. The portion of the original town of Willink retaining the name now contained the area of Aurora, Wales, Holland and Colden; Hamburg, Eden and Concord were now, by an act of legislation separate entities. Hamburg became comprised of the present towns of Hamburg and Orchard Park [then known as East Hamburg]. Eden comprised the present towns of Eden, Evans and Boston. Concord was now comprised of the present towns of Concord, Collins, North Collins, Sardinia and a small section of the town of Brant.

Despite the remote locale, news of a pending disaster filtered through the wilderness. France and Britain, the two most powerful European countries had been at war since 1793, their conflict directly hindering American trade. American Presidents; Washington, Adams, Jefferson and Madison had each struggled to remain neutral, but France and Britain continued to flagrantly disregard our right to neutrality, with Britain being the literal *thorn in the side* of the United States.

Their practice of *impressment*, or seizing American seamen and forcing them into service within the British Navy had become uncontrolled. The British, claiming that she was merely seizing what was hers, [deserters] had also captured more than six thousand Americans forcing them into service as well. Although it had been an ongoing practice of the British, the United States had kept silent about the intrusion until the 1807 incident between the American Naval frigate; *Chesapeake*, and the British Vessel, *Leopard*, just off the American coast. When ordered to halt so the British could inspect the ship, Chesapeake's Commander, James Barron refused. The Leopard opened fire, killing several American sailors. The British then boarded the ship confiscating four men. At Jefferson's demand a public apology was issued and restitution made, yet the British continued their impressment policy. Between the years 1803 and 1812 both the British and French had confiscated nearly 1500 American ships.

In an attempt to stop the confiscation of ships and sailors, the United States passed the *Embargo Act of 1807*, which prohibited all United States vessels from trading with European Nations during the Napoleonic Wars. Trade restrictions with both British and Spanish possessions in Canada and Florida were enacted in 1808 and 1809, but all attempts failed to peaceably halt British impressment. A pro-war faction in Congress known as the *War-Hawks*, looking for the means to both declare a war against Native Americans they believed still to be British allies and seize more territory; essentially Canada and Florida instigated another war with Britain. [NOTE – one such war hawk was John Caldwell Calhoun, an ancestor of my own children.] In June 18, 1812, war was declared.

A great deal of this war would be played across the Niagara Frontier. Many of the young settlement's women and children fled the area as operations began, seeking safer grounds on which to live. Their actual fears being that the native would once again side with Britain. Male settlers however, eagerly answered their country's call for assistance, even though the efforts of the revolution hung clearly in their brains, the losses clinging in their hearts. Soldiers from the Collins area included; Benjamin Albee Sr., Jehiel Albee, Darius Crandall, James Tyrer, Henry Palmerton, Luke Crandall Jr., Stephen Peters, Jesse Frye, Simeon Waterman, Luther Pratt, Phineus Orr, Elisha Cox, Amasa Chaffee, Truman B Payne, Mr. Slaight [father of Edwin T.], Rex Brown, David Nivers and Samuel Clark. [NOTE – this is the most accurate list we have been able to obtain to date.] Although he may have not fought in the war, Benjamin Albee Jr. should be noted for his bravery during this time. As families fled the area and men enlisted in the Army, sixteen year-old Benjamin was left behind to tend and defend to not only the possessions of his family, but also the possessions of the other settlers. His body, along with others from the Albee family, now rests in a deserted, destroyed local cemetery on the original triangle of land donated by his father as a cemetery.

Initially when war again broke out between the young United States and Britain the Iroquois of both the United States and Canada met, agreeing to remain neutral in the white man's war. Most important was their decision that no Indian warrior would meet his brother in battle. However, as the curse of the white man invaded the Iroquois' heart in a call for assistance, the Iroquois chose sides. Chief John Norton of the Mohawk Tribe siding with the British while Red Jacket and Farmers Brother of the Seneca Tribe sided with the Americans. Once the choice of the native had been made, settlers began returning to their homes within the town's boundaries [approximately six weeks later.]

American dreams of capturing Canada died within the first months of the war. Although Americans won a series of single ship battles, most land engagements were lost between 1812 and 1813.

The *Burning of Buffalo* on December 30, 1813 in retaliation for the burning of Newark [Niagara-on-the-Lake] immediately appeared to locals as an ending to the freedom they had recently fought so hard to secure, but after a second thought, the Americans persevered.

By the spring of 1814 Buffalo was being rebuilt. The *Battle of Chippewa*, July 5, 1814, lasted about three hours, resulted in a decisive American victory. This would become the first time during the War of 1812 that regular forces of both nations would faced one another across an open battle field, in a major action. This date and battle would also violate a centuries old tradition of peaceful coexistence between members of the Iroquois Nation; as Seneca leader Red Jacket led warriors against Mohawk Chief John Norton. Finally, on September 11 of the same year a decisive battle was won under the leadership of American Captain, Thomas Macdonough. Upturned events led the Americans to a final victory and on December 24, 1814, the Treaty of Ghent was signed, successfully ending the war without meeting any of the American objectives and without the most decisive British loss of the war yet to be fought.

From the fall of 1814 until the biggest battle of the war was fought and won by the Americans on January 8, 1815, New Orleans would feel the fallout of the War of 1812. News of the Peace Treaty and ending of the war did not reach the area until February of that year. The population had more than doubled between the Revolutionary War through the War of 1812; from 3.5 million settlers to 7.6 million. Two hundred and eighty six thousand persons enrolled in the War of 1812, eighty six thousand more than during the Revolution, but casualties were far less. About half as many men were killed during the War of 1812 then during the revolution; a total of 2,260 deaths and 4,505 men were wounded, again far less than during the revolution. Although many historians claim that the United States was not militarily ready when war was declared, it appears the troops were indeed well rehearsed.

The outstanding American debt at the time the War of 1812 began was $45 million. At the end of three years of fighting the national debt increased to $123 million. Twenty three years later America had repaid all her debts in full.

Besides the war, settlers found themselves fighting strange weather patterns from 1811 through 1817; the worse weather and most devastation occurring during the year 1816. As calendars turned to welcome in the year 1816, settlers had little knowledge of what they would soon be facing. January 1 was cold, but then again, January 1 is normally cold in Western New York, the weather patterns appeared relatively normal until spring began. The bizarre weather pattern seemed to hover across the entire north east section of the country, beginning in March when the temperatures started plunging to below normal highs and rains seemed to forget to moisten the earth. Due to the draught and cold weather, farmers were being forced to feed their animals the corn reserve originally set aside for human consumption. The *Albany Advertiser* reported: "*no recollection of so backward a season.*"

Pioneers kept their hopes high and their prayers repeating. In May, they would begin to feel the true effects of the peculiar weather patterns when night after night the area suffered from frost. Similar weather conditions were being reported from as far north as Quebec City, Canada and as far south as Virginia. Daily frosts became a normal occurrence but ice storms in May and snow in June brought the disastrous truth to light. The people in the town were beginning to get hungry. Children began wandering the woods in search of edible roots. The bitter cold, frost and irregular weather patterns continued until winter finally breathed a sigh of relief upon the settlers. The best news the settlers received throughout the entire year would be the admission of Indiana as the nineteenth state [December 11, 1816].

Originally created by a group of philanthropists calling themselves *the Society for the Prevention of Pauperism*, in 1816, the *New York House of Refuge* of which the State of New York was involved from beginning of organization to funding, establishing inmate procedures and developing treatment programs, would become the first juvenile reformatory in the nation.

1817 brought relief to the settlers as weather patterns returned to normal. On July 4, 1817, the country's independence was celebrated in unusual fashion in New York State; Governor Dewitt Clinton broke ground for the construction of the Erie Canal. Later that same year, December 10, Mississippi would become the twentieth state admitted to the union.

What would become the town of Collins was growing by leaps and bounds with *Collins Centre* being the active hub of the community, even though the area was still known as the town of Concord. Illinois would become the twenty first state admitted to the union on December 3, 1818.

While locals continued to welcome more settlers into their community, meeting for raisings where within one to two days a log home or barn would be built by the neighbors to assist the newest resident, they remained unprepared for the *Panic of 1819*. With several inducements, including; a dramatic decline in cotton prices, the unwillingness of the Bank of the United States to allow credit towards the purchase of land [this factor had been placed as a means to curb inflation] due to the 1817 congressional order requiring only hard-currency payments for land purchases and last, but not least foreign competition. In New York alone, property values fell by one third, from a high of $315 million in 1818 to a low of $256 million by 1820. Debtors were calling for *stay laws* to provide relief from debts, for abolishment of all debtors' prisons and for protection against foreign imports. This crisis had passed by 1823.

While the panic affected all Americans in general, there was also good news to be reported. The New York shipyard of Crocket and Fickett, located at Corlear's Hook, NY built the first 350 ton full-rigged steam powered ship complete with thirty two staterooms that would cross the Atlantic. The historic voyage began at Savannah, Georgia on August 22, 1818.

From Savannah she sailed to Liverpool, England, St. Petersburg, Russia and back to Savannah. During the same year Congress granted The *American Colonization Society* [ACS] $100,000. A group of white, upper middle class males whose goals were to satisfy two extreme American groups; the abolitionist who wanted to free African slaves and slave owners who typically feared free people of color. This group took African-American citizens to Liberia for the sole purpose of colonization in their native lands.

On the federal level, things were heating up in the south. After 1783, Americans immigrants had begun relocating to the area known as West Florida. After the American settlers rebelled, declaring independence from Spain in 1810, President James Madison and Congress realizing I that the Spanish government had been seriously weakened by Napoleon's invasion of Spain, now claimed the region. General Andrew Jackson seized the Spanish forts at Pensacola and St. Marks in his 1818 authorized raid against Seminoles and escaped slaves both groups having been viewed as a threat to Georgia. Jackson, who had executed two British citizens on charges of inciting the Indians and runaways was defended by Adams citing the necessity to restrain the Indians and escaped slaves since the Spanish failed to do so.

Adams took this issue one step further, demanding that Spain either control the inhabitants of East Florida or cede the area to the United States. An agreement was reached: Spain ceded East Florida to the United States while at the same time renouncing all claim to West Florida. While Spain received no compensation for the actual land, the United States agreed to assume liability for the $5 million in damages caused by the Americans who had originally rebelled against her.

The Onís-Adams Treaty of 1819 [ratified in 1821] Spain surrendered its claims to the Pacific Northwest in exchange for the United States' recognition of Spanish sovereignty over Texas. On December 14, 1819, Alabama became the twenty second state to be admitted to the union.

January 1820 marked the sailing of the ship *Elizabeth* with three white ACS members and eighty eight persons of African descent left New York harbor heading for West Africa in hopes of starting a new life. Yet, the controversy concerning the black population in America was just beginning to boil. When Missouri applied for statehood, New York representative, James Tallmadge proposed an amendment which would forbid the importation of slaves into the new states while slowly emancipating all slaves presently within the territory. While the bill passed the House, it did not pass the Senate.

Maine was admitted to the union on March 15, 1820, allowing Missouri into the union as a slave state would maintain the non-slave/slave state balance. Rather than attempt a forced non-slave position onto Missouri a different bill was drafted; this time forbidding slavery in the remainder of the Louisiana Purchase. This bill became known as *the Missouri Compromise*. In retaliation for what the editor of Connecticut's Hartford Courant considered a sellout by the politicians, he became the first editor to print a *black list* of all northern members of Congress who either voted for the Missouri Compromise or vacated their seats during the vote.

The male landowners of Collins had casts their votes for the fifth President of the United States. James Monroe would be inaugurated on March 5 rather than the traditional March 4 date which fell on a Sunday. Later that same month, March 16, 1821, Concord would be divided into three townships, Concord, Collins and Sardinia.

An Act to divide the town of Concord in the County of Niagara.

Passed March 16 1821

Section One: Be it enacted by the people of the State of New York represented in Senate and Assembly, that from and after the thirty first day of March, instant, all that part of the town of Concord, in the County of Niagara, comprehending township number seven in the eighth range, and all that part of township number six in the eighth range lying within the county Niagara together with three tiers of lots on the west side of township number seven in the seventh range, and three tiers of lots on the west side of township number seven in the seventh range, and three tiers of lots on the west side of township number six in the seventh range, within the county of Niagara, of the Holland Company, shall be and is hereby erected into a separate town by the name of Collins, and that the first town meeting shall be held at the dwelling house of George Southwick in said town.

The town of Collins had finally arrived, but geographic changes would continue to occur until the present day boundaries finally existed. However smaller committees had already risen up within the limits of the town.

The community of Zoar lies in the southeast corner of Collins and the northeast corner of Otto, the valley and county lines being divided by the waters of the Cattaraugus. It is said that in its primeval state, the valley was beautiful and when looked upon by the early pioneers from the surrounding hills, it caused in them a feeling of wonder and surprise, as it appeared to then a new Canaan, and they entered into the valley as did the Israelites of old with thoughts of rest and thanksgiving. It is believed that the name Zoar is of scriptural origin, given by Ahaz Allen one of the first settlers in the area.

The first family to inhabit the Zoar area was the Peter Pratt family. The Pratt family had left Taunton, Massachusetts in 1806 moving first to

Clarence, NY and finally to Zoar. Peter built his family a double log home, split the *shakes* of pine [shingles three feet long which had not been shaved] and nailed them to poles which had been themselves nailed to the rafters, complete with puncheon floors [a heavy slab of roughly dressed timber]. All in all, the Pratt home was exceptionally stylish in those days.

There had been no trails into Zoar when the Pratt family settled there. In order to move their good into the house they were forced, with the assistance of some local boys, to tie canoes together, load their household good in the canoes and float them up river. It was in the Pratt abode shortly thereafter that the second child was born within the limits of the town of Collins, Peter Pratt Jr.

The family survived on *Johnny Cake* which Mrs. Pratt would make on her Johnny Cake Board. According to the pioneers, the larger the family, the greater the board, the Pratt family's Johnny Cake Board was two feet long and eight inches wide. It had been split out of clean, white ash and polished smooth. Meal would be mixed into stiff dough and spread upon the board then set before the fire to bake until done. Another staple of the Pratt family was baked potatoes. Since there were no stoves, the family would use a flat bottomed kettle with an iron lid which would be placed into a Dutch Fireplace [a hearth built into the floor, masonry or stone wall behind, and a chimney resting on a beam arching around the hearth.]. The kettle would then literally be buried in the coals. The same kettles would be used to bake beans or bread.

The Centre would soon become Collins Centre. [The spelling would later be changed by one of our many postmasters.] The hamlet had always been the hub of the area, centrally located in what is now the town of Collins; the hamlet would be the first to host a church and a school.

Lawton Hollow, [now simply Lawtons] received its name from settler John Lawton. Taylor's Hollow received its name from Jacob Taylor. Bagdad was given its name by Bernard Cook. It was named after an ancient Asian city. Aldrich Mills [now Gowanda located half in the town of Collins, County of Erie and half in the town of Persia, County of Cattaraugus] received its name from Turner Aldrich, the area's first settler.

The first school house had been built nearly as quickly as the settlement began. A simple single roomed log structure was built near the Centre by the King family in 1811. This building was heated by a fireplace that is said to have taken up an entire wall with no more than a stick chimney. Benches were made from slabs of wood with holes drilled in for legs. There were very little books or other materials to teach from. John King was the first teacher and the list of his students has been preserved. The students were; David Paulina, Elma and John Wilbur; Isaac, George, Angeline and Phila King; Benjamin Jr., Hannah and Enoch Albee. Whenever possible, Isaac Aldrich from Aldrich Mills also attended classes here.

The first tannery was built by Smith Bartlett in 1815, soon after he moved to the area from Danby, Vermont. Even by the standards of the times this tannery was considered primitive. Large troughs were dug out to be used as tanning vats. To grind bark, Smith constructed a circular platform with a rim around the outer edge. Locating a large circular stone, more than six feet in diameter, he drilled a hole through the center of the stone, through which he fitted a shaft. A horse was then attached to the outer edge of the platform; the other end of his tether was attached to an upright revolving shaft in the center of the platform. As the horse was led around the platform, the stone would roll over the bark crushing it. The hides would be soaked in a mixture of water and crushed bark, then hung to dry.

Mills were essential to the pioneers. They needed a place where they would be able to grind their corn and wheat. By the time Collins had become a town six mills existed throughout the area. Jacob Taylor's mill was built in 1812 at Taylor's Hollow. Joseph Adams built a mill in Zoar in 1814; Stephen Lapham built his mill at Bagdad the same year. Turner Aldrich built his mill at Aldrich Mills about 1818. David Pound would be the last to build a mill prior to the organization of the town. His mill would be built just after David Pound's mill was built.

Collins would have two Quaker meeting houses built within a few years of settlement [approximately 1813]. The first was located on the property of Nathaniel Sisson just over the line that would later become North Collins. The second meeting house was located in Bagdad. Next to the meeting house was a large cemetery where more than three hundred of our pioneers were buried. To date we have not been able to locate the exact location of either the meeting house or cemetery.

Undetermined denominational meetings were also held at the home of William King. Preachers would take turns tending to the needs of their congregation. One local preacher, Elder Bartlett would share responsibilities with visiting preachers from Boston, NY; Talcott Patchin, Richard Carey and Sylvester Carey.

The town of Collins and the people who originally settled the area had made their marks on local, state and national history, but times were changing. It would take another thirty one years before the boundaries of the town would become the same as what we now know them as.

A GROWING TOWN
1821 – 1830

    A law enacted on 16 March 1821 stated that the town of Concord would be divided into three towns. All of the land included in townships 6 & 7, range 8 and in three tiers of lots on the west side of townships 6 & 7, Range 7 was to become the town of Collins.

    Two weeks later, on 2 April, 1821, a law was enacted stating that all lands in the part of the County known as Niagara, north of the center of the Tonawanda Creek would from that time foreword be known as Niagara County. All of the remaining land was to become known as Erie County. With such a split, Erie retained more than one half the land area of the former Niagara County. It also retained the county seat, the county records and most of the county officers. In every aspect except name, Erie County was no more than the continuation of the old Niagara County which had been originally established in 1808. Rather than Erie being the new county, one can correctly assume that Niagara was the new county.

    Prior to the year 1821 the area, then known as Niagara County had been known as a pioneer county, one of which pioneers settled. From the time of the split between Niagara and Erie Counties, Erie County would become known as a farming county.

    During the era when Niagara County included all lands of the present Niagara and Erie Counties, most townships were still comprised of vast forest. Nearly every home, with the exception of those in the Buffalo metropolis was a log cabin. By the time Erie became a county, a great deal of the wilderness had been tamed. Forest had been cleared and log cabins were being replaced by frame buildings.

    The new county of Erie was comprised of thirteen towns, serviced by ten post offices, known as; Buffalo, Black Rock, Clarence, Willink, Williamsville, Smithville, Barkersville, Boston, Springville & Eden. The Eden post office was located in the present town of Evans. The Barkersville post office was located at, what was known as the old Barker's Stand, the present day Hamburg. The Willink post office was located at the village of Aurora. References have also been made to a post office located within Hamburg at the Tavern owned by John Green. Villages such as Cayuga Creek, the present day Lancaster, Alden, Hall's Mills [AKA Hall's Hollow],

Holland, Griffins Mills, East Hamburg and Gowanda had no post office at all.

Pioneers were now keeping sheep, necessary for the manufacture of their clothing. Wolves, not previously a concern, were now becoming a great nuisance. Bounties were established, ranging from $10 - $90 per wolf with one half as much per each whelp. Whether this is an urban legend or fact many local historians tend to report that in one afternoon, an unnamed native made $360 shooting whelps alone.

According to documentation, the wiliest of all of the wolves within the county roamed the area of the present towns of Collins and North Collins. A she-wolf, she is said to have used her cunning to seduce half of the large male dogs in the area. Those she could not seduce she whipped; sometimes in death other times leaving her victims in massive agony of defeat. It is written that she destroyed her victims by the hundreds, consistently evading all attempts to shoot or trap her. Once she was finally trapped and disposed of, men gathered from all over the county to celebrate her death.

It is written that one of the great treats to the local native was the pigeon. The banks of the Cattaraugus Creek from Springville to Gowanda were known to nests thousands of these birds. The native from as far north as the Buffalo Creek Reservation would join their southern counterparts in an annual rush for food. There is documentation indicating that some trees held as many as fifty to sixty nests and by cutting the trees, the native could secure at least one *squab* per nest. [A fat young pigeon big enough to eat but not yet old enough to fly away] The native would scald, salt and dry their catch, preserving the food for the upcoming winter months.

History tells us that the first murder in the new Erie County was a young Native American female. According to some historians, a young Seneca Indian died of a disease that was unknown to their medicine man; therefore the squaw that had nursed him, Kauquatau became branded a witch. Knowing the fate that awaited her, she fled to Canada but Chief So-onongise [AKA Tommy Jimmy] who had been designated her executioner, sought her out as a friend, convincing her to return to the United States with him.

Taking her back to their reservation, Tommy Jimmy killed her. Her body was found by local white men the following morning. A coroner's inquest named Tommy Jimmy as her murderer. Despite the sovernity that Indians had been granted by the Federal Government, the local white residents felt that Tommy Jimmy should be tried for his crime. A warrant was issued, but the constable refused to go to Reservation and arrest Tommy Jimmy, an extremely popular chief. Pascal P Pratt, a friend of Red-Jacket, was deputized to execute the warrant. Red Jacket ascertained that Tommy Jimmy would be at the Reservation the following morning. Despite the fact that white men held no jurisdiction over the reservation where the murder had been committed according to Indian Law, Tommy Jimmy was arrested.

A trial was held in June of 1821 at the Erie County Oyer and Terminer. The jury found that the execution of Kauquatau was upheld by Indian Law, therefore the case was sent to the New York Supreme Court for review. The court decided that since the native was subject to Independent authority Tommy Jimmy could not be tried in a white man's court, thus releasing Tommy Jimmy. Shortly thereafter, laws were passed subjecting Indians, even those committing crimes on reservation lands to the same penalties white men would endure for similar crimes.

Law and order was by far not the only thing on the pioneer's minds, they were increasingly interested in the education of their youth. By 1815, what would become the town of Collins hosted five schools, some in buildings actually constructed as schools, others were held in private homes or businesses. The same five schools existed when Collins first became a town; one in Collins Center, one in Lapham's Mills [Bagdad] one in Zoar and the remaining two near what would become the line separating the towns of Collins and North Collins. By the time the town boundary lines would become the same as present; twenty nine schools existed within the town of Collins.

The schools were far different from what we have grown accustomed to. Most of the schools were not free which meant that not all of the children could attend. Those that did attend would sometimes go to class six days a week, unless they were needed at home to help especially during harvest time. There would be only one teacher per district which meant that all children, no matter what their age, attended the same classroom.

The basics of reading, writing and ciphering were taught in the pioneer schools. [To cipher was to do a simplified math problem.] Since teaching materials were few and far between, the normal classroom had but two books, the Bible and a primer which contained spelling words, the alphabet and poems; children would learn by repeating the same information day after day. Paper was a scare commodity; therefore the basic tools used by the students would be the hornbook, a wooden paddle with a piece of paper attached which hung from their belts. The paper would include the alphabet, numbers and normally either a prayer or verse from the Bible. To save on paper the children would draw small lines, writing extremely tiny so as not to run out of paper.

Of course, the pioneer child always looked forward to recess, where, especially when the weather was nice, he or she would be given a specific time outside to spend with their friends during the school day. The pioneer child had much to keep them busy; their need for the imagination of others [i.e. computer games] would not develop for nearly two centuries. Instead, they would play such games as *Blind man's Bluff, Cricket, Quoits [tossing a ring on a peg] or simply lay in the grass and talk to their friends.*

Voting within New York State would also become more universal during 1821. Prior to this time, the only people allowed to vote for Senators or the Governor were male landowners holding property worth at least $250.00 without debt. In order to vote for representatives of the New York Assembly, the qualifications were males owning property worth at least $50.00 without debts or those renting property that paid annual taxes in excess of $5.00 annually.

Under the new voting laws, all males who were citizens of the United States, had lived in the area for at least six months and/or offered a service which would continue would be allowed to vote. The landowner option had been dropped. Male residents were now becoming more involved in the political field. By 1822, the positions of both Sheriff and County Clerks became elected positions rather than appointed positions, offering the men of the area the opportunity to participate in all levels of government.

The early settlers had established themselves within the area. They supported their families by raising crops and animals. Some of the residents specialized in woodcrafts, tanning or milling. Most everything was made within the home or upon their own property. From food to clothing to furniture, the pioneer made his own way.

Once the area had been cleared and the rough log cabins had served their purpose, the early settler began to improve his property. In the early days a tree stump would suffice for a table and a stick chimney would be barely sufficient for heat and cooking. The modern world was what the pioneer had left behind and what he now longed to have.

The common marketplace, where the pioneer would take his crops, his animals, his eggs or his crafts to sell was being replaced with regular stores known as mercantile establishments. The extended family of mothers, fathers grandparents, aunts and uncles all living under the same roof was changing, people were now able to build their own homes, residing in close proximity to their relatives, but no longer living in one home.

The men continued to plow fields, tend to animals, hunt or work at a specific trade while the women continued to tend to the child rearing, the gardening, cooking, cleaning and manufacture of cloth and clothing.

Local pioneers had but one main worry, making payments to the Holland Land Company for the property they had purchased. Few had access to a steady monetary income, making the payment for their property near impossible. In 1824 the ability of the landowner to pay his debt to the Holland Land Company would change. Rather than requesting cash only from those who had purchased claims from the land company, the company now offered the land owners the option to pay with goods, specifically the products that they farmed. This act lessened the reality of not only losing the property the pioneer had worked so intensely to develop, it kept them from becoming classified as a pauper and being placed in jail.

News traveled rapidly through the quickly expanding settlements. In late 1824, news reached residents of the town of Collins concerning a missing man, John Love, a farmer from the nearby town of Boston, NY. Several months later, Love's body was discovered in a shallow, frozen grave near Israel Thayer's cabin, another Boston, NY farmer. The following summer the three Thayer brothers, Nelson, Isaac and Israel Jr. were tried and convicted of Love's murder. On June 7, 1825, the Thayer brother's were executed by public hanging. It has been claimed that more than 30,000 persons showed up to witness the execution, including several entire families from the Collins area.

In August of 1826, after extensive deliberations the Seneca nation ceded an additional 5,120 acres of the Cattaraugus Indian Reservation to towns in both Erie and Chautauqua Counties. The ceded property included one square mile in Chautauqua County plus a strip of land along the northern boundary of the Reservation one mile wide and six miles long, which became known as the *mile strip*. An additional one mile block [AKA *Mile Block*] of land just south of the eastern end of the original Reservation line was also ceded in Erie County. Today these areas continue to retain the names Mile Strip and Mile Block, a remembrance of the final ceding of land from the Cattaraugus Reservation.

By the next year travel between the original colonies and the newer areas of development would become easier for the pioneer looking to move his family to a new area. Turnpikes, roads that charge a fee to be used were now open throughout many areas of the state. No longer were the pioneers relying on the old Indian trails that were originally traveled to reach the Western New York area. Stagecoaches traveling along these turnpikes now reduced the time for the weary pioneer to less than half the normal time the pioneers' travels would have taken. Taverns and Inns had been built along the turnpike, offering the traveler a place to stay and a hearty meal while traveling, which offered a great deal more comfort than what the original traveler experienced. The original settlers traveling between the Danby, Vermont and Collins, NY area noted their travel time as being from twenty three to thirty three days. Later settlers, taking the Erie Canal noted their travel time as thirteen days.

On October 26, 1825, the Erie Canal would officially open. This travel option appeared to be even quicker than the turnpike. The Inns and Taverns were located along the canal route just as they were located on the turnpike. However, the Inns and Taverns of yesteryear were not what one experiences today. During the days of the pioneer, the traveler received a hot meal and drink before being sent to his unheated room where he would share a single bed with up to five strangers.

There were no locks on any room doors. If a travel was accompanied by a servant or slave, the servant or slave would be sent to the barn and forced to sleep with the horses. Women did not stay at the tavern or inn, instead they would be sent into the local community to spend the night with a local family.

1826 marked the year of a great mystery; a mystery so intense it created political parties and cast an eerie air of doubt on world wide members of the Freemasons. The mystery entails the disappearance of fifty two year old William Morgan.

Morgan, born in Virginia in 1774 would marry a sixteen year old female in 1819. Two years later, he would move his family to Canada, where he opened a distillery. Shortly thereafter, Morgan's distillery would burn forcing him and his family to move yet again, back to the United States, this time to New York. Although the actual movements of Morgan and his family remain sketchy, evidence that he settled in Rochester and then Batavia does exist.

While no evidence has been located to state without a doubt that Morgan had been a member of the Freemasons, there have been notations noted which indicate that he had made visits to lodges in various areas. Evidence is said to exists which stipulates that Morgan did indeed receive the *York Rite* [a collection of Masonic degrees] while in Leroy, NY in 1825.

Trouble is said to have begun when a new Masonic Chapter was proposed in Morgan's hometown of Batavia. According to legend, Morgan's name was on the original petition to charter a local lodge. However, an objection was raised and the petition was rewritten, this time leaving Morgan's name off. Filled with resentment over the action, Morgan vowed revenge. Entering into a conspiracy with the local newspaper editor, David Miller, Morgan began to exact his revenge threatening to write an expose of Freemasonry, something that had never been attempted in the United States.

Revenge seemed to be taken when the newspaper office was set ablaze, September 10, 1826, leading to the arrest of four Freemasons. Masons exerted that Miller had set his own newspaper office on fire in order to place the blame on their indicted brothers. Stories concerning the occurrences leading to the disappearance of Morgan vary. Some claim that over the next several months Morgan and Miller would be targeted by trumped up charges that would lead them to being jailed. At other times, they would be jailed when caught in the act of revenge. Others state that Morgan would be arrested the night after the fire, September 11, 1826 at the behest of a local innkeeper for a debt Morgan had incurred several months earlier. Whether the arrest came immediately or later will take more in-depth research to discover, but the results are eerily the same.

Some say a single man came to the jail to bail Morgan out, others claim that Nicholas Cheesboro, Master of the local lodge accompanied by two assistants simply persuaded the jailer's wife to release Morgan. No matter how the release was managed William Morgan would supposedly never be seen alive after that night.

Several *eyewitnesses* came forward to report that they had seen Morgan being taken away by a group of men; other *eyewitnesses* reported that Morgan drove off alone. Approximately one month later, a badly decomposed body would be found. Morgan's widow would at first emphatically deny that the body was that of her *lost* husband. Later, she would recant her original story, claiming the body was indeed that of her husband. Over the years several *sightings* of Morgan were reported, but for all practical purposes, he was assumed dead.

The controversy over the disappearance of Morgan and Freemason members would lead to the closing of several lodges across the Western New York area. The fear induced by the *Morgan Affair* led to the belief that Freemasonry was a powerful secret society which was attempting to rule the United States in a manner against all Republican principals. Paranoia gripped the country; people began to believe that Freemasons were an occult practicing ceremonial magic and witchcraft to further their cause. By 1827 this paranoia had spread becoming a religious crusade as well as a unique Western New York Political issue. Persons across the region had come to terms, agreeing to withhold support from any Masons seeking public office. The following year, the formation of the Anti-Mason political party would help stave off the Masonic craze.

Nearing election, the Anti-Mason party would make *bodies floating* a fear inducing statement which lead to strengthening the party until it would supersede even the National Republican Party within the state of New York. [Here is proof that people learn from history. Today the Republican Party utilizes the *terrorist threat* at election time to bolster fear and win elections.]

In 1828, Millard Fillmore would be elected to New York State Assembly by the Anti-Mason Party. This political party would continue to increase in strength and control, maintaining their vigilance through 1843 when finally, the generation that remembered the Morgan Affair had dwindled, and the party's threat was no longer considered.

Over the next two years things seemed to remain on an even keel within the town of Collins. People continued to upgrade their homes replacing the log homes of the original settlers with frame dwellings. Settlers continued to move into the area, while others moved westward, their pioneer spirit yet unfulfilled, they were continuously seeking another wilderness to tame.

The mail was becoming a more organized industry, with twenty seven post offices now being spread throughout Erie County, most of which were organized between 1825 and 1830. Within the county, nine townships now had a single post office to handle the mail. Four townships now had two post offices servicing their citizens. Two townships boasted three post offices to service their residents; but only one town within the entire county found the need for four post offices; the town of Collins.

There literally existed one post office in each corner of the town. One post office serviced the Zoar area. One post office serviced the hamlet of Collins. One post office serviced the hamlet of Collins Center. The final post office, known as Angola, serviced the present Lawtons area. Three out of four of these post offices remain in existence today; Collins, Collins Center and Lawtons.

The forest animals that had once reigned in the area had all but disappeared. Townsfolk were no longer bothered by the wolf or bear, even those residing along the Cattaraugus Creek found the creatures to be few. The human population increase had driven the few remaining wild creatures into hiding.

On January 20, 1830 New York State lost a great man, *Sagoyewatha* better known as Red Jacket died at his home on the Buffalo Creek Reservation.

Red Jacket's year of birth varies, ranging from 1750 to 1758 many historians have chosen 1756 as a date of birth. His place of birth is just as elusive as his birth date. Some list his place of birth as Seneca Lake; others say it was Cayuga Lake.

Red Jacket rose to notoriety during the Revolutionary War, although he is said to have pleaded with the Iroquois to remain neutral. It is often stated that Joseph Brant continuously harassed Red Jacket calling him a coward for wanting to remain neutral. We have located various historians who claim that Red Jacket fled during many battles, although as we have earlier stated, Red Jacket led his brethren against other members of the Iroquois Confederacy during the War of 1812. Many now feel that Red Jacket was more a political figure than a warrior.

He was a staunch opponent of Christianity and preached across the state to fellow Iroquois against conversion. Historians across the country often dub him as the most eloquent orator in all of history. Many of his speeches have been written, transcribed and preserved.

Red Jacket was also known for his opposition towards the Iroquois selling their lands to the white man. This may have been meant to protect his people from assimilated into white culture or it may be due to the fact that the white man's ploy, alcohol had diseased Red Jacket himself. All of these years later, I am positive that those of Iroquois heritage wish that their ancestors would have listened to Red Jacket.

The final years of Red Jacket's life were extremely unhappy. Despite his aversion to Christianity, his second wife and her children converted. Red Jacket died on January 20, 1830, on the Buffalo Reservation. Claims have been made that Red Jacket left his family, only to reconcile shortly before his death. Some say his wife proceeded with a Christian burial and cemetery, others claim that it was Red Jacket's last wish to convert to Christianity. He was buried in a local cemetery that has long since been removed. In 1884, his remains were reinterred in Forest Lawn Cemetery in Buffalo.

For many years a local urban legend concerning the bones of Red Jacket circulated the area. Recently we have located documentation which suggests this was never a legend, but fact. Apparently, when it was learned that the cemetery where Red Jacket had been buried was to be removed, someone dug up Red Jacket's bones, presenting them to his great-niece for safe keeping. The niece protected the bones of her great-uncle at her home on the Cattaraugus Reservation until she could turn them over to the Buffalo and Erie County Historical Society.

CHANGES IN THE AIR

1831-1840

Following the death of Red Jacket, would be the death of Mary Jamison Dehhewamis, the white woman who had been captured when a Shawnee war party raided her hometown in Pennsylvania, massacring her parents and taking Mary hostage.

Mary was born in 1743 on the ship carrying her Irish immigrant parents to the new world. Mary was twelve years old when she was taken captive and sold to the Seneca Tribe where she was assimilated into the tribe, becoming one with her captives. The Seneca treated Mary with compassion and respect.

At the age of seventeen, [1760] while living in the village of Wiishto on the Ohio River, Mary would marry Sheninjee, a member of the Delaware Tribe. Sheninjee and Mary had two children. Her first child was a girl born in 1761, who lived but two days. Her second child was a son named Thomas, born in the winter of 1762. Mary and Sheninjee were making their way to the Genesee Valley when Sheninjee died of disease. Mary would continue to the Genesee Valley alone, carrying her young son upon her back. Today a statue of Mary Jamison carrying her son Thomas stands at the Council Grounds at Letchworth State Park.

Hiokatoo, a Seneca Chief, would be Mary's second husband. They would marry in the Genesee Valley in 1765. Hiokatoo fathered six children with Mary; John born 1766, Nancy born 1773, Betsey birth date unknown, Polly born in late 1778 or early 1779, Jane born in 1782 and Jesse born in either 1784 or 1785.

Over many years Mary had made her way to the Buffalo Creek Reservation where she lived out the remaining years of her life. In 1824 at the age of 80, Mary spoke with James Everett Seaver, sharing the recollections of her life. At that time she had lived through the massacre of her parents and withstood Butler's Raid, refusing to rejoin the white culture she had been stripped away from. She had been sold and assimilated into a strange lifestyle with a strange language. She had outlived two husbands and eight children.

Each of Mary's daughters had died young, her first child and first daughter at the age of two days. Her daughter Jane died at the age of fifteen in 1797. The remaining three daughters, Nancy, Betsey and Polly each died in 1839 within nine months of one another. John, the eldest son of Hiokatoo, fell victim to alcoholism. Driving by alcohol and rage, John would murder first his half brother Thomas in 1811 and then his brother Jesse in 1812. Fueled by alcohol, John's life would end at the hands of another during a drunken brawl in 1817.

Mary lived amongst the Seneca for nearly eight decades. She was finally freed from life's hardships at the age of 88. [Note: some claim that Mary's death was in 1833 rather than 1831.]

The following years would bring more changes into the town of Collins. Prior to this time German immigrants migrated to the City of Buffalo. Beginning in 1832 these immigrants migrated to the south towns, settling in the area of New Oregon, now part of the town of North Collins. Some of these immigrants would be my ancestors.

German immigrants were not the only changes the settlers were considering in 1832. In February, the New York State Agricultural Society was founded in Albany by a group of farmers, legislators, and others to promote agricultural improvement and local fairs.

With good news comes bad. The first railroad accident in the history of the United States would occur on July 25 near Quincy, Massachusetts, when four people were thrown from a vacant car on the Granite Railway. Each of the victims had been invited to view the process of transporting large loads of stone. On the return trip, a cable on a vacant car snapped, throwing the four off from the train and over a thirty four foot cliff. One man was killed, the others were seriously injured.

The Treaty of Payne's Landing was concluded when some Seminole chiefs in Florida accepted a resettlement plan in allotted lands west of the Mississippi River. When some chiefs, along with their follows demurred, remaining in Florida, white settlers stepped up their campaign of harassment towards the natives, while insisting the U.S. government force the Seminoles to obey the provisions of the treaty. Continued resistance to resettlement would eventually lead to the Second Seminole War (1835-1842)

Millard Fillmore would be elected to Congress from Erie County in the fall of 1832. At the r age of thirty two, he would become one of the youngest men to ever be elected to Congress. This would be a title he would hold until 1873 when John R Lynch, a young black man, age twenty six, would become the youngest Congressman ever to be elected.

Politics often took center stage in both local and national debate, political scuttlebutt being as old as politics. President Andrew Jackson provided his constituents with plenty of material for debate, beginning with his extreme unpopularity despite his reelection. Jackson had truly sought to act as protector and representative to the common man, yet his actions hailed drastically differing results.

Jackson himself brought opponents to the Bank of the United States with his election to President. Jackson himself severely opposed the Bank of the U.S. Not only did he feel that Congress did not hold the authority to create such an institution, he also felt that the bank operated primarily for the benefit of the upper class at the expense of the working people.

In 1832, four years before the bank's charter was due to expire, Nicholas Biddle, President of the Bank of the U.S., at the urging of Henry Clay applied to Congress for the renewal of the bank's charter. Jackson immediately vetoed the charter, stirring vicious debates in his bid for reelection. Once reelected, Jackson mistakenly assumed that his reelection voiced approval of his veto and immediately began withdrawing the government's money from the Bank of the U.S., depositing it into several *State* Banks.

State banks began issuing a vast amount of paper money without adequate foundation, resulting in a generalized inflation in business and advance in prices. Although countrywide, the Great Lakes area spawned the greatest inflation rates. Speculators fueled the inflation and by 1835 Erie County was on the verge of financial disaster. Yet no one took heat like President Jackson for his initial vetoing of the Charter of the Bank of the United States.

A large portion of Jackson's constituents felt that his actions in regards to the Bank of the U.S. made him a tyrant and a dictator. His popularity began to falter; people began referring to him as *King Andrew I, destroyer of our liberties*. Congress censured Jackson [a formal condemnation by the Congressional body] stating that he had *assumed upon himself authority and power not conferred by the Constitution and laws*. Congress may have felt this way due to the fact that Jackson's belief in a strong presidency and thus used the veto extensively. It has been written that Jackson vetoed more legislation than the first six presidents vetoed together. [Near the end of Jackson's second Presidential term Senator Thomas Hart Benton of Missouri led a coup to expunge the censure vote from the Senate Journal. It has been stated that a black line was drawn around the resolution and the word *expunged* was written across it. Some historians have stated that Benton's loyalty to Jackson may have been a result of the guilt that Benton felt towards a confrontation with Jackson during his youth which resulted in Jackson being shot and forever carrying Benton's bullet in his body.]

Andrew Jackson is most well known as being the President of firsts. He was the first populist president [an advocate of Democratic principals] reared a commoner rather than an aristocrat. He was the first of two Presidents to have a Vice president resign. John Caldwell Calhoun was elected Vice President in 1824 under President John Quincy Adams. Calhoun was elected Vice President a second time in 1828 under President Andrew Jackson. Calhoun resigned December 28, 1832 to serve as Democratic Republican [later a nullifier, a person who believes that a state can resist federal laws] to the U.S. Senate.

The only other Vice President to have resigned during his term was Spiro T Agnew, Vice President under Richard Nixon. Agnew resigned on October 10, 1973, before pleading *no contest* to criminal tax evasion for income allegedly received while Governor of Maryland. President Richard Nixon would resign from office less than one year later on August 9, 1974 for his part in the Watergate scandal.

Jackson was also the first American President to be nominated at a national convention, which actually occurred in his second term. The very first national convention to ever be held had been hosted by the Anti-Mason party on September 21, 1831 in Baltimore, Maryland. Realizing how popular the event had been, supporters of Henry Clay called for a National Republican Convention, also held in Baltimore, Maryland on December 12, 1831. Finally, on May 12, 1832 the Democratic Party would host their first National Convention, also held in Baltimore, Maryland. Jackson, the incumbent, was nominated not by vote, but rather by resolution.

Jackson was the first president to utilize an informal cabinet of advisors; dubbed the *Kitchen Cabinet* because Jackson often met with his friends to discuss governmental business in the White House kitchen. He was also the first president to use the *pocket veto* to kill Congressional Bills. [This is accomplished when Congress adjourns prior to the President signing a bill into law. The legislation automatically fails.]

Of course, one mustn't forget that Jackson also holds the title as the first president to marry a divorcee; which is far better to be remembered for than the adultery charges his opponent brought forward during the 1828 Presidential Campaign. While the charges were indeed true; it had been naivety rather than sin on the young couple's part.

Andrew Jackson married Rachel Donelson Robards in 1791; Rachel having earlier been unhappily married to Lewis Robards. After appealing to the Kentucky legislature, a resolution was passed granting Robards permission to sue for divorce. Despite the resolution, Robards did not act upon the resolution.

Neither Andrew nor Rachel realized that the declaration passed by legislature had merely granted permission for a divorce, it did not grant a divorce. The young couple, assuming that Rachel had thusly been divorced, married. Two years later, 1793, Robards finally sued for divorce, citing adultery as grounds. Although malicious and embarrassing rumors would haunt the couple, they would remarry in 1794 after Rachel's divorce had truly been granted.

In January of 1835 President Jackson was quoted as saying, "*Let us commemorate the payment of the public debt as an event that gives us increased power as a nation and reflects luster on our Federal Union.*" For the first and only time in American history, the United States was debt free! Unfortunately the same did not hold true for the American public, the recession continued to roll throughout the country. Banks everywhere were failing. Paper money was becoming worth less than the paper it had been printed upon. Personal fortunes would literally disappear at the blink of an eye. Mortgages were being foreclosed on. Property value was falling; what had been purchased for fifty dollars per foot now brought half that amount per acre. While settlers throughout Erie County were feeling the weight of the recession, it was the Buffalo area that suffered greatest.

At the end of January of the same year, Andrew Jackson would earn another *first* title; the first assassination attempt on a U.S. President. On January 30 a house painter, Richard Lawrence, working at the Capitol Building aimed two flintlock pistols at President Jackson and fired. Both pistols misfired; the first at a distant of approximately thirteen feet, the second at point blank range. It has been claimed that the man was subdued after the president beat him with a cane. Lawrence was found to be insane and confined to a mental institution for the remainder of his life.

The recession continued to rock the country. As Buffalo suffered, now the entire county suffered. Even the more rural towns such as Collins found themselves trapped by the recession. Those who once felt that they were wealthy now found themselves scratching to assure they could provide mere necessities for their families.

Despite the recession and the hard times it brought, all New Yorkers found a reason to celebrate in 1836, for the first time in U.S. history, the President hailed from New York State. Known as *the Little Magician*, five foot six inch Martin Van Buren was elected to office three months before the panic of 1837 hit; a result of Andrew Jackson's policies yet Van Buren would be blamed for the tragedy that would cause the worse economic depression that the young country had ever seen.

Immediately clear was the fact that banks were in trouble, some closing shortly after the panic struck. Businesses began to fail, closing their doors. Thousands of people lost their jobs; many more lost their homes and land. Despite the economic crises, Van Buren stuck to the political philosophy of his predecessor; the federal government should exercise only limited power over the economy.

Many advised Van Buren to assist the people and the failing economy by taking control and creating a new Bank of the United States. Van Buren refused. He trusted neither a federal or state bank; instead he created an independent treasury where all governmental monies were relocated. While protecting the federal funds, this move did nothing to assist the economy. Van Buren was decisively defeated in his bid for reelection.

People all across Western New York were not only feeling the pinch of the depression, they were also suffocating under the intolerable terms that the Holland Land Company was demanding of them. [Note: we have located a great deal of documentation regarding this issue, yet specific towns were most often not mentioned. Since this issue seemed to entail the entire Holland Land Purchase, we felt a mention was deserved.] Land owners began to meet, denouncing the Holland Land Company and its supporters. Resolutions were passed and demands were made of the Attorney General to *contest the company's title to the land*.

In some areas, whenever a land agent would appear to take possession of a land which had fallen to arrears, armed men would stand their ground, intimidating the agents until they gave up on their pursuit to repossess the properties. Since the legislature deemed that there were no legal grounds by which to contest original title to the properties, they refused to become involved in the dispute. Eventually, most of the settlers were able to pay the arrears, finally enabling themselves to claim deeds to their property. In some areas however, the settlers refused to buckle under the pressure of the Land Company and their enormous interest penalties. Since the Land Company took a great amount of time to enforce their claims to the properties, the settlers were able to take possession of their deeds by *adverse possession* [A process by which a person acquires title to property by possessing the property for a specific period of time.] To the dismay of the Land Company courts found for the settlers in the adverse possession cases.

At times such as these a diversion sometimes helps to put things into perspective; a diversion is what Western New Yorkers would soon get. Insurrections [organized oppositions to authority] were rocking both Upper and Lower Canada. [Upper Canada was a British Colony covering the southern portion of the present day Province of Ontario. Lower Canada, also a British Colony, on the lower St. Lawrence River. It covered the southern portion of the present day Province of Quebec as well as the Labrador Region of the present day Provinces of Newfoundland and Labrador.]

1838 found the Seneca, Mohawk, Cayuga & Oneida Indian Nations along with the Onondaga and Tuscarora tribes entering a Treaty with the United States government which allowed for the sale of the four remaining New York State Reservations; Buffalo Creek, Tonawanda, Cattaraugus and Allegany. In return, all residents of these Reservations were to be removed to a tract of land west of Missouri. According to the details of the treaty, the Ogden Land Company would be purchasing all Reservation lands. This would create a rife between the white man and his red brethren which would take years to resolve.

In 1841, a separate Treaty between the Seneca Tribe and the United States indicated that Ogden would be purchasing only two of the four Seneca Reservations; one being the Tonawanda Reservation. However, not one Chief from the Tonawanda Reservation had signed either treaty, thus the Seneca residing on the Tonawanda Reservation refused to leave their land. The Treaty with the Seneca of 1857, more commonly known as the Treaty with the Seneca, Tonawanda Band, granted the Tonawanda Reservation lands back to the Seneca. Money which had originally been set aside for the removal of the New York Indian was now used to purchase the Tonawanda Reservation back from the Ogden Land Company.

By this time, the fate of the Redman had been pushed aside, while the American public negotiated the fate of the Black man. By 1838, The *Underground Railroad* was in full swing, providing escape routes for

Southern Slaves. The *railroad* would lead the slaves to the Northern states and onward to Canada where they could truly be free. Along the way, if a runaway slave was discovered, he would be seized, shackled and returned to his owner in the south. He would be denied a trial of any sort. Many times, even freed slaves were captured and returned south. Northerners became awed by the necessity to free the black man that included many persons who lived within the town of Collins. Even today there are many local reminders of the Underground Railroad operation throughout the town.

On March 25, 1839, the town of Brant would be formed by an act of Legislation. The town was formed from the southern part of the town of Evans and a portion of the Cattaraugus Indian Reservation belonging to the town of Collins. It also included the land purchased from the Reservation in 1826, both the Mile Strip and Mile Block purchases. Brant, upon its founding, had believed that the sale of the Cattaraugus Indian Reservation would be finalized, and all of the land within the Reservation would thusly be granted to the new town. Subsequent treaties which allowed the Indian to retain Reservation lands left Brant as the smallest of all town ships in Erie County.

The year 1840 would find Federal Legislction created to protect Federal employees. On March 31, 1840; legislation was signed establishing a ten hour work day for all Federal employees. The following year New York Legislature would appropriate $8000 to *promote agriculture and household manufacture in the state through an annual fair.* This would be come the first sate fair in the entire United States.

The first fair was held in Syracuse due to its location. First, the city was in the midst of New York State's farming interest. Besides that it was the central point of the Erie Canal and it had become a promising way-station for the developing railroads. The first fair was a great success with crowds estimated at ten to fifteen thousand persons in attendance; mainly farmers. For the next half century, the State fair traveled throughout the state.

Many felt that the state fair needed a single site where it could be held year after year and more permanent structures could be built. The two cities biding for the fair were Buffalo and Syracuse, both proving to bring the greatest success to the annual fair. Syracuse became the first city to host the fair three times in 1858, but it would not be until 1890 that the fair would permanently locate in Syracuse.

The Erie County Fair had actually begun in the 1820's under the auspice of the Niagara County Horticultural Society. The following year, the agricultural society would split with the counties. It would be at that time that the annual county fair would be suspended. It would remain suspended until 1841 when a renewed interest in the agricultural fair surfaced. The Erie County Fair has been held at the same site ever since, with the exception of the year 1943, when the fair was suspended due to the war.

The economy would slowly rekindle throughout Erie County, loosening the financial belt that most were wearing. Most of the houses were now frame or plank rather than log cabins. While the state and country were finding themselves wracked by havoc, the town of Collins was settling well.

In 1846 a new State Constitution would make nearly all public offices including those of Judges and District Attorneys, offices to be filled by public election. Senators would now hold a seat for a mere two year period and assemblymen would each have their own district. The Court of Common Pleas would now become County Court. New York State was also divided into eight Judicial Districts, each being allowed to elect four Judges to State Supreme Court.

The following year the Postal Service would for the first time issue adhesive backed postage stamps. Prior to this postage was paid to the local post master in cash and he would write that postage was paid on the envelope. Now, people could purchase stamps in advance of mailing a letter. For a nickel they could purchase a stamp bearing the image of Benjamin Franklin; for ten cents the stamp would bear the image of George Washington.

After two years [1848] the Treaty of Guadalupe Hidalgo was signed by the United States and Mexico on February 2, ending the two-year Mexican war. In the treaty, Mexico agreed to recognize Texas as an American territory. Mexico, for the price of $15 million, ceded five hundred thousand square miles of land to the United States; including, land which now comprises the present states of California, Nevada, Utah, New Mexico, Arizona and part of the land comprising the states of Colorado and Wyoming. The United States also agreed to assume the claims of all its citizens against Mexico, the claims totaled $3,250.00.

During the same year, laws were passed which granted women rights to pre-marital assets. To date, this was the biggest act of legislation geared towards the rights of women. The following year, 1849, New York State would grant women equal property rights with men.

American citizens would be granted an historical event, when on March 4, 1849 David Rice Atkinson would become President of the United States for one day. Former President Polk's term had expired and President-elect Zachery Taylor was not due to be inaugurated until Monday the 5th of March. Rather than leave the country without a Commander in Chief, the *President Pro Tempore* of the Senate assumed the responsibilities.

The following year on July 9, 1850, Erie County resident Millard Fillmore would become president when General Taylor died. The growth of the United States was phenomenal. Fillmore had a great deal on his plate. It is estimated that more than 20,000 blacks had escaped slavery via the Underground Railroad and Fillmore was now resided in Washington DC, the largest slave market in North America.

Earlier, on March 4, John C Calhoun, near death, attended a session of Congress, his colleague; James Mason read his final formal speech to Congress. Calhoun called for decisive action regarding the slavery issue, without which the Southern States would be forced to secede from the Union. Calhoun stated that the issue was about equity and 51% of the population should not be able to coerce 49% to meet their demands.

Later that year, [August] a compromise, a series of bills meant mainly to deal with the issues of slavery, was passed. California was admitted to the Union as a free state. New Mexico and Utah were organized as territories without mention of slavery. The status of slavery would be left up to each territory when it became prepared to be admitted to the Union as a state [AKA popular sovereignty]. A stricter fugitive slave law was enacted and the slave trade became prohibited within the District of Columbia. Finally, the Texas boundary dispute was settled by a federal payment of $10 million towards the debt contracted by the Republic of Texas.

With the division of the town of Amherst in 1839, the town of Collins had become the largest township in Erie County. On November 24, 1852 Collins would become equally proportioned to the other towns of Erie County, when all of the land north of the line between townships seven and eight, with the exception of the southern most tier of lots were taken from the town of Collins to form the town of Shirley. The following spring the town of Shirley would change its name to the town of North Collins.

FINALLY

We have covered the History of the town of Collins from before recorded history until its present boundaries were established. Our next volume will cover the history from that moment in time through the year 1900.

During this time frame many things happened which either directly or indirectly affected residents of the town of Collins; things such as the Civil War and the Spanish American War. We will also take a closer look at a few town of Collins residents, including those residents who secured patents for their inventions. We will take a closer look at Orra L C Hughes, an African American attorney who not only gained recognition in Erie County but also across the entire country, working as a member of the Federal Government. We will also follow the trial of Frederick Bruce, a young Collins resident who was charged with the murder of his Paternal Grandmother, Nancy Harrington-Bruce.

The trial would be as publicized as the O J Simpson trial. All of the evidence will be presented to our readers, including the Judge's charge to the jury. The question remains, will you agree with the outcome.

After that we will be publishing a volume covering 1900 to 1950, which will cover not only both world wars, but a civil defense plan you have to see to believe. Our final volume will bring us up to date. In each volume we will carry genealogies of town of Collins families. We will also attempt to include biographies of members of the Seneca Tribe specifically those residing on the Cattaraugus Indian Reservation. We sincerely hope that the time you have spent with us has been one of learning and enjoyment.

May God Bless.

PICTORAL HISTORY OF THE TOWN OF COLLINS, ERIE COUNTY, NEW YORK

PRE-HISTORY - 1852

THE ORIGINAL LOG CABINS OF THE TOWN OF COLLINS

In upcoming volumes of the History and Genealogy of the town of Collins, this section will be more easily filled. At this time, we have been unable to locate pictures of the town or surrounding area from pre-history through 1852; however, we have been able to affix pictures which will not only enhance the history that you have previously read, they will also allow you, our readers to see for yourselves what the homes of pioneers looked like.

As noted in the previous history, the land mass now known as the town of Collins was once lumped into a portion of land mass known originally as the towns of Willink and Concord. In 1975, the Bicentennial Commission of the town of Concord located detailed data concerning an early settler in the town of Concord, Christopher Stone. To celebrate the bicentennial the commission had an exact duplicate of the log home Christopher Stone had built on property he had originally owned.

The cabin remains standing; an historical marker erected in front of the cabin tells a short story concerning Christopher Stone. The cabin remains unlocked so those interested can get a closer look at an actual log home from the early nineteenth century. The following are actual pictures of the log cabin built in 1975 to the exact specifications of Christopher Stone's original cabin.

We hope you enjoy the pictures, but more so, we hope anyone traveling through the Western New York area will take a few moments of time to at least view the cabin and see for oneself the difficulties endured by those who settled the land we today call home.

LOG CABINS OF THE PIONEERS

Situated on land originally owned by Christopher Stone this exact replica of the first log cabin he built to house his family can still be viewed today.

My eldest half-sister, five foot six inch Betty George stands before the door of the cabin to show how small the doorway entrance actually is. It has been noted that Christopher Stone, builder and owner of the original cabin stood over six foot tall.

Note; there are no windows. Original log cabins would not have cut window openings within their structure. Glass was not only difficult to come by, it was also quite expensive. Most of the early pioneers waited upwards of two years or longer to cut windows into their log cabins, and then the opening would probably be covered with grease paper which would allow entrance for light.

This un-vented fireplace served to keep the Stone family warm as well as giving them a place to cook their meals. Note the iron posts on either side of the fireplace with a pole extended through them; this was where a cast iron kettle would hang, directly over the fire, allowing the family to cook.

Attached to the wall was the family bed. This particular cabin was so small; there was only room for a single bed which would have been shared by Christopher Stone and his wife. Note the dirt floor; during the early years many of the area settlers became accustomed to the dirt floor. Puncheon floors would come in later years after the initial lands had been cleared and the cabins became large enough to comfortably shelter an entire family.

This is indicative of the crude furniture made by early pioneers. This table would be used as a place to help the wives preserve food or prepare food for their meals. It could also be used as a reading desk, or a central point for visitors to gather. Note that the logs of the outer walls do not fit together. In order to resist inclement weather, the pioneer would fill these gaps with mud which would not only help seal out the weather, but was also a fantastic insulation.

Here is yet another necessity of the Pioneer, a storage bin. While the bin could be used as a place to store everything from clothing to wood, it was most likely used as a place to store the vegetables that the pioneers grew in their own gardens. Squash and potatoes were a hardy staple for the pioneer and stayed fresh for a great deal of time, especially when stored in these bins which were attached to the outside, cooler walls of the early log cabins.

DEATH NOTICE OF JACOB TAYLOR
AS PRINTED IN THE FREEMAN AND MESSENGER, LODI NY MAY 7, 1840 NEWSPAPER [LODI IS NOW THE VILLAGE OF GOWANDA]

Died – At his residence in Collins, on Sunday morning last, Jacob Taylor, aged 84 years. He was one of the earliest settlers of Erie County, and for a period of nearly forty years was an accredited faithful agent of the Friend's Society, to take care of, and provide for the wants of the Indians. For a few years past, owing to his advanced age, he retired from that agency, and at last like a shock of corn fully ripe has been by his Father gathered to his garner. He fully sustained a character for sobriety, prudence, economy and strict integrity, and is endeared to his friends by the recollection of his many virtues. He has left a property valued at $40,000, which descends to his connections without a will. – *Communicated.*

GENEALOGICAL INFORMATION & FAMILY GENEALOGIES OF EARLY SETTLERS OF THE TOWN OF COLLINS, ERIE COUNTY, NEW YORK

Genealogies of Families that Inhabited the Town of Collins
The Early Years

The following are genealogies of a few of the early settlers of the town of Collins. In each of the four volumes of the history of the town of Collins, we will include two in-depth family genealogies that coincide with the settlement of that family in the area and the parts the ancestors played in the history of the area and/or our country. We will also include a few short biographies of settlers who settled in the area during the period of history that the volume is covering.

Please note the following genealogies are of families that not only helped found the town of Collins but also played distinct parts throughout the history of our Country, State and County as well. We have chosen the families of Lawrence Southwick and Christopher Smith.

The family of Lawrence Southwick suffered physical, mental and emotional persecution from the American Puritans for their religious convictions, yet they persevered, holding strong, going on to secure their religion. The wife of Lawrence, Cassandra Burnell, was immortalized in a poem by John Greenleaf Whittier entitled; *Cassandra Southwick*. Their descendents lived on, fighting in various American wars and helping to settle the town now known as Collins.

Christopher Smith married the widow Metcalf, daughter of Jonathan Fayerbankes [Fairbanks] original ancestor of many American Presidents and builder of a home in Dedham, Massachusetts. The home not only served many generations of his own family, but stands yet today, allowing not only his descendants but all who want to take a glimpse into the past the ability. The Smith family also served in many American wars and helped to settle the area now known as the town of Collins.

Future volumes of the history of the town of Collins may contain any updates or revisions to the following genealogies.

Our plans had been to provide our readers with genealogies of our Native American citizens, but the information we have retrieved to date is sketchy at best. Therefore, rather than skip this portion entirely, we have included a list of Reservation landowners as listed on an 1866 town of Collins map.

We have also learned that many people seeking their ancestors have difficulty locating those who lived in the town of Collins prior to the 1830 Federal census. This is most likely due to the changing land masses which would become new towns and counties in the New York State area. To assist those who are finding the early records troublesome or indecipherable, we have spent many hours attempting to decipher both the 1810 and 1820 area census records.

The 1810 census records are listed under the County of Niagara and the town of Willink. The 1820 Census records are listed under the County of Niagara and the town of Concord. The knowledge of the actual names of the area is sometimes not enough to assist those seeking information; handwriting from the early nineteenth century must be deciphered. Many of the letters of yesteryear do not easily represent what we have come to know as the same letters today. Those looking at census records also must deal with poor mimeograph or microfilm records. Those lucky enough to have actual copies of the census records must deal with smeared ink, and poor storage methods which have left many names unreadable or undecipherable.

We will start this section with the 1810 and 1820 census lists, followed by the names we were able to decipher from an 1866 map which listed land owners on the Cattaraugus Indian Reservation. We sincerely hope this will assist those of you seeking ancestral records.

Following these lists, will be actual researched genealogies of the families who were amongst the early settlers in the town of Collins area.

One final note, names within each genealogical record have been verified by at least two public documents for accuracy.

1810 FEDERAL CENSUS TOWN OF WILLINK, COUNTY OF NIAGARA, STATE OF NEW YORK

PLEASE NOTE [?] INDICATE THAT WE WERE UNSURE OF OUR TRANSCRIPTION

1. D EDDY
2. J WEAVER
3. H HIBBARD
4. D TUBBS
5. W WINNERO [?]
6. J CUMMINS
7. T STEVENS
8. L FRANCIS
9. C POOL
10. G IRISH
11. R EARL
12. E GOODRICH
13. L ABBOT
14. J TAYLOR
15. W JOHNSON
16. E ENOS
17. J HAMILTON
18. N PETERS
19. D THURSTON
20. J ADAMS
21. J PAIN
22. L BLIP
23. T BLIP
24. L HANARIE [?]
25. D ROWLEY 1ST
26. D ROWLEY
27. L CALKINS
28. O P PETTINGILL
29. J HARRENSON
30. J SAGA
31. HARVEY HIBBARD
32. J HOAG
33. C VIDS
34. J NEWTON
35. SAM ABBOT
36. O NEWTON
37. J POTTER
38. T BROWN
39. A KING
40. J BROWNING
41. J W CURIR [?]
42. J BENIRS [?]
43. A TAYLOR
44. H GRIFFIN
45. E GATES
46. A SMITH
47. J LATON
48. J GREEN
49. L TOMERSY
50. J FRANCIS
51. N IVES
52. JOB GRIFFIN
53. C B UTLEY
54. A WILSON
55. E DUDLEY
56. A ELDRIDGE
57. W C DUDLEY
58. J MAYO
59. J HARRIS
60. N TITUS
61. M SPRAGUE
62. H SPRAGUE
63. E WOODRUFF
64. J WALKER
65. A FULLER
66. R PERRY
67. D PETTINGILL
68. J LURDERVANT [?]
69. ELIKER ENNOS
70. L MILLER
71. J MILLER
72. C PIERCE
73. L PIERCE
74. W PIERCE
75. N WHITICAN [?]
76. A AMSDEN
77. B J CLUGH
78. C CLUGH
79. SETH HERSEY
80. L HERSEY
81. J FISK
82. J SALSBURY
83. A SALLSBURY
84. D CASK
85. T WEBB
86. J KINNEY
87. J PALMER
88. J HAWKINS
89. N HALL
90. A ROADS
91. W MOP
92. C CURTIS
93. A ABBOT
94. MRS SMITH
95. N CUMMINS
96. L ROBERTS
97. L SPRAGUE
98. J SHERMAN
99. J W DANA
100. A PARKER
101. L KINNEY
102. J RIGHT
103. G PIERCE
104. G RICHMOND
105. W COLTSIN
106. E COOK
107. J BOWMAN
108. A STUTSON
109. J EDDY
110. D WATERS
111. T WATERS
112. J HOLMES
113. A C SAIR
114. D ANATOW [?]
115. A FERGUSON
116. E SPRAGUE
117. D BAKER

1810 FEDERAL CENSUS TOWN OF WILLINK, COUNTY OF NIAGARA, STATE OF NEW YORK

PLEASE NOTE [?] INDICATE THAT WE WERE UNSURE OF OUR TRANSCRIPTION

118. A SPRAGUE
119. S STARKWEATHER
120. G HALL
121. T WARREN
122. J WATSON
123. N MILLER
124. J FITCH
125. J HUTCHKISS
126. L MCKAY
127. H WARREN
128. H GODFREY
129. L WARREN
130. L SARLIO [?]
131. T EARLS
132. J ALWARD
133. J CONNANT
134. T PIATT
135. W PAIN
136. W WARREN
137. A W KAY
138. J HAMPTON
139. J R SAUNGERS
140. T PAIN
141. A BURT
142. B EARL
143. W ALLEN
144. E HALL
145. E ALLEN
146. L MORRIS
147. J MORRIS
148. M SPRAGUE
149. C BLACKMAN
150. L HAVINS
151. W MOORE
152. M HORISE
153. F M HOLMES
154. E BENJAMIN
155. J CADDIN
156. A SWAN
157. A VANKURSER
158. E SANFORD
159. W HOIT
160. E HOLMES
161. [?] CLARK
162. A PETTINGILL
163. N EMMERSON
164. D HARSHAL
165. L HURRY
166. J THURSTON
167. J ADAMS
168. T CASK
169. J LEWIS
170. O LUNN
171. A LEWIS
172. C CALKINS
173. D JONES
174. E ADAMS
175. J MERRIAM
176. J SUMNER
177. U HARSHAL
178. T TRACY
179. E RICHARDSON
180. L STARY
181. C ERNEST
182. H CHILD
183. E CLILLIS
184. J HILLS
185. L COLLINS
186. D FULLER
187. D W KIRN
188. A UMPHREY
189. W DAVIS
190. L MILLER
191. T BALDWIN
192. L GRANT
193. J DAKE
194. J DAVIS
195. N COLBY
196. L DAVIS
197. L DREW
198. E COLBY
199. L COLBY
200. H COLBY
201. T FULLER
202. A CURRIER
203. J COLBY
204. T CARNEY
205. J PHELPS
206. T TREAT
207. H SMITH
208. B HENSHAW
209. L HENSHAW
210. J L HENSHAW
211. J HENSHAW
212. JONATHAN HENSHAW
213. L DEARA
214. L PARMELY
215. C KING
216. D GRIFFIN
217. IRISH GRIFFIN
218. E COLS
219. JOSIAH GRIFFIN
220. J AKINS
221. L COOK
222. L COLVIN
223. J COLVIN
224. L COLVIN
225. A CURRIER 1ST
226. A W CURRIER
227. J TAYLOR
228. T FRANCIS
229. E SMITH
230. B WHATEY
231. C BEVINS
232. R BARTAM

1810 FEDERAL CENSUS TOWN OF WILLINK, COUNTY OF NIAGARA, STATE OF NEW YORK

PLEASE NOTE [?] INDICATE THAT WE WERE UNSURE OF OUR TRANSCRIPTION

233. J IRISH
234. L HARRINGTON
235. L KISTER
236. J GREEN
237. L HALL
238. C C KINNEY
239. K PRATT
240. C FLETCHER
241. J ELDRIDGE
242. J BOUTWELL
243. E SMITH 1ST
244. R SMITH
245. W PRATT
246. D SMITH
247. B ENOS
248. E LOUIS [?]
249. R PALMER
250. J CROW
251. L CLARK
252. A RICE
253. W WEAVER
254. D TOLLS
255. J CLARK [?]
256. J CHERRY [?]
257. J TUPPER
258. J MARSH
259. L EASTER
260. C SAMPSON
261. J GALE
262. T GORDEN
263. L PARRISH [?]
264. J M WELCH
265. B GROVER
266. L TUBBS
267. J BARBER
268. M [?] HOWARD
269. L SISON
270. E SOUTHWICK
271. N SISON
272. A TUCKER
273. D WOOD
274. T ALDRICH
275. L LAPHAM
276. G WEBSTER
277. A HOWARD
278. A LINDSLEY
279. T TUBBS
280. J CIMMONS
281. L BROWNURLE [?]
282. J PEARSON
283. L COOPER
284. S MCGEE [?]
285. A ARMAN
286. L SMITH
287. J STEWART
288. J J DRAKE
289. J DRAKE
290. C STONE
291. E DUNHAM
292. W SMITH
293. E PARMERTON
294. J AKANS
295. R EATON
296. L COCHRAN
297. J RUPELL
298. G PIERSONS
299. D BROOK
300. G HUMPHREY
301. J ALBRO
302. J YAW
303. L BARRET
304. A ALGER
305. E HOWARD
306. A EASTMAN
307. R BUFFUM
308. T POPE
309. E STREATER
310. J BUMP
311. J ADAMS
312. T THURBER
313. J H CUMMINS
314. W COOK
315. C DOOLITTLE
316. M MIDDLEWAIT [?]
317. A CARY
318. E JOHNSON
319. R CARY
320. L CARY
321. D JOHNSON
322. L BUBE
323. L EATON
324. A SHINER
325. D LANE
326. J TWINNING
327. A J TUPPER
328. G COLVIN
329. L RICE
330. G [?] KINNEY
331. W CLARK
332. H CLARK 1ST
333. H CLARK
334. E MOORE
335. M MILLER
336. H JIMMERSON
337. L PARISH
338. P GIBBONS
339. N AUSTIN

1820 FEDERAL CENSUS TOWN OF CONCORD, COUNTY OF NIAGARA, STATE OF NEW YORK

PLEASE NOTE [?] INDICATE THAT WE WERE UNSURE OF OUR TRANSCRIPTION

1. ISAAC ALLEN
2. WILLIAM HARRIS
3. CLIVE [?] HARRIS
4. SOLOMON DUNHAM
5. LUTHER ROLL
6. SILVANUS BATES
7. JAMES NICHOLS
8. ARNOLD KING
9. ASA SMITH
10. ISAAC WILBER
11. JOEL PHILIPS
12. JOB SMITH
13. NATHANIEL BALLARD
14. ADAM BALLARD
15. SAMUEL HILL
16. JOSEPH BARTELL
17. JOHN BOLINSKI [?]
18. WILLIAM CORK
19. WILLIAM BALLIOM [?]
20. CHARLES BARBER [?]
21. LUCIAN CODDING
22. JOSIAH PRATT
23. PODAH [?] PRATT
24. SINFELD SAGE [?]
25. ELIJAH PRAMBALL [?]
26. PHIEAS ORR
27. ELIAS BACON
28. HEZKIAH SIPPLE
29. DAVID PRATT [?]
30. JOSIAH A GOSA [?]
31. ISRAEL PRATT [?]
32. JASON MILLER [?]
33. JOHN WILLIAMS
34. DAVID WILLIAMS
35. OTIS BULLEMONT
36. CHARLES CHAFFEE
37. PATIENCE CHAFFEE
38. ISREAL BOWMAN [?]
39. ELIAS BOWMAN [?]
40. HILLIKER HORDAN [?]
41. THOMAS JOHNSON
42. LUCAS AUSTIN
43. HELORA [?] AUSTIN
44. PERRY GORAN
45. JERAMIAH ISANSON
46. JAMES RUSSELL
47. SYLVESTER RUSSELL
48. JEDEDIAH WATERS
49. EZEKIAL JACOB [?]
50. JOSIAH PIKE
51. SERIUS [?] IRISH
52. BLAKE COLE
53. GEORGE MILLER
54. JOHN BROWNGLER [?]
55. JOHN TYRER
56. FIDEAS [?] GRISWALD
57. HENRY PALMERTON
58. JERUPA REED [?]
59. JOHN J BROWN
60. WARREN TANNER
61. TRINKLEY [?] CLARK
62. JOHN METTIS
63. JONATHAN IRISH
64. NATHANIEL KNIGHT
65. WILBER IRISH
66. PILICE [?] SKEGS
67. SILVANUS PARKINSON
68. REUBAN PARKINSON
69. DAVID BEARDSLEY
70. JULIUS AIKERS
71. GEUMMAR [?] HUITT
72. IRIGHS URIB [?]
73. NATHAN KING
74. STEPHEN WILBER

1820 FEDERAL CENSUS TOWN OF CONCORD, COUNTY OF NIAGARA, STATE OF NEW YORK

PLEASE NOTE [?] INDICATE THAT WE WERE UNSURE OF OUR TRANSCRIPTION

75. JUSHUA PALLMERTON
76. EZRA NICHOLS
77. AUGUSTUS SMITH
78. ASA LAPHAM
79. ANABEST [?] HASKINS
80. JOSEPH SISSON
81. ALLEN KING
82. JOHN GRIFFITH
83. HADEN ARNOLD [?]
84. ELKARIAH SHERMAN
85. SISSON FRANCIS
86. DAVID PRINDLE
87. THADDEUS STUART
88. BELLEN MCCRACK [?]
89. GEORGE PHILESA [?]
90. HENRY SISSON
91. HENRY PIKE
92. WILLIAM SISSON
93. ERASTUS CLARK
94. DAVID WHITE
95. SAMUEL WHITE
96. JOSEPH NEEDHAM [?]
97. WILLIAM PICKENS
98. SILLY STAFFORD 1ST
99. DAVID CONGER
100. JOB SOUTHWICK
101. JOHN SIERS [?]
102. JOHN HUNLENT [?]
103. JOSPEH HANFORD
104. JOHN MACK
105. BENJAMIN GODFREY
106. GEORGE SOUTHWICK
107. DAVID HURLY
108. SMITH BARTLETT
109. WILLIAM PALMER
110. JAMES STARKS
111. LUTHER LYONS
112. STUEBAN HUSKS
113. SAMUEL HALL
114. ANDREAS HALL
115. HENRY HALL
116. JOHN ARNOLD
117. HIRAM ARNOLD
118. JAMES GOODELL
119. KENDALL JOHNSON
120. CHARLES MCBARDEN
121. GILBERT MCBARDEN
122. BENJAMIN ALBEE
123. LUKE CRANDALL 1ST
124. LUKE CRANDALL
125. WILLIAM CRANDALL
126. JOHN GIBBONS
127. WANTON HATHAWAY
128. JAHIAL ALBEE
129. ADOLPHUS ALBEE
130. OESDOT [?] INGERSOLL
131. DARIUS CRANDALL
132. ABIGAIL ALBEE
133. DAVID STICKNEY
134. JOHN CAYBER [?]
135. JOHN MENN [?]
136. EZIKIAL SWIAK
137. DAVID KENNEL [?]
138. ARCHIBALD RANDALL
139. LALLATIA L BURROW [?]
140. DONALD SAMUEL
141. JOHN SCHULCK
142. HIRAM CHAULKIN
143. BISHOP COSLIN

1820 FEDERAL CENSUS TOWN OF CONCORD, COUNTY OF NIAGARA, STATE OF NEW YORK

PLEASE NOTE [?] INDICATE THAT WE WERE UNSURE OF OUR TRANSCRIPTION

144. BENJAMIN GEORGE
145. SAMUEL HASS [?]
146. JOHN PALISON
147. HEILER CRASSY
148. JONATHAN PINGUY
149. NEHEMIAH ROGERS
150. CHARLES G HALLS
151. SABER HUCHEN [?]
152. GEORGE RICHMOND 1ST
153. ASA GODDLING
154. CURES RICHMOND
155. JOEL PALMER
156. BENJAMIN KELLER
157. SAMUEL SLAGG
158. AARON SHULTZ
159. PETER LAMPHAM
160. WILLIAM SKULKS
161. PHINEAS SCOTT
162. HEREZ ULIA [?]
163. JEROME SCOTT
164. DANIEL BEARDSLEY
165. SAMUEL FOX
166. FRANCIS WHITE
167. REFEAL SUGAR [?]
168. ISSAC WHITE
169. GEORGE SHELTERS
170. ISAAC TUCKMAN
171. HARVEY SEALD
172. DANIEL INGLES
173. STEPHEN LAPHAM
174. AARON LINDSLEY
175. ALI LAPHAM
176. AARON WHITE
177. JAMES HERON
178. CLASIAK [?] CASK
179. ZANDER L SMITH
180. JOHN BLANCHARD
181. BENEJAH BOLECK [?]
182. PAUL AHHECK
183. ELISHA BECKER
184. WILLIAM SISSON
185. JONATHAN SELE
186. PHILEAS GUILE
187. JOHN KIMBLE
188. JOHN H LINDSLER
189. WILLIAM SISSON
190. NATHANIEL SISSON
191. JOHN LAWTON
192. STEPHEN SISSON
193. PERRY SISSON
194. BENJAMIN SISSON
195. LILLE RIELER [?]
196. HUGH MC MILLAN
197. LENI HARDWARD
198. JOHN HARWARD
199. LEAH HUFF
200. RUSSELL THISEA [?]
201. JONATHAN SOUTHWICK
202. DAVID ALLEN
203. HUMPHREY SMITH
204. PUNDERON [?] BALLON
205. HAMMS BOWERS [?]
206. ISAIH BRIGGS
207. HUMPHREY RUSSELL
208. JOHN REYNOLDS
209. JOHN DAVID
210. STEPHEN SMITH
211. LEON PARKER
212. ISAAC RANSOM

1820 FEDERAL CENSUS TOWN OF CONCORD, COUNTY OF NIAGARA, STATE OF NEW YORK

PLEASE NOTE [?] INDICATE THAT WE WERE UNSURE OF OUR TRANSCRIPTION

213. ADAM CLARK
214. RUSSELL SEUEL [?]
215. ISREAL CARMUTH [?]
216. JOHN M PARKER
217. LEVI PARKER 1ST
218. RICHARD ROGERS
219. JAMES RATHBUN
220. HORACE LANDON
221. JOHN JAMES
222. SECOURD REED 1ST
223. JAMES MCMILLAN
224. TIMOTHY STANCLIFF
225. WILLIAM STANCLIFF
226. NATHAN LAMB
227. JOHN DANIELS
228. HERMUS STANCLIFF
229. JESSE STANCLIFF
230. JOHN STANCLIFF 1ST
231. BENJAMIN HUSSEY
232. GESSIE HERD
233. SAMUEL TUCKER
234. ABRAM GRIFFITH
235. HUGHES GRIFFITH
236. RUFUS EASSERT [?]
237. DANIEL HUNT
238. KOREAS HUNT
239. BARTLETT ALLEN
240. CROMMWELL LUTHER
241. ANNA HEARLARK [?]
242. MOSES TUCKER
243. QILLIAM O'BRIEN
244. DAVID BUND
245. SIDNEY TRACY
246. JACOB TAYLOR
247. HOSEA STUART
248. JOHN STRANG
249. GABRIEL STRANG
250. THOMAS WEST
251. JAMES WEST
252. TURNER ALDRICH
253. SUBINNA ADAMS
254. TURNER ALDRICH 1ST
255. ENOS SOUTHWICK
256. PARKER DAILEY
257. JOHN JOHNSON
258. DAVID BRANDT
259. CHARLES SMITH
260. JOHN RUSSELL
261. ELISHA RUSSELL
262. ISREAL KNOX
263. SAMUEL COCHRAN
264. JOSEPH YAW
265. WILLIAM SMITH
266. JOHN M RICHARDS
267. RUFUS A EATON
268. SILVESTER PATINA [?]
269. THOMAS RICHMOND
270. JUDUAK RICHMOND
271. JOHN ALLEN
272. GILES CHUSSELL [?]
273. JOSEPH HARMON
274. DANIEL TICE
275. SULA [?] SQUIRE
276. JACOB PARKER
277. ELIJAH DUNHAM
278. BENJAMIN WHEELER
279. JOSHUA WHEELER 1ST
280. NEHEMIAH JAY
281. LORICA STRATTON [?]
282. ZEBADAN STRATTON

1820 FEDERAL CENSUS TOWN OF CONCORD, COUNTY OF NIAGARA, STATE OF NEW YORK

PLEASE NOTE [?] INDICATE THAT WE WERE UNSURE OF OUR TRANSCRIPTION

283. ORIN SERERIDGE
284. JAMES FLEETINGS
285. THURBER ORRIN
286. JONATHAN SHEDING
287. ERASTUS BASEDICKS [?]
288. JUSTUS BASEDICKS [?]
289. JAMES ELLIS
290. PETER POLLARD
291. JAMES BROWN
292. ROSUCH [?] OLCOTT
293. ASA PHILIPS
294. SOPHRONIA BARKER
295. SAMUEL CREPES
296. HIRAM HERRICK
297. ASA HERRICK
298. DANIEL PARSONS
299. SAMUEL LAPHAM
300. PINSKY LAPHAM
301. SILVESTER PEABODY
302. JOSEPH HERRICK
303. PERRY GREEN
304. SAMUEL BRODY
305. RUFUS EASTON
306. HUGH GARDNER
307. SOLOMON HOLMAN
308. ABEL HOLMAN
309. ELISABETH GEIGER
310. ELIKIAM KESSER
311. JONATHON JENNINGS
312. BENJAMIN SHOWER
313. JAMES HIRAM
314. JOSHUA GALASSER
315. SHEFFLER [?] DOUGLAS
316. SELMONN SLAGG
317. ALMON FULLER
318. SIMPSON PHILIPS
319. SAMUEL SEARS
320. ELIJACK PERRIGE
321. HALE MATTESON
322. SCHOE HIMANN
323. ELIJAH MATTESON
324. CHARLES HALLS
325. ABNER CHAR
326. JEREMIAH MILLER
327. ASA MILLS
328. WILLIAM KNIGHT
329. IRA LARL [?]
330. NATHAN GOODRICH
331. PERSUS ABRAM
332. SABATIAN GRIFFIS
333. JONATHAN NICHOLS
334. JONATHAN ALBEGE [?]
335. GEORGE EDWARDS
336. JONATHAN BALLMAN
337. BERE EWING
338. BENJAMIN R BERTA [?]
339. JOHN FULLER
340. HAILSON STONE
341. STUCKLEY STONE
342. ALLEN BRIGGS
343. ISREAL SWANSON [?]
344. BENJAMIN GAY
345. JENSTER SWANSON [?]
346. JAMES BENCH
347. ABNER COLBY
348. EZEKIAL BALLARD
349. HENRY DAVID
350. RUFUS WAIT
351. GEORGE BROWN
352. NATHAN POLLEY [?]

1820 FEDERAL CENSUS TOWN OF CONCORD, COUNTY OF NIAGARA, STATE OF NEW YORK

PLEASE NOTE [?] INDICATE THAT WE WERE UNSURE OF OUR TRANSCRIPTION

353. DANIEL HALL
354. JONATHAN GEEK
355. SMITH FIELD BALLARD
356. BENJAMIN WILLBER
357. ISAIAH WILSON
358. HENRY BOWEN
359. JOHN COLBY
360. STUCKLEY HUDSON
361. ELISHA RICE
362. JOSEPH RICE
363. CALEB NICHOLS
364. FRANCIS PETERS
365. HEMAN GEGER
366. ABRAM GEWALD [?]
367. ALLEN GREEN
368. GEORGE PULLMAN 1ST
369. GEORGE PULLMAN
370. HANNAH FLINT
371. CHARLES ABBE
372. HOSEA CLARK
373. REUBAN LONG
374. ANDRIAS CROCKER
375. JOHN HAMER
376. EZRA VETT
377. DANIEL SUDHAM
378. NATHANIEL GRIMMS
379. DANIEL HALL
380. HIRAM MAGEN
381. ACKY BRIGGS
382. DAVID BRIGGS
383. STEPHEN BRITT
384. ROSWELL FRISKY
385. THOMAS MANN
386. ESAK BRIGGS
387. ARNOLD FENRAN [?]
388. SEYMOR HODGES
389. DAVID BIGHTON
390. CHARLES MATTESON
391. ABEL WILLIAMS
392. JOHN MATTES
393. TERRANCE SQUIRE
394. JOHN BURKY
395. ROBERT RUTLEDGE
396. WILLIAM SERE
397. ISAIAH KENSON
398. EDWARD SCOTT
399. STEPHEN B PARKINSON
400. DANIEL SPRAGUE
401. BENJAMIN RANSOM
402. MATTHEW BROWN
403. WILLIAM HEUE [?]
404. SAMUEL SHEPPARD
405. JONATHAN KERNS
406. JOHN BUTLER
407. STEPHEN PRATT 1ST
408. URIEL STERNS
409. ISIAH COMSTOCK
410. BENINI PRATT
411. POLARD MANNA [?]
412. JAMES SECORD
413. JOHN W GOODRICH
414. JERUSHIA BLAKE
415. EILAS BRIGGS
416. JACOB KITSEY
417. KONAS CARNEY
418. ELMER HEISLER
419. JOHN HEISLER
420. HORACE REDM [?]
421. JEREMIAH OLIN
422. PETER SCARS
423. SAMUEL WINNERS

1820 FEDERAL CENSUS TOWN OF CONCORD, COUNTY OF NIAGARA, STATE OF NEW YORK

PLEASE NOTE [?] INDICATE THAT WE WERE UNSURE OF OUR TRANSCRIPTION

424. WILLIAM LINDSLER
425. ISAAC SEARS
426. ISAAC SMITH
427. JAMES MARTIN
428. ELISHA RANDALL
429. CORNELIUS SNIDER
430. RICHARD SMITH
431. SAMUEL EATON
432. BENJAMIN LIAT [?]
433. KENDREAS HENSEN
434. JOHN ANDERD
435. JOHN LEMPICA [?]
436. JAMES PERRY
437. AMASA LORIDAN
438. ISREAL TURNSER [?]
439. AMOS HAMPSON
440. JONATHAN LAVENDER
441. PHINY GILDEN
442. LUTHER KEMPSON
443. PHILIP HURL
444. JOHN L SMALL
445. LAZERUS NICHOLS
446. EBENEZER SHRINER
447. ADOLP NICHOLS
448. ELIJAH RICHARDSON
449. NEHEMMIAH PRIME
450. SIMEON HELLEN
451. CALEB KNIGHT
452. JERAMIAH RICHARDSON
453. STEOHEN KNIGHT
454. JOHN BUTLER
455. SOLOMON FIELERS [?]
456. JOSEPH PARKS
457. ISREAL PARKMAN
458. SHERMAN STARKS
459. NATHANIEL BROWN
460. JOHN BROWN
461. JOHN MCADAMS
462. HEMAN HARDIN
463. DAVID J ERMKKIA
464. JOB TURNER
465. GEORGE BURN
466. JOHN UTLEY
467. HENRY SNIDER
468. PETER SNIDER
469. EZEKIAL HARDEN
470. LAPHERTY DANIEL
471. JAMES BHRUMBULIAN
472. REUBAN RIDER
473. JOSEPH HILAS
474. LAKEY CHAPIN
475. AARON COLE
476. LEBIAH [?] CANFIELD
477. LAUDSON LUTHER
478. DAVID CUNNINGHAM
479. ELTHENA JUDSON
480. BRIAN SIBLEY
481. WILLIAM SOUTHWORTH
482. GEORGE BABCOCK
483. ISAIAH AGARTH [?]
484. BENJAMIN SIBLEY
485. STEPHEN FORDHAM
486. OLIVER FORDHAM
487. HENA POTTER
488. RUFUS WILBER
489. AMOS HICKNEY
490. JOHN BURKES
491. LYONIS JANAS
492. RUFUS INGLES
493. WILLIAM DYE

1820 FEDERAL CENSUS TOWN OF CONCORD, COUNTY OF NIAGARA, STATE OF NEW YORK

PLEASE NOTE [?] INDICATE THAT WE WERE UNSURE OF OUR TRANSCRIPTION

494. ABEL GRIFFITH
495. JAMES WILBER
496. CLARK CARR
497. STEPHEN CHAPMAN
498. SAMUEL SMITH
499. EDUM PUTMAN
500. COMFORT KNAPP
501. FILLMORE KNAPP
502. WILLIAM KNAPP
503. TYMAN HARLEN
504. JOHN HARLEN
505. THOMAS BAIRD
506. ISAAC DRAKE
507. JEHOLED FRENCH
508. SEFER KINGSLEY
509. JOHN EUNIS

CATTARAUGUS RESERVATION: 1866

1. MRS. CROUSE
2. F TALLCHIEF
3. W LOGAN
4. L JONES
5. A PIERCE
6. J PIERCE
7. J P CROE
8. J TALL CHIEF
9. MRS. J YOUNG
10. C LOGAN
11. F JIMERSON
12. A THOMPSON
13. G TALLCHIEF
14. M SILVERHEELS
15. S LOGAN
16. M TWOGUNS
17. C KENNEDY
18. H JOHNSON
19. J KENNEDY
20. H JAMISON
21. D WHITE
22. D TWOGUNS
23. H HUFF
24. N GORDER
25. W BLACKSNAKE
26. H JONES
27. MRS BENNETT
28. D JIMESON
29. T JIMESON 2ND
30. MRS N WHITE
31. MRS SENECA
32. WILLIAM GSW SNYDER
33. J A ARMSTRONG
34. A JOHN
35. W BENNETT
36. J JACKET
37. J BENNETT
38. Z JIMESON
39. J SPRING
40. S C LEIGH
41. C S YORK
42. W CROUSE
43. J JIMESON
44. I SENECA
45. I BENNETT
46. MRS. S JIMESON
47. W PIERCE
48. J TSAARS
49. M E PIERCE
50. J PEIERCE
51. C KENNEDY
52. A JOHN
53. A WRIGHT
54. J LOGAN
55. J GREY-BEARD
56. MRS GREENBLARK
57. A BUTTON
58. J JOHN
59. WILLIAM DAVIS
60. G COOPER
61. S JIMMERSON
62. BURBER
63. C CROW
64. MRS SNOW
65. A KENNEDY
66. W TALLCHIEF
67. G WASHINGTON
68. H JACOB
69. D CROW
70. A JOHN
71. J HERNLOCK
72. P CONJOCKETY
73. H PHILLIPS
74. J PHILLIPS
75. S TOJOHN
76. G JONES
77. W JONES
78. W CROW
79. M LAYL DORSTATER
80. A SNOW
81. J JACK
82. G MOSES
83. G THOMAS
84. G JOHN
85. W CAYUGAR
86. W SCOTT
87. J BENNETT
88. G CROW
89. P WHITE
90. F HALFTOWN
91. G DENNIS
92. F CONJOCKETY
93. A FOX
94. A MOHAWK
95. P PETERS
96. S JOHNSON
97. N WILSON
98. MRS TURKEY
100. A CROW
101. MRS HALFTOWN
102. TURKEY
103. G BUTTON
104. C JOHNY JOHN
105. S JOE
106. M J SCOTT
107. C DAVIS
108. J DUDLEY
109. S NISICK

Descendants of Christopher Smith

Descendants of Christopher Smith

Generation No. 1

1. CHRISTOPHER^1 SMITH was born about 1615 in Plymouth, Devon, England, and died November 07, 1676 in Dedham, Norfolk County, Massachusetts. He married MARY FAIRBANKS June 02, 1654 in Dedham, Norfolk County, Massachusetts, daughter of JONATHAN FAYERBANKES and GRACE LEE. She was born April 18, 1622 in Sowerby, Halifax Parish, Yorkshire, England, and died March 10, 1675/76 in Dedham, Norfolk County, Massachusetts.

More about CHRISTOPHER SMITH:
Fact: October 1642, Admitted to Church of Dedham
Immigration: 1640

More about MARY FAIRBANKS:
Fact: It appears that Mary Fairbanks was previously married to a Metcalf which causes much confusion with genealogists
Immigration: 1633

Child of CHRISTOPHER SMITH and MARY FAIRBANKS is:
2.   i. JOHN^2 SMITH, b. November 19, 1655, Dedham, Suffolk County, Massachusetts; d. October 07, 1722, Needham, Suffolk County, Massachusetts.

Generation No. 2

2. JOHN² SMITH *(CHRISTOPHER¹)* was born November 19, 1655 in Dedham, Suffolk County, Massachusetts, and died October 07, 1722 in Needham, Suffolk County, Massachusetts. He married ABIGAIL DAY December 21, 1677 in Dedham, Suffolk County, Massachusetts, daughter of RALPH DAY and ABIGAIL CRAFT. She was born April 20, 1661 in Dedham, Norfolk County, Massachusetts, and died June 15, 1725 in Needham, Norfolk County, Massachusetts.

Children of JOHN SMITH and ABIGAIL DAY are:

      i. **ABIGAIL³ SMITH**, b. October 27, 1678, Dedham, Essex County, Massachusetts; d. March 1682/83, Dedham, Essex County, Massachusetts.

3.   ii. **JOHN SMITH**, b. February 16, 1678/79, Dedham, Essex County, Massachusetts; d. December 15, 1752, Ashford, Windham County, CT.

4.   iii. **CHRISTOPHER SMITH**, b. November 29, 1681, Dedham, Essex County, Massachusetts; d. 1724, Needham, Norfolk County, Massachusetts.

      iv. **ABIGAIL SMITH**, b. March 02, 1682/83, Dedham, Essex County, Massachusetts; d. November 12, 1730, Sudbury, Middlesex County, Massachusetts; m. JAMES BREWER, March 12, 1718/19, Sudbury, Middlesex County, Massachusetts; b. September 10, 1675, Sudbury, Middlesex County, Massachusetts

More about ABIGAIL SMITH:
Fact: Received bequest in his father's will

5.   v. **JONATHAN SMITH**, b. February 11, 1685/86, Dedham, Essex County, Massachusetts; d. April 22, 1752, Needham, Norfolk County, Massachusetts.

6.   vi. **SAMUEL SMITH**, b. 1687, Dedham, Essex County, Massachusetts; d. March 01, 1753, Ashford, Windham County, Connecticut.

7.   vii. **JOSHUA SMITH**, b. April 06, 1691, Dedham, Essex County, Massachusetts; d. August 23, 1727, Needham, Norfolk County, Massachusetts.

8.   viii. **CALEB SMITH**, b. March 15, 1692/93, Dedham, Essex County, Massachusetts; d. March 01, 1753, Ashford, Windham County, Connecticut.
9.   ix. **MOSES SMITH**, b. August 05, 1695, Dedham, Essex County, Massachusetts; d. Ashford, Windham County, Connecticut.
         x. **AARON SMITH**, b. 1699, Dedham, Essex County, Massachusetts; d. April 15, 1776, Needham, Norfolk County, Massachusetts; m. MARTHA WARE, June 29, 1725, Massachusetts; b. June 12, 1699, Dedham, Essex County, Massachusetts; d. Aft. 1754.

More about AARON SMITH:
Burial: Old Burying Ground, Dedham, Norfolk, Mass
Fact: Received bequest in his father's will
Military service: Lieutenant
Political: Bet. 1747 - 1751, Selectmen of Dedham, Also in; 1737, 1740, 1742, 1744

More about MARTHA WARE:
Fact: Alternate birth day 13th

Generation No. 3

3. JOHN³ SMITH *(JOHN², CHRISTOPHER¹)* was born February 16, 1678/79 in Dedham, Essex County, Massachusetts, and died December 15, 1752 in Ashford, Windham County, CT. He married MARY ACCORS March 18, 1702/03 in Brookline, Norfolk County, Massachusetts, daughter of JOHN ACKERS and DESIRE THORNE. She was born May 26, 1682 in Dunstable, Middlesex County, Massachusetts, and died October 30, 1757 in Connecticut.

More about JOHN SMITH:
Fact: Alternate birth date: February 16, 1679

6. SAMUEL³ SMITH *(JOHN², CHRISTOPHER¹)* was born 1687 in Dedham, Essex County, Massachusetts, and died March 01, 1753 in Ashford, Windham County, Connecticut. He married ZAPORRA MORSE May 30, 1722 in Needham, Suffolk County, Massachusetts, daughter of JOSHUA MORSE and ELIZABETH. She was born April 10, 1702 in Medfield, Suffolk County, Massachusetts, and died 1780 in Ashford, Windham County, Connecticut.

More about SAMUEL SMITH:
Burial: Ashford, Windham Co., Connecticut, Old Ashford Cemetery
Fact: Alternate birth place: Needham

7. JOSHUA³ SMITH *(JOHN², CHRISTOPHER¹)* was born April 06, 1691 in Dedham, Essex County, Massachusetts, and died August 23, 1727 in Needham, Norfolk County, Massachusetts. He married ELIZABETH WADKINS August 23, 1709 in Dedham, Norfolk County, Massachusetts, daughter of ANDREW WADKINS and ELIZABETH. She was born 1682 in Roxbury, Suffolk County, Massachusetts.

More about JOSHUA SMITH:
Fact: Received bequest in his father's will

8. CALEB³ SMITH *(JOHN², CHRISTOPHER¹)* was born March 15, 1692/93 in Dedham, Essex County, Massachusetts, and died March 01, 1753 in Ashford, Windham County, Connecticut. He married RACHEL FISHER July 04, 1717 in Medway, Massachusetts, daughter of JONATHAN FISHER and

RACHEL FAIRBANKS. She was born September 04, 1698 in Medfield, Suffolk County, Massachusetts.

More about CALEB SMITH:
Fact: Received bequest in his father's will

Children of CALEB SMITH and RACHEL FISHER are:
27.   i. **CALEB⁴ SMITH**, b. May 17, 1718, Oxbridge, Worcester County, Massachusetts; d. January 23, 1797, Danby, Rutland County, Vermont.
    ii. **JEMIMA SMITH**, b. October 16, 1722, Needham, Norfolk County, Massachusetts.

       More about JEMIMA SMITH:
       Baptism: December 23, 1722, Needham, MA

    iii. **RACHEL SMITH**, b. September 18, 1720, Needham, Norfolk County, Massachusetts.

       More about RACHEL SMITH:
       Baptism: October 02, 1720, Needham, MA

    iv. **NATHANIEL SMITH**, b. October 27, 1724, Needham, Norfolk County, Massachusetts.

       More about NATHANIEL SMITH:
       Baptism: November 29, Needham, MA

    v. **ESTHER SMITH**, b. June 25, 1726, Needham, Norfolk County, Massachusetts.
    vi. **MIRIAM SMITH**, b. January 31, 1727/28, Needham, Norfolk County, Massachusetts.

       More about MIRIAM SMITH:
       Baptism: February 23, Needham, MA

    vii. **ICHABOD SMITH**, b. June 14, 1730, Needham, Norfolk County, Massachusetts.

       More about ICHABOD SMITH:
       Baptism: July 19, Needham, MA
       Fact: May 06, 1771, Purchased land, he then lived in Natck

    viii. **HANNAH SMITH**, b. May 12, 1732, Needham, Norfolk County, Massachusetts.

More about HANNAH SMITH:
Baptism: July 09, 1732, Needham, MA

    ix. **MARY SMITH**, b. June 06, 1734, Needham, Norfolk County, Massachusetts.

More about MARY SMITH:
Baptism: February 02, 1734/35, Needham, MA

9. MOSES³ SMITH *(JOHN², CHRISTOPHER¹)* was born August 05, 1695 in Dedham, Essex County, Massachusetts, and died in Ashford, Windham County, Connecticut. He married MARY PARKER September 16, 1723 in Needham, Suffolk County, Massachusetts.

More about MOSES SMITH:
Fact: 1717, Received 8 acres of Chestnut Trees from his father

Generation No. 4

10. JOHN⁴ SMITH *(JOHN³, JOHN², CHRISTOPHER¹)* was born November 13, 1704 in Needham, Norfolk County, Massachusetts. He married SARAH YEOMANS March 01, 1736/37 in Needham, Suffolk County, Massachusetts.

More about JOHN SMITH:
Baptism: February 18, Needham, MA

11. WILLIAM⁴ SMITH *(JOHN³, JOHN², CHRISTOPHER¹)* was born November 01, 1707 in Needham, Norfolk County, Massachusetts, and died September 21, 1811 in Needham, Norfolk County, Massachusetts. He married JEMIMA KINGSBURY August 27, 1747 in Needham, Suffolk County, Massachusetts, daughter of JOSIAH JOSEPH KINGSBURY. She was born January 31, 1725/26 in Needham, Norfolk County, Massachusetts, and died March 13, 1813 in Needham, Norfolk County, Massachusetts.

More about WILLIAM SMITH:
Baptism: February 18, Needham, MA

12. NEHEMIAH⁴ SMITH *(JOHN³, JOHN², CHRISTOPHER¹)* was born April 25, 1709 in Needham, Norfolk County, Massachusetts, and died December 10, 1800 in Ashford, Windham County, Connecticut. He married ANN TIFFANY December 25, 1745 in Ashford, Windham County, Connecticut, daughter of THOMAS TIFFANY and MERCY. She was born July 07, 1723 in Ashford, Windham County, Connecticut, and died September 09, 1801 in Ashford, Windham County, Connecticut.

More about NEHEMIAH SMITH:
Baptism: February 18, Needham, MA

13. EZRA⁴ SMITH *(JOHN³, JOHN², CHRISTOPHER¹)* was born October 06, 1711 in Needham, Norfolk County, Massachusetts. He married (1) ELIZABETH KINGSBURY May 30, 1732 in Needham, Suffolk County, Massachusetts.   He married (2) JUDITH BOSWORTH May 23, 1745 in Ashford, Windham County, Connecticut. She died July 12, 1754 in Ashford, Windham County, Connecticut. He married (3) CATHERINE SPRING November 13, 1755 in Ashford, Windham County, Connecticut.

More about EZRA SMITH:
Baptism: February 18, Needham, MA

Fact: Received bequest in his grandfather's will

More about ELIZABETH KINGSBURY:
Fact: a widow at time of marriage

14. ISAIAH⁴ SMITH *(JOHN³, JOHN², CHRISTOPHER¹)* was born May 07, 1721 in Needham, Norfolk County, Massachusetts. He married SUSANNAH.

15. ASAPH⁴ SMITH *(JOHN³, JOHN², CHRISTOPHER¹)* was born June 12, 1725 in Needham, Norfolk County, Massachusetts. He married SARAH PLACE December 19, 1749 in Ashford, Windham County, Connecticut, daughter of NATHAN PLACE and SARAH. She was born 1725.

16. ABIJAH⁴ SMITH *(JOHN³, JOHN², CHRISTOPHER¹)* was born December 11, 1727 in Needham, Norfolk County, Massachusetts, and died Aft. 1780. He married MARY BLANCHER in Connecticut, daughter of SAMUEL BLANCHER and MERCY RICHARDSON. She was born January 21, 1720/21 in Ashford, Windham County, Connecticut, and died in Vermont.

More About ABIJAH SMITH:
Military service: Revolutionary War Soldier

17. TIMOTHY⁴ SMITH *(JONATHAN³, JOHN², CHRISTOPHER¹)* was born July 03, 1725 in Needham, Norfolk County, Massachusetts, and died 1803 in Natick, Massachusetts. He married (1) ESTHER DEWING October 02, 1750 in Needham, Suffolk County, Massachusetts, daughter of HENRY DEWING and MEHITABLE ELLIS. She was born May 25, 1727, and died July 25, 1775 in Natick, Massachusetts. He married (2) ABIGAIL SAWIN 1780.

More about TIMOTHY SMITH:
Baptism: January 19, 1727/28, Needham, MA
Fact: Settled in Natick, MA
Military service: 1755, Captain Morse's Muster Role

More about ABIGAIL SAWIN:
Fact: April 18, 1775, came to warn the Sawins of the Marching of the British from Boston

18. DAVID⁴ SMITH *(JONATHAN³, JOHN², CHRISTOPHER¹)* was born May 06, 1727 in Needham, Norfolk County, Massachusetts, and died December 23, 1807. He married (1) ELIZABETH DEWING March 27, 1751 in Needham, Suffolk County, Massachusetts, daughter of HENRY DEWING and MEHITABLE ELLIS. She was born October 29, 1729 in Needham, MA, and died April 05, 1764. He married (2) ABIGAIL PARKER December 16, 1768 in Boston, Suffolk County, Massachusetts.

More about DAVID SMITH:
Baptism: January 19, 1727/28, Needham, MA
Fact: 1807, Purchased a house
Military service: Revolutionary War Soldier

19. AARON[4] SMITH *(JONATHAN[3], JOHN[2], CHRISTOPHER[1])* was born March 28, 1730 in Needham, Norfolk County, Massachusetts, and died December 04, 1796 in Needham, Norfolk County, Massachusetts. He married BEULAH WOODWARD December 04, 1755 in Needham, Suffolk County, Massachusetts, daughter of BENONI WOODWARD and ELIZABETH MIRICK. She was born October 24, 1734, and died April 11, 1796 in Needham, Norfolk County, Massachusetts.

More about AARON SMITH:
Baptism: April 12, Needham, MA
Burial: West Parish Cemetery, Needham, Norfolk County, Massachusetts
Fact: Large landowner in Needham & Natick
Military service: Revolutionary War Soldier

More about BEULAH WOODWARD:
Burial: West Parish Cemetery, Needham, Norfolk County, Massachusetts

20. SAMUEL[4] SMITH *(SAMUEL[3], JOHN[2], CHRISTOPHER[1])* was born May 17, 1723 in Needham, Norfolk County, Massachusetts. He married MEHITABEL WATKINS November 07, 1745 in Ashford, Windham County, Connecticut. She was born June 03, 1728.

More about SAMUEL SMITH:
Baptism: April 05, 1824, Needham, MA

21. RUTH[4] SMITH *(SAMUEL[3], JOHN[2], CHRISTOPHER[1])* was born November 01, 1724 in Needham, Norfolk County, Massachusetts, and died August 1813 in Ashford, Windham County, Connecticut. She married JACOB WILLSON May 21, 1741 in Ashford, Windham County, Connecticut. He was born July 10, 1718 in Ashford, Windham County, Connecticut, and died December 27, 1807 in Ashford, Windham County, Connecticut.

More about RUTH SMITH:
Baptism: December 27, Needham, MA

23. PELATIA⁴ SMITH *(SAMUEL³, JOHN², CHRISTOPHER¹)* was born September 24, 1728 in Needham, Norfolk County, Massachusetts. He married MARY DANIELS November 01, 1753 in Pomfret, Windham County, Connecticut.

More about PELATIA SMITH:
Baptism: September 29, 1728, Needham, MA

24. HEZEKIAH⁴ SMITH *(SAMUEL³, JOHN², CHRISTOPHER¹)* was born March 30, 1732 in Needham, Norfolk County, Massachusetts, and died 1789 in Ashford, Windham County, Connecticut. He married MIRIAM STOWELL 1757 in Ashford, Windham County, Connecticut. She was born May 29, 1737 in Ashford, Windham County, Connecticut, and died January 10, 1795 in Ashford, Windham County, Connecticut.

More about HEZEKIAH SMITH:
Baptism: April 02, 1732, Needham, MA

More about MIRIAM STOWELL:
Burial: Old Ashford Cemetery, Ashford, Windham County, CT

25. EBENEZER⁴ SMITH *(SAMUEL³, JOHN², CHRISTOPHER¹)* was born August 12, 1741 in Ashford, Windham County, Connecticut, and died 1791. He married MARTHA ELDRIDGE. She was born 1747.

26. ITHAMAR⁴ SMITH *(JOSHUA³, JOHN², CHRISTOPHER¹)* was born March 09, 1716/17 in Needham, Norfolk County, Massachusetts. He married ELIZABETH PARMENTER June 04, 1741 in Needham, Suffolk County, Massachusetts.

27. CALEB⁴ SMITH *(CALEB³, JOHN², CHRISTOPHER¹)* was born May 17, 1718 in Oxbridge, Worcester County, Massachusetts, and died January 23, 1797 in Danby, Rutland County, Vermont. He married DEBORAH CHICKERING 1748 in Mendon, Massachusetts, daughter of NATHANIEL CHICKERING and DEBORAH WRIGHT. She was born April 09, 1722 in Dedham, Norfolk County, Massachusetts, and died January 10, 1818 in Danby, Rutland County, Vermont.

More about CALEB SMITH:
Fact: Alternate birth place Needham
Military service: acted as spy for colonial troops
Religion: Quaker

Children of CALEB SMITH and DEBORAH CHICKERING are:
  i. EBENEZER[5] SMITH, b. September 03, 1749, Uxbridge, Massachusetts; d. June 06, 1826, Danby, Rutland County, Vermont; m. PHEBE LAPHAM, about 1798; b. January 18, 1759, Danby, Rutland County, Vermont; d. July 20, 1819, Danby, Rutland County, Vermont.

  More about EBENEZER SMITH:
  Baptism: April 30, 1758, Medway, Massachusetts
  Religion: Quaker

  More about PHEBE LAPHAM:
  Fact: alternate birth year 1758

  ii. **ASA SMITH**, b. February 14, 1750/51, Uxbridge, Massachusetts; m. (1) CATHERINE STEER; m. (2) LYDIA WILBUR.

  More about ASA SMITH:
  Baptism: April 30, 1758, Medway, Massachusetts

  iii. **NATHAN SMITH**[1,2], b. May 08, 1753, Bellingham, Massachusetts[2]; d. May 17, 1824, Danby, Rutland County, Vermont[2]; m. ELIZABETH ROGERS[3,4], 1786, Massachusetts; b. May 16, 1767, Pembroke, Plymouth County, Massachusetts[4]; d. December 28, 1817, Danby, Rutland County, Vermont[4].

  More about NATHAN SMITH:
  Baptism: April 30, 1758, Medway, Massachusetts
  Fact: Lived in Massachusetts until after Revolutionary War[7,8]
  Military service: Revolutionary War Soldier[9,10]
  Religion: Quaker

  iv. **DEBORAH SMITH**, b. February 11, 1755, Holliston, Middlesex County, Massachusetts; d. 1848, Stillwater, New York; m. KEITH.

  More about DEBORAH SMITH:
  Baptism: April 30, 1758, Medway, Massachusetts
  Fact: Twin to Barak

  v. **BARAK SMITH**, b. February 11, 1755, Holliston, Middlesex County, Massachusetts; d. December 02, 1828, Danby, Rutland County, Vermont; m. ABIGAIL BATTLE; b. January 18, 1764; d. February 20, 1831.

More about BARAK SMITH:
Baptism: April 30, 1758, Medway, Massachusetts
Fact: Twin to Deborah

vi. **LYDIA SMITH**, b. 1758, Uxbridge, Massachusetts; d. 1837, Bemus Heights, Saratoga County, NY; m. JOSEPH WALKER.

More about LYDIA SMITH:
Baptism: April 30, 1758, Medway, Massachusetts
Fact: Moved to Bemus Heights, NY

vii. **RHODA SMITH**, b. 1762, Uxbridge, Massachusetts; d. 1850, Danby, Rutland County, Vermont.

More about RHODA SMITH:
Baptism: May 30, 1762, Medway, Massachusetts

viii. **GEORGE SMITH**, b. June 15, 1757, Massachusetts; m. RACHEL, 1782, Danby, Rutland County, Vermont; b. September 19, 1764.

ix. **ABIAL SMITH**, b. about 1805; d. 1863; m. ROSWELL LILLIE; b. about 1783; d. 1846.

Generation No. 5

2. EBENEZER⁵ SMITH *(CALEB⁴, CALEB³, JOHN², CHRISTOPHER¹)* was born September 03, 1749 in Uxbridge, Massachusetts, and died June 06, 1826 in Danby, Rutland County, Vermont. He married PHEBE LAPHAM Abt. 1798. She was born January 18, 1759 in Danby, Rutland County, Vermont, and died July 20, 1819 in Danby, Rutland County, Vermont.

More about EBENEZER SMITH:
Baptism: April 30, 1758, Medway, Massachusetts
Religion: Quaker

More about PHEBE LAPHAM:
Fact: alternate birth year 1758

4. NATHAN⁵ SMITH *(CALEB⁴, CALEB³, JOHN², CHRISTOPHER¹)* was born May 08, 1753 in Bellingham, Massachusetts², and died May 17, 1824 in Danby, Rutland County, Vermont². He married ELIZABETH ROGERS 1786 in Massachusetts, daughter of WING ROGERS and MERCY HATCH. She was born May 16, 1767 in Pembroke, Plymouth County, Massachusetts⁴, and died December 28, 1817 in Danby, Rutland County, Vermont.

More about NATHAN SMITH:
Baptism: April 30, 1758, Medway, Massachusetts
Fact: Lived in Massachusetts until after Revolutionary War
Military service: Revolutionary War Soldier
Religion: Quaker

Children of NATHAN SMITH and ELIZABETH ROGERS are:

12.   i.   **BARAK⁶ SMITH**, b. April 28, 1787, Danby, Rutland County, Vermont; d. March 22, 1868, Springdale, Iowa.

     ii.   **MERCY SMITH¹²**, b. October 13, 1789, Danby, Rutland County, Vermont¹²; m. DAVID MORRISON, October 18, 1810, Danby, Rutland County, Vermont.

        More about MERCY SMITH:
        Fact: May have been married to a Morrison not Boyce

13.   iii.   **AUGUSTUS SMITH**, b. April 27, 1792, Danby, Rutland County, Vermont; d. June 05, 1886, Collins, Erie County, NY.

14.	iv.	**DANIEL SMITH**, b. August 16, 1794, Danby, Rutland County, Vermont; d. November 16, 1830, Danby, Rutland County, Vermont.	
15.	v.	**FRIEND ROGERS SMITH**, b. December 01, 1796, Danby, Rutland County, Vermont.	
16.	vi.	**RUTH SMITH**, b. January 13, 1799, Danby, Rutland County, Vermont.	
17.	vii.	**KATHERINE SMITH**, b. October 05, 1802, Danby, Rutland County, Vermont.	
	viii.	**LYDIA SMITH**, b. December 13, 1805, Danby, Rutland County, Vermont; m. AUGUSTUS SWEET.	

5. BARAK^5 **SMITH** *(CALEB*^{4}*, CALEB*^{3}*, JOHN*^{2}*, CHRISTOPHER*^{1}*)* was born February 11, 1755 in Holliston, Middlesex County, Massachusetts, and died December 02, 1828 in Danby, Rutland County, Vermont. He married ABIGAIL BATTLE. She was born January 18, 1764, and died February 20, 1831.

More about BARAK SMITH:
Baptism: April 30, 1758, Medway, Massachusetts
Fact: Twin to Deborah

Children of BARAK SMITH and ABIGAIL BATTLE are:
18.	i.	**JABEZ**^{6} **SMITH**, b. April 13, 1784; d. November 08, 1874.
	ii.	**BARACH SMITH**, b. September 16, 1791, Dover, Massachusetts.

6. GEORGE^5 **SMITH** *(CALEB*^{4}*, CALEB*^{3}*, JOHN*^{2}*, CHRISTOPHER*^{1}*)* was born June 15, 1757 in Massachusetts. He married RACHEL 1782 in Danby, Rutland County, Vermont. She was born September 19, 1764.

7. ABIAL^5 **SMITH** *(CALEB*^{4}*, CALEB*^{3}*, JOHN*^{2}*, CHRISTOPHER*^{1}*)* was born about 1805, and died 1863. She married ROSWELL LILLIE. He was born about 1783, and died 1846.

Generation No.6

8. ASA[6] SMITH *(EBENEZER[5], CALEB[4], CALEB[3], JOHN[2], CHRISTOPHER[1])* was born May 20, 1779 in Danby, Rutland County, Vermont, and died March 20, 1845 in Danby, Rutland County, Vermont. He married RHODA BAKER. She was born May 20, 1789 in Easton, Washington County, NY, and died February 20, 1866 in Danby, Rutland County, Vermont.

More about ASA SMITH:
Burial: Quaker Cemetery, Danby, Rutland County, Vermont
Fact: Said to have been deranged from receiving a blow on the back of his head

More about RHODA BAKER:
Burial: Quaker Cemetery, Danby, Rutland County, Vermont

9. LYDIA[6] SMITH *(EBENEZER[5], CALEB[4], CALEB[3], JOHN[2], CHRISTOPHER[1])* was born September 06, 1783 in Danby, Rutland County, Vermont, and died 1863 in Shrewsbury, Vermont. She married WILLIAM HITT after 1809 in Danby, Rutland County, Vermont. He was born about 1782 in New York, and died 1856 in Shrewsbury, Vermont.

More about WILLIAM HITT:
Fact: Moved to Addison Vermont

10. MARY[6] SMITH *(EBENEZER[5], CALEB[4], CALEB[3], JOHN[2], CHRISTOPHER[1])* was born October 16, 1794 in Danby, Rutland County, Vermont, and died Bet. 1870 - 1880 in Vermont. She married (1) PHILLIP POTTER. She married (2) JOSEPH BARTLETT. He was born about 1791 in New Hampshire, and died Bet. 1870 - 1880 in Vermont.

More about PHILLIP POTTER:
Fact: lived in Granville, NY

11. MARY[6] SMITH *(ASA[5], CALEB[4], CALEB[3], JOHN[2], CHRISTOPHER[1])* was born about 1780 in Uxbridge, Massachusetts, and died 1809. She married WILLIAM HITT. He was born about 1782 in New York, and died 1856 in Shrewsbury, Vermont.

More about WILLIAM HITT:
Fact: Moved to Addison Vermont

12. BARAK⁶ SMITH *(NATHAN⁵, CALEB⁴, CALEB³, JOHN², CHRISTOPHER¹)* was born April 28, 1787 in Danby, Rutland County, Vermont[12], and died March 22, 1868 in Springdale, Iowa[12]. He married MARY PALMER September 01, 1808 in Danby, Rutland County, Vermont, daughter of GILBERT PALMER and MARY SHERMAN. She was born December 05, 1788 in Danby, Rutland County, Vermont[12], and died 1874 in Springdale, Iowa.

More about BARAK SMITH:
Burial: Hickory Grove Cemetery, Iowa
Fact: Alternate death year: 1868
Religion: Spiritualist Mignonette Circle

More about MARY PALMER:
Burial: Hickory Grove Cemetery, Iowa
Fact: Twin to Elizabeth

Children of BARAK SMITH and MARY PALMER are:

24.   i.   **OPRAH⁷ SMITH**, b. October 06, 1809, Danby, Rutland County, Vermont; d. July 12, 1866, Liscomb Township, Marshall County, Iowa.

      ii.   **NATHAN SMITH**[12], b. February 08, 1810, Danby, Rutland County, Vermont[12]; d. January 15, 1837, Collins, Erie County, NY[12]; m. RACHEL SISSON[12], December 05, 1833, Collins, Erie County, New York[12].

      More about NATHAN SMITH:
      Burial: Collins Center Cemetery, Collins Center, town of Collins, Erie County, NY

25.   iii.   **GILBERT PALMER SMITH**, b. October 19, 1812, Danby, Rutland County, Vermont; d. July 19, 1900, Wichita, Guthrie County, Iowa.
26.   iv.   **DANIEL CHICKERING SMITH**, b. October 25, 1814, Danby, Rutland County, Vermont; d. 1899, Wood Lake, Cass County, Minnesota.
27.   v.   **JOSEPH ADDISON SMITH**, b. May 06, 1817, Danby, Rutland County, Vermont; d. March 01, 1872, Collins, Erie County, NY.
28.   vi.   **ELIZABETH SMITH**, b. June 25, 1820, Danby, Rutland County, Vermont; d. November 1900, Collins, Erie County, NY.
29.   vii.   **EBENEZER R SMITH**, b. October 29, 1829, Collins, Erie County, NY; d. March 23, 1885, Collins, Erie County, NY.

      viii.   **DEBORAH CHICKERING SMITH**[12], b. September 03, 1831, Collins, Erie County, NY[12]; d. March 11, 1905, High Grove, Riverside County, California[12]; m. GEORGE PIERSON[12], 1854, Gowanda,

NY[12]; b. about 1832, New York; d. March 01, 1864, Brownsville, Hinds County, Mississippi[12].

More about DEBORAH CHICKERING SMITH:
Religion: Spiritualist Mignonette Circle[12]

13. AUGUSTUS[6] SMITH *(NATHAN[5], CALEB[4], CALEB[3], JOHN[2], CHRISTOPHER[1])* was born April 27, 1792 in Danby, Rutland County, Vermont[15,16], and died June 05, 1886 in Collins, Erie County, NY[16]. He married ELIZABETH WHITE October 29, 1812 in Danby, Rutland County, Vermont, daughter of REUBEN WHITE and DEBORAH WILBUR. She was born September 21, 1793 in Nine Partners, Dutchess County, NY, and died April 27, 1875 in Collins, Erie County, New York.

More about AUGUSTUS SMITH:
Burial: Quaker Cemetery, Route 39, Collins, Erie County, New York
Fact: March 1816, Moved from Danby, VT to Collins, NY
Religion: Quaker

More about ELIZABETH WHITE:
Burial: Quaker Cemetery, Route 39, Collins, Erie County, New York
Fact: Member of Quaker Church: Augustus Smith Meeting House
Religion: Quaker

Children of AUGUSTUS SMITH and ELIZABETH WHITE are:

30.   i. **RHODA[7] SMITH**, b. October 09, 1813, Danby, Rutland County, Vermont.
31. ii. **RACHEL SMITH**, b. October 20, 1814, Danby, Rutland County, Vermont; d. August 20, 1896.
     iii. **MARIA SMITH**, b. May 13, 1819, Collins, Erie County, New York; d. February 19, 1840, Farmington, Michigan; m. EZRA SOUTHWICK; b. 1809, Mount Holly, Vermont.

        More about EZRA SOUTHWICK:
        Fact: June 18, 1850, quit Phoenix Senior Band of Philo-Howards rather than give up tea & tobacco

32. iv. **REUBEN W SMITH**, b. September 11, 1821, Collins, Erie County, New York; d. April 19, 1868, Leon, Cattaraugus County, New York.
     v. **LYDIA SMITH**, b. August 07, 1823, Collins, Erie County, New York; d. August 13, 1846, Collins, Erie County, NY.

        More about LYDIA SMITH:

Burial: Quaker Cemetery, Route 39, Collins, Erie County, New York

33. vi. **AMY W SMITH**, b. June 10, 1825, Collins, Erie County, New York; d. 1902.
34. vii. **HANNAH SMITH**, b. September 26, 1827, Collins, Erie County, New York; d. August 22, 1902, Perry, NY.
35. viii. **STEPHEN WHITE SMITH**, b. September 06, 1829, Collins, Erie County, New York; d. August 14, 1907, Collins, Erie County, NY.
36. ix. **PHOEBE L SMITH**, b. March 08, 1832, Collins, Erie County, New York; d. Bet. 1910 - 1920, Pontiac, Oakland County, Michigan.
    x. **FLORA ROLFE**, b. about 1850, New York; m. WILLIAM P PRATT, June 15, 1870, Collins, Erie County, NY; b. October 06, 1847, Concord, Erie County, NY.

14. DANIEL6 SMITH *(NATHAN5, CALEB4, CALEB3, JOHN2, CHRISTOPHER1)* was born August 16, 1794 in Danby, Rutland County, Vermont, and died November 16, 1830 in Danby, Rutland County, Vermont. He married (1) ANNA BOYCE November 02, 1815 in Easton, Washington County, New York[66]. She was born October 27, 1794, and died January 27, 1822 in Danby, Rutland County, Vermont. He married (2) HANNAH POTTER July 13, 1823. She was born October 04, 1798 in Granville, Washington County, New York, and died February 07, 1859 in Danby, Rutland County, Vermont.

More about DANIEL SMITH:
Burial: Cemetery at Danby Four Corners Danby Hill Road, Danby, Rutland County, VT

More about ANNA BOYCE:
Burial: Cemetery at Danby Four Corners Danby Hill Road, Danby, Rutland County, VT

More about HANNAH POTTER:
Burial: Scottsville Cemetery, Danby, Rutland County, Vermont

15. FRIEND ROGERS6 SMITH *(NATHAN5, CALEB4, CALEB3, JOHN2, CHRISTOPHER1)* was born December 01, 1796 in Danby, Rutland County, Vermont. He married SYLVIA SOUTHWICK February 22, 1821 in Danby, Rutland County, Vermont, daughter of ISSAC SOUTHWICK and THANKFUL. She was born March 21, 1805, and died before 1880.

More about FRIEND ROGERS SMITH:
Fact: Moved to Erie County, NY

Children of FRIEND SMITH and SYLVIA SOUTHWICK are:
39.   i. **EDNA THANKFUL[7] SMITH**, b. October 24, 1822, Danby, Rutland County, Vermont.
40.   ii. **TRUMAN MOTT SMITH**, b. January 19, 1825, Danby, Rutland County, Vermont; d. September 19, 1909, St Paul, Minnesota.
     iii. **ARTHUR SMITH**, b. 1829.
     iv. **ISAAC N SMITH**, b. 1834, Danby, Rutland County, Vermont.
     v. **JOHN N SMITH**, b. about 1835, Vermont.

16. **RUTH[6] SMITH** *(NATHAN[5], CALEB[4], CALEB[3], JOHN[2], CHRISTOPHER[1])* was born January 13, 1799 in Danby, Rutland County, Vermont[66]. She married JOSEPH DILLINGHAM. He was born September 07, 1795 in Granville, Washington County, NY, and died 1870.

17. **KATHERINE[6] SMITH** *(NATHAN[5], CALEB[4], CALEB[3], JOHN[2], CHRISTOPHER[1])* was born October 05, 1802 in Danby, Rutland County, Vermont. She married BENJAMIN BOYCE, son of WILLIAM BOYCE and ALICE WEAVER. He was born April 07, 1796 in Danby, Rutland County, Vermont.

More about KATHERINE SMITH:
Fact: Moved to Collins, NY

Children of KATHERINE SMITH and BENJAMIN BOYCE are:
     i. **ANNA[7] BOYCE**, b. about 1826, Vermont.
     ii. **SARAH H BOYCE**, b. about 1832, Collins, Erie County, NY.
     iii. **DANIEL BOYCE**, b. about 1833, Collins, Erie County, NY.
     iv. **RHODA M BOYCE**, b. about 1838, Collins, Erie County, NY.

18. **JABEZ[6] SMITH** *(BARAK[5], CALEB[4], CALEB[3], JOHN[2], CHRISTOPHER[1])* was born April 13, 1784, and died November 08, 1874. He married CHLOE RICHARDS March 05, 1807. She was born December 08, 1785, and died March 11, 1844.

19. **ASA[6] SMITH** *(GEORGE[5], CALEB[4], CALEB[3], JOHN[2], CHRISTOPHER[1])* was born 1784 in Danby, Rutland County, Vermont. He married SYLVIA WILBER February 23, 1809 in Danby, Rutland County, Vermont.

Generation No. 7

20. REUBEN B[7] SMITH *(ASA[6], EBENEZER[5], CALEB[4], CALEB[3], JOHN[2], CHRISTOPHER[1])* was born 1823 in Vermont. He married ELIZABETH WELLS. She was born about 1823 in New York.

More about REUBEN B SMITH:
Fact: Moved to Illinois

21. PHEBE[7] SMITH *(ASA[6], EBENEZER[5], CALEB[4], CALEB[3], JOHN[2], CHRISTOPHER[1])* was born 1822 in Danby, Rutland County, Vermont. She married C M BRUCE. He died between 1860 - 1870 in Danby, Rutland County, Vermont.

22. SAMUEL[7] HITT *(LYDIA[6] SMITH, EBENEZER[5], CALEB[4], CALEB[3], JOHN[2], CHRISTOPHER[1])* was born about 1815 in Vermont, and died 1853 in Addison, Vermont. He married EMILY MERRILL. She was born about 1820 in Vermont.

23. SMITH[7] HITT *(MARY[6] SMITH, ASA[5], CALEB[4], CALEB[3], JOHN[2], CHRISTOPHER[1])* He married MARIA RANDALL, daughter of CALEB RANDALL.

More about SMITH HITT:
Fact: 1841, Moved to Pawlet, Vermont

24. OPRAH[7] SMITH *(BARAK[6], NATHAN[5], CALEB[4], CALEB[3], JOHN[2], CHRISTOPHER[1])* was born October 06, 1809 in Danby, Rutland County, Vermont, and died July 12, 1866 in Liscomb Township, Marshall County, Iowa. She married ROYAL STRANG October 27, 1831 in Collins, Erie County, New York, son of JOHN STRANG and ELIZABETH HISTED. He was born 1801 in New York, and died 1901.

Children of OPRAH SMITH and ROYAL STRANG are:
- i. **SARAH ANN[8] STRANG**, b. September 07, 1832, Collins, Erie County, NY; d. Correctionville, Woodbury County, Iowa; m. MORRIS KELLOGG, March 29, 1853; b. May 20, 1824, Leon, Cattaraugus County, NY; d. September 08, 1907, Correctionville, Woodbury County, Iowa.
- ii. **JOHN STRANG**, b. July 12, 1834, Collins, Erie County, NY; d. February 27, 1848, Collins, Erie County, NY.

iii. **DANIEL STRANG**, b. May 17, 1836, Collins, Erie County, NY; d. 1855, Collins, Erie County, NY.
iv. **MARY PALMER STRANG**, b. September 22, 1838, Collins, Erie County, NY; d. 1912, Westphalia, Anderson County, Kansas; m. JOHN RUSSELL, July 06, 1856, Felix Township, Grundy County, Iowa; b. March 20, 1821, Sandy Township, Tuscarawas County, Ohio; d. July 21, 1900, Westphalia, Anderson County, Kansas.
v. **BARAK SMITH STRANG**, b. September 24, 1840, Collins, Erie County, NY; d. July 16, 1852, Collins, Erie County, NY.
vi. **WILLIAM STRANG**, b. September 24, 1842, Collins, Erie County, NY; d. 1928, Pasadena, Los Angeles County, California; m. CAROLINE BALDWIN, 1878; b. March 1854, Indiana; d. 1943.
vii. **DAVID STRANG**, b. September 13, 1844, Collins, Erie County, NY; d. February 28, 1845, Collins, Erie County, NY.
viii. **ROBERT EDWIN STRANG**, b. February 23, 1846, Collins, Erie County, NY; d. March 21, 1909, los Angeles, Los Angeles County, California; m. HARRIET LEMERT, December 12, 1878; b. July 23, 1849, Ohio; d. December 01, 1911, los Angeles, Los Angeles County, California.

More about ROBERT EDWIN STRANG:
Fact: twin to Rhoda

ix. **RHODA ELLEN STRANG**, b. February 23, 1846, Collins, Erie County, NY; d. January 22, 1930, Albion, Marshall County, Iowa; m. REUBEN TABER, August 18, 1875, Colorado Springs, El Paso County, Colorado; b. January 20, 1845, Mount Pleasant, Clinton County, Ohio; d. March 10, 1923, Agra, Lincoln County, Oklahoma.

25. GILBERT PALMER[7] SMITH *(BARAK[6], NATHAN[5], CALEB[4], CALEB[3], JOHN[2], CHRISTOPHER[1])* was born October 19, 1812 in Danby, Rutland County, Vermont, and died July 19, 1900 in Wichita, Guthrie County, Iowa. He married (1) LYDIA PALMERTON October 14, 1837 in Collins, Erie County, New York. She was born December 08, 1818 in Collins, Erie County, New York, and died December 25, 1848 in Collins, Erie County, New York. He married (2) CLARISSA RATHBORN October 04, 1850. She was born about 1822 in New York, and died December 04, 1884 in Iowa.

More about GILBERT PALMER SMITH:
Fact: Member of Quaker Church: Augustus Smith Meeting House
Religion: Quaker

More about LYDIA PALMERTON:
Burial: Collins Center Cemetery, Collins Center, Collins, Erie County, NY
Fact: Member of Quaker Church: Augustus Smith Meeting House
Religion: Quaker

Children of GILBERT SMITH and LYDIA PALMERTON are:
  i. **NATHAN E^8 SMITH**, b. November 01, 1838, Collins, Erie County, NY d. July 07, 1877, Cedar River, Cedar County, Iowa m. REBECCA HOOPES MARIS, December 14, 1865, Cedar River, Cedar County, Iowa b. May 05, 1837, Chesterfield, Ohio, d. March 20, 1924, Brownville, Texas.

  More about NATHAN E SMITH:
  Burial: Springdale Cemetery, Iowa

  ii. **EMILY ADELINE SMITH**, b. May 02, 1841, New York d. January 30, 1918 m. ERASTUS L HARRIS, February 11, 1863, Springdale, Cedar County, Iowa[143]; b. January 04, 1831, Collins, Erie County, NY.

  More about ERASTUS L HARRIS:
  Military service: Civil War Soldier

  iii. **DANIEL WHEELER SMITH**, b. May 03, 1843, Collins, Erie County, NY d. March 30, 1918, Norwalk, California m. NARCISSA MACY, May 28, 1870, Springdale, Cedar County, Iowa.
  iv. **HANNAH ARLETTA SMITH**, b. June 17, 1845, Collins, Erie County, NY d. January 28, 1927, Albion, Marshall County, Iowa m. JESSE BINFORD, November 17, 1864, Tipton, Cedar County, Iowa b. 1832, Ohio; d. Bet. 1910 - 1915, Iowa.
  v. **MARY ELIZABETH SMITH**, b. August 21, 1847, Collins, Erie County, NY d. December 12, 1931, Waukon, Allamakee County, Iowa m. GEORGE JENKINS MARIS, June 02, 1865, Tipton, Cedar County, Iowa; b. June 17, 1841, Chesterfield, Ohio d. November 10, 1915, Utah.

26. DANIEL CHICKERING^7 SMITH *(BARAK^6, NATHAN^5, CALEB^4, CALEB^3, JOHN^2, CHRISTOPHER^1)* was born October 25, 1814 in Danby, Rutland County, Vermont, and died 1899 in Wood Lake, Cass County, Minnesota. He married ELIZA JAMES. She was born about 1824 in England.

Child of DANIEL SMITH and ELIZA JAMES is:
  i. **GEORGE A^8 SMITH**, b. about 1862, Iowa.

27. JOSEPH ADDISON⁷ SMITH *(BARAK⁶, NATHAN⁵, CALEB⁴, CALEB³, JOHN², CHRISTOPHER¹)* was born May 06, 1817 in Danby, Rutland County, Vermont, and died March 01, 1872 in Collins, Erie County, NY. He married MARY JANE SHOTWELL June 01, 1842 in Collins, Erie County, New York. She was born September 15, 1822 in Elba, Genesee County, NY, and died February 05, 1894 in Cleveland, Cuyahoga County, Ohio.

More about JOSEPH ADDISON SMITH:
Burial: Collins Center Cemetery, Collins Center, town of Collins, Erie County, NY

Children of JOSEPH SMITH and MARY SHOTWELL are:
  i. **ALBERT G⁸ SMITH**, b. April 1844, Collins, Erie County, NY; d. 1920; m. (1) VICTORIA; b. about 1859, New York; m. (2) LUVINA L; b. March 1855, New York; d. before 1930.

  More about ALBERT G SMITH:
  Burial: Collins Center cemetery, town of Collins, Erie County, NY

  More about LUVINA L:
  Fact: Had 4 children; 2 died young

  ii. **SARAH SMITH**, b. about 1847, Collins. Erie County, NY.
  iii. **GERTRUDE SMITH**, b. about 1852, New York.
  iv. **MARY SMITH**, b. about 1855, New York.
  v. **LIBBIE SMITH**, b. about 1864, Collins, Erie County, NY.

28. ELIZABETH⁷ SMITH *(BARAK⁶, NATHAN⁵, CALEB⁴, CALEB³, JOHN², CHRISTOPHER¹)* was born June 25, 1820 in Danby, Rutland County, Vermont, and died November 1900 in Collins, Erie County, NY. She married ABRAM LAPHAM SOUTHWICK August 25, 1841. He was born August 04, 1809 in Mount Holly, Vermont, and died October 1892 in Gowanda, NY.

Children of ELIZABETH SMITH and ABRAM SOUTHWICK are:
  i. **ALBERT⁸ SOUTHWICK**, b. 1838, New York; d. 1915; m. PHEOBE A, about 1863, New York; b. 1842, New York; d. 1925.

  More about ALBERT SOUTHWICK:
  Burial: Pine Grove Cemetery, Gowanda, town of Collins, Erie County, NY

More about PHEOBE A:
Burial: Pine Grove Cemetery, Gowanda, town of Collins, Erie County, NY

ii. **GILBERT S SOUTHWICK**, b. April 10, 1843, Michigan; d. December 21, 1866, Collins, Erie County, NY.

More about GILBERT S SOUTHWICK:
Burial: Pine Grove Cemetery, Gowanda, town of Collins, Erie County, NY
Military service: Civil War Soldier

iii. **JOSEPH ADDISON SOUTHWICK**, b. November 1847, Collins, Erie County, NY; d. Bet. 1920 - 1930; m. JULIA, Abt. 1891; b. February 1861, New York.
iv. **ROSE GRIFFITH**, b. about 1855, New York.

More about ROSE GRIFFITH:
Fact: adopted daughter

29. EBENEZER R[7] SMITH (BARAK[6], NATHAN[5], CALEB[4], CALEB[3], JOHN[2], CHRISTOPHER[1]) was born October 29, 1829 in Collins, Erie County, NY, and died March 23, 1885 in Collins, Erie County, NY. He married CAROLINE ESTHLER January 31, 1856 in Collins, Erie County, New York. She was born October 20, 1829 in Libertytown, Frederick County, Maryland[164], and died October 10, 1919 in Buffalo, Erie County, NY.

More about EBENEZER R SMITH:
Burial: Pine Grove Cemetery, Gowanda, town of Collins, Erie County, NY

More about CAROLINE ESTHLER:
Burial: Pine Grove Cemetery, Gowanda, town of Collins, Erie County, NY

Children of EBENEZER SMITH and CAROLINE ESTHLER are:
i. **CATHERINE[8] SMITH**, b. about 1869, Collins, Erie County, NY; m. EDWARD H RUSSELL; b. about 1871.
ii. **CORA SMITH**, b. June 04, 1858, Iowa; d. Collins, Erie County, NY.

More about CORA SMITH:
Burial: Pine Grove Cemetery, Gowanda, town of Collins, Erie County, NY

iii. **ARTHUR E SMITH**, b. November 06, 1864; d. Collins, Erie County, NY.

More about ARTHUR E SMITH:
Burial: Pine Grove Cemetery, Gowanda, town of Collins, Erie County, NY

30. RHODA[7] SMITH *(AUGUSTUS[6], NATHAN[5], CALEB[4], CALEB[3], JOHN[2], CHRISTOPHER[1])* was born October 09, 1813 in Danby, Rutland County, Vermont. She married CALEB TARBOX 1833, son of BENJAMIN TARBOX and HULDAH. He was born February 17, 1799, and died October 21, 1874 in Collins, Erie County, New York.

More about RHODA SMITH:
Fact: Teacher Collins
Religion: Quaker

More about CALEB TARBOX:
Burial: Quaker Cemetery, Route 39, Collins, Erie County, New York
Religion: Quaker

Children of RHODA SMITH and CALEB TARBOX are:
    i. **CHESTER[8] TARBOX**, b. September 29, 1834, Collins, Erie County, NY d. February 02, 1890.

    More about CHESTER TARBOX:
    Fact: 1878, Lived in Collins, Erie County, NY
    ii. **STEPHEN S TARBOX**, b. December 20, 1835, Collins, Erie County, NY d. March 26, 1918, Collins, Erie County, NY; m. JULIA ANN CLARK, September 14, 1856, Collins, Erie County, NY; b. June 04, 1836, Collins, Erie County, NY; d. September 17, 1916, Collins, Erie County, NY.

    More about STEPHEN S TARBOX:
    Burial: Collins Center Cemetery, town of Collins, Erie County, NY
    Fact: 1878, Lived in Collins, Erie County, NY

    More about JULIA ANN CLARK:
    Burial: Collins Center Cemetery, town of Collins, Erie County, NY

    iii. **FRANCIS TARBOX**, b. July 12, 1839, Collins, Erie County, NY m. MARY BALDWIN, about 1868; b. about 1845, New York.

More about FRANCIS TARBOX:
Fact: 1878, Lived in East Otto, Cattaraugus County, NY

iv. **LEONARD TARBOX**, b. April 10, 1845, Collins, Erie County, NY, m. ADDIE STONE.

More about LEONARD TARBOX:
Fact: 1878, Lived in Evans, Erie County, NY

v. **EMILY L TARBOX**, b. January 27, 1847, Collins, Erie County, NY d. July 16, 1905, Collins, Erie County, NY m. HIRAM W COOK b. September 28, 1834, New York d. December 22, 1920.

More about EMILY L TARBOX:
Burial: Shaw Cemetery, Foster Road, town of Collins, Erie County, NY
Fact: 1878, Lived in Collins, Erie County, NY

More about HIRAM W COOK:
Burial: Shaw Cemetery, Foster Road, town of Collins, Erie County, NY

vi. **ALDEN TARBOX**, b. November 17, 1848, Collins, Erie County, NY m. MARTHA WEST b. Abt. 1848, New York.

More about ALDEN TARBOX:
Fact: 1878, Lived in Morris County, Kansas

vii. **REUBAN TARBOX**, b. March 18, 1851, Collins, Erie County, NY d. 1927 m. EVA STEWART; b. about 1860, New York.

More about REUBAN TARBOX:
Burial: Collins Center Cemetery, Route 39, Collins Center, town of Collins, Erie County, NY
Fact: 1878, Lived in Collins, Erie County, NY

viii. **HANNAH MELINDA TARBOX**, b. January 29, 1853, Collins, Erie County, NY d. 1893; m. CHARLES BABCOCK, 1875.

More about HANNAH MELINDA TARBOX:
Fact: 1878, Lived in Collins, Erie County, NY

ix. **OLIVE TARBOX**, b. October 29, 1854, Collins, Erie County, NY d. August 30, 1878, Collins, Erie County, NY, m. JAMES PARKINSON.

More about OLIVE TARBOX:
Burial: Pine Grove Cemetery, Gowanda, town of Collins, Erie County, NY

31. RACHEL[7] SMITH *(AUGUSTUS[6], NATHAN[5], CALEB[4], CALEB[3], JOHN[2], CHRISTOPHER[1])* was born October 20, 1814 in Danby, Rutland County, Vermont[308], and died August 20, 1896. She married (1) ALMOND LINDSLEY, son of AARON LINDSLEY. He was born 1805 in New York. She married (2) ISAIAH MONSON.

More about RACHEL SMITH:
Fact: 1878, Lived in Iowa

More about ALMOND LINDSLEY:
Fact: Bet. 1825 - 1826, Taught Winter Sessions at Hazard Corner School

More about ISAIAH MONSON:
Fact: May Be Isaiah Morrison

Children of RACHEL SMITH and ALMOND LINDSLEY are:
  i. **ASA S[8] LINDSLEY**, b. about 1835, New York; m. CHLOE ROSETTA SOPER; b. about 1849.
  ii. **AMELIA LINDSLEY**, b. about 1846, New York.

32. REUBEN W[7] SMITH *(AUGUSTUS[6], NATHAN[5], CALEB[4], CALEB[3], JOHN[2], CHRISTOPHER[1])* was born September 11, 1821 in Collins, Erie County, New York, and died April 19, 1868 in Leon, Cattaraugus County, New York. He married MARY WHITE. She was born March 19, 1825 in New York, and died Bet. 1910 - 1920 in New York.

More about REUBEN W SMITH:
Burial: Treat Cemetery, Leon, Cattaraugus County, NY

Children of REUBEN SMITH and MARY WHITE are:
  i. **ISAAC[8] SMITH**, b. 1845 d. 1877 m. CHARLOTTE BUMP b. August 21, 1845, Perrysburg, Cattaraugus County, NY; d. September 28, 1910, Dayton, Cattaraugus County, NY.

  More about ISAAC SMITH:
  Burial: Treat Cemetery, Leon, Cattaraugus County, NY

More about CHARLOTTE BUMP:
Burial: Cottage Cemetery, Cottage, Cattaraugus, NY

    ii. **LAWTON W SMITH**, b. October 23, 1855 m. MARY, about 1899; b. about 1871, New York; d. Bet. 1910 - 1920, New York.

    iii. **MARY SMITH**, b. May 08, 1856, Leon, Cattaraugus County, NY; d. October 23, 1938; m. DEWITT HIBBARD, about 1878; b. January 20, 1855, North Collins, Erie County, NY d. August 04, 1933.

More about MARY SMITH:
Burial: North Collins, NY

More about DEWITT HIBBARD:
Burial: North Collins, Erie County, NY

    iv. **FRANK W SMITH**, b. March 15, 1864 d. 1929 m. FLORA TOWN, Abt. 1893; b. April 11, 1867 d. 1946.

More about FRANK W SMITH:
Burial: Rutledge Cemetery, Conewango, Cattaraugus County, NY

More about FLORA TOWN:
Burial: Rutledge Cemetery, Conewango, Cattaraugus County, NY

33. AMY W^7 SMITH *(AUGUSTUS^6, NATHAN^5, CALEB^4, CALEB^3, JOHN^2, CHRISTOPHER^1)* was born June 10, 1825 in Collins, Erie County, New York, and died 1902. She married WILLIAM O TYRER before 1850. He was born about 1825 in New York, and died before 1900.

More about AMY W SMITH:
Fact: 1878, Lived in Pontiac, Michigan

Children of AMY SMITH and WILLIAM TYRER are:
    i. **SARAH H^8 TYRER**, b. about February 1850, New York.
    ii. **SMITH H TYRER**, b. about 1857, New York.
    iii. **ERNEST J TYRER**, b. about 1859, New York; m. MARY H; b. about 1867, Michigan.
    iv. **MELVA TYRER**, b. about 1859, New York.

34. HANNAH[7] SMITH *(AUGUSTUS[6], NATHAN[5], CALEB[4], CALEB[3], JOHN[2], CHRISTOPHER[1])* was born September 26, 1827 in Collins, Erie County, New York, and died August 22, 1902 in Perry, NY. She married JOHN WILBUR WOOD January 02, 1856 in Collins, Erie County, New York. He was born 1825 in Collins Center, Erie County, NY, and died before 1900 in Leon, Cattaraugus County, NY.

More about HANNAH SMITH:
Fact: 1878, Lived in Leon, Cattaraugus County, NY

More about JOHN WILBUR WOOD:
Career: farmer
Fact: Moved from Collins, NY to Leon, Cattaraugus County, NY

Children of HANNAH SMITH and JOHN WOOD are:
  i. **AUGUSTUS[8] WOOD**, b. 1857, Leon, Cattaraugus County, NY d. 1956, Leon, Cattaraugus County, NY; m. CLARA, about 1899, New York; b. about 1871, New York.
  ii. **ELIZABETH WOOD**, b. February 1857, Leon, Cattaraugus County, NY d. 1920 m. JOHN HARMON, July 23, 1876, Leon, Cattaraugus County, NY b. September 1851, New York; d. 1928.
  iii. **ADDIE WOOD**, b. 1860, Leon, Cattaraugus County, NY; d. before 1870.

35. STEPHEN WHITE[7] SMITH *(AUGUSTUS[6], NATHAN[5], CALEB[4], CALEB[3], JOHN[2], CHRISTOPHER[1])* was born September 06, 1829 in Collins, Erie County, New York, and died August 14, 1907 in Collins, Erie County, NY. He married (1) MAHALA DOUGLAS. He married (2) MARY E KNIGHT April 06, 1857 in Collins, Erie County, New York, daughter of EDWIN KNIGHT and SARAH. She was born May 10, 1838 in Collins, Erie County, NY, and died March 30, 1875 in Collins, Erie County, NY. He married (3) LUCINDA KNIGHT Bet. 1875 - 1880, daughter of EDWIN KNIGHT and SARAH. She was born Abt. 1841 in New York.

More about STEPHEN WHITE SMITH:
Fact: 1878, Lived in Collins, Erie County, NY

Children of STEPHEN SMITH and MARY KNIGHT are:
  i. **FREDERICK D[8] SMITH**, b. about 1858, Collins, Erie County, NY d. 1894; m. ELLEN HILLDEBRAND.
  ii. **EDWIN KNIGHT SMITH**, b. April 24, 1862, Collins, Erie County, NY d. June 07, 1924, Jerome, Jerome County, Idaho m. REBECCA MINNIE SAYER, November 04, 1914, Lincoln, Lancaster County,

Nebraska b. March 09, 1881, Norwich, England d. October 25, 1947, Portland, Multnomah County, Oregon.
   iii. **GEORGE LAVETT SMITH**, b. about 1865, Collins, Erie County, NY d. 1901; m. MARY MAGDELENA FOOT, April 20, 1893.
   iv. **REUBEN AUGUSTUS SMITH**, b. November 22, 1873, Collins, Erie County, NY d. November 30, 1932; m. SARAH PEARL BAKER, June 28, 1906, Franklin, Venango County, Pennsylvania; b. 1884, New York; d. October 20, 1976.

More about REUBEN AUGUSTUS SMITH:
Burial: Collins Center Cemetery, Collins Center, Collins, Erie County, NY

More about SARAH PEARL BAKER:
Burial: Collins Center Cemetery, Collins Center, Collins, Erie County, NY

Child of STEPHEN SMITH and LUCINDA KNIGHT is:
   v. **CLARENCE ORVILLE[8] SMITH**, b. about 1878, Collins, Erie County, NY d. 1944.

36. **PHOEBE L[7] SMITH** *(AUGUSTUS[6], NATHAN[5], CALEB[4], CALEB[3], JOHN[2], CHRISTOPHER[1])* was born March 08, 1832 in Collins, Erie County, New York, and died Bet. 1910 - 1920 in Pontiac, Oakland County, Michigan. She married **RICHARD BARTLETT** 1851 in Collins, Erie County, NY, son of SMITH BARTLETT and SARAH ALLEN. He was born November 28, 1829 in Collins, Erie County, NY, and died 1909 in Pontiac, Oakland County, Michigan.

More about PHOEBE L SMITH:
Fact: 1878, Lived in Pontiac, Michigan

More about RICHARD BARTLETT:
Fact: May 1865, Moved to Oakland County, Michigan
Political: Republican

Children of PHOEBE SMITH and RICHARD BARTLETT are:
   i. **CHARLES S[8] BARTLETT**, b. about 1849, Collins, Erie County, NY d. July 25, 1917, Pontiac, Oakland County, Michigan; m. (1) CARRIE B OSMUN, 1881, Michigan b. May 1862, New York m. (2) HELENA CAITLIN, February 25, 1917, Michigan b. March 24, 1862, Persia, Cattaraugus County, New York d. April 25, 1939, Pontiac, Elizabeth Lake, Oakland, Michigan.
   ii. **SMITH AUGUSTUS BARTLETT**, b. May 1860, New York m. LOUISE D CARR, 1883, Pontiac, Oakland County, Michigan b. May 1864, Germany.

iii. **AUGUSTA M BARTLETT**, b. about 1850, Collins, Erie County, NY.
iv. **CHARLES BARTLETT**, b. about 1857, Collins, Erie County, NY.

37. AUGUSTUS D[7] SMITH *(DANIEL[6], NATHAN[5], CALEB[4], CALEB[3], JOHN[2], CHRISTOPHER[1])* was born March 09, 1825 in Danby, Rutland County, Vermont, and died April 07, 1887 in Danby, Rutland County, Vermont. He married CHARITY HERRICK January 28, 1845 in Danby, Rutland County, Vermont, and daughter of WILLIAM HERRICK. She was born 1827 in Vermont, and died November 09, 1898 in Danby, Rutland County, VT.

More about AUGUSTUS D SMITH:
Burial: Scottsville Cemetery, Danby, Rutland County, Vermont
Fact: 1862, Vice President of Rutland County Agricultural Society
Political: Bet. 1861 - 1868, Justice of the Peace, Danby, VT
Religion: Congregational Church

More about CHARITY HERRICK:
Burial: Scottsville Cemetery, Danby, Rutland County, Vermont

38. ANNA ELIZA[7] SMITH *(DANIEL[6], NATHAN[5], CALEB[4], CALEB[3], JOHN[2], CHRISTOPHER[1])* was born December 07, 1828 in Danby, Rutland County, Vermont, and died May 03, 1874 in Danby, Rutland County, Vermont. She married CHARLES HENRY CONGDON January 22, 1846 in Danby, Rutland County, Vermont. He was born October 06, 1820 in Sugar Hill, East Wallingford County, Vermont, and died August 25, 1891 in Wallingford, Vermont.

39. EDNA THANKFUL[7] SMITH *(FRIEND ROGERS[6], NATHAN[5], CALEB[4], CALEB[3], JOHN[2], CHRISTOPHER[1])* was born October 24, 1822 in Danby, Rutland County, Vermont. She married EDWIN KELLOGG February 26, 1852 in Leon, Cattaraugus County, New York. He was born 1820 in New York, and died February 08, 1892 in Leon, Cattaraugus County, NY.

Children of EDNA SMITH and EDWIN KELLOGG are:
i. **SMITH EDWIN[8] KELLOGG**, b. January 18, 1854, Leon, Cattaraugus County, NY; d. October 01, 1854, Leon, Cattaraugus County, NY.
ii. **SYLVIA ANNA KELLOGG**, b. March 04, 1856; m. EMORY ADELBERT TAYLOR.

40. TRUMAN MOTT[7] SMITH *(FRIEND ROGERS[6], NATHAN[5], CALEB[4], CALEB[3], JOHN[2], CHRISTOPHER[1])* was born January 19, 1825 in Danby, Rutland County, Vermont, and died September 19, 1909 in St Paul, Minnesota. He married (1) MARY BACHUS. She was born about 1826 in Vermont. He married (2) LYDIA COMSTOCK November 19, 1845 in Geneva, Wisconsin. She was born September 24, 1822 in Luzerne, New York, and died December 01, 1854 in St Paul, Minnesota.

More about TRUMAN MOTT SMITH:
Fact: Moved to St Paul, Minnesota

Child of TRUMAN SMITH and MARY BACHUS is:
    i. MARY FRANCES[8] SMITH, b. about 1856, Minnesota.

Children of TRUMAN SMITH and LYDIA COMSTOCK are:
    ii. **SYLVIA ANTOINETTE[8] SMITH**, b. April 28, 1848, Walworth County, Wisconsin d. July 09, 1928, St Paul, Minnesota m. JACOB G MILLER, December 25, 1866, St Paul, Minnesota b. January 03, 1838, Wittenberg, Germany d. October 23, 1909, St Paul, Minnesota.
    iii. **EMMA S SMITH**, b. about 1850, Vermont.

41. HOWELL[7] DILLINGHAM (RUTH[6] SMITH, NATHAN[5], CALEB[4], CALEB[3], JOHN[2], CHRISTOPHER[1]) was born March 07, 1820 in Granville, Washington County, NY. He married EMILY. She was born about 1822 in New York, and died before 1880 in Vermont.

42. REUEL[7] SMITH (JABEZ[6], BARAK[5], CALEB[4], CALEB[3], JOHN[2], CHRISTOPHER[1]) was born April 19, 1811, and died January 29, 1882. He married LUCINDA ADAMS March 03, 1833. She was born September 03, 1810, and died November 11, 1845.

Child of Reuel Smith and Lucinda Adams is:
    i. MARY ABIGAIL[8] SMITH, b. April 05, 1834; d. September 29, 1864; m. CHAUNCEY PARMELEE, February 22, 1854; b. August 05, 1824, Wilmington, Vermont; d. January 23, 1904, Vineland, New Jersey.

Generation No. 8

9. STEPHEN S⁸ TARBOX *(RHODA⁷ SMITH, AUGUSTUS⁶, NATHAN⁵, CALEB⁴, CALEB³, JOHN², CHRISTOPHER¹)* was born December 20, 1835 in Collins, Erie County, NY, and died March 26, 1918 in Collins, Erie County, NY. He married JULIA ANN CLARK September 14, 1856 in Collins, Erie County, NY. She was born June 04, 1836 in Collins, Erie County, NY, and died September 17, 1916 in Collins, Erie County, NY.

More about STEPHEN S TARBOX:
Burial: Collins Center Cemetery, town of Collins, Erie County, NY
Fact: 1878, Lived in Collins, Erie County, NY

More about JULIA ANN CLARK:
Burial: Collins Center Cemetery, town of Collins, Erie County, NY

Children of STEPHEN TARBOX and JULIA CLARK are:
- 25. i. **WARD TIMOTHY⁹ TARBOX**, b. March 17, 1871, Collins, Erie County, NY; d. June 24, 1951.
- 26. ii. **IRWIN RAYMOND TARBOX**, b. May 16, 1873, Collins, Erie County, NY; d. January 04, 1936, Collins, Erie County, NY.

10. FRANCIS⁸ TARBOX *(RHODA⁷ SMITH, AUGUSTUS⁶, NATHAN⁵, CALEB⁴, CALEB³, JOHN², CHRISTOPHER¹)* was born July 12, 1839 in Collins, Erie County, NY. He married MARY BALDWIN about 1868. She was born about 1845 in New York.

More about FRANCIS TARBOX:
Fact: 1878, Lived in East Otto, Cattaraugus County, NY

Child of FRANCIS TARBOX and MARY BALDWIN is:
- 27. i. **IDA M⁹ TARBOX**, b. about 1870, New York.

11. EMILY L⁸ TARBOX *(RHODA⁷ SMITH, AUGUSTUS⁶, NATHAN⁵, CALEB⁴, CALEB³, JOHN², CHRISTOPHER¹)* was born January 27, 1847 in Collins, Erie County, NY, and died July 16, 1905 in Collins, Erie County, NY. She married

HIRAM W COOK. He was born September 28, 1834 in New York, and died December 22, 1920.

More about EMILY L TARBOX:
Burial: Shaw Cemetery, Foster Road, town of Collins, Erie County, NY
Fact: 1878, Lived in Collins, Erie County, NY

More about HIRAM W COOK:
Burial: Shaw Cemetery, Foster Road, town of Collins, Erie County, NY

Children of EMILY TARBOX and HIRAM COOK are:
      i. **ETHEL⁹ COOK**, b. May 1878, Collins, Erie County, NY.
28.   ii. **ARTHUR COOK**, b. May 1870, Collins, Erie County, NY.

12. **ALDEN⁸ TARBOX** *(RHODA⁷ SMITH, AUGUSTUS⁶, NATHAN⁵, CALEB⁴, CALEB³, JOHN², CHRISTOPHER¹)* was born November 17, 1848 in Collins, Erie County, NY. He married MARTHA WEST. She was born Abt. 1848 in New York.

More about ALDEN TARBOX:
Fact: 1878, Lived in Morris County, Kansas

Children of ALDEN TARBOX and MARTHA WEST are:
      i. **NEWTON⁹ TARBOX**, b. about 1876, Kansas; m. ELLA A; b. about 1883, Wisconsin.
      ii. **JOHN A TARBOX**, b. about 1879, Kansas.
      iii. **FRANCIS TARBOX**, b. about 1862, Michigan.

13. **REUBAN⁸ TARBOX** *(RHODA⁷ SMITH, AUGUSTUS⁶, NATHAN⁵, CALEB⁴, CALEB³, JOHN², CHRISTOPHER¹)* was born March 18, 1851 in Collins, Erie County, NY, and died 1927. He married EVA STEWART. She was born about 1860 in New York.

More about REUBAN TARBOX:
Burial: Collins Center Cemetery, Route 39, Collins Center, town of Collins, Erie County, NY
Fact: 1878, Lived in Collins, Erie County, NY

Children of REUBAN TARBOX and EVA STEWART are:
29.   i. **MINNIE⁹ TARBOX**, b. about 1882, New York.
30.   ii. **EARL R TARBOX**, b. about 1890, Collins, Erie County, NY.
      iii. **GERTRUDE TARBOX**, b. about 1893, Collins, Erie County, NY.

14. HANNAH[8] MELINDATARBOX *(RHODA[7] SMITH, AUGUSTUS[6], NATHAN[5], CALEB[4], CALEB[3], JOHN[2], CHRISTOPHER[1])* was born January 29, 1853 in Collins, Erie County, NY, and died 1893. She married CHARLES BABCOCK 1875.

More about HANNAH MELINDATARBOX:
Fact: 1878, Lived in Collins, Erie County, NY

Children of HANNAH MELINDATARBOX and CHARLES BABCOCK are:
      i. **FRED[9] BABCOCK**, b. 1876; d. 1939.
31.   ii. **CLAIR A BABCOCK**, b. June 23, 1885; d. September 17, 1967, New Port Richie, Florida.

15. ASA S[8] LINDSLEY *(RACHEL[7] SMITH, AUGUSTUS[6], NATHAN[5], CALEB[4], CALEB[3], JOHN[2], CHRISTOPHER[1])* was born about 1835 in New York[299]. He married CHLOE ROSETTA SOPER. She was born about 1849.

Children of ASA LINDSLEY and CHLOE SOPER are:
      i. **CORA[9] LINDSLEY**, b. about 1869, Michigan.
      ii. **EDNA LINDSLEY**, b. about 1873, Michigan.
      iii. **DAUGHTER LINDSLEY**, b. about 1878, Michigan.

16. ISAAC[8] SMITH *(REUBEN W[7], AUGUSTUS[6], NATHAN[5], CALEB[4], CALEB[3], JOHN[2], CHRISTOPHER[1])* was born 1845, and died 1877. He married CHARLOTTE BUMP. She was born August 21, 1845 in Perrysburg, Cattaraugus County, NY, and died September 28, 1910 in Dayton, Cattaraugus County, NY.

More about ISAAC SMITH:
Burial: Treat Cemetery, Leon, Cattaraugus County, NY

More about CHARLOTTE BUMP:
Burial: Cottage Cemetery, Cottage, Cattaraugus, NY

Children of ISAAC SMITH and CHARLOTTE BUMP are:
32.   i. **NELLIE L[9] SMITH**, b. November 18, 1866; d. December 24, 1934, Dayton, Cattaraugus County, NY.
      ii. **EMMA SMITH**, b. October 12, 1868 d. September 1934 m. C A MCGARREL.

17. LAWTON W[8] SMITH *(REUBEN W[7], AUGUSTUS[6], NATHAN[5], CALEB[4], CALEB[3], JOHN[2], CHRISTOPHER[1])* was born October 23, 1855. He married MARY about 1899. She was born about 1871 in New York, and died Bet. 1910 - 1920 in New York.

Children of LAWTON SMITH and MARY are:
33.   i.   **ALFRED^9 SMITH.**
34.   ii. **MABLE SMITH.**

18. Mary Smith *(REUBEN W^7, AUGUSTUS^6, NATHAN^5, CALEB^4, CALEB^3, JOHN^2, CHRISTOPHER^1)* was born May 08, 1856 in Leon, Cattaraugus County, NY, and died October 23, 1938. She married DEWITT HIBBARD about 1878. He was born January 20, 1855 in North Collins, Erie County, NY, and died August 04, 1933.

More about MARY SMITH:
Burial: North Collins, NY

More about DEWITT HIBBARD:
Burial: North Collins, Erie County, NY

Children of MARY SMITH and DEWITT HIBBARD are:
35.   i.   **INEZ^9 HIBBARD**, b. December 19, 1878, North Collins, Erie County, NY; d. August 1963, Olean, Cattaraugus County, NY.
       ii. **GRACE L HIBBARD**, b. 1882; d. 1883.

          More about GRACE L HIBBARD:
          Burial: North Collins, Erie County, NY

       iii. **DEE E HIBBARD**, b. 1888 d. January 10, 1892.

          More about DEE E HIBBARD:
          Burial: North Collins, Erie County, NY

19. **FRANK W^8 SMITH** *(REUBEN W^7, AUGUSTUS^6, NATHAN^5, CALEB^4, CALEB^3, JOHN^2, CHRISTOPHER^1)* was born March 15, 1864, and died 1929. He married FLORA TOWN about 1893. She was born April 11, 1867, and died 1946.

More about FRANK W SMITH:
Burial: Rutledge Cemetery, Conewango, Cattaraugus County, NY

More about FLORA TOWN:
Burial: Rutledge Cemetery, Conewango, Cattaraugus County, NY

Child of FRANK SMITH and FLORA TOWN is:
  i. **JOSEPHINE LUCILLE[9] SMITH**, b. February 03, 1907.

  More about JOSEPHINE LUCILLE SMITH:
  Fact: Lucile is adopted[299]

20. ELIZABETH[8] WOOD *(HANNAH[7] SMITH, AUGUSTUS[6], NATHAN[5], CALEB[4], CALEB[3], JOHN[2], CHRISTOPHER[1])* was born February 1857 in Leon, Cattaraugus County, NY, and died 1920. She married JOHN HARMON July 23, 1876 in Leon, Cattaraugus County, NY. He was born September 1851 in New York, and died 1928.

Children of ELIZABETH WOOD and JOHN HARMON are:
36.	i.	**GEORGIANNA[9] HARMON**, b. July 25, 1877, Leon, Cattaraugus County, NY; d. 1924, Little Valley, Cattaraugus County, NY.
37.	ii.	**ADDIE HARMON**, b. February 24, 1880, Leon, Cattaraugus County, NY; d. June 23, 1939, Akron, NY.
38.	iii.	**JENNIE L HARMON**, b. October 10, 1882, Leon, Cattaraugus County, NY; d. November 07, 1965, Perry, New York.
39.	iv.	**HERBERT HARMON**, b. May 17, 1887, Albion, Cattaraugus County, NY; d. August 23, 1960, Rochester, Monroe County, NY.
40.	v.	**CLARA ELIZABETH HARMON**, b. June 13, 1891, Allegany, New York; d. October 16, 1969, Gerry, Chautauqua County, NY.
41.	vi.	**LULA RUTH HARMON**, b. January 28, 1893, Bolivar, NY; d. November 26, 1973, Albion, Cattaraugus County, NY.
42.	vii.	**LIDA HARMON**, b. September 30, 1896, Cattaraugus, NY; d. September 22, 1972, Churchville, NY.

21. EDWIN KNIGHT[8] SMITH *(STEPHEN WHITE[7], AUGUSTUS[6], NATHAN[5], CALEB[4], CALEB[3], JOHN[2], CHRISTOPHER[1])* was born April 24, 1862 in Collins, Erie County, NY, and died June 07, 1924 in Jerome, Jerome County, Idaho. He married REBECCA MINNIE SAYER November 04, 1914 in Lincoln, Lancaster County, Nebraska. She was born March 09, 1881 in Norwich, England, and died October 25, 1947 in Portland, Multnomah County, Oregon.

Children of EDWIN SMITH and REBECCA SAYER are:
43.	i.	**EDWIN JAMES[9] SMITH**, b. May 26, 1916, Jerome, Jerome County, Idaho; d. March 15, 1997, Long Beach, Pacific County, Washington.
	ii.	**ROLAND M SMITH**, b. about 1908, Idaho.

22. REUBEN AUGUSTUS⁸ SMITH *(STEPHEN WHITE⁷, AUGUSTUS⁶, NATHAN⁵, CALEB⁴, CALEB³, JOHN², CHRISTOPHER¹⁹)* was born November 22, 1873 in Collins, Erie County, NY, and died November 30, 1932. He married SARAH PEARL BAKER June 28, 1906 in Franklin, Venango County, Pennsylvania, daughter of UNKNOWN BAKER and SARAH A. She was born 1884 in New York, and died October 20, 1976.

More about REUBEN AUGUSTUS SMITH:
Burial: Collins Center Cemetery, Collins Center, Collins, Erie County, NY

More about SARAH PEARL BAKER:
Burial: Collins Center Cemetery, Collins Center, Collins, Erie County, NY

Children of REUBEN SMITH and SARAH BAKER are:
  i. **CHARLEY ADELBERT⁹ SMITH**, b. January 02, 1915, New York; d. March 09, 1988; m. WANDAA MUHLESTEIN; b. July 26, 1917, Manti, Sanpete County, Utah; d. May 05, 2001.
  ii. **FEMALE SMITH**, b. August 04, 1910, Concord, Erie County, NY; d. August 09, 1910.
  iii. **G MORRIS SMITH**, b. about 1914, New York.
  iv. **S ELIZABETH SMITH**, b. about 1917, New York.

23. CHARLES S⁸ BARTLETT *(PHOEBE L⁷ SMITH, AUGUSTUS⁶, NATHAN⁵, CALEB⁴, CALEB³, JOHN², CHRISTOPHER¹)* was born about 1849 in Collins, Erie County, NY, and died July 25, 1917 in Pontiac, Oakland County, Michigan. He married (1) CARRIE B OSMUN 1881 in Michigan, daughter of WILLIAM H OSMUN. She was born May 1862 in New York. He married (2) HELENA CAITLIN February 25, 1917 in Michigan. She was born March 24, 1862 in Persia, Cattaraugus County, New York, and died April 25, 1939 in Pontiac, Elizabeth Lake, Oakland, Michigan.

Children of CHARLES BARTLETT and CARRIE OSMUN are:
44. i. **LENA I⁹ BARTLETT**, b. June 08, 1885, Michigan; d. November 11, 1973.
  ii. **BEULAH B BARTLETT**, b. June 28, 1889, Michigan d. June 11, 1977.
  iii. **CHARLES R BARTLETT**, b. August 12, 1895, Michigan d. September 1971.

   More about CHARLES R BARTLETT:
   Fact: Last address: Washington, Macomb County, Michigan
   Social Security Number: 369-07-0335: Issued in Michigan

24. SMITH AUGUSTUS⁸ BARTLETT *(PHOEBE L⁷ SMITH, AUGUSTUS⁶, NATHAN⁵, CALEB⁴, CALEB³, JOHN², CHRISTOPHER¹)* was born May 1860 in New York.

He married LOUISE D CARR 1883 in Pontiac, Oakland County, Michigan. She was born May 1864 in Germany.

Children of SMITH BARTLETT and LOUISE CARR are:
  i. **LOLA B[9] BARTLETT**, b. April 1884, Ponticc, Oakland County, Michigan.
  ii. **PHEBE L BARTLETT**, b. September 1890, Pontiac, Oakland County, Michigan m. CLARK TERRY, about 1914, Michigan; b. about 1882, Michigan.
  iii. **NETTIE L BARTLETT**, b. July 1895, Michigan.

25. SARAH ANN[8] STRANG *(OPRAH[7] SMITH, BARAK[6], NATHAN[5], CALEB[4], CALEB[3], JOHN[2], CHRISTOPHER[1])* was born September 07, 1832 in Collins, Erie County, NY, and died in Correctionville, Woodbury County, Iowa. She married MORRIS KELLOGG March 29, 1853. He was born May 20, 1824 in Leon, Cattaraugus County, NY, and died September 08, 1907 in Correctionville, Woodbury County, Iowa.

Children of SARAH STRANG and MORRIS KELLOGG are:
  i. **LUELLA[9] KELLOGG**, b. about 1854, Iowa.
  ii. **MARY KELLOGG**, b. about 1856, Iowa.
  iii. **ABBIE KELLOGG**, b. about 1865, Iowa.
  iv. **EDITH KELLOGG**, b. about 1868, Iowa.

26. MARY PALMER[8] STRANG *(OPRAH[7] SMITH, BARAK[6], NATHAN[5], CALEB[4], CALEB[3], JOHN[2], CHRISTOPHER[1])* was born September 22, 1838 in Collins, Erie County, NY, and died 1912 in Westphalia, Anderson County, Kansas. She married JOHN RUSSELL July 06, 1856 in Felix Township, Grundy County, Iowa. He was born March 20, 1821 in Sandy Township, Tuscarawas County, Ohio, and died July 21, 1900 in Westphalia, Anderson County, Kansas.

Children of MARY STRANG and JOHN RUSSELL are:
  i. **MARY[9] RUSSELL**, b. November 13, 1864; d. August 06, 1933, Hall's Summit, Coffey County, Kansas; m. DANIEL BOUSE.
  ii. **CORA RUSSELL**, b. February 14, 1860; d. August 23, 1861.
  iii. **EDWIN RUSSELL**, b. June 26, 1857, Burlington, Coffey County, Kansas; d. Texas; m. (1) ANNA MEFFORD; b. April 01, 1867, Marion County, Missouri; d. Texas; m. (2) EMMA SEELEY, September 09, 1880, Burlington, Coffey County, Kansas.
  iv. **ELLEN RUSSELL**, b. September 09, 1873.
  v. **ANN RUSSELL**, b. September 04, 1871; d. November 29, 1871.
  vi. **HUGH RUSSELL**, b. September 06, 1869; d. October 29, 1870.

vii. **ROYAL RUSSELL**, b. February 08, 1867; d. April 24, 1867.

27. WILLIAM[8] STRANG *(OPRAH[7] SMITH, BARAK[6], NATHAN[5], CALEB[4], CALEB[3], JOHN[2], CHRISTOPHER[1])* was born September 24, 1842 in Collins, Erie County, NY, and died 1928 in Pasadena, Los Angeles County, California. He married CAROLINE BALDWIN 1878. She was born March 1854 in Indiana, and died 1943.

Children of WILLIAM STRANG and CAROLINE BALDWIN are:
- i. **JOHN R[9] STRANG**, b. August 1879, Iowa.
- ii. **LOTTIE M STRANG**, b. May 1880, Iowa.
- iii. **BENJAMIN STRANG**, b. January 1882, Iowa.
- iv. **GRACE STRANG**, b. July 1883, Iowa.
- v. **WILLIAM STRANG**, b. October 1886, Iowa.

28. ROBERT EDWIN[8] STRANG *(OPRAH[7] SMITH, BARAK[6], NATHAN[5], CALEB[4], CALEB[3], JOHN[2], CHRISTOPHER[1])* was born February 23, 1846 in Collins, Erie County, NY, and died March 21, 1909 in los Angeles, Los Angeles County, California. He married HARRIET LEMERT December 12, 1878. She was born July 23, 1849 in Ohio, and died December 01, 1911 in Los Angeles, Los Angeles County, California.

More about ROBERT EDWIN STRANG:
Fact: twin to Rhoda

Child of ROBERT STRANG and HARRIET LEMERT is:
- i. **CARL[9] STRANG**, b. October 1879, Iowa.

29. RHODA ELLEN[8] STRANG *(OPRAH[7] SMITH, BARAK[6], NATHAN[5], CALEB[4], CALEB[3], JOHN[2], CHRISTOPHER[1])* was born February 23, 1846 in Collins, Erie County, NY, and died January 22, 1930 in Albion, Marshall County, Iowa. She married REUBEN TABER August 18, 1875 in Colorado Springs, El Paso County, Colorado. He was born January 20, 1845 in Mount Pleasant, Clinton County, Ohio, and died March 10, 1923 in Agra, Lincoln County, Oklahoma.

Children of RHODA STRANG and REUBEN TABER are:
- i. **EDWIN STRANG[9] TABER**, b. June 18, 1876, Colorado Springs, Colorado; m. SADIR STAHL, February 12, 1901; b. October 09, 1875, Newton, Iowa.
- ii. **OPRAH TABER**, b. November 11, 1878, Lacombe, Marshall County, Iowa; m. CURTISS GREEN, August 22, 1901.

iii. **SARAH TABER**, b. December 31, 1881, Spencer, Iowa; m. CARLTON HAWK, September 11, 1915.

30. **NATHAN E[8] SMITH** *(GILBERT PALMER[7], BARAK[6], NATHAN[5], CALEB[4], CALEB[3], JOHN[2], CHRISTOPHER[1])* was born November 01, 1838 in Collins, Erie County, NY, and died July 07, 1877 in Cedar River, Cedar County, Iowa. He married REBECCA HOOPES MARIS December 14, 1865 in Cedar River, Cedar County, Iowa. She was born May 05, 1837 in Chesterfield, Ohio, and died March 20, 1924 in Brownville, Texas.

More about NATHAN E SMITH:
Burial: Springdale Cemetery, Iowa

Children of NATHAN SMITH and REBECCA MARIS are:
i. **GEORGE C[9] SMITH**, b. June 15, 1871, Springdale, Iowa
ii. **NATHAN EDWIN SMITH**, b. September 12, 1876, Springdale, Iowa

31. **EMILY ADELINE[8] SMITH** *(GILBERT PALMER[7], BARAK[6], NATHAN[5], CALEB[4], CALEB[3], JOHN[2], CHRISTOPHER[1])* was born May 02, 1841 in New York, and died January 30, 1918. She married ERASTUS L HARRIS[90] February 11, 1863 in Springdale, Cedar County, Iowa[90], son of ESEK HARRIS and SUSANNAH. He was born January 04, 1831 in Collins, Erie County, NY.

More about ERASTUS L HARRIS:
Military service: Civil War Soldier

Children of EMILY SMITH and ERASTUS HARRIS are:
i. **HOWARD L[9] HARRIS**, b. October 27, 1864, Collins, Erie County, NY.
ii. **EARL W HARRIS**, b. April 28, 1868, Collins, Erie County, NY.
iii. **ALICE L HARRIS**, b. March 13, 1871, Collins, Erie County, NY.
iv. **MARY HARRIS**, b. March 18, 1873, Collins, Erie County, NY.
v. **GILBERT PALMER HARRIS**, b. November 12, 1875, Collins, Erie County, NY; m. MABEL J HOLLENBACK, Abt. 1903, New York; b. about 1877, New York.

More about GILBERT PALMER HARRIS:
Military service: WWI

32. **HANNAH ARLETTA[8] SMITH** *(GILBERT PALMER[7], BARAK[6], NATHAN[5], CALEB[4], CALEB[3], JOHN[2], CHRISTOPHER[1])* was born June 17, 1845 in Collins, Erie County, NY:, and died January 28, 1927 in Albion, Marshall County, Iowa. She married JESSE BINFORD[90] November 17, 1864 in Tipton, Cedar

County, Iowa. He was born 1832 in Ohio, and died between 1910 - 1915 in Iowa.

Children of HANNAH SMITH and JESSE BINFORD are:
    i. **GILBERT[9] BINFORD**, b. about 1866, Iowa.
    ii. **ACGUILLA BINFORD**, b. March 1868, Iowa.
    iii. **ROBERT O BINFORD**, b. June 1870, Iowa.
44.   iv. **JESSIE BINFORD**, b. November 1893, Iowa.

33. MARY ELIZABETH[8] SMITH *(GILBERT PALMER[7], BARAK[6], NATHAN[5], CALEB[4], CALEB[3], JOHN[2], CHRISTOPHER[1])* was born August 21, 1847 in Collins, Erie County, NY, and died December 12, 1931 in Waukon, Allamakee County, Iowa. She married GEORGE JENKINS MARIS June 02, 1865 in Tipton, Cedar County, Iowa. He was born June 17, 1841 in Chesterfield, Ohio, and died November 10, 1915 in Utah.

Children of MARY SMITH and GEORGE MARIS are:
45.   i. **EMOR BONSALL[9] MARIS**, b. August 31, 1866, Cedar Rapids, Iowa; d. October 15, 1945, Memphis, Tennessee.
    ii. **EVA PENROSE MARIS**, b. February 06, 1868, Iowa d. May 23, 1937 m. DAVID C SPEAR, April 03, 1890 b. March 22, 1862 d. April 13, 1940.
46.   iii. **LYDIA CLARISSA MARIS**, b. November 26, 1869, Iowa; d. May 02, 1957.
    iv. **EMILY REBECCA MARIS**, b. March 24, 1872, Iowa; d. December 30, 1961 m. WILLIAM HENRY COLE[111], August 22, 1906; b. April 17, 1857 d. March 09, 1915.
    v. **WALTER SCOTT MARIS**, b. March 30, 1877, Iowa d. April 23, 1901.
    vi. **FLORENCE LOUISE MARIS**, b. January 24, 1883 d. April 04, 1967 m. FREDERICK WILLIAM SCHALK[111], November 30, 1924 b. Abt. 1879.

34. ALBERT G[8] SMITH *(JOSEPH ADDISON[7], BARAK[6], NATHAN[5], CALEB[4], CALEB[3], JOHN[2], CHRISTOPHER[1])* was born April 1844 in Collins, Erie County, NY, and died 1920. He married (1) VICTORIA. She was born Abt. 1859 in New York. He married (2) LUVINA L. She was born March 1855 in New York, and died before 1930.

More about ALBERT G SMITH:
Burial: Collins Center cemetery, town of Collins, Erie County, NY

More about LUVINA L:
Fact: Had 4 children; 2 died young

Child of ALBERT SMITH and VICTORIA is:
   i. **GLENHAM⁹ SMITH**, b. about 1878, Collins, Erie County, NY.

Children of ALBERT SMITH and LUVINA L are:
   ii. **SUMNER⁹ SMITH**, b. August 12, 1885, Collins, Erie County, NY; d. 1964, `.

   More about SUMNER SMITH:
   Burial: Collins Center cemetery, town of Collins, Erie County, NY
   Military service: WWI

   iii. **ROBERT SMITH**, b. August 1895, Collins, Erie County, NY.

35. JOSEPH ADDISON⁸ SOUTHWICK *(ELIZABETH⁷ SMITH, BARAK⁶, NATHAN⁵, CALEB⁴, CALEB³, JOHN², CHRISTOPHER¹)* was born November 1847 in Collins, Erie County, NY, and died Bet. 1920 - 1930. He married JULIA about 1891. She was born February 1861 in New York.

Children of JOSEPH SOUTHWICK and JULIA are:
   i. **RUTH⁹ SOUTHWICK**, b. December 1891, New York.
   ii. **RACHEL SOUTHWICK**, b. October 1892, New York.
47. iii. **CHARLOTTE SOUTHWICK**, b. June 1895, New York.
   iv. **MARSHALL SOUTHWICK**, b. about 1901, New York.

36. CATHERINE⁸ SMITH *(EBENEZER R⁷, BARAK⁶, NATHAN⁵, CALEB⁴, CALEB³, JOHN², CHRISTOPHER¹)* was born about 1869 in Collins, Erie County, NY. She married EDWARD H RUSSELL. He was born about 1871.

Children of CATHERINE SMITH and EDWARD RUSSELL are:
   i. **VIRGINIA⁹ RUSSELL**, b. about 1895, New York.
   ii. **CORY RUSSELL**, b. about 1897, New York.
   iii. **RALPH RUSSELL**, b. about 1899, New York.

   iv. **ERICKA RUSSELL**, b. about 1900, New York.
   v. **KENNETH RUSSELL**, b. about 1905, Ohio.

37. SYLVIA ANTOINETTE⁸ SMITH *(TRUMAN MOTT⁷, FRIEND ROGERS⁶, NATHAN⁵, CALEB⁴, CALEB³, JOHN², CHRISTOPHER¹)*[1] was born April 28, 1848 in Walworth County, Wisconsin[1], and died July 09, 1928 in St Paul, Minnesota[1]. She married JACOB G MILLER[1] December 25, 1866 in St Paul, Minnesota[1]. He was born January 03, 1838 in Wittenberg, Germany[1], and died October 23, 1909 in St Paul, Minnesota[1].

Child of SYLVIA SMITH and JACOB MILLER is:
48.i.   TRUMAN SMITH[9] MILLER, b. January 25, 1884, St Paul, Minnesota; d. July 13, 1953, Los Gatos, California

Generation No. 9

38. WARD TIMOTHY[9] TARBOX *(STEPHEN S[8], RHODA[7] SMITH, AUGUSTUS[6], NATHAN[5], CALEB[4], CALEB[3], JOHN[2], CHRISTOPHER[1])* was born March 17, 1871 in Collins, Erie County, NY, and died June 24, 1951. He married ELIZABETH about 1894 in Collins, Erie County, NY. She was born September 1870 in New York.

Child of WARD TARBOX and ELIZABETH is:
  i. **ERWIN[10] TARBOX**, b. March 1896, Collins, Erie County, NY: Sheet 5B; m. OLIVE; b. about 1895, New York.

39. IRWIN RAYMOND[9] TARBOX *(STEPHEN S[8], RHODA[7] SMITH, AUGUSTUS[6], NATHAN[5], CALEB[4], CALEB[3], JOHN[2], CHRISTOPHER[1])* was born May 16, 1873 in Collins, Erie County, NY, and died January 04, 1936 in Collins, Erie County, NY. He married MARY 1898. She was born June 1868 in New York.

More about MARY:
Fact: 1910, Had 5 children, 4 were living

Children of IRWIN TARBOX and MARY are:
  i. **HOWARD STEPHEN[10] TARBOX**, b. November 20, 1898, New York; d. March 1966.

  ### More about HOWARD STEPHEN TARBOX:
  Military service: WWI
  Social Security Number: 111-14-0977 Last address Collins Center: Issued in NY before 1951

  ii. **CLAYTON TARBOX**, b. March 12, 1901, New York; d. July 1983; m. MERCEDA, about 1920; b. September 18, 1898, New York; d. March 1980.

  ### More about CLAYTON TARBOX:
  Social Security Number: 054-14-5088 : Last address Lancaster, Erie County, NY: Issued in NY before 1951

  ### More about MERCEDA:
  Social Security Number: 106-12-2152 : Last address: Lancaster, Erie County, NY: Issued NY before 1951

 iii. **ELIZABETH TARBOX**, b. about 1907, New York.
 iv. **CHARLES TARBOX**, b. August 31, 1909, New York; d. February 1978.

More about CHARLES TARBOX:
Social Security Number: 122-07-6681 : Last known address, Springville, Erie County, NY: Issued in NY before 1951

40. IDA M^9 TARBOX *(FRANCIS^8, RHODA^7 SMITH, AUGUSTUS^6, NATHAN^5, CALEB^4, CALEB^3, JOHN^2, CHRISTOPHER^1)* was born about 1870 in New York. She married UNKNOWN CAMPBELL about 1891.

Child of IDA TARBOX and UNKNOWN CAMPBELL is:
 i. **HOMER E^{10} CAMPBELL**, b. about 1892, New York.

41. ARTHUR^9 COOK *(EMILY L^8 TARBOX, RHODA^7 SMITH, AUGUSTUS^6, NATHAN^5, CALEB^4, CALEB^3, JOHN^2, CHRISTOPHER^1)* was born May 1870 in Collins, Erie County, NY. He married JOSEPHINE V about 1910. She was born about 1869 in New York.

Children of ARTHUR COOK and JOSEPHINE are:
 i. **RICHARD^{10} COOK**, b. about 1915, Collins, Erie County, NY.
 ii. **LLOYD A COOK**, b. about 1918, Collins, Erie County, NY.
 iii. **ALICE E COOK**, b. about 1918, Collins, Erie County, NY.

42. MINNIE^9 TARBOX *(REUBAN^8, RHODA^7 SMITH, AUGUSTUS^6, NATHAN^5, CALEB^4, CALEB^3, JOHN^2, CHRISTOPHER^1)* was born about 1882 in New York. She married LEON J SMITH about 1905. He was born about 1880 in New York.

More about LEON J SMITH:
Fact: AKA Leo
Military service: Soldier WWI

Children of MINNIE TARBOX and LEON SMITH are:
 i. **ORLIN L^{10} SMITH**, b. about 1902, New York.
 ii. **ROLAND T SMITH**, b. November 12, 1909, New York; d. February 1973; m. HAZEL MAE; b. May 30, 1911; d. April 01, 2000.

More about ROLAND T SMITH:
Social Security Number: 066-20-9377: Last known address: Collins Center, Erie, NY: Issued NY before 1951

Notes for HAZEL MAE:
4/3/2000 - Hazel Mae Smith - 4/1/2000

Age 89, of Collins Center, NY, April 1, 2000, beloved wife of the late Roland T. Smith; mother of Mrs. Richard (Bonnie) DiBlasi of Spring Hill, FL, Mrs. Robert (Marlene) Valentine of Collins Center and Arnold (Judy) Smith of Collins Center; also surviving 11 grand, 14 great-grand and 2 great-great-grandchildren. No prior visitation. Funeral service at the convenience of the family. Memorials made to the Collins Center Volunteer Fire Dept. Arrangements by MENTLEY FUNERAL HOME, INC., 105 E. Main St., Gowanda, NY.

More about HAZEL MAE:
Social Security Number: 106-28-6079: Last known address: Springville, Erie County, NY: Issued in NY

   iii. **LEIGHTON R SMITH**, b. about 1916, New York.

43. EARL R^9 TARBOX *(REUBAN^8, RHODA^7 SMITH, AUGUSTUS^6, NATHAN^5, CALEB^4, CALEB^3, JOHN^2, CHRISTOPHER^1)* was born about 1890 in Collins, Erie County, NY. He married ELLA H. She was born about 1891 in New York.

Children of EARL TARBOX and ELLA H are:
   i. **DONALD H^{10} TARBOX**, b. October 05, 1912, New York; d. September 23, 1991.

    More about DONALD H TARBOX:
    Social Security Number: 084-18-5827: Last address Collins, Erie, NY: Issued in NY before 1951

   ii. **CLIFFORD E TARBOX**, b. about 1917, New York; d. 1934.

    More about CLIFFORD E TARBOX:
    Burial: Collins Center Cemetery, town of Collins, Erie County, NY

44. CLAIR A^9 BABCOCK *(HANNAH^8 MELINDA TARBOX, RHODA^7 SMITH, AUGUSTUS^6, NATHAN^5, CALEB^4, CALEB^3, JOHN^2, CHRISTOPHER^1)* was born June 23, 1885, and died September 17, 1967 in New Port Richie, Florida. He married EDA COOK June 22, 1911 in Otto, Cattaraugus County, NY.

She was born September 08, 1885, and died October 1971 in St Petersburg, Florida.

Children of CLAIR BABCOCK and EDA COOK are:
    i. **DOROTHY JANE[10] BABCOCK**, b. September 12, 1914, Otto, Cattaraugus County, NY; d. March 27, 1988, Charlotte, North Carolina; m. (1) PAUL LINDSLER; b. 1914, Collins Center, Erie County, NY; d. 1962; m. (2) LAWRENCE PIPER; b. April 02, 1900; d. April 18, 1994, Charlotte, North Carolina.
    ii. **DONALD W BABCOCK**.
    iii. **CAROL BABCOCK**.

45. NELLIE L[9] SMITH *(ISAAC[8], REUBEN W[7], AUGUSTUS[6], NATHAN[5], CALEB[4], CALEB[3], JOHN[2], CHRISTOPHER[1])* was born November 18, 1866, and died December 24, 1934 in Dayton, Cattaraugus County, NY. She married HOYT M ALLEN February 27, 1890 in Dayton, Cattaraugus County, NY, son of NORMAN ALLEN and HULDA. He was born October 23, 1863 in Dayton, Cattaraugus County, NY, and died October 12, 1892 in Dayton, Cattaraugus County, NY.

More about NELLIE L SMITH:
Burial: Cottage Cemetery, Cottage, Cattaraugus, NY[299]

More about HOYT M ALLEN:
Burial: Cottage Cemetery, Cottage, Cattaraugus, NY[299]

Child of NELLIE SMITH and HOYT ALLEN is:
    i. **NORMAN BOYD[10] ALLEN**, b. May 02, 1892, Dayton, Cattaraugus County, NY d. August 21, 1936 m. (1) LYDIA WARNER HOLDEN m. (2) ETHEL EMMA SPRINGER, May 31, 1913, Perrysburg, Cattaraugus County, NY b. 1885, Cherry Creek, Chautauqua County, NY d. 1918.

    More about NORMAN BOYD ALLEN:
    Burial: Cottage Cemetery, Cottage, Cattaraugus, NY

    More about ETHEL EMMA SPRINGER:
    Burial: Cottage Cemetery, Cottage, Cattaraugus, NY

46. ALFRED[9] SMITH *(LAWTON W[8], REUBEN W[7], AUGUSTUS[6], NATHAN[5], CALEB[4], CALEB[3], JOHN[2], CHRISTOPHER[1])*[299]. He married FEMALE.

Child of ALFRED SMITH and FEMALE is:

i. ALBERT HOWARD[10] SMITH, b. April 06, 1910.

47. MABLE[9] SMITH *(LAWTON W[8], REUBEN W[7], AUGUSTUS[6], NATHAN[5], CALEB[4], CALEB[3], JOHN[2], CHRISTOPHER[1])*. She married MALE HERMAN.

Child of MABLE SMITH and MALE HERMAN is:
i. **DOROTHY[10] HERMAN**, m. MALE PRICE.

48. INEZ[9] HIBBARD *(MARY[8] SMITH, REUBEN W[7], AUGUSTUS[6], NATHAN[5], CALEB[4], CALEB[3], JOHN[2], CHRISTOPHER[1])* was born December 19, 1878 in North Collins, Erie County, NY, and died August 1963 in Olean, Cattaraugus County, NY. She married BURTON CURRIE[299] September 05, 1900 in 70 Summer Street, Bradford, PA. He was born April 03, 1877 in North East, Pennsylvania, and died March 06, 1938 in St Petersburg, Florida.

More about INEZ HIBBARD:
Burial: Chestnut Hill, Portville, NY
Social Security Number: 105-28-5249: Issued in NY between 1952-1954

More about BURTON CURRIE:
Burial: Chestnut Hill, Portville, NY[299]
Military service: Soldier WWI

Child of INEZ HIBBARD and BURTON CURRIE is:
i. **EDITH JULIA[10] CURRIE**, b. June 11, 1907, Bradford, McKean County, PA; d. October 14, 1984, Olean, Cattaraugus County, NY m. HARVEY COMSTOCK b. July 05, 1904, Sartwell, McKean County, PA d. August 03, 1978, Olean, Cattaraugus County, NY.

More about EDITH JULIA CURRIE:
Burial: Chestnut Hill Cemetery, Portville, NY
Social Security Number: 065-38-0760: Last known Address: Olean, Cattaraugus County, NY; Issued in NY 1963

More about HARVEY COMSTOCK:
Burial: Chestnut Hill Cemetery, Portville, NY

49. GEORGIANNA[9] HARMON *(ELIZABETH[8] WOOD, HANNAH[7] SMITH, AUGUSTUS[6], NATHAN[5], CALEB[4], CALEB[3], JOHN[2], CHRISTOPHER[1])* was born July 25, 1877 in Leon, Cattaraugus County, NY, and died 1924 in Little Valley, Cattaraugus County, NY. She married DAVID EUGENE WHIPPLE September 08, 1897. He was born August 22, 1877 in Mansfield, Cattaraugus County, NY, and died December 30, 1944.

More about DAVID EUGENE WHIPPLE:
Military service: WWI

Children of GEORGIANNA HARMON and DAVID WHIPPLE are:
i. **HARMON OLIN[10] WHIPPLE**, b. July 22, 1899, New York d. October 30, 1965 m. (1) CAROLINE GERWITZ b. July 10, 1904 d. June 24, 1996, Salamanca Nursing Home, Salamanca, NY m. (2) LENA ANN BACKUS, May 26, 1920, Jamestown, Chautauqua County, NY; b. 1901, Onoville, New York d. June 16, 1933.

More about HARMON OLIN WHIPPLE:
Military service: WWI
Social Security Number: 094-10-4660: Issued in NY before 1951

More about CAROLINE GERWITZ:
Burial: Crawford Cemetery, Salamanca, NY[299]

ii. **MORGAN JOHN WHIPPLE**, b. June 05, 1901, Little Valley, Cattaraugus County, NY d. March 12, 1942, Little Valley, Cattaraugus County, NY m. ELVA LOUISE STEVENS, June 22, 1920, Jamestown, Chautauqua County, NY b. September 13, 1903, New Albion, Cattaraugus County, NY d. September 18, 1977, Salamanca, Cattaraugus County, NY.

More about MORGAN JOHN WHIPPLE:
Burial: Little Valley, Cattaraugus County, NY

More about ELVA LOUISE STEVENS:
Burial: Little Valley, Cattaraugus County, NY

iii. **LIDA ANN WHIPPLE**, b. September 05, 1907, Little Valley, Cattaraugus County, NY d. April 26, 1959, Warsaw, New York m. LEON SLOCUM b. May 02, 1907 d. December 10, 1958.

50. ADDIE[9] HARMON (*ELIZABETH[8] WOOD, HANNAH[7] SMITH, AUGUSTUS[6], NATHAN[5], CALEB[4], CALEB[3], JOHN[2], CHRISTOPHER[1]*) was born February 24, 1880 in Leon, Cattaraugus County, NY, and died June 23, 1939 in Akron, NY. She married BURTON HITCHCOCK October 20, 1903 in Rochester, Monroe County, NY. He was born March 30, 1869 in Gerry, Chautauqua County, NY[299], and died December 04, 1955 in Gowanda, NY.

Children of ADDIE HARMON and BURTON HITCHCOCK are:

i. **FOREST BURTON¹⁰ HITCHCOCK**, b. November 10, 1904, Buffalo, Erie County, NY d. September 19, 1976, Toronto, Ontario, Canada m. EVELYN SMITH, June 16, 1928, Rochester, Monroe County, NY b. September 21, 1905, Brantford, Ontario, Canada d. October 10, 1998, Florida.

More about FOREST BURTON HITCHCOCK:
Burial: North Chili, New York
Social Security Number: 104-09-3642: Last known address: Clearwater, Pinellas County, FL: Issued in NY before 1951

ii. **FLOYD PRESTON HITCHCOCK**, b. February 22, 1909, Villanova, New York; d. January 23, 1991, Amherst, Erie County, NY; m. IVA COOK, June 12, 1928, Olean, Cattaraugus County, NY b. September 13, 1908, Murdo, South Dakota d. September 10, 1985, Gerry, Chautauqua County, NY.

More about FLOYD PRESTON HITCHCOCK:
Burial: Pioneer Cemetery, Akron, NY
Social Security Number: 114-12-7361: issued in NY before 1951

More about IVA COOK:
Burial: Pioneer Cemetery, Akron, NY
Social Security Number: 089-38-5605: Last Known Address; Akron, Erie County, NY: issued in NY 1963

iii. **RAYMOND CLIFFORD HITCHCOCK**, b. January 23, 1916, Brockport, NY d. January 02, 1929, Akron, NY.
iv. **GERTRUDE R HITCHCOCK**, b. October 04, 1918, Batavia, NY m. CARL BRACKETT, February 14, 1938, Akron, NY b. June 07, 1918, Akron, NY.
v. **ONNOLEE GERTRUDE HITCHCOCK**, b. July 07, 1920, Akron, NY m. (1) LESTER ROESCH, August 22, 1953, Akron, NY m. (2) CLAUDE RISLEY, December 31, 1976, Williamsville, Erie County, NY b. February 05, 1925, Buffalo, Erie County, NY.

51. JENNIE L⁹ HARMON *(ELIZABETH⁸ WOOD, HANNAH⁷ SMITH, AUGUSTUS⁶, NATHAN⁵, CALEB⁴, CALEB³, JOHN², CHRISTOPHER¹)* was born October 10, 1882 in Leon, Cattaraugus County, NY, and died November 07, 1965 in Perry, New York. She married CHARLES CATTON BLYTHE July 15, 1903 in Rochester, Monroe County, NY. He was born October 03, 1877 in Perry, New York, and died June 18, 1953.

More about JENNIE L HARMON:

Burial: Glenwood Cemetery, Perry, NY

More about CHARLES CATTON BLYTHE:
Burial: Glenwood Cemetery, Perry, NY
Military service: WWI

Children of JENNIE HARMON and CHARLES BLYTHE are:
- i. **JOHN HARMON[10] BLYTHE**, b. May 29, 1904, Perry, New York d. May 02, 1993 m. MILDRED BRAINARD, June 22, 1927 b. July 11, 1904, New York d. December 08, 1977.

    More about JOHN HARMON BLYTHE:
    Burial: Glenwood Cemetery, Perry, NY
    Social Security Number: 081-01-7849: Last known address: Webster, Monroe County, NY: Issued in NY

    More about MILDRED BRAINARD:
    Burial: Glenwood Cemetery, Perry, NY
    Social Security Number: 081-32-0036: Last known Address: Geneseo, Livingston County, NY: Issued in NY

- ii. **ROBERT C BLYTHE**, b. March 31, 1908, Perry, New York d. December 28, 1980 m. MARY JENKS June 28, 1932, Perry, New York b. July 30, 1910 d. June 1980.

    More about ROBERT C BLYTHE:
    Social Security Number: 122-10-2549: Last known address: Valrico, Hillsborough County, FL: Issued in NY

    More about MARY JENKS:
    Social Security Number: 118-34-5820: Last known address: Perry, Wyoming County, NY: Issued in NY

- iii. **LEWIS EVERITT BLYTHE**, b. August 29, 1912, New York d. March 07, 1973 m. AGNES ROGERS, August 07, 1941, Perry, New York b. July 06, 1914.
- iv. **JAMES MILTON BLYTHE**, b. July 12, 1917, New York; d. October 18, 2003, Geneseo, New York; m. MARIE REED, August 10, 1940, Canandaigua, NY b. May 19, 1920.

    More about JAMES MILTON BLYTHE:
    Burial: Glenwood Cemetery, Perry, NY
    Census: April 02, 1930, Perry, Wyoming County, NY: Sheet 3B

52. HERBERT[9] HARMON *(ELIZABETH[8] WOOD, HANNAH[7] SMITH, AUGUSTUS[6], NATHAN[5], CALEB[4], CALEB[3], JOHN[2], CHRISTOPHER[1])* was born May 17, 1887 in Albion, Cattaraugus County, NY, and died August 23, 1960 in Rochester, Monroe County, NY. He married MILLIE METCALF July 16, 1913. She was born March 31, 1891 in Rushford, Cattaraugus County, NY, and died March 29, 1981 in Rochester, Monroe County, NY.

More about MILLIE METCALF:
Social Security Number: 053-52-3583: last known address: Rochester, Monroe County, NY: issued in NY 1973

Children of HERBERT HARMON and MILLIE METCALF are:
  i. **ELIZABETH[10] HARMON**, b. September 04, 1914, Brockport, NY d. August 13, 1990, Rochester, Monroe County, NY m. PRITCHARD DOUGLASS, July 16, 1938, North Chili, NY b. March 22, 1913, Jamestown, Chautauqua County, NY.
  ii. **ELLEN HARMON**, b. June 04, 1916, Rochester, Monroe County, NY.
  iii. **MARION HARMON**, b. October 04, 1918, Rochester, Monroe County, NY m. VICTOR MURPHY b. December 12, 1919 d. January 1996.
  iv. **RICHARD HARMON**, b. January 16, 1924, Rochester, Monroe County, NY m. JOYCE RUTTER, May 11, 1946, Rochester, Monroe County, NY b. June 12, 1925, London, England, United Kingdom.

53. CLARA ELIZABETH[9] HARMON *(ELIZABETH[8] WOOD, HANNAH[7] SMITH, AUGUSTUS[6], NATHAN[5], CALEB[4], CALEB[3], JOHN[2], CHRISTOPHER[1])* was born June 13, 1891 in Allegany, New York, and died October 16, 1969 in Gerry, Chautauqua County, NY. She married WILBOR WARBOYS December 16, 1913 in Rochester, Monroe County, NY. He was born June 15, 1886, and died July 20, 1962.

Children of CLARA HARMON and WILBOR WARBOYS are:
  i. **WILSON THOMAS[10] WARBOYS**, b. September 03, 1916, Rochester, Monroe County, NY d. August 05, 1979, Rochester, Monroe County, NY m. ALISON MCINTYRE, May 03, 1941, Alton, New York[299]; b. April 20, 1917 d. April 26, 1979.
  ii. **RUTH ADELLA WARBOYS**, b. May 07, 1918 d. March 29, 1982, Pultneyville, NY m. ROBERT JOHNSON, April 25, 1954, Buffalo, Erie County, NY.
  iii. **LAWRENCE WILBUR WARBOYS**, b. February 24, 1921, North Chili, New York d. 1962, Cleveland, Ohio; m. JULIA ANN NEWSOME, June 27, 1944, Titusville, Pennsylvania b. May 17, 1920, Titusville, PA d. 2003, Louisville, Kentucky.

iv. **LUCILLE ELIZABETH WARBOYS**, b. November 09, 1923, North Chili, New York d. 2003, Mableton, Georgia m. WILLIAM BRUCE, October 09, 1943, Buffalo, Erie County, NY b. April 08, 1921, Penn Run, Pennsylvania d. September 25, 1972, Warsaw, Indiana.

54. LULA RUTH[9] HARMON *(ELIZABETH[8] WOOD, HANNAH[7] SMITH, AUGUSTUS[6], NATHAN[5], CALEB[4], CALEB[3], JOHN[2], CHRISTOPHER[1])* was born January 28, 1893 in Bolivar, NY, and died November 26, 1973 in Albion, Cattaraugus County, NY. She married JOHN W PARKER. He was born July 09, 1890, and died October 24, 1978.

Children of LULA HARMON and JOHN PARKER are:
   i. **JOHN ELLWYN[10] PARKER**, b. February 26, 1926.
   ii. **PHYLLIS PARKER**, b. August 14, 1932 m. MALE MULLINS.

55. LIDA[9] HARMON *(ELIZABETH[8] WOOD, HANNAH[7] SMITH, AUGUSTUS[6], NATHAN[5], CALEB[4], CALEB[3], JOHN[2], CHRISTOPHER[1])* was born September 30, 1896 in Cattaraugus, NY, and died September 22, 1972 in Churchville, NY. She married EDGAR L GOULD September 25, 1917 in North Chili, NY. He was born January 05, 1897 in New York, and died February 18, 1961.

More about LIDA HARMON:
Burial: North Chili, New York
Social Security Number: 066-24-5490 : Last known address: Rochester, Monroe County, NY: Issued in NY before 1951

More about EDGAR L GOULD:
Military service: WWI

Children of LIDA HARMON and EDGAR GOULD are:
   i. **EDGAR EVERETT[10] GOULD**, b. August 17, 1918, Rochester, Monroe County, NY d. November 25, 1967 m. MILDRED SCHOENTHALER b. May 02, 1915 d. April 18, 1967.

   More about EDGAR EVERETT GOULD:
   Burial: Myrtle Hill Memorial Park, Tampa, FL
   Social Security Number: 128-07-2089: Issued in NY before 1951

   More about MILDRED SCHOENTHALER:
   Burial: Myrtle Hill Memorial Park, Tampa, FL

ii. **LOUISE GOULD**, b. January 20, 1927, Irondequoit, NY m. DAVID GEORGE STEEDMAN, October 12, 1946 b. November 13, 1923, Churchville, NY d. November 17, 2006.

More about DAVID GEORGE STEEDMAN:
Social Security Number: 094-16-2048: Last known address: North Chili, Monroe County, NY: Issued in NY before 1951

iii. **GEORGIANNA GOULD**, b. January 1930, New York; m. WILLIAM FARROW.

56. EDWIN JAMES[9] SMITH *(EDWIN KNIGHT[8], STEPHEN WHITE[7], AUGUSTUS[6], NATHAN[5], CALEB[4], CALEB[3], JOHN[2], CHRISTOPHER[1])* was born May 26, 1916 in Jerome, Jerome County, Idaho, and died March 15, 1997 in Long Beach, Pacific County, Washington. He married CLARICE TOBIE May 13, 1945 in Portland, Multnomah County, Oregon. She was born Abt. 1919.

More about EDWIN JAMES SMITH:
Social Security Number: 540-12-5093: Issued in Oregon

Children of EDWIN SMITH and CLARICE TOBIE are:
iii. **WARREN KNIGHT SMITH**, b. November 22, 1952, Portland, Multnomah County, Oregon; d. November 02, 1999, Salem, Marion County, Oregon.

More about WARREN KNIGHT SMITH:
Social Security Number: 541-80-1683: Issued in Oregon

57. LENA I[9] BARTLETT *(CHARLES S[8], PHOEBE L[7] SMITH, AUGUSTUS[6], NATHAN[5], CALEB[4], CALEB[3], JOHN[2], CHRISTOPHER[1])* was born June 08, 1885 in Michigan, and died November 11, 1973. She married ALFRED W GALE Abt. 1906 in Michigan. He was born about 1878 in Michigan.

More about LENA I BARTLETT:
Census: June 23, 1900, Pontiac, Oakland County, Michigan: Sheet 19B
Social Security Number: 369-52-3452: Last address: Pontiac, Oakland County, Michigan: issued in Michigan 1965

Children of LENA BARTLETT and ALFRED GALE are:
i. **ESTHER M[10] GALE**, b. about 1908, Michigan.
ii. **FLOYD B GALE**, b. April 1910, Michigan.
iii. **BEULAH I GALE**, b. about 1913, Michigan.

iv. **CHARLES W GALE**, b. about 1915, Michigan.

58. JESSIE[9] BINFORD *(HANNAH ARLETTA[8] SMITH, GILBERT PALMER[7], BARAK[6], NATHAN[5], CALEB[4], CALEB[3], JOHN[2], CHRISTOPHER[1])* was born November 1893 in Iowa. She married CHRIS J SORENSEN. He was born Abt. 1896 in Chicago, Illinois.

Children of JESSIE BINFORD and CHRIS SORENSEN are:
    i. BETTIE L[10] SORENSEN, b. about 1922, Iowa.

    More About BETTIE L SORENSEN:
    Census: 1925, Iowa State census: Liscomb, Marshall County, Iowa

    ii. ROBERT J SORENSEN, b. about 1921, Iowa.

    More About ROBERT J SORENSEN:
    Census: 1925, Iowa State census: Liscomb, Marshall County, Iowa

59. EMOR BONSALL[9] MARIS *(MARY ELIZABETH[8] SMITH, GILBERT PALMER[7], BARAK[6], NATHAN[5], CALEB[4], CALEB[3], JOHN[2], CHRISTOPHER[1])* was born August 31, 1866 in Cedar Rapids, Iowa, and died October 15, 1945 in Memphis, Tennessee. He married NELLIE MCCONNELL May 05, 1887 in Iowa. She was born September 15, 1866 in Illinois, and died July 16, 1946 in San Jose, California.

Children of EMOR MARIS and NELLIE MCCONNELL are:
    i. **WILLIS LESLIE[10] MARIS**, b. February 07, 1888, Iowa.
    ii. **CECIL W MARIS**, b. December 1899, Iowa.
    iii. **LAURA B MARIS**, b. September 1892, Iowa.
    iv. **GEORGE JOSEPH MARIS**, b. November 1894, Iowa.

60. LYDIA CLARISSA[9] MARIS *(MARY ELIZABETH[8] SMITH, GILBERT PALMER[7], BARAK[6], NATHAN[5], CALEB[4], CALEB[3], JOHN[2], CHRISTOPHER[1])* was born November 26, 1869 in Iowa, and died May 02, 1957. She married (1) PRINCE SOLOMON MACY April 09, 1896 in Texas. He was born 1869, and died April 28, 1896. She married (2) FRED GRANGER STILLWELL February 22, 1899. He was born about 1865.

Child of LYDIA MARIS and FRED STILLWELL is:
    i. **FLORENCE GERTRUDE[10] STILLWELL**.

61. CHARLOTTE[9] SOUTHWICK *(JOSEPH ADDISON[8], ELIZABETH[7] SMITH, BARAK[6], NATHAN[5], CALEB[4], CALEB[3], JOHN[2], CHRISTOPHER[1])* was born June 1895 in New York. She married FRED C MERRILL. He was born about 1890 in New York.

Children of CHARLOTTE SOUTHWICK and FRED MERRILL are:
    i. **FAYE M[10] MERRILL**, b. about 1925, New York.
    ii. **CLAIR R MERRILL**, b. about 1928, New York.

62. TRUMAN SMITH[9] MILLER *(SYLVIA ANTOINETTE[8] SMITH, TRUMAN MOTT[7], FRIEND ROGERS[6], NATHAN[5], CALEB[4], CALEB[3], JOHN[2], CHRISTOPHER[1])*[1] was born January 25, 1884 in St Paul, Minnesota[1], and died July 13, 1953 in Los Gatos, California[1]. He married MARY E FAHEY[1] November 07, 1906 in St Paul, Minnesota[1]. She was born May 14, 1885 in iowa[1], and died October 09, 1939 in St Paul, Minnesota[1].

Child of TRUMAN MILLER and MARY FAHEY is:
    i. **WALTER TRUMAN[10] MILLER**[1], b. August 28, 1907, St Paul, Minnesota[1]; d. October 12, 1990, St Anthony, Minnesota[1]; m. LILLIAN AUGUSTA DECKER[1], September 17, 1932, St Paul, Minnesota[1]; b. April 11, 1909, St Paul, Minnesota[1]; d. October 08, 1999, St Anthony, Minnesota[1]

Descendants of Lawrence Southwick

Descendants of Lawrence Southwick

Generation No. 1

1. **LAWRENCE1 SOUTHWICK** was born in Lancashire, England, and died 1660 in Shelter Island, Long Island, NY. He married CASSANDRA BURNELL. She was born in Lancashire, England, and died 1660 in Shelter Island, Long Island, NY.

More about LAWRENCE SOUTHWICK:
Baptism: February 24, 1638/39, First Church of Salem
Fact: Died within 3 days of his wife
Immigration: 1629 on ship Mayflower
Religion: Quaker
Will: July 10, 1659, Will Dated

More about CASSANDRA BURNELL:
Baptism: February 24, 1638/39, First Church of Salem
Fact: Died within 3 days of her husband
Immigration: 1629 on ship Mayflower
Religion: Quaker

Children of LAWRENCE SOUTHWICK and CASSANDRA BURNELL are:

JOHN2 SOUTHWICK, b. 1620, England; d. October 25, 1672.
MARY SOUTHWICK, b. 1630; d. 1693.
JOSIAH SOUTHWICK, b. 1632; d. 1693.
PROVIDED SOUTHWICK, b. 1635; d. 1640.
   More about PROVIDED SOUTHWICK:
   Baptism: December 06, 1639, First Church of Salem
DANIEL SOUTHWICK, b. 1637; d. 1718.
PROVIDED SOUTHWICK, b. December 1641; m. SAMUEL GASKILL, December 30, 1662.
   More about PROVIDED SOUTHWICK:
   Baptism: December 06, 1639, First Church of Salem, MA
DEBORAH SOUTHWICK.

Generation No. 2

2. **JOHN2 SOUTHWICK** *(LAWRENCE1)* was born 1620 in England, and died October 25, 1672. He married (1) SARAH BURNETT, daughter of JOHN BURNETT. He married (2) SARAH 1642. He married (3) HANNAH May 12, 1668.
> More about SARAH BURNETT:
> Fact: Last name may be Burnell not Burnett
> More about HANNAH:
> Fact: She was a widow when she married John

Children of JOHN SOUTHWICK and SARAH are:
  SARAH3 SOUTHWICK, b. June 16, 1644.
  MARY SOUTHWICK, b. October 10, 1646; m. THOMAS BURT, November 18, 1872.
  SAMUEL SOUTHWICK, b. February 19, 1657/58; d. 1709.

Children of JOHN SOUTHWICK and HANNAH are:
  JOHN3 SOUTHWICK, b. January 1668/69; d. 1742.
  ISAAC SOUTHWICK, b. November 1669; d. February 1669/70.
  ISAAC SOUTHWICK, b. January 27, 1670/71.

3. MARY2 SOUTHWICK *(LAWRENCE1)* was born 1630, and died 1693. She married HENRY TRASK 1650, son of CAPTAIN WILLIAM TRASK.

Children of MARY SOUTHWICK and HENRY TRASK are:
  MARY3 TRASK, b. August 14, 1652.
  ANN TRASK, b. April 14, 1654.
  SARAH TRASK, b. July 27, 1656.
  HENRY TRASK, b. April 1669.

4. **JOSIAH2 SOUTHWICK** *(LAWRENCE1)* was born 1632, and died 1693. He married MARY BOYCE 1658, daughter of JOSEPH BOYCE and ELLENOR. She was born in Salem, Massachusetts.

Children of JOSIAH SOUTHWICK and MARY BOYCE are:
  DEBORAH3 SOUTHWICK, b. 1667.
  JOSIAH JR. SOUTHWICK, b. January 27, 1659/60, Salem, Massachusetts; d. Northampton, Burlington County, New Jersey.
  JOSEPH SOUTHWICK, b. April 1662; m. ANN.
  MARY SOUTHWICK, b. November 1664.

CASSANDRA SOUTHWICK, b. 1666; d. Abt. 1719.
SOLOMON SOUTHWICK, b. 1672.
RUTH SOUTHWICK, b. February 21, 1673/74.
JONATHAN SOUTHWICK, b. 1676.
DELIVERANCE SOUTHWICK, b. 1678.
HOPESTILL SOUTHWICK, b. 1680.

5. **DANIEL2 SOUTHWICK** *(LAWRENCE1)* was born 1637, and died 1718. He married ESTHER BOYCE February 23, 1662/63, daughter of JOSEPH BOYCE and ELLENOR. She was born in Salem, Massachusetts.

> **More about DANIEL SOUTHWICK:**
> Baptism: February 21, 1639/40, First Church of Salem, MA
> Fact: owned slaves at the time of his death
> Will: Proved February 10, 1717/18

> **More about ESTHER BOYCE:**
> Baptism: December 12, 1640, Salem, Massachusetts
> Fact: December, Alternate Marriage month

Children of DANIEL SOUTHWICK and ESTHER BOYCE are:

LAWRENCE3 SOUTHWICK, b. 1664, Salem, Massachusetts; d. 1718.
DANIEL SOUTHWICK, b. March 25, 1671, Salem, Massachusetts; d. 1732.
ELEANOR SOUTHWICK, b. June 25, 1674, Salem, Massachusetts; d. October 26, 1702.
MERCY SOUTHWICK, b. 1676, Salem, Massachusetts; m. JOHN OSBORNE, May 09, 1704; b. August 22, 1677; d. August 1744.
ELIZABETH SOUTHWICK, b. June 24, 1668, Salem, Massachusetts; m. UNKNOWN WILKINS.
HANNAH SOUTHWICK, b. August 07, 1667, Salem, Massachusetts; m. THOMAS BUFFINGTON.

> **More about THOMAS BUFFINGTON:**
> Fact: 1670, Alternate wedding year
> Immigration: Aft. 1650, From Scotland
> Note: Crane & Cutter disagree about who Thomas Buffington married: both are listed as wives

Generation No. 3

7. SARAH3 SOUTHWICK *(JOHN2, LAWRENCE1)* was born June 16, 1644. She married THOMAS BUFFINGTON December 30, 1670.

More about THOMAS BUFFINGTON:
Fact: 1670, Alternate wedding year
Immigration: Aft. 1650, From Scotland

Children of SARAH SOUTHWICK and THOMAS BUFFINGTON are:
1. THOMAS4 BUFFINGTON, b. March 01, 1671/72, Salem, Massachusetts.
2. BENJAMIN BUFFINGTON, b. July 24, 1675, Salem, Massachusetts; m. HANNAH.

    More about BENJAMIN BUFFINGTON:
    Fact: 1700, Moved to Swansea
    Religion: Quaker

    More about HANNAH:
    Religion: Quaker

3. JOSEPH BUFFINGTON.

8. SAMUEL3 SOUTHWICK *(JOHN2, LAWRENCE1)* was born February 19, 1657/58, and died 1709. He married MARY.

Children of SAMUEL SOUTHWICK and MARY are:
1. SAMUEL 2ND4 SOUTHWICK, b. January 30, 1687/88; d. Bef. 1709.
2. EBENEZER SOUTHWICK, b. November 09, 1690.
3. HANNAH SOUTHWICK, b. February 24, 1690/91.
4. JONATHAN SOUTHWICK, b. about 1694.
5. BENJAMIN SOUTHWICK, b. about 1696; d. 1795.
6. DAVID SOUTHWICK, b. 1701, Salem, Massachusetts; d. 1792.
7. MERCY SOUTHWICK, b. 1698.
8. MARY SOUTHWICK, b. 1700; m. HENRY HUTCHINS, October 16, 1736.
9. ELIZABETH SOUTHWICK, b. 1702.
10. PROVIDED SOUTHWICK, b. 1704.

9. JOHN3 SOUTHWICK *(JOHN2, LAWRENCE1)* was born January 1668/69, and died 1742. He married HANNAH BLACK, daughter of ROBERT BLACK and PERSIS.

More about JOHN SOUTHWICK:
Will: Proved November 24, 1743

More about Hannah Black:
Fact: Widow of Unknown Flint when she married John

Children of JOHN SOUTHWICK and HANNAH BLACK are:
1. JOHN4 SOUTHWICK, b. December 13, 1688; d. about 1771.
2. JOSEPH SOUTHWICK, b. January 01, 1689/90; d. October 01, 1691.
3. SARAH SOUTHWICK, b. February 09, 1692/93.
4. ABRAHAM SOUTHWICK, b. July 27, 1696; d. before 1769.
5. HANNAH SOUTHWICK, b. November 01, 1698.
6. BENJAMIN SOUTHWICK, b. January 22, 1700/01.
7. ISAAC SOUTHWICK, b. September 23, 1704.

10. **ISAAC3 SOUTHWICK** *(JOHN2, LAWRENCE1)* was born January 27, 1670/71. He married ANNA 1691.

> **More about ISAAC SOUTHWICK:**
> Fact: 1696, Lived at Reading

Children of ISAAC SOUTHWICK and ANNA are:
1. ANNA4 SOUTHWICK, b. 1694; m. JONATHAN HERBERT, 1713.
2. SARAH SOUTHWICK, b. 1696; d. 1696.
3. SARAH SOUTHWICK, b. 1699.
4. ISAAC JR SOUTHWICK, b. 1703; m. MARY DALTON, April 12, 1741.

> **More about ISAAC JR SOUTHWICK:**
> Fact: Lived in the East part of the West Parish of Reading, MA

5. MEHITABLE SOUTHWICK, b. 1706; m. EBENEZER WESTON, 1726.

11. **JOSIAH JR.3 SOUTHWICK** *(JOSIAH2, LAWRENCE1)* was born January 27, 1659/60 in Salem, Massachusetts, and died in Northampton, Burlington County, New Jersey. He married RUTH SYMONDS, daughter of JAMES SYMONDS and ELIZABETH BROWNING. She was born February 19, 1662/63.

> **More about JOSIAH JR. SOUTHWICK:**
> Fact: 1660, Alternate birth year

> **More about RUTH SYMONDS:**
> Fact: From Salem, MA

Children of JOSIAH SOUTHWICK and RUTH SYMONDS are:
1. JOSIAH4 SOUTHWICK, b. about 1686.
2. JAMES SOUTHWICK, b. about 1685.
3. RUTH SOUTHWICK, b. about 1692; m. WILLIAM CRANMER, 1716.

More about WILLIAM CRANMER:
Fact: From Northampton, NJ

12. **CASSANDRA3 SOUTHWICK** *(JOSIAH2, LAWRENCE1)* was born 1666, and died about 1719. She married JACOB MOTT 1689. He was born 1661.

   More about CASSANDRA SOUTHWICK:
   Fact: 1680, Alternate birth year

   More about JACOB MOTT:
   Fact: From Portsmouth, MA

Children of CASSANDRA SOUTHWICK and JACOB MOTT are:
   1. CASSANDRA4 MOTT, b. November 01, 1714.
   2. DORCAS MOTT, b. March 01, 1715/16.
   3. ANN MOTT, b. October 22, 1718.

13. **SOLOMON3 SOUTHWICK** *(JOSIAH2, LAWRENCE1)* was born 1672. He married MARY about 1712.

Children of SOLOMON SOUTHWICK and MARY are:
   1. HANNAH4 SOUTHWICK, b. 1713; m. WILLIAM JEFFRIES, October 22, 1739.
   2. MARY SOUTHWICK, b. 1715; m. WILLIAM WEST, 1739.
   3. RUTH SOUTHWICK, b. 1717; m. HENRY BRIGHTMAN, December 26, 1751.

      More about HENRY BRIGHTMAN:
      Fact: From Portsmouth, RI

   4. JOSEPH SOUTHWICK, b. 1719; d. September 15, 1780.
   5. MARTHA SOUTHWICK, b. 1722; m. JOSEPH DAVOL, 1765.

      More about JOSEPH DAVOL:
      Fact: From Portsmouth, RI

   6. JEREMIAH SOUTHWICK, b. 1725; m. ELIZABETH SHEFFIELD, 1766.
   7. ELIZABETH SOUTHWICK, b. 1728; m. PETER WILKEY, October 1767.
   8. SOLOMON SOUTHWICK, b. 1731; d. December 23, 1797.

14. **LAWRENCE3 SOUTHWICK** *(DANIEL2, LAWRENCE1)* was born 1664 in Salem, Massachusetts, and died 1718. He married TAMSON BUFFUM August 04, 1704, daughter of CALEB BUFFUM.

   More about LAWRENCE SOUTHWICK:

Fact: February 15, 1705/06: Deeded 1/2 of father's house & barn

Children of LAWRENCE SOUTHWICK and TAMSON BUFFUM are:
1. LAWRENCE4 SOUTHWICK, b. January 11, 1710/11, Salem, Massachusetts; d. 1795, at home of his son Joseph in Uxbridge, MA.
2. DANIEL SOUTHWICK, b. 1705, Salem, Massachusetts; d. November 19, 1776.
3. CALEB SOUTHWICK, b. 1709.
4. JOSIAH 3RD SOUTHWICK, b. 1709; m. MARY.

   More about JOSIAH 3RD SOUTHWICK:
   Fact: 1707, Alternate birth year

5. ESTHER SOUTHWICK, b. 1712; m. EPHRAIM SILSBEE.

   More about EPHRAIM SILSBEE:
   Fact: blacksmith at Boston, MA

6. DAVID SOUTHWICK, b. 1714.
7. . JOSEPH SOUTHWICK, b. 1716; d. June 01, 1791.

15. **DANIEL3 SOUTHWICK** *(DANIEL2, LAWRENCE1)* was born March 25, 1671 in Salem, Massachusetts, and died 1732. He married JANE 1696.

    More about DANIEL SOUTHWICK:
    Will: Proved February 14, 1731/32.

Children of DANIEL SOUTHWICK and JANE are:
1. ELIZABETH4 SOUTHWICK, b. 1702; m. JONATHAN BUXTON, 1742.
2. HANNAH SOUTHWICK, b. 1704; m. UNKNOWN GIRDLER, 1724.
3. JOHN SOUTHWICK, b. May 1709; d. October 01, 1784.
4. DANIEL SOUTHWICK, b. 1721; d. March 03, 1804.
5. JONATHAN SOUTHWICK, b. 1697; d. June 28, 1786.

16. **ELEANOR3 SOUTHWICK** *(DANIEL2, LAWRENCE1)* was born June 25, 1674 in Salem, Massachusetts, and died October 26, 1702. She married SAMUEL OSBORNE, son of WILLIAM OSBORNE and HANNAH BURTON. He was born April 27, 1675 in Salem, Massachusetts, and died Abt. 1750.

Children of ELEANOR SOUTHWICK and SAMUEL OSBORNE are:
1. SAMUEL4 OSBORNE, b. February 04, 1696/97.
2. ELIZABETH OSBORNE, b. January 14, 1698/99.
3. HANNAH OSBORNE, b. November 14, 1700.
4. JOSEPH OSBORNE, b. August 26, 1702; d. Aft. November 26, 1780.

5. ELEANOR OSBORNE.
6. MERCY OSBORNE.
7. ESTHER OSBORNE.
8. JOHN OSBORNE.
9. MARY OSBORNE.

Generation No. 4

17. THOMAS4 BUFFINGTON *(SARAH3 SOUTHWICK, JOHN2, LAWRENCE1)* was born March 01, 1671/72 in Salem, Massachusetts. He married HANNAH ROSS in Salem, Massachusetts.

Children of THOMAS BUFFINGTON and HANNAH ROSS are:
1. ABIGAIL5 BUFFINGTON, b. July 25, 1695, Salem, Massachusetts.
2. HANNAH BUFFINGTON, b. May 11, 1701, Salem, Massachusetts; m. ELEAZER POPE; d. August 02, 1734.
3. JAMES BUFFINGTON.
4. MARY BUFFINGTON.

> **More about MARY BUFFINGTON:**
> Baptism: Baptized as an adult; March 31, 1728.

18. JOSEPH BUFFINGTON *(SARAH3 SOUTHWICK, JOHN2, LAWRENCE1)*

Child of JOSEPH BUFFINGTON is:
1. JOSEPH5 BUFFINGTON

19. EBENEZER4 SOUTHWICK *(SAMUEL3, JOHN2, LAWRENCE1)* was born November 09, 1690. He married (1) SARAH PROCTOR April 09, 1724. He married (2) MARY WHITMAN October 18, 1727.

> **More about SARAH PROCTOR:**
> Fact: Had no children

Children of EBENEZER SOUTHWICK and MARY WHITMAN are:
1. SARAH5 SOUTHWICK, b. May 24, 1728; m. JOSEPH STACEY, May 16, 1749.
2. MARY SOUTHWICK, b. December 22, 1729; m. UNKNOWN UPTON.
3. LOIS SOUTHWICK, b. March 03, 1732/33.
4. EBENEZER SOUTHWICK, b. February 03, 1735/36; d. January 08, 1820; m. SUSANNAH ORR, 1758; b. February 02, 1734/35; d. August 09, 1811.

> **More about SUSANNAH ORR:**
> Fact: From North Yarmouth, MA

5. HANNAH SOUTHWICK, b. 1738; m. UNKNOWN LAFAVOUR.
6. LYDIA SOUTHWICK, b. 1740; d. Bef. 1771.

More about LYDIA SOUTHWICK:
Baptism: August 24, 1760

20. **JONATHAN4 SOUTHWICK** *(SAMUEL3, JOHN2, LAWRENCE1)* was born about 1694. He married ELIZABETH DOWTY December 16, 1727.

More about JONATHAN SOUTHWICK:
Fact: November 17, 1727, Alternate Marriage date

Children of JONATHAN SOUTHWICK and ELIZABETH DOWTY are:

1. ICHABOD5 SOUTHWICK, b. 1730; d. March 05, 1822, West Pittsfield, Massachusetts; m. UNKNOWN, 1759.

   More about ICHABOD SOUTHWICK:
   Baptism: 1832, Williamstown, MA

2. MARY SOUTHWICK, b. 1732.
3. REBECCA SOUTHWICK, b. 1734.
4. SAMUEL SOUTHWICK, b. 1736; m. HANNAH.

   More about SAMUEL SOUTHWICK:
   Religion: Joined Shakers after marriage

5. LEMUEL SOUTHWICK, b. 1738; d. September 20, 1831; m. MARY SPENCER, about 1772; b. November 02, 1754.
6. JONATHAN SOUTHWICK, b. 1740.
7. ELIZABETH SOUTHWICK, b. August 08, 1741.
8. JESSE SOUTHWICK, b. 1728; m. COPIA WRIGHT, 1757.

   More about JESSE SOUTHWICK:
   Fact: Moved from Williamstown, MA to west Pittsfield, MA

21. **BENJAMIN4 SOUTHWICK** *(SAMUEL3, JOHN2, LAWRENCE1)* was born about 1696, and died 1795. He married ABIGAIL BURT April 22, 1722 in Congregational Church, New Salem, Massachusetts.

More about BENJAMIN SOUTHWICK:
Fact: Moved to New Salem

Children of BENJAMIN SOUTHWICK and ABIGAIL BURT are:

1. SAMUEL5 SOUTHWICK, b. 1722; d. March 04, 1756; m. ABIGAIL, 1741.

   More about SAMUEL SOUTHWICK:
   Baptism: November 19, 1742

2. BENJAMIN JR SOUTHWICK, b. 1723; m. SARAH, 1745.

   More about BENJAMIN JR SOUTHWICK:
   Baptism: November 19, 1742

3. ABIGAIL SOUTHWICK, b. 1725; m. JAMES COOK, March 26, 1740.

   More about ABIGAIL SOUTHWICK:
   Baptism: November 19, 1742

4. HANNAH SOUTHWICK, b. 1727; m. EZEKIAL KELLOGG, May 10, 1750.

   More about HANNAH SOUTHWICK:
   Baptism: November 19, 1742

5. SARAH SOUTHWICK, b. 1729; m. JAMES WHEELER, January 13, 1747/48.
6. REBECCA SOUTHWICK, b. 1731; m. JOSEPH BALLARD, January 12, 1759.
7. SIMEON SOUTHWICK, b. 1733; m. RUTH FELTON, December 15, 1755.

22. **DAVID4 SOUTHWICK** *(SAMUEL3, JOHN2, LAWRENCE1)* was born 1701 in Salem, Massachusetts, and died 1792. He married THANKFUL GRIGG 1726.

    More about DAVID SOUTHWICK:
    Fact: Over age 90 at death

    More about THANKFUL GRIGG:
    Fact: She was a widow when she married David

Child of DAVID SOUTHWICK and THANKFUL GRIGG is:
1. SAMUEL5 SOUTHWICK, b. 1727; m. ABIGAIL WARNER, about 1755.

23. **JOHN4 SOUTHWICK** *(JOHN3, JOHN2, LAWRENCE1)* was born December 13, 1688, and died about 1771. He married MARY TRASK January 08, 1709/10.

    More about JOHN SOUTHWICK:
    Baptism: May 1690
    Fact: Lived in Danvers, MA
    Will: Proved October 07, 1771.

Children of JOHN SOUTHWICK and MARY TRASK are:
1. JOHN5 SOUTHWICK, b. about 1725; d. before 1785; m. (1) ELIZABETH WILSON; m. (2) EUNICE.

More about JOHN SOUTHWICK:
Will: Made January 04, 1785.

2. WILLIAM SOUTHWICK, b. 1719; d. before 1767; m. SARAH ELIZABETH KING, August 06, 1748.
3. . MARY SOUTHWICK, b. 1717; d. September 24, 1796; m. EBENEZER KING, March 23, 1733/34.
4. ANNA SOUTHWICK, b. 1719; m. ZACHARIA KING, November 09, 1736.
5. ELIZABETH SOUTHWICK, b. 1721; m. ROBERT JR WILSON, May 26, 1744.
6. JOSEPH SOUTHWICK, b. 1723, Salem, Massachusetts [Now Peabody]; m. MARY WILSON, September 13, 1743.

More about JOSEPH SOUTHWICK:
Fact: Lived at Danvers, MA

7. GEORGE SOUTHWICK, b. about 1736; d. about 1808; m. SARAH SITCHEL.

More about GEORGE SOUTHWICK:
Will: Made June 06, 1803.

More about SARAH SITCHEL:
Fact: She was a widow when she married George.

24. **ABRAHAM4 SOUTHWICK** *(JOHN3, JOHN2, LAWRENCE1)* was born July 27, 1696, and died before 1769. He married SARAH 1729.

More about ABRAHAM SOUTHWICK:
Fact: bricklayer

Children of ABRAHAM SOUTHWICK and SARAH are:
1. ISAAC5 SOUTHWICK, d. before 1764.

More about ISAAC SOUTHWICK:
Baptism: April 26, 1730

2. ABRAHAM JR SOUTHWICK, m. MARY ABORN, January 11, 1755.

More about ABRAHAM JR SOUTHWICK:
Baptism: April 26, 1730

3. SARAH SOUTHWICK, m. NATHANIEL CLARK, October 24, 1751.

More about SARAH SOUTHWICK:

Baptism: April 26, 1730

More about NATHANIEL CLARK:
Fact: From Wells, Maine

4. JOSEPH SOUTHWICK, d. before 1754.

More about JOSEPH SOUTHWICK:
Baptism: July 18, 1731

5. MARGARET SOUTHWICK, m. AMOS NEWHALL, December 07, 1750.

More about MARGARET SOUTHWICK:
Baptism: October 06, 1734

More about AMOS NEWHALL:
Fact: From Lynn, MA

24. **BENJAMIN4 SOUTHWICK** (JOHN3, JOHN2, LAWRENCE1) was born January 22, 1700/01. He married (1) SARAH SOUTHWICK, daughter of ISAAC SOUTHWICK and ANNA. He married (2) SARAH SOUTHWICK, daughter of ISAAC SOUTHWICK and ANNA. She was born 1699.

More about BENJAMIN SOUTHWICK:
Fact: Lived at Reading, MA

Children of BENJAMIN SOUTHWICK and SARAH SOUTHWICK are:
1. ISAAC5 SOUTHWICK, b. 1720.
2. BENJAMIN SOUTHWICK, b. 1722; m. MIRIAM BENSON, 1737.

More about BENJAMIN SOUTHWICK:
Fact: Settled at Mendon, MA

3. SARAH SOUTHWICK, b. 1724.
4. MERCY SOUTHWICK, b. 1730.

25. **ISAAC4 SOUTHWICK** (JOHN3, JOHN2, LAWRENCE1) was born September 23, 1704. He married ESTHER CLARK June 05, 1731.

More about ISAAC SOUTHWICK:
Baptism: October 04, 1705
Will: Made September 27, 1774,

More about ESTHER CLARK:
Fact: From Wells, Maine

Children of ISAAC SOUTHWICK and ESTHER CLARK are:

1. ISAAC5 SOUTHWICK, b. 1732; m. ELIZABETH DRESSER.

More about ISAAC SOUTHWICK:
Baptism: June 24, 1733, Middle Precinct
Fact: Moved to Amherst, NH after marriage

2. NATHANIEL SOUTHWICK, b. 1734.

More about NATHANIEL SOUTHWICK:
Baptism: May 28, 1738

3. ESTHER SOUTHWICK, b. 1736.

More about ESTHER SOUTHWICK:
Baptism: June 15, 1740

4. JOHN SOUTHWICK, b. 1738.

More about JOHN SOUTHWICK:
Baptism: May 06, 1744

5. SUSANNAH SOUTHWICK, b. 1740; m. UNKNOWN JAFREY.
6. BENJAMIN SOUTHWICK, b. 1742.

24A. **SARAH4 SOUTHWICK** *(ISAAC3, JOHN2, LAWRENCE1)* was born 1699. She married BENJAMIN SOUTHWICK, son of JOHN SOUTHWICK and HANNAH BLACK. He was born January 22, 1700/01.

More about BENJAMIN SOUTHWICK:
Fact: Lived at Reading

Children are listed above under (24) Benjamin Southwick

26. **JOSIAH4 SOUTHWICK** *(JOSIAH JR.3, JOSIAH2, LAWRENCE1)* was born about 1686. He married ELIZABETH COLLINS 1705, daughter of FRANCIS COLLINS.

Children of JOSIAH SOUTHWICK and ELIZABETH COLLINS are:
1. JOSIAH5 SOUTHWICK, b. 1706; m. ELIZABETH, 1737.
2. JAMES SOUTHWICK, b. 1708; m. RACHEL DAWSON, 1737.
3. RUTH SOUTHWICK, b. 1710.
4. ABRAHAM SOUTHWICK, b. 1712.

27. JOSEPH4 SOUTHWICK *(SOLOMON3, JOSIAH2, LAWRENCE1)* was born 1719, and died September 15, 1780. He married MARY PITTMAN 1738. She was born 1722, and died October 16, 1788.

Children of JOSEPH SOUTHWICK and MARY PITTMAN are:
1. JOHN5 SOUTHWICK, b. 1740; d. November 09, 1803; m. REBECCA MOSHER, 1767; b. 1747; d. February 09, 1805.
2. MARY SOUTHWICK, b. 1743; d. 1819; m. JOHN TRIPP GRIERS, October 03, 1765.
3. HANNAH SOUTHWICK, b. 1743; d. 1830; m. HENRY BLIVEN.
4. CATHERINE SOUTHWICK, b. 1745; m. JEREMY SHEFFIELD.
5. JOSEPH SOUTHWICK, b. 1746; d. June 19, 1829; m. (1) SUSANNAH PITTS; b. 1756; d. December 21, 1839; m. (2) MARY IRISH, 1768.
6. DEBORAH SOUTHWICK, b. 1749; d. May 09, 1765.
7. JONATHAN SOUTHWICK, b. 1764; d. March 15, 1832; m. LYDIA A HANDY; b. 1762; d. May 17, 1855.
8. JOSIAH SOUTHWICK, b. 1748, Rhode Island; m. REBECCA MEGGS.

28. SOLOMON4 SOUTHWICK *(SOLOMON3, JOSIAH2, LAWRENCE1)* was born 1731, and died December 23, 1797. He married ANN GARDNER June 20, 1769, daughter of JOHN GARDNER. She was born 1748.

More about ANN GARDNER:
Fact: Ann was a widow when she married Solomon

Children of SOLOMON SOUTHWICK and ANN GARDNER are:
1. ELIZABETH ANN5 SOUTHWICK, b. April 10, 1770; m. (1) RICHARD WOODMAN; m. (2) JAMES CHACE.
2. JOHN P SOUTHWICK, b. June 30, 1771.

More about JOHN P SOUTHWICK:
Fact: Went to sea at young age and was never heard from again

3. MARY SOUTHWICK, b. July 20, 1772; d. July 24, 1772.
4. HENRY COLLINS SOUTHWICK, b. July 20, 1772, Newport, Rhode Island; d. 1821; m. MARY WOOL, July18, 1797.

More about HENRY COLLINS SOUTHWICK:
Fact: Twin

More about MARY WOOL:
Fact: May have been Margaret

5. **SOLOMON SOUTHWICK**, b. December 25, 1773; d. November 18, 1839, Albany, NY; m. JANE BARBER, March 31, 1795.

More about JANE BARBER:
Fact: From Albany, NY

6. WILMARTH SOUTHWICK, b. 1775, Newport, Rhode Island; d. August 19, 1843; m. HANNAH, November 20, 1800.

More about HANNAH:
Fact: Hannah was a widow when she married Wilmarth

29. LAWRENCE4 SOUTHWICK *(LAWRENCE3, DANIEL2, LAWRENCE1)* was born January 11, 1710/11 in Salem, Massachusetts, and died 1795 in At home of his son Joseph in Uxbridge, MA. He married (1) HANNAH SHOVE May 08, 1739, daughter of EDWARD SHOVE and LYDIA. She died Abt. 1754. He married (2) PATIENCE HANDY 1754, daughter of UNKNOWN HANDY and UNKNOWN FRANKLIN. She was born 1739.

More about LAWRENCE SOUTHWICK:
Fact: Cordwainer at Dighton, MA

More about HANNAH SHOVE:
Fact: From Dighton, MA

More about PATIENCE HANDY:
Fact: May be Handee

Children of LAWRENCE SOUTHWICK and HANNAH SHOVE are:

1. EDWARD5 SOUTHWICK, b. March 18, 1739/40, Smithfield, Rhode Island; d. March 18, 1833; m. ELIZABETH SOUTHWICK, June 01, 1761; b. February 18, 1744/45; d. June 18, 1834.

    More about EDWARD SOUTHWICK:
    Fact: June, alternate death month

    More about ELIZABETH SOUTHWICK:
    Fact: June 26, 1806, Moved from Mendon, MA to Danby, VT

2. ELIZABETH SOUTHWICK, b. 1748; m. MOSES FARNUM, May 02, 1777.
3. JOSEPH SOUTHWICK, b. February 21, 1744/45; d. March 19, 1814; m. ABIGAIL SAYLES, April 01, 1779; b. February 05, 1756; d. November 11, 1844.

    More about ABIGAIL SAYLES:
    Fact: From Smithfield, RI

4. NATHANIEL SOUTHWICK, b. May 02, 1752; m. ELIZABETH SOUTHGATE, 1775.
5. DAVID SOUTHWICK, b. March 21, 1754; d. April 16, 1819; m. ELIZABETH SWEET, April 16, 1779; b. June 29, 1760.

Children of LAWRENCE SOUTHWICK and PATIENCE HANDY are:

6. ISSAC5 SOUTHWICK, b. December 13, 1761, Dighton, Massachusetts; d. 1823, Danby, Rutland County, Vermont; m. THANKFUL PARRIS; b. 1765; d. 1830, Danby, Rutland County, Vermont.

More about ISSAC SOUTHWICK:
Fact: Early settler in Danby, VT

7. DANIEL SOUTHWICK, b. 1756; d. 1846, Holland Purchase, Erie County, New York; m. JEMIMA BARTLETT, May 02, 1792, Smithfield, Rhode Island; d. 1840.

More about DANIEL SOUTHWICK:
Fact: Came with his brother Josiah to Danby
Religion: Quaker

8. CALEB SOUTHWICK, b. February 04, 1757; d. December 28, 1819; m. PHEBE OSBORN, October 1793; b. November 24, 1764; d. February 15, 1843.

More about CALEB SOUTHWICK:
Fact: Settled in Peru, Clinton County, NY

More about PHEBE OSBORN:
Fact: From Danvers, MA

9. AMOS SOUTHWICK, b. 1760; d. before 1762.
10. AMOS SOUTHWICK, b. 1762.
11. LYDIA SOUTHWICK, b. 1764; m. OBADIAH FRYE, January 12, 1791; b. 1763.

More about LYDIA SOUTHWICK:
Fact: Moved to Farmington, Ontario County, NY

12. ASA SOUTHWICK, b. August 03, 1766; m. LYDIA SHERMAN, 1787.

More about ASA SOUTHWICK:
Fact: 1826, Settled at North Adams, Massachusetts

13. MOSES SOUTHWICK, b. September 30, 1768; d. June 11, 1836, Killed in accident; m. ANNA HARKNESS, 1792; b. September 29, 1759; d. August 16, 1824.

More about MOSES SOUTHWICK:
Fact: Shoe maker

14. ESTHER SOUTHWICK, b. 1770; m. UNKNOWN CASE.

More about ESTHER SOUTHWICK:
Fact: Settled at Hoosick, NY

15. ABIGAIL SOUTHWICK, b. 1772; m. ASA WHEELER, 1789.

More about ABIGAIL SOUTHWICK:
Fact: Moved to Bolton, Massachusetts

16. MARY SOUTHWICK, b. July 12, 1772; d. February 26, 1851, Clarksborough, Massachusetts; m. (1) ISRAEL CHILSON, 1791; d. 1805, Clarksburgh, Massachusetts; m. (2) JACOB BROWN, 1805.

More about ISRAEL CHILSON:
Burial: Stamford, Vermont

17. JACOB SOUTHWICK, b. 1774; m. UNKNOWN OSBORNE.

More about JACOB SOUTHWICK:
Fact: Settled at Peru, NY

18. ANNA SOUTHWICK, b. 1775; d. 1794.
19. JOSIAH SOUTHWICK, b. January 27, 1777, Massachusetts; d. March 04, 1874, Danby, Rutland County, Vermont; m. (1) MARY BAKER, 1818; m. (2) RACHEL BROWN, March 1832; b. February 06, 1789; d. April 25, 1876.

More about JOSIAH SOUTHWICK:
Fact: About 1801, Moved to Danby, VT
Political: Republican
Religion: Quaker

More about MARY BAKER:
Fact: From Granville, NY

More about RACHEL BROWN:
Fact: From Queensbury, NY

20. HANNAH SOUTHWICK, b. 1779; m. SETH BALLARD, St. Lawrence County, NY.

More about HANNAH SOUTHWICK:
Fact: Preacher for Society of Friends

30. **DANIEL4 SOUTHWICK** *(LAWRENCE3, DANIEL2, LAWRENCE1)* was born 1705 in Salem, Massachusetts, and died November 19, 1776. He married RUTH SHOVE February 08, 1729/30 in Swansea, Massachusetts, daughter of EDWARD SHOVE and LYDIA.

More about DANIEL SOUTHWICK:
Fact: Moved to Mendon after marriage [later Uxbridge]
Religion: Quaker

Children of DANIEL SOUTHWICK and RUTH SHOVE are:
1. LAWRENCE5 SOUTHWICK, b. January 11, 1730/31; d. 1810; m. (1) DORCAS BROWN, January 1753; d. December 17, 1757; m. (2) HANNAH SOUTHWICK, September 06, 1759; b. December 02, 1741; d. 1809.

    More about LAWRENCE SOUTHWICK:
    Fact: tanner

2. LYDIA SOUTHWICK, b. December 22, 1735; m. AMOS OSBORNE, December 03, 1761.
3. DANIEL SOUTHWICK, b. October 18, 1737; m. MARY MABBETT.
4. ELEANOR SOUTHWICK, b. February 02, 1738/39; m. DANIEL READ, July 01, 1762.
5. JOSIAH SOUTHWICK, b. July 17, 1742; d. killed wrestling in father's barn with hired man.
6. ELIZABETH SOUTHWICK, b. September 04, 1744; m. SOLOMON HAIGHT, September 03, 1779.
7. GEORGE SOUTHWICK, b. December 14, 1747; d. April 07, 1807; m. JUDITH SOUTHWICK, June 05, 1777; b. October 23, 1757; d. February 11, 1837.
8. THEOPHILUS SOUTHWICK, b. November 29, 1750; d. January 10, 1825; m. ANNA REMINGTON; d. August 20, 1824.

31. **CALEB4 SOUTHWICK** *(LAWRENCE3, DANIEL2, LAWRENCE1)* was born 1709. He married RUTH GOULD April 08, 1732, daughter of THOMAS GOULD and ABIGAIL.

More about CALEB SOUTHWICK:

Fact: blacksmith

Child of CALEB SOUTHWICK and RUTH GOULD is:
1. TAMSON5 SOUTHWICK, b. 1736; m. DANIEL ALDRICH, May 01, 1759.

32. **DAVID4 SOUTHWICK** *(LAWRENCE3, DANIEL2, LAWRENCE1)* was born 1714. He married HANNAH 1736.

> **More about DAVID SOUTHWICK:**
> Fact: Settled in Dudley, MA
>
> **More about HANNAH:**
> Fact: About 1735, Alternate Marriage year

Children of DAVID SOUTHWICK and HANNAH are:
1. SAMUEL5 SOUTHWICK, b. November 19, 1736; m. ABIGAIL, 1759.
2. HANNAH SOUTHWICK, b. August 24, 1739.
3. SARAH SOUTHWICK, b. 1742; m. (1) NATHAN EATON, about 1762; m. (2) NATHANIEL DANIELS, about 1762.

> **More about Nathan Eaton:**
> Fact: First husband of Sarah

33. **JOSEPH4 SOUTHWICK** *(LAWRENCE3, DANIEL2, LAWRENCE1)* was born 1716, and died June 01, 1791. He married BETHIA CALLUM March 31, 1739 in Uxbridge, Massachusetts, daughter of CALEB CALLUM. She died April 08, 1803.

> **More about JOSEPH SOUTHWICK:**
> Fact: Was a tanner at Salem, MA
>
> **More about BETHIA CALLUM:**
> Fact: From Uxbridge, MA

Children of JOSEPH SOUTHWICK and BETHIA CALLUM are:
1. BETHIA5 SOUTHWICK, b. October 02, 1741; m. UNKNOWN HANSON, Brunswick, Maine.
2. ANNE SOUTHWICK, b. December 30, 1743; d. July 30, 1775; m. JEREMIAH HACKER.
3. JOSEPH SOUTHWICK, b. September 03, 1746; d. November 19, 1773.
4. ESTHER SOUTHWICK, b. October 24, 1748; d. June 26, 1772; m. JAMES TORREY, Falmouth, Maine.
5. TAMSON SOUTHWICK, b. October 28, 1750; d. January 27, 1836; m. WILLIAM FRYE; b. August 1749; d. October 11, 1831.

> **More about WILLIAM FRYE:**

Fact: From Andover, MA

6. JOSIAH SOUTHWICK, b. September 14, 1752; d. October 18, 1775.
7. CASSANDRA SOUTHWICK, b. March 11, 1755; d. August 15, 1755.
8. EDWARD SOUTHWICK, b. March 01, 1757; d. January 03, 1836; m. ABIGAIL ROWELL, November 25, 1790; b. June 14, 1764; d. February 10, 1856.

More about EDWARD SOUTHWICK:
Fact: Lived in Danvers, MA

More about ABIGAIL ROWELL:
Fact: From Amesbury, MA

9. CALEB SOUTHWICK, b. April 03, 1763; d. October 04, 1775.

34. JOHN4 SOUTHWICK *(DANIEL3, DANIEL2, LAWRENCE1)* was born May 1709, and died October 01, 1784. He married MARY GASKILL December 12, 1730, daughter of SAMUEL GASKILL and MARY. She was born June 1703, and died May 12, 1790.

More about JOHN SOUTHWICK:
Fact: Known as Shop keeper

More about MARY GASKILL:
Fact: Mary was a widow when she married John

Children of JOHN SOUTHWICK and MARY GASKILL are:
1. MEHITABLE5 SOUTHWICK, b. August 19, 1725; d. October 06, 1778; m. UNKNOWN VARNEY, October 06, 1758.
2. ZACHEUS SOUTHWICK, b. April 14, 1732.
3. HANNAH SOUTHWICK, b. August 22, 1734; d. March 14, 1793; m. ABIJAH PURINGTON.

More about ABIJAH PURINGTON:
Fact: From Salem, MA

4. DANIEL SOUTHWICK, b. August 10, 1736.
5. ELIZABETH SOUTHWICK, b. February 08, 1737/38; d. June 28, 1786; m. JONATHAN BUXTON, 1767, Friend's Meeting Salem, Massachusetts.
6. JOSIAH SOUTHWICK, b. July 17, 1742; m. ELIZABETH SOUTHWICK, at Quaker Meeting, Salem, Massachusetts; d. February 15, 1818.

More about JOSIAH SOUTHWICK:
Fact: tanner
Religion: Quaker

35. **DANIEL4 SOUTHWICK** *(DANIEL3, DANIEL2, LAWRENCE1)* was born 1721, and died March 03, 1804. He married RUTH MUSSEY February 08, 1741/42, daughter of JAMES MUSSEY. She was born February 18, 1721/22, and died January 16, 1790.

Children of DANIEL SOUTHWICK and RUTH MUSSEY are:
1. JUDITH5 SOUTHWICK, b. October 23, 1757; d. February 11, 1837; m. GEORGE SOUTHWICK, June 05, 1777; b. December 14, 1747; d. April 07, 1807.
2. DAVID SOUTHWICK, b. September 27, 1743; d. July 19, 1746.
3. ELIZABETH SOUTHWICK, b. March 29, 1746; m. JEREMIAH WILKINSON, December 04, 1777.

   More about JEREMIAH WILKINSON:
   Fact: From Cumberland, RI

4. JANE SOUTHWICK, b. September 14, 1748; d. June 24, 1772.

   More about JANE SOUTHWICK:
   Fact: unmarried

5. HANNAH SOUTHWICK, b. March 19, 1749/50; m. JESSE DARLING, January 04, 1771, Smithfield, Rhode Island.

   More about JESSE DARLING:
   Fact: From Gloucester, MA

6. RUTH SOUTHWICK, b. March 20, 1755; d. June 10, 1813; m. BENEDICT REMINGTON, October 05, 1780.
7. LYDIA SOUTHWICK, b. February 04, 1761; d. October 08, 1848; m. JAMES CONGDON, December 06, 1781.

36. **JONATHAN4 SOUTHWICK** *(DANIEL3, DANIEL2, LAWRENCE1)* was born 1697, and died June 28, 1786. He married (1) ELIZABETH BUFFUM. He married (2) HANNAH OSBORNE March 21, 1734/35, daughter of JOHN OSBORNE and HANNAH BUFFUM. She was born January 18, 1716/17, and died 1775.

   More about ELIZABETH BUFFUM:
   Fact: Elizabeth was a widow when she married Jonathan

Children of JONATHAN SOUTHWICK and ELIZABETH BUFFUM are:
1. JONATHAN5 SOUTHWICK, b. July 10, 1736; m. JUDITH MUSSEY, November 01, 1759.

More about JONATHAN SOUTHWICK:
Fact: Farmer

2. ENOCH SOUTHWICK, b. 1738.

   More about ENOCH SOUTHWICK:
   Fact: died young

3. ZACHEUS SOUTHWICK, b. 1740.

   More about ZACHEUS SOUTHWICK:
   Fact: died young

Children of JONATHAN SOUTHWICK and HANNAH OSBORNE are:

4. HANNAH5 SOUTHWICK, b. December 02, 1741; d. 1809; m. LAWRENCE SOUTHWICK, September 06, 1759; b. January 11, 1730/31; d. 1810.

   More about LAWRENCE SOUTHWICK:
   Fact: tanner

5. ELIZABETH SOUTHWICK, b. February 18, 1744/45; d. June 18, 1834; m. EDWARD SOUTHWICK, June 01, 1761; b. March 18, 1739/40, Smithfield, Rhode Island; d. March 18, 1833.

   More about ELIZABETH SOUTHWICK:
   Fact: June 26, 1806, Moved from Mendon, MA to Danby, VT

   More about EDWARD SOUTHWICK:
   Fact: June, alternate death month

6. JOHN SOUTHWICK, b. September 06, 1744; d. January 23, 1831; m. CHLOE A BARTLETT; b. October 04, 1749; d. April 25, 1817.

   More about JOHN SOUTHWICK:
   Fact: Farmer

7. ESTHER SOUTHWICK, b. 1748, Mendon, Massachusetts; m. JAMES BUXTON, 1773.
8. GEORGE SOUTHWICK, b. February 08, 1753, Smithfield, Rhode Island; d. October 12, 1825, Collins, Erie County, NY {area now North Collins}; m. LYDIA SARGENT, February 05, 1778; b. July 09, 1757, Smithfield, Rhode Island; d. July 27, 1845, Collins, Erie County, NY {area now North Collins}.

More about GEORGE SOUTHWICK:
Fact: 1810, brought family to area which would become North Collins

9. JACOB SOUTHWICK, b. June 04, 1751; d. August 19, 1833; m. SARAH FOWLER, June 04, 1778; b. October 20, 1753; d. July 28, 1829.
10. ENOCH SOUTHWICK, b. April 04, 1753; m. MARY SWETT, 1778; b. May 11, 1758.

More about ENOCH SOUTHWICK:
Fact: 1811, Moved from Vermont to Holland Purchase [area now known as Colden, NY]

11. MERCY SOUTHWICK, b. 1757.
12. ZACHEUS SOUTHWICK, b. September 04, 1760; d. June 04, 1845; m. LAVINIA SAYLES, January 04, 1787; b. September 05, 1760.

37. **JOSEPH4 OSBORNE** *(ELEANOR3 SOUTHWICK, DANIEL2, LAWRENCE1)* was born August 26, 1702, and died after November 26, 1780. He married (1) RACHEL FOSTER. She died before 1734. He married (2) SARAH GARDNER.

More about JOSEPH OSBORNE:
Will: Proved: December 04, 1780.

Child of JOSEPH OSBORNE and RACHEL FOSTER is:

1. JOSEPH5 OSBORN, b. August 06, 1726, Salem, Massachusetts; d. July 09, 1804; m. MARY PROCTOR, January 06, 1756; b. December 13, 1733; d. January 06, 1791.

More about MARY PROCTOR:
Fact: Descendant of John Proctor: Witchcraft Martyr

Children of JOSEPH OSBORNE and SARAH GARDNER are:

2. RACHEL5 OSBORNE.

More about RACHEL OSBORNE:
Baptism: September 29, 1734

3. GINGER OSBORNE.

More about GINGER OSBORNE:
Baptism: September 29, 1734

4. EUNICE OSBORNE.

More about EUNICE OSBORNE:

Baptism: December 19, 1736

5. ISRAEL OSBORNE.

More about ISRAEL OSBORNE:
Baptism: May 27, 1739

6. MEHITABLE OSBORNE, m. (1) SYLVESTER PROCTOR; m. (2) EZRA PORTER, February 09, 1764.

More about MEHITABLE OSBORNE:
Baptism: November 15, 1741

7. ABEL OSBORNE.

More about ABEL OSBORNE:
Baptism: August 18, 1745
Fact: died young

8. ABEL OSBORNE, m. LYDIA FOSTER.

More about ABEL OSBORNE:
Baptism: November 09, 1746

9. AARON OSBORNE, b. November 15, 1742; d. February 08, 1803; m. LYDIA PROCTOR, March 24, 1774.

Generation No. 5

38. **THOMAS5 BUFFINGTON** *(Thomas4 Buffington, SARAH3 SOUTHWICK, JOHN2, LAWRENCE1)* was born March 01, 1671/72 in Salem, Massachusetts. He married HANNAH ROSS in Salem, Massachusetts.

Children of THOMAS BUFFINGTON and HANNAH ROSS are:
1. ABIGAIL3 BUFFINGTON, b. July 25, 1695, Salem, Massachusetts
2. HANNAH BUFFINGTON, b. May 11, 1701, Salem, Massachusetts.
3. JAMES BUFFINGTON
4. MARY BUFFINGTON.

39. JOSEPH5 BUFFINGTON *(Thomas4 Buffington, SARAH3 SOUTHWICK, JOHN2, LAWRENCE1* His wife is unknown.

Child of JOSEPH BUFFINGTON is:
1. JOSEPH3 BUFFINGTON.

40. **ICHABOD5 SOUTHWICK** *(JONATHAN4, SAMUEL3, JOHN2, LAWRENCE1)* was born 1730, and died March 05, 1822 in West Pittsfield, Massachusetts. He married UNKNOWN 1759.

> **More about ICHABOD SOUTHWICK:**
> Baptism: 1832, Williamstown, MA

Children of ICHABOD SOUTHWICK and UNKNOWN are:
1. JONATHAN6 SOUTHWICK, b. 1760.

   > **More about JONATHAN SOUTHWICK:**
   > Fact: Leader of Shakers at West Pittsfield, Massachusetts
   > Religion: Shaker

2. LEMUEL SOUTHWICK, b. 1761.
3. ISRAEL SOUTHWICK, b. 1763.
4. ICHABOD SOUTHWICK, b. 1765; m. BUELAH.
5. JACOB SOUTHWICK, b. 1770.
6. BENJAMIN FRANKLIN SOUTHWICK, b. July 19, 1774; m. CHARLOTTE HADDOCK, 1797.

41. **LEMUEL5 SOUTHWICK** *(JONATHAN4, SAMUEL3, JOHN2, LAWRENCE1)* was born 1738, and died September 20, 1831. He married MARY SPENCER about 1772. She was born November 02, 1754.

Children of LEMUEL SOUTHWICK and MARY SPENCER are:
1. LEMUEL6 SOUTHWICK, b. 1773; d. September 1857; m. JOANNA RICE.

   More about LEMUEL SOUTHWICK:
   Military service 1: Served 3 months
   Military service 2: war of 1812

2. SAMUEL SOUTHWICK, b. 1775; d. Iowa.
3. HENRY SOUTHWICK, b. 1777.
4. POLLY SOUTHWICK, b. 1780.
5. DAVID SOUTHWICK, b. 1784.
6. JONATHAN SOUTHWICK, b. September 29, 1798; d. November 02, 1875; m. ESTHER CORWIN, November 30, 1823.
7. ARNOLD SOUTHWICK, b. June 02, 1802; m. SALLY, August 05, 1838.

   More about SALLY:
   Fact: Sally was a widow when she married Arnold

43. **JESSE5 SOUTHWICK** *(JONATHAN4, SAMUEL3, JOHN2, LAWRENCE1)* was born 1728. He married COPIA WRIGHT 1757.

   More about JESSE SOUTHWICK:
   Fact: Moved from Williamstown, MA to west Pittsfield, MA

Children of JESSE SOUTHWICK and COPIA WRIGHT are:
1. JESSE6 SOUTHWICK, b. 1758, New Lebanon, Massachusetts; d. September 1826.
2. LEMUEL SOUTHWICK, b. 1761; m. MARY SPENCER, 1790.

   More about LEMUEL SOUTHWICK:
   Baptism: 1761, Congregational Church, New Salem, MA

3. MARY SOUTHWICK, b. November 29, 1763; d. 1830, West Pittsfield, Massachusetts.

   More about MARY SOUTHWICK:
   Fact: unmarried
   Religion: Shaker

4. SARAH SOUTHWICK, b. 1766; m. UNKNOWN PIERCE.

More about SARAH SOUTHWICK:
Fact: Moved to Illinois

5. SAMUEL SOUTHWICK, b. 1768.
6. DAVID SOUTHWICK, b. 1770; d. June 1843.

44. SAMUEL5 SOUTHWICK *(BENJAMIN4, SAMUEL3, JOHN2, LAWRENCE1)* was born 1722, and died March 04, 1756. He married ABIGAIL 1741.

More about SAMUEL SOUTHWICK:
Baptism: November 19, 1742

Children of SAMUEL SOUTHWICK and ABIGAIL are:
1. DAVID6 SOUTHWICK, b. 1742.

More about DAVID SOUTHWICK:
Fact: Married three times

2. SAMUEL SOUTHWICK, b. 1743; d. March 04, 1756.
3. MARY SOUTHWICK, b. 1744.

More about MARY SOUTHWICK:
Baptism: June 19, 1784
Fact: Married to unknown person: November 18, 1765.

4. RELIEF SOUTHWICK, b. 1746.

More about RELIEF SOUTHWICK:
Fact: Married to unknown person, October 04, 1767.

5. JOHN SOUTHWICK, b. 1748.

More about JOHN SOUTHWICK:
Baptism: September 16, 1795

45. BENJAMIN JR5 SOUTHWICK *(BENJAMIN4, SAMUEL3, JOHN2, LAWRENCE1)* was born 1723. He married SARAH 1745.

More about BENJAMIN JR SOUTHWICK:
Baptism: November 19, 1742

Children of BENJAMIN SOUTHWICK and SARAH are:
1. SAMUEL6 SOUTHWICK, b. December 08, 1750; m. ELIZABETH, September 19, 1779.

More about SAMUEL SOUTHWICK:

Baptism: New Salem
Fact: Married three times

2. HANNAH SOUTHWICK, b. 1752.

More about HANNAH SOUTHWICK:
Baptism: April 23, 1758, New Salem

3. MARY SOUTHWICK, b. 1754.
4. JEREMIAH SOUTHWICK, b. 1756.

More about JEREMIAH SOUTHWICK:
Baptism: May 13, 1766, New Salem

5. BENJAMIN SOUTHWICK, b. 1760; d. 1801; m. SARAH FISKE, December 23, 1787.

More about BENJAMIN SOUTHWICK:
Baptism: September 19, 1779, New Salem

6. SIMEON SOUTHWICK, b. 1764; m. RUTH FELTON, 1785.
7. RACHEAL SOUTHWICK, b. July 1768; d. June 12, 1842.

46. **SIMEON5 SOUTHWICK** *(BENJAMIN4, SAMUEL3, JOHN2, LAWRENCE1)* was born 1733. He married RUTH FELTON December 15, 1755.

Child of SIMEON SOUTHWICK and RUTH FELTON is:
1. SIMEON6 SOUTHWICK, b. about 1763; d. May 1805.

47. **SAMUEL5 SOUTHWICK** *(DAVID4, SAMUEL3, JOHN2, LAWRENCE1)* was born 1727. He married ABIGAIL WARNER about 1755.

Children of SAMUEL SOUTHWICK and ABIGAIL WARNER are:
1. DAVID6 SOUTHWICK, b. 1756; d. 1841; m. BETSEY STACEY.

More about DAVID SOUTHWICK:
Baptism: November 07, 1762, Congregational Church of New Salem, MA

More about BETSEY STACEY:
Fact: From Benson, VT

2. JONATHAN SOUTHWICK, b. August 22, 1772; d. August 18, 1863, died at son Masa's Home in St Hilaire, Canada.
3. DANIEL SOUTHWICK, b. June 11, 1773; d. January 15, 1839; m. POLLY CHURCHILL, October 05, 1797.

More about POLLY CHURCHILL:
Fact: From Benson, VT

4. SAMUEL SOUTHWICK, b. 1775; m. PHEBE SOUTHWICK, 1843; b. February 20, 1798; d. December 29, 1878.

More about SAMUEL SOUTHWICK:
Fact: Settled in Western, NY

48. **JOHN5 SOUTHWICK** *(JOHN4, JOHN3, JOHN2, LAWRENCE1)* was born About 1725, and died before 1785. He married (1) ELIZABETH WILSON, daughter of ISAAC WILSON and MARY. He married (2) EUNICE.

More about JOHN SOUTHWICK:
Will 1: Made; January 04, 1785.
Will 2: Proved; February 08, 1785.

Children of JOHN SOUTHWICK and ELIZABETH WILSON are:
1. GEORGE6 SOUTHWICK, b. 1750; d. April 17, 1775, Killed at Battle of Lexington.
2. PRUDENCE SOUTHWICK, d. before 1795; m. STEPHEN SOUTHWICK, February 24, 1785; b. December 27, 1759.

More about PRUDENCE SOUTHWICK:
Baptism: May 25, 1766

3. JOHN FLOOD SOUTHWICK.
4. MARY SOUTHWICK, b. 1766; d. January 14, 1862; m. JONATHAN DAY.

49. **WILLIAM5 SOUTHWICK** *(JOHN4, JOHN3, JOHN2, LAWRENCE1)* was born 1719, and died before 1767. He married SARAH ELIZABETH KING August 06, 1748.

Children of WILLIAM SOUTHWICK and SARAH KING are:
1. STEPHEN6 SOUTHWICK, b. December 27, 1759.
2. WILLIAM SOUTHWICK, b. May 17, 1754; d. September 11, 1828.
3. JOHN SOUTHWICK, b. 1756.
4. JAMES SOUTHWICK, b. October 12, 1768.

50. **JOSEPH5 SOUTHWICK** *(JOHN4, JOHN3, JOHN2, LAWRENCE1)* was born 1723 in Salem, Massachusetts [Now Peabody]. He married MARY WILSON September 13, 1743, daughter of ISAAC WILSON and MARY.

More about JOSEPH SOUTHWICK:
Fact 1: Lived at Danvers, MA
Fact 2: a potter

Children of JOSEPH SOUTHWICK and MARY WILSON are:
1. MARY6 SOUTHWICK, b. about 1744.

   More about MARY SOUTHWICK:
   Baptism: June 15, 1754

2. SUSAN SOUTHWICK, b. 1746; d. September 22, 1791.

   More about SUSAN SOUTHWICK:
   Baptism: 1754

3. HANNAH SOUTHWICK, b. November 16, 1756; d. May 17, 1806.
4. ELIZABETH SOUTHWICK, b. August 21, 1759; d. January 25, 1844.

51. **GEORGE5 SOUTHWICK** *(JOHN4, JOHN3, JOHN2, LAWRENCE1)* was born about 1736, and died about 1808. He married SARAH SITCHEL.

    More about GEORGE SOUTHWICK:
    Will 1: Made; June 06, 1803.
    Will 2: Proved; July 19, 1808.

    More about SARAH SITCHEL:
    Fact: Sarah was a widow when she married George

Children of GEORGE SOUTHWICK and SARAH SITCHEL are:
1. GEORGE JR6 SOUTHWICK.
2. FRANCIS SOUTHWICK, b. April 08, 1764.
3. SARAH SOUTHWICK.

   More about SARAH SOUTHWICK:
   Baptism: August 24, 1766.
   Fact: Died young.

4. MERCY SOUTHWICK.
5. NATHAN SOUTHWICK, d. July 20, 1836.
6. REBECCA SOUTHWICK.
7. MARY SOUTHWICK.

   More about MARY SOUTHWICK:
   Baptism: June 15, 1777

52. **ISAAC5 SOUTHWICK** *(ISAAC4, JOHN3, JOHN2, LAWRENCE1)* was born 1732. He married ELIZABETH DRESSER.

    More about ISAAC SOUTHWICK:

Baptism: June 24, 1733, Middle Precinct
Fact: Moved to Amherst, NH after marriage

Children of ISAAC SOUTHWICK and ELIZABETH DRESSER are:
1. NATHANIEL6 SOUTHWICK.

More about NATHANIEL SOUTHWICK:
Baptism: August 16, 1762, First Church of Salem

2. BETSEY SOUTHWICK.

More about BETSEY SOUTHWICK:
Baptism: July 07, 1765, First Church of Salem

3. ESTHER SOUTHWICK.

More about ESTHER SOUTHWICK:
Baptism: August 14, 1768, First Church of Salem

4. ISAAC DRESSER SOUTHWICK.

More about ISAAC DRESSER SOUTHWICK:
Baptism: July 29, 1770, First Church of Salem

5. AMOS SOUTHWICK.

More about AMOS SOUTHWICK:
Baptism: August 20, 1775, First Church of Salem

53. **BENJAMIN5 SOUTHWICK** *(SARAH4, ISAAC3, JOHN2, LAWRENCE1)* was born 1722. He married MIRIAM BENSON 1737.

> **More about BENJAMIN SOUTHWICK:**
> Fact: Settled at Mendon, MA

Child of BENJAMIN SOUTHWICK and MIRIAM BENSON is:
1. JOSEPH6 SOUTHWICK, b. 1738; d. March 23, 1813.

54. **JOSIAH5 SOUTHWICK** *(JOSIAH4, JOSIAH JR.3, JOSIAH2, LAWRENCE1)* was born 1706. He married ELIZABETH 1737.

Children of JOSIAH SOUTHWICK and ELIZABETH are:
1. SOLOMON6 SOUTHWICK, b. 1738; m. RACHEAL ZELLEY.
2. JOSIAH SOUTHWICK, b. 1740.

55. **JAMES5 SOUTHWICK** *(JOSIAH4, JOSIAH JR.3, JOSIAH2, LAWRENCE1)* was born 1708. He married RACHEL DAWSON 1737.

Children of JAMES SOUTHWICK and RACHEL DAWSON are:
1. SARAH6 SOUTHWICK, b. 1740; m. FRANCIS DAWSON, 1758.
2. WILLIAM SOUTHWICK, b. 1742; m. ELIZABETH ALLEN, Abt. 1772.
3. SAMUEL SOUTHWICK, b. 1744.

56. **JOHN5 SOUTHWICK** *(JOSEPH4, SOLOMON3, JOSIAH2, LAWRENCE1)* was born 1740, and died November 09, 1803. He married REBECCA MOSHER 1767. She was born 1747, and died February 09, 1805.

Children of JOHN SOUTHWICK and REBECCA MOSHER are:
1. BENJAMIN6 SOUTHWICK, b. 1768; d. October 28, 1854.
2. DEBORAH SOUTHWICK, b. 1769; d. 1851; m. WILLIAM SWANN.
3. SILAS SOUTHWICK, b. 1780; d. October 03, 1864; m. HANNAH HEATH; b. 1772; d. September 13, 1856.

   More about HANNAH HEATH:
   Fact: Hannah was a widow when she married Silas

4. FRANCIS SOUTHWICK, b. 1788; d. 1820, Richmond, Virginia; m. (1) MARIA EASTON; m. (2) UNKNOWN COGGESHELL.

57. **JOSEPH5 SOUTHWICK** *(JOSEPH4, SOLOMON3, JOSIAH2, LAWRENCE1)* was born 1746, and died June 19, 1829. He married (1) SUSANNAH PITTS. She was born 1756, and died December 21, 1839. He married (2) MARY IRISH 1768.

Children of JOSEPH SOUTHWICK and SUSANNAH PITTS are:
1. TILLEY6 SOUTHWICK, b. 1774; d. 1829.
2. SARAH SOUTHWICK, b. 1779; d. 1849; m. PELEG TURNER, April 1802.

   More about PELEG TURNER:
   Fact: From Middletown

3. JOSEPH SOUTHWICK, b. October 11, 1780; d. March 06, 1864; m. (1) DORCAS EASTON; m. (2) DORCAS SWEET.
4. DAVID SOUTHWICK, b. 1785; d. May 1807, Lost at Sea; m. BETSEY DUNELL, 1804; b. 1773; d. August 07, 1829, Providence, Rhode Island.

   More about BETSEY DUNELL:
   Fact: Betsey was w widow when she married David

5. BETSEY SOUTHWICK, d. 1844; m. JAMES BRIGHTMAN.
6. SUSAN SOUTHWICK, b. 1792; d. 1860; m. ARNOLD PIERCE.
7. PITTS SOUTHWICK, b. 1795; m. (1) MARY ELDRED; b. 1796; d. 1879; m. (2) SARAH SWEET, 1817; b. December 25, 1799; d. July 20, 1822.

More about MARY ELDRED:
Fact: Mary was a widow when she married Pitts

8. CATHERINE SOUTHWICK.

More about CATHERINE SOUTHWICK:
Fact: Died young

9. GEORGE H SOUTHWICK, b. 1798; m. ELIZABETH.

More about GEORGE H SOUTHWICK:
Military service 1: War of 1812
Military service 2: Served with Commander Perry on Lake Erie

More about ELIZABETH:
Fact: Last name is either Sweet or Larvet

10. RUTH SOUTHWICK.

Children of JOSEPH SOUTHWICK and MARY IRISH are:
11. JOSIAH6 SOUTHWICK, b. 1769; m. MARY CONGDON, Maine.

More about JOSIAH SOUTHWICK:
Fact: Moved to Maine

12. MARY SOUTHWICK, b. 1770; d. 1835; m. JOSEPH LEW.

58. **JONATHAN5 SOUTHWICK** *(JOSEPH4, SOLOMON3, JOSIAH2, LAWRENCE1)* was born 1764, and died March 15, 1832. He married LYDIA A HANDY. She was born 1762, and died May 17, 1855.

Children of JONATHAN SOUTHWICK and LYDIA HANDY are:
1. SOLOMON6 SOUTHWICK, b. 1786; d. June 06, 1823.
2. JOSEPH SOUTHWICK, b. December 18, 1782; d. December 25, 1861; m. SARAH HERSWELL; b. 1788; d. June 03, 1818.

More about JOSEPH SOUTHWICK:
Military service 1: War of 1812
Military service 2: With Com. Perry on Lake Erie

3. SARAH SOUTHWICK, m. N WHITE.

59. **JOSIAH5 SOUTHWICK** *(JOSEPH4, SOLOMON3, JOSIAH2, LAWRENCE1)* was born 1748 in Rhode Island. He married REBECCA MEGGS.

Child of JOSIAH SOUTHWICK and REBECCA MEGGS is:
    1. STEPHEN6 SOUTHWICK, b. October 17, 1783; d. September 13, 1853; m. LYDIA BACKUS; b. November 04, 1789; d. February 02, 1860.

More about LYDIA BACKUS:
Fact: Last name may be spelled Baccus

59. **HENRY COLLINS5 SOUTHWICK** *(SOLOMON4, SOLOMON3, JOSIAH2, LAWRENCE1)* was born July 20, 1772 in Newport, Rhode Island, and died 1821. He married MARY WOOL July 18, 1797, daughter of JOSIAH WOOL.

More about HENRY COLLINS SOUTHWICK:
Fact: Twin

More about MARY WOOL:
Fact 1: May have been Margaret
Fact 2: From NYC

1. **Children of HENRY SOUTHWICK and MARY WOOL are**: MARGARET6 SOUTHWICK, b. 1798.
2. MARY ANN SOUTHWICK, b. 1799; m. MOWRY OSBORN, December 13, 1818.
3. WILLAIM SOUTHWICK, b. 1800.
4. CATHERINE SOUTHWICK, b. 1804; m. UNKNOWN KEELER.
5. HENRY COLLINS JR SOUTHWICK, b. December 28, 1806; m. MARY PARKINSON; b. June 14, 1808; d. March 20, 1879.

More about MARY PARKINSON:
Fact: From Mayfield, Fulton County, NY

6. CHARLES SOUTHWICK, b. 1808.
7. JOHN SOUTHWICK, b. 1810.
8. EDWIN SOUTHWICK, b. 1812.
9. JANE SOUTHWICK, b. 1814.

More about JANE SOUTHWICK:
Fact: Moved to Sand Lake after marriage

10. SARAH SOUTHWICK, b. 1816; m. FRANK MCGUIGAN.

More about FRANK MCGUIGAN:

Fact 1: Drover
Fact 2: Lived in Albany, NY

60. **SOLOMON5 SOUTHWICK** *(SOLOMON4, SOLOMON3, JOSIAH2, LAWRENCE1)* was born December 25, 1773, and died November 18, 1839 in Albany, NY. He married JANE BARBER March 31, 1795.

> **More about JANE BARBER:**
> Fact: From Albany, NY

Children of SOLOMON SOUTHWICK and JANE BARBER are:

1. ANN GOULDBURY6 SOUTHWICK, b. July 02, 1796; d. October 16, 1799.
2. FRANCIS MOORE SOUTHWICK, b. October 12, 1798; d. October 21, 1821.
3. MARY SOUTHWICK, b. June 21, 1801; d. July 20, 1801.
4. ELIZABETH SOUTHWICK, b. December 22, 1802; d. October 16, 1803.
5. JOHN BARBER SOUTHWICK, b. December 03, 1805; d. July 23, 1833.
6. HENRY COLLINS SOUTHWICK, b. July 05, 1808; d. January 30, 1866; m. JULIA CATHERINE BUEL; b. December 20, 1816.

   More about JULIA CATHERINE BUEL:
   Fact: From Albany, NY

7. SOLOMON SOUTHWICK, b. July 12, 1810; d. August 11, 1866.
8. ALFRED SOUTHWICK, b. August 23, 1812; d. December 05, 1862.
9. ARTHUR CUMMINGS SOUTHWICK, b. February 22, 1815; d. December 10, 1846.

61. **WILMARTH5 SOUTHWICK** *(SOLOMON4, SOLOMON3, JOSIAH2, LAWRENCE1)* was born 1775 in Newport, Rhode Island, and died August 19, 1843. He married HANNAH November 20, 1800.

More about HANNAH:
Fact: Hannah was a widow when she married Wilmarth.

Children of WILMARTH SOUTHWICK and HANNAH are:

1. WILLIAM6 SOUTHWICK, b. August 18, 1801, Plymouth, Massachusetts.
2. SOLOMON SOUTHWICK, b. January 12, 1804, Plymouth, Massachusetts; d. July 31, 1835, Albany, New York; m. SARAH RICE.

   More about SOLOMON SOUTHWICK:
   Fact: No children

   More about SARAH RICE:

Fact: From Waterford, NY

3. MARY ANN SOUTHWICK, b. September 30, 1807; d. 1807.
4. MARY ANN SOUTHWICK, b. June 30, 1808; d. August 28, 1824.
5. SARAH SHERMAN SOUTHWICK, b. April 12, 1812, Plymouth, Massachusetts; m. WILLIAM GREENE FRY, May 07, 1829, Albany, new York; b. Albany, NY.

62. **EDWARD5 SOUTHWICK** *(LAWRENCE4, LAWRENCE3, DANIEL2, LAWRENCE1)* was born March 18, 1739/40 in Smithfield, Rhode Island, and died March 18, 1833. He married ELIZABETH SOUTHWICK June 01, 1761, daughter of JONATHAN SOUTHWICK and HANNAH OSBORNE. She was born February 18, 1744/45, and died June 18, 1834.

More about EDWARD SOUTHWICK:
Date Born 2: March 15, 1733/34
Fact 1: June, alternate death month
Fact 2: Captain of a whaling boat
Fact 3: October 29, 1807, Moved from Mendon, MA to Danby, VT

More about ELIZABETH SOUTHWICK:
Fact: June 26, 1806, Moved from Mendon, MA to Danby, VT

Children of EDWARD SOUTHWICK and ELIZABETH SOUTHWICK are:
1. ELIZABETH6 SOUTHWICK, b. 1790; m. MOSES CHILSON, 1812, Danby, Rutland County, Vermont; b. 1792, Hoosick, New York.

More about ELIZABETH SOUTHWICK:
Fact: June 26, 1806, Moved from Mendon, MA to Danby, VT

2. HANNAH SOUTHWICK, b. October 03, 1773; d. September 16, 1862; m. (1) ANTHONY COMSTOCK, 1787; d. 1808; m. (2) SAMUEL GASKILL, 1843; d. 1847.

More about HANNAH SOUTHWICK:
Fact: Lived in Smithfield, RI when she married Anthony Comstock

3. DAVID SOUTHWICK, b. February 04, 1777, Rhode Island; d. 1850; m. MARY SHERMAN, March 01, 1804; b. November 15, 1783.

More about DAVID SOUTHWICK:
Fact 1: Farmer
Fact 2: About 1805, Moved to Danby, Vermont
Religion: Quaker

4. MERCY SOUTHWICK, b. October 18, 1779; m. ELIJAH BULL.

5. OLIVE SOUTHWICK, b. July 02, 1780; m. CYRUS CARPENTER, February 03, 1800.

More about OLIVE SOUTHWICK:
Fact: January 29, 1801, Moved to Danby, Vermont

6. EZRA SOUTHWICK, b. July 25, 1782; d. September 25, 1845, Collins, Erie County, NY; m. DEBORAH SMITH.

More about EZRA SOUTHWICK:
Fact 1: June 26, 1806, Moved from Mendon, MA to Danby, VT
Fact 2: Farmer
Fact 3: Moved from Mount Holly to Danby Vermont
Fact 4: shoemaker
Fact 5: Came to Buffalo via Erie Canal

63. **JOSEPH5 SOUTHWICK** *(LAWRENCE4, LAWRENCE3, DANIEL2, LAWRENCE1)* was born February 21, 1744/45, and died March 19, 1814. He married ABIGAIL SAYLES April 01, 1779, daughter of JONATHAN SAYLES. She was born February 05, 1756, and died November 11, 1844.

More about ABIGAIL SAYLES:
Fact 1: From Smithfield, RI
Fact 2: Name may be Ailsie

Children of JOSEPH SOUTHWICK and ABIGAIL SAYLES are:

1. EZRA6 SOUTHWICK, b. February 22, 1780; d. April 19, 1847; m. (1) CHLOE TAFT; m. (2) SUSAN TAFT; m. (3) NANCY TURTLOTTE.
2. SARAH SOUTHWICK, b. July 02, 1781; d. January 01, 1867; m. GERSHOM KEITH; b. 1783; d. October 1841.
3. MOSES SOUTHWICK, b. May 06, 1783; d. October 04, 1828; m. SARAH PULSIFER, December 08, 1804; b. May 25, 1786, Douglas, Massachusetts; d. August 19, 1859.

More about MOSES SOUTHWICK:
Fact 1: Farmer
Fact 2: blacksmith
Fact 3: Millwright

4. ELIZABETH SOUTHWICK, b. March 03, 1785; d. April 13, 1859.
5. MARY SOUTHWICK, b. July 15, 1787; d. August 26, 1872.

More about MARY SOUTHWICK:
Fact: Name may be Ruth

6. LUKE SOUTHWICK, b. September 11, 1789; d. March 24, 1814.

7. JOSEPH SOUTHWICK, b. March 02, 1793; d. August 08, 1860; m. MIRANDA LAPHAM; b. September 05, 1800; d. November 01, 1879.
8. DUTY SOUTHWICK, b. July 15, 1794; d. February 02, 1803.
9. ARNOLD SOUTHWICK, b. February 14, 1798; d. November 15, 1869, Paralysis of the Kidneys: Uxbridge, Massachusetts; m. PATIENCE LAPHAM, March 08, 1827; b. January 30, 1803, Burrillville, Rhode Island.

More about ARNOLD SOUTHWICK:
Fact: Mechanic

64. NATHANIEL5 SOUTHWICK *(LAWRENCE4, LAWRENCE3, DANIEL2, LAWRENCE1)* was born May 02, 1752. He married ELIZABETH SOUTHGATE 1775.

Children of NATHANIEL SOUTHWICK and ELIZABETH SOUTHGATE are:
    1. PAULINA6 SOUTHWICK, b. 1776.

More about PAULINA SOUTHWICK:
Fact: Never married

    2. AMASA SOUTHWICK, b. November 13, 1778; d. March 27, 1867; m. POLLY RICHARDSON; b. November 29, 1780; d. December 21, 1868.
    3. CASSANDRA SOUTHWICK, b. 1780; d. 1871; m. JOEL KELLY.
    4. ABIGAIL SOUTHWICK, b. 1782.

More about ABIGAIL SOUTHWICK:
Fact: Never married

    5. BETSEY SOUTHWICK, b. 1790.

More about BETSEY SOUTHWICK:
Fact: Never married

    6. SEBE MARIA SOUTHWICK, b. 1792; m. UNKNOWN KENT.
    7. REBECCA SOUTHWICK, b. January 15, 1796.

65. DAVID5 SOUTHWICK *(LAWRENCE4, LAWRENCE3, DANIEL2, LAWRENCE1)* was born March 21, 1754, and died April 16, 1819. He married ELIZABETH SWEET April 16, 1779. She was born June 29, 1760.

Children of DAVID SOUTHWICK and ELIZABETH SWEET are:
    1. TAMSON6 SOUTHWICK, b. March 19, 1780; m. JOHN HOAG; d. April 10, 1807, died of Consumption.

2. HULDAH SOUTHWICK, b. April 06, 1783; d. October 22, 1800, Berlin, Massachusetts.
3. HANNAH SOUTHWICK, b. February 20, 1785; d. April 23, 1809, Berlin, Massachusetts.
4. DAVID JR SOUTHWICK, b. January 11, 1787; m. POLLY COOLEDGE.
5. GEORGE SOUTHWICK, b. April 10, 1789.

More about GEORGE SOUTHWICK:
Fact: About 1818, Moved to Upper Canada

6. ELIZABETH SOUTHWICK, b. January 11, 1791; m. HENRY POWERS, December 10, 1810.
7. DANIEL SOUTHWICK, b. June 02, 1793.

More about DANIEL SOUTHWICK:
Fact: About 1818, Moved to Upper Canada

8. ELISHA SOUTHWICK, b. March 31, 1795; d. August 13, 1830; m. LYDIA H HOUGHTON.
9. MARY SOUTHWICK, b. April 23, 1797; d. August 30, 1797.
10. MARY SOUTHWICK, b. October 27, 1798; m. TIMOTHY VARNEY, November 05, 1819.
11. MARMADUKE SOUTHWICK, b. December 23, 1800; d. March 24, 1870, Centerville, St Joseph County, Michigan.

More about MARMADUKE SOUTHWICK:
Fact 1: Never married
Fact 2: blacksmith

12. RUTH SOUTHWICK, b. May 17, 1804.

More about RUTH SOUTHWICK:
Fact: Never married

66. ISSAC5 SOUTHWICK *(LAWRENCE4, LAWRENCE3, DANIEL2, LAWRENCE1)* was born December 13, 1761 in Dighton, Massachusetts, and died 1823 in Danby, Rutland County, Vermont. He married THANKFUL PARRIS, daughter of ELKANAH PARRIS. She was born 1765, and died 1830 in Danby, Rutland County, Vermont.

More about ISSAC SOUTHWICK:
Fact 1: Early settler in Danby, VT
Fact 2: Blacksmith
Fact 3: Worked with David Bartlett Manufacturing edge tools

Children of ISSAC SOUTHWICK and THANKFUL PARRIS are:

1. TRUMAN6 SOUTHWICK, b. 1802.

More about TRUMAN SOUTHWICK:
Fact: Died young

2. SYLVIA SOUTHWICK, b. 1805; m. FRIEND SMITH.

More about FRIEND SMITH:
Fact: Moved to Erie County, NY

3. EDNA SOUTHWICK, b. 1808.

More about EDNA SOUTHWICK:
Fact: Died young

4. ISSAC JR SOUTHWICK, b. October 10, 1809, Danby, Rutland County, Vermont; d. October 11, 1832, Starksboro, Vermont; m. ELIZABETH OTIS, June 10, 1828; b. December 09, 1809, Danby, Rutland County, Vermont; d. 1841.

More about ISSAC JR SOUTHWICK:
Fact: Was in mercantile business with his father.

5. ARTHUR SOUTHWICK, b. 1817.

More about ARTHUR SOUTHWICK:
Fact: Died young

67. DANIEL5 SOUTHWICK *(LAWRENCE4, LAWRENCE3, DANIEL2, LAWRENCE1)* was born 1756, and died 1846 in Holland Purchase, Erie County, New York. He married JEMIMA BARTLETT May 02, 1792 in Smithfield, Rhode Island, daughter of JACOB BARTLETT and JUDITH. She died 1840.

More about DANIEL SOUTHWICK:
Fact: Came with his brother Josiah to Danby
Religion: Quaker

Children of DANIEL SOUTHWICK and JEMIMA BARTLETT are:
1. SAMUEL6 SOUTHWICK, b. February 11, 1793; m. PHEBE SOUTHWICK.

More about SAMUEL SOUTHWICK:
Fact 1: Settled in Collins, NY
Fact 2: Farmer
Fact 3: No children

2. SARAH SOUTHWICK, b. 1795; m. LUTHER COLVIN, July 1814.

More about SARAH SOUTHWICK:
Fact: Moved to Brant, NY

More about LUTHER COLVIN:
Fact: Moved to Western NY

3. ANNA SOUTHWICK, b. 1797; m. DAVID CLARK.

More about ANNA SOUTHWICK:
Fact: Moved to Hamburg, NY

4. GEORGE SOUTHWICK, b. February 14, 1800; m. LOUISA FINNEY, 1827.

More about GEORGE SOUTHWICK:
Fact 1: Moved west.
Fact 2: School teacher.

More about LOUISA FINNEY:
Fact 1: Last name may be Tenny.
Fact 2: From Danby, VT.

5. ASA SOUTHWICK, b. March 19, 1804; m. SALLY FINNEY; b. 1809.

More about ASA SOUTHWICK:
Fact 1: Farmer.
Fact 2: Moved from Brant, NY to Ohio.
Fact 3: Moved to Brant, NY.

More about SALLY FINNEY:
Fact 1: Last name may be Tenny.
Fact 2: From Danby, VT.
Fact 3: Name may be Sarah rather than Sally.

6. NATHAN SOUTHWICK, b. April 19, 1808; d. September 22, 1867, killed while falling trees; m. CLARINDA HALL.

More about NATHAN SOUTHWICK:
Fact 1: Moved to Brant, NY.
Fact 2: Farmer.

7. DANIEL JR SOUTHWICK, b. April 13, 1813; m. (1) SALLY ANN FISK, November 16, 1853; d. before 1869; m. (2) LYDIA SISSON, December 24, 1859.

More about DANIEL JR SOUTHWICK:
Fact: Moved to Brant, NY

More about SALLY ANN FISK:

Fact: From Danby, VT.

More about LYDIA SISSON:
Fact: From Queensbury, NY.

8. JACOB SOUTHWICK, b. May 20, 1820; m. MARY ANNA WEALTHY, January 11, 1857.

More about JACOB SOUTHWICK:
Fact 1: Moved to Brant, NY.
Fact 2: Farmer.

9. MARIAH SOUTHWICK, b. January 09, 1809; m. AUSTIN SHAW.

More about MARIAH SOUTHWICK:
Fact 1: Moved to Collins, NY
Fact 2: Name may be Maria

10. NAOMI SOUTHWICK, b. 1812.

   More about NAOMI SOUTHWICK:
   Fact: died young

11. LYDIA SOUTHWICK, b. 1807; m. CALVIN HITCHCOCK.

More about LYDIA SOUTHWICK:
Fact: Moved with family to Brant, NY.

More about CALVIN HITCHCOCK:
Fact: From Brant, NY.

12. JUDITH SOUTHWICK, b. 1801; m. JOHN ROBERTS.
13. PATIENCE SOUTHWICK, b. 1803; d. 1833; m. EBENEAZER HOLTON.

More about EBENEAZER HOLTON:
Fact: From Dorset, Vermont.

14. PHEBE SOUTHWICK, b. January 08, 1817; m. GEORGE CORY.

More about PHEBE SOUTHWICK:
Fact: No children.

68. CALEB5 SOUTHWICK *(LAWRENCE4, LAWRENCE3, DANIEL2, LAWRENCE1)* was born February 04, 1757, and died December 28, 1819. He married PHEBE OSBORN October 1793. She was born November 24, 1764, and died February 15, 1843.

More about CALEB SOUTHWICK:
Fact: Settled in Peru, Clinton County, NY

More about PHEBE OSBORN:
Fact: From Danvers, MA

Children of CALEB SOUTHWICK and PHEBE OSBORN are:

1. PAUL6 SOUTHWICK, b. May 15, 1797; d. November 14, 1858; m. SARAH COFFEE, November 08, 1826.
2. ABIGAIL SOUTHWICK, b. August 09, 1801; d. December 04, 1870.

More about ABIGAIL SOUTHWICK:
Fact: Unmarried

3. MARY SOUTHWICK, b. August 30, 1804; d. November 04, 1818.

More about MARY SOUTHWICK:
Fact: Unmarried

4. DAVID SOUTHWICK, b. November 04, 1794; d. February 20, 1824; m. PRISCILLA MASON, October 1817.
5. EDWARD SOUTHWICK, b. March 12, 1807; m. MARIA MILLER, January 03, 1833.

More about MARIA MILLER:
Fact: From Clinton County, NY

6. INFANT SOUTHWICK.

More about INFANT SOUTHWICK:
Fact: Died young

7. INFANT SOUTHWICK.

More about INFANT SOUTHWICK:
Fact: Died young

8. DANIEL SOUTHWICK, b. November 04, 1799; d. April 1800.

69. LYDIA5 SOUTHWICK *(LAWRENCE4, LAWRENCE3, DANIEL2, LAWRENCE1)* was born 1764. She married OBADIAH FRYE January 12, 1791. He was born 1763.

More about LYDIA SOUTHWICK:
Fact: Moved to Farmington, Ontario County, NY

Children of LYDIA SOUTHWICK and OBADIAH FRYE are:
1. JOHN6 FRYE, b. February 03, 1793.
2. MIRIAM FRYE, b. September 16, 1794.
3. MARY FRYE, b. March 08, 1796.
4. SARAH FRYE, b. September 14, 1797.
5. LYDIA FRYE, b. June 05, 1799.

70. **ASA5 SOUTHWICK** *(LAWRENCE4, LAWRENCE3, DANIEL2, LAWRENCE1)* was born August 03, 1766. He married LYDIA SHERMAN 1787.

> **More about ASA SOUTHWICK:**
> Fact: 1826, Settled at North Adams, Massachusetts

Children of ASA SOUTHWICK and LYDIA SHERMAN are:
1. LEMUEL6 SOUTHWICK, b. December 04, 1793; d. 1875, Ohio; m. (1) JULIA; m. (2) RHODA ARNOLD, 1814; d. October 14, 1855.

> **More about JULIA:**
> Fact: Julia was a Widow when she married Lemuel

2. LYDIA SOUTHWICK, b. 1795; m. SAMUEL WILBUR.

> **More about LYDIA SOUTHWICK:**
> Fact: Moved to Detroit, Michigan

3. EDMUND SOUTHWICK, b. 1797; m. CHLOE CLARK.

> **More about EDMUND SOUTHWICK:**
> Fact: Lived entire life in North Adams, MA.

4. HANNAH SOUTHWICK, b. 1797; m. IRA WILBUR.

> **More about HANNAH SOUTHWICK:**
> Fact: Moved to Detroit, Michigan

5. NANCY SOUTHWICK, b. 1799; d. about 1817, North Adams, Massachusetts.

71. **MOSES5 SOUTHWICK** *(LAWRENCE4, LAWRENCE3, DANIEL2, LAWRENCE1)* was born September 30, 1768, and died June 11, 1836. Killed in an accident. He married ANNA HARKNESS 1792, daughter of ADAM HARKNESS and HANNAH. She was born September 29, 1759, and died August 16, 1824.

> **More about MOSES SOUTHWICK:**

Fact: Shoemaker

Children of MOSES SOUTHWICK and ANNA HARKNESS are:
1. MARY6 SOUTHWICK, b. June 27, 1792; d. June 17, 1827; m. ROYAL TYLER, April 28, 1811.
2. ANNIE SOUTHWICK, b. April 18, 1794; d. April 06, 1851; m. JOSHUA TRASK, November 07, 1819.
3. PHEBE SOUTHWICK, b. April 25, 1796; d. February 09, 1853.

   More about PHEBE SOUTHWICK:
   Fact: unmarried

4. NATHAN SOUTHWICK, b. March 19, 1798; m. (1) ELIZA A INMAN, March 05, 1829; d. September 25, 1829; m. (2) ELIZA A ARNOLD, June 26, 1832; d. October 26, 1837; m. (3) SARAH DARLING, August 19, 1839; d. January 09, 1841; m. (4) CLARA DARLING, October 27, 1841.
5. RACHEAL SOUTHWICK, b. October 25, 1799; d. May 14, 1806.

72. **ABIGAIL5 SOUTHWICK** *(LAWRENCE4, LAWRENCE3, DANIEL2, LAWRENCE1)* was born 1772. She married ASA WHEELER 1789.

   More about ABIGAIL SOUTHWICK:
   Fact: Moved to Bolton, Massachusetts

Children of ABIGAIL SOUTHWICK and ASA WHEELER are:
1. ABEL6 WHEELER, b. September 10, 1790; d. February 18, 1838.
2. ANNA WHEELER, b. June 27, 1792.
3. ASA JR WHEELER, b. January 19, 1796; d. May 21, 1862.
4. DINAH WHEELER, b. November 13, 1797; d. December 05, 1872.
5. AARON WHEELER, b. June 14, 1800; d. November 22, 1838.
6. ABIGAIL WHEELER, b. October 08, 1803; d. August 08, 1852.
7. ASCHA WHEELER, b. October 29, 1804.
8. SEBA WHEELER, b. December 29, 1806; d. January 16, 1845.
9. ALLEN WHEELER, b. January 26, 1809; d. April 13, 1873.
10. ROENA WHEELER, b. December 24, 1810; d. April 25, 1812.
11. OBEDIAH WHEELER, b. August 13, 1813; d. January 24, 1814.
12. ELIZA WHEELER, b. April 06, 1815; d. August 23, 1829.

73. **MARY5 SOUTHWICK** *(LAWRENCE4, LAWRENCE3, DANIEL2, LAWRENCE1)* was born July 12, 1772, and died February 26, 1851 in Clarksborough, Massachusetts. She married (1) ISRAEL CHILSON 1791. He died 1805 in Clarksburgh, Massachusetts. She married (2) JACOB BROWN 1805.

   More about ISRAEL CHILSON:

Burial: Stamford, Vermont

Children of MARY SOUTHWICK and ISRAEL CHILSON are:

1. MOSES6 CHILSON, b. 1792, Hoosick, New York; m. ELIZABETH SOUTHWICK, 1812, Danby, Rutland County, Vermont; b. 1790.

   More about ELIZABETH SOUTHWICK:
   Fact: June 26, 1806, Moved from Mendon, MA to Danby, VT

2. SERIEL CHILSON, b. 1794.

   More about SERIEL CHILSON:
   Fact: Moved to Michigan

3. JASON CHILSON, b. October 28, 1798.

   More about JASON CHILSON:
   Fact 1: had only one child that died young
   Fact 2: Was married four times
   Fact 3: 1880, Lived at Clarksburgh, MA

4. JUDSON CHILSON, b. June 24, 1800, Uxbridge, Massachusetts; d. June 04, 1874; m. SOPHIA SMITH, October 03, 1821; b. February 09, 1802; d. June 04, 1871.

   More about JUDSON CHILSON:
   Fact: 1880, Lived with sons: Andrew & Chester

   More about SOPHIA SMITH:
   Fact: From Pownel, VT

5. VELORAS CHILSON, b. 1802; d. 1877.
6. ISRAEL CHILSON, b. 1804.

   More about ISRAEL CHILSON:
   Fact 1: Lived near Ontario County, NY
   Fact 2: Married

Children of MARY SOUTHWICK and JACOB BROWN are:

7. GEORGE SOUTHWICK6 BROWN, b. February 07, 1807; d. October 04, 1828, Ontario, NY.

   More about GEORGE SOUTHWICK BROWN:
   Fact: unmarried

8. HENRY CUMMINGS BROWN, b. May 17, 1808; m. CLARISSA M BAKER, January 01, 1828.

More about HENRY CUMMINGS BROWN:
Fact: Lived in Ontario, NY

9. HIRAM BROWN, b. August 31, 1809; d. October 10, 1812.
10. MARIA FENWICK BROWN, b. April 13, 1811; m. QUARTUS JOSLIN, September 08, 1836.

More about MARIA FENWICK BROWN:
Fact: Moved to Fenwick Michigan

11. HULDAH BROWN, b. October 14, 1817; d. December 29, 1844, North Adams, Massachusetts; m. ALVIN W LEONARD, October 1836.
12. HIRAM BROWN, b. January 19, 1814; m. JANE SMITH, February 14, 1840; b. October 30, 1817; d. March 1878.

74. JOSIAH5 SOUTHWICK *(LAWRENCE4, LAWRENCE3, DANIEL2, LAWRENCE1)* was born January 27, 1777 in Massachusetts, and died March 04, 1874 in Danby, Rutland County, Vermont. He married (1) MARY BAKER 1818, daughter of WILLIAM BAKER and PHEBE GRIFFIN. He married (2) RACHEL BROWN March 1832, daughter of HOWGILL BROWN and LYDIA. She was born February 06, 1789, and died April 25, 1876.

More about JOSIAH SOUTHWICK:
Fact 1: About 1801, Moved to Danby, VT
Fact 2: 1801, alternate marriage date
Political: Republican
Religion: Quaker

More about MARY BAKER:
Fact 1: From Granville, NY
Fact 2: Mary had two children, both died young

More about RACHEL BROWN:
Fact: From Queensbury, NY

Children of JOSIAH SOUTHWICK and RACHEL BROWN are:

1. HANNAH6 SOUTHWICK, b. May 17, 1825; m. JOSEPH FLETCHER, December 26, 1861; b. April 11, 1837.

More about JOSEPH FLETCHER:
Fact: From Mount Holly, VT

2. WILLIAM SOUTHWICK, b. December 10, 1819, Danby, Rutland County, Vermont.

3. PHEBE SOUTHWICK, b. September 04, 1821.
4. INFANT SOUTHWICK, b. 1827; d. 1827.

75. **LAWRENCE5 SOUTHWICK** *(DANIEL4, LAWRENCE3, DANIEL2, LAWRENCE1)* was born January 11, 1730/31, and died 1810. He married (1) DORCAS BROWN January 1753. She died December 17, 1757. He married (2) HANNAH SOUTHWICK September 06, 1759, daughter of JONATHAN SOUTHWICK and HANNAH OSBORNE. She was born December 02, 1741, and died 1809.

> **More about LAWRENCE SOUTHWICK:**
> Fact: tanner

Children of LAWRENCE SOUTHWICK and DORCAS BROWN are:

1. SARAH6 SOUTHWICK, b. April 27, 1754; d. February 14, 1836; m. BENEDICT ARNOLD, November 04, 1774.

   > **More about BENEDICT ARNOLD:**
   > Fact: Not the famed traitor

2. ELISHA SOUTHWICK, b. February 17, 1757; d. 1841; m. MARGARET MOSHER, August 16, 1777; b. August 16, 1758.
3. RUTH SOUTHWICK, b. 1757.

   > **More about RUTH SOUTHWICK:**
   > Fact: died young

Children of LAWRENCE SOUTHWICK and HANNAH SOUTHWICK are:

4. ROYAL6 SOUTHWICK, b. December 06, 1760; m. PHEBE FARNUM.
5. RUTH SOUTHWICK, b. March 04, 1763; d. March 17, 1851, Grafton, Massachusetts; m. DAVID FARNUM, December 02, 1781, Uxbridge, Massachusetts; b. September 29, 1753; d. February 29, 1844, Grafton, Massachusetts.

   > **More about DAVID FARNUM:**
   > Fact: Farmer

6. ZADOCK SOUTHWICK, b. May 08, 1765; d. October 23, 1823; m. ELIZABETH CARPENTER, September 27, 1786; b. September 17, 1766; d. October 10, 1847.
7. EDWARD SOUTHWICK, b. November 02, 1767; d. December 13, 1847; m. CATHERINE WILKINSON, 1802; b. July 25, 1772; d. February 13, 1813.

   > **More about CATHERINE WILKINSON:**

Fact: From Duchess County, NY

8. DORCAS SOUTHWICK, b. August 12, 1770; m. ABRAM STAPLES.
9. JESSE SOUTHWICK, b. December 05, 1772; d. 1832; m. CHARLOTTE MARSH, 1794, Dorset, Vermont; d. 1856.
10. HANNAH SOUTHWICK, b. 1778; m. JAMES C MOORE.
11. CHADE SOUTHWICK, b. October 01, 1774; d. March 16, 1841, Palmyra, Wayne County, NY; m. (1) CHLOE GIDDINS; b. August 02, 1773; d. August 04, 1823, Walcott, Wayne County, NY; m. (2) MARGARET JENNINGS.

More about CHADE SOUTHWICK:
Fact: tanner & Currier at Union Springs, NY

12. LYDIA SOUTHWICK, b. 1781; m. TIMOTHY ALEXANDER.

76. **GEORGE5 SOUTHWICK** *(DANIEL4, LAWRENCE3, DANIEL2, LAWRENCE1)* was born December 14, 1747, and died April 07, 1807. He married JUDITH SOUTHWICK June 05, 1777, daughter of DANIEL SOUTHWICK and RUTH MUSSEY. She was born October 23, 1757, and died February 11, 1837.

Children of GEORGE SOUTHWICK and JUDITH SOUTHWICK are:
1. THOMAS MUSSEY6 SOUTHWICK, b. March 17, 1778, Uxbridge, Massachusetts; m. MATILDA CAREY.
2. DANIEL SOUTHWICK, b. May 28, 1780, Uxbridge, Massachusetts; d. June 13, 1817; m. LUCINA THAYER, 1803.
3. RUTH SOUTHWICK, b. November 28, 1782, Uxbridge, Massachusetts; d. November 29, 1861; m. ASAHAL ALDRICH, February 08, 1817.
4. ELIZABETH SOUTHWICK, b. October 02, 1785, Uxbridge, Massachusetts; d. October 24, 1872; m. NATHANIEL DAY; b. October 09, 1783, Uxbridge, Massachusetts; d. May 1860.

More about NATHANIEL DAY:
Fact: From Uxbridge, MA

5. GEORGE SOUTHWICK, b. January 11, 1789, Uxbridge, Massachusetts; m. BETSEY CHILSON, 1820.
6. JAMES SOUTHWICK, b. Uxbridge, Massachusetts.

More about JAMES SOUTHWICK:
Fact: Died young

7. JUDITH SOUTHWICK, b. July 21, 1791, Uxbridge, Massachusetts; m. OTIS ALDRICH.

8. JAMES SOUTHWICK, b. September 01, 1795, Uxbridge, Massachusetts.

More about JAMES SOUTHWICK:
Fact: unmarried

9. LYDIA SOUTHWICK, b. January 01, 1800, Uxbridge, Massachusetts; d. November 30, 1828, Lee, NY; m. DANIEL MORSE, December 1822.

77. **THEOPHILUS5 SOUTHWICK** *(DANIEL4, LAWRENCE3, DANIEL2, LAWRENCE1)* was born November 29, 1750, and died January 10, 1825. He married ANNA REMINGTON. She died August 20, 1824.

Children of THEOPHILUS SOUTHWICK and ANNA REMINGTON are:
1. REMINGTON6 SOUTHWICK, b. November 26, 1779; d. April 22, 1807; m. PHILENA COOK.
2. NATHAN SOUTHWICK, b. May 18, 1783; d. December 11, 1845; m. AMY WILKINSON.
3. WILLIAM SOUTHWICK, b. June 04, 1786; d. July 19, 1828; m. REBECCA BOWDITCH.
4. LUCY SOUTHWICK, b. March 08, 1789; d. July 19, 1873; m. PARLEY BROWN.
5. DANIEL SOUTHWICK, b. August 17, 1793; m. LUCINDA BROWN, February 14, 1822.
6. MARBRA SOUTHWICK, b. January 08, 1795; d. March 12, 1866; m. MANNING WHEELOCK.
7. KEZIAH SOUTHWICK, b. September 30, 1803; d. July 16, 1804.

78. SAMUEL5 SOUTHWICK *(DAVID4, LAWRENCE3, DANIEL2, LAWRENCE1)* was born November 19, 1736. He married ABIGAIL 1759.

Children of SAMUEL SOUTHWICK and ABIGAIL are:
1. MARY6 SOUTHWICK, b. 1760.

More about MARY SOUTHWICK:
Baptism: June 19, 1784, New Salem, MA

2. JOHN SOUTHWICK, b. 1762.

More about JOHN SOUTHWICK:
Baptism: September 06, 1795

3. BETSEY SOUTHWICK, b. 1764.

More about BETSEY SOUTHWICK:

Baptism: May 07, 1780, New Salem, MA

79. SARAH5 SOUTHWICK *(DAVID4, LAWRENCE3, DANIEL2, LAWRENCE1)* was born 1742. She married (1) NATHAN EATON about 1762. She married (2) NATHANIEL DANIELS about1762.

> **More about NATHAN EATON:**
> Fact: First husband of Sarah

Children of SARAH SOUTHWICK and NATHAN EATON are:
1. LUCINDA6 EATON, b. 1763.
2. DEBORAH EATON, b. 1765; m. ADAM LAMBERTON, Paris, Oneida County, NY.

> **More about ADAM LAMBERTON:**
> Fact 1: Farmer
> Fact 2: Lived in Paris, NY

3. SARAH EATON, b. 1767.
4. CHARLOTTE EATON, b. 1769.
5. LUANA EATON, b. 1770.

80. ANNE5 SOUTHWICK *(JOSEPH4, LAWRENCE3, DANIEL2, LAWRENCE1)* was born December 30, 1743, and died July 30, 1775. She married JEREMIAH HACKER.

Children of ANNE SOUTHWICK and JEREMIAH HACKER are:
1. ESTHER6 HACKER, m. THOMAS JONES.

> **More about THOMAS JONES:**
> Fact: From Brunswick, ME

2. JOSEPH HACKER.
3. ANNA HACKER, m. WILLIAM PURINGTON.

> **More about WILLIAM PURINGTON:**
> Fact: From Falmouth, Maine

4. EUNICE HACKER, m. STEPHEN JONES.

> **More about STEPHEN JONES:**
> Fact: From Brunswick, ME

81. ESTHER5 SOUTHWICK *(JOSEPH4, LAWRENCE3, DANIEL2, LAWRENCE1)* was born October 24, 1748, and died June 26, 1772. She married JAMES TORREY in Falmouth, Maine.

Child of ESTHER SOUTHWICK and JAMES TORREY is:
1. ESTHER6 TORREY, m. BUTLER WEEKS.

   More about BUTLER WEEKS:
   Fact: From Vasselboro, Maine

82. TAMSON5 SOUTHWICK *(JOSEPH4, LAWRENCE3, DANIEL2, LAWRENCE1)* was born October 28, 1750, and died January 27, 1836. She married WILLIAM FRYE. He was born August 1749, and died October 11, 1831.

   More about WILLIAM FRYE:
   Fact: From Andover, MA

Children of TAMSON SOUTHWICK and WILLIAM FRYE are:
1. WILLIAM6 FRYE, b. November 27, 1774; d. 1860; m. UNKNOWN BUFFUM.
2. CASSANDRA FRYE, b. November 27, 1777; m. ICHABOD NICHOLS.
3. TAMSON FRYE, b. April 28, 1779; m. UNKNOWN PURINGTON.
4. HANNAH FRYE, b. October 04, 1781; m. JOSEPH BUXTON.

   More about JOSEPH BUXTON:
   Fact: From Danvers, MA

5. BETHIA FRYE, b. February 26, 1784; d. December 18, 1826; m. UNKNOWN PURINGTON.
6. ANNA FRYE, b. May 06, 1786; m. EZRA JOHNSON.

   More about EZRA JOHNSON:
   Fact: From Lynn, MA

7. GERTRUDE FRYE, b. September 24, 1789; d. December 09, 1818; m. MOSES WHITTIER, December 15, 1814.

   More about MOSES WHITTIER:
   Fact: From Dover, NH

83. **EDWARD5 SOUTHWICK** *(JOSEPH4, LAWRENCE3, DANIEL2, LAWRENCE1)* was born March 01, 1757, and died January 03, 1836. He married ABIGAIL ROWELL November 25, 1790. She was born June 14, 1764, and died February 10, 1856.

   More about EDWARD SOUTHWICK:
   Fact 1: Lived in Danvers, MA
   Fact 2: Hide dealer

More about ABIGAIL ROWELL:
Fact: From Amesbury, MA

Children of EDWARD SOUTHWICK and ABIGAIL ROWELL are:

1. **JOSEPH6 SOUTHWICK**, b. September 11, 1791; d. May 10, 1866; m. THANKFUL HUSSEY.

    More about THANKFUL HUSSEY:
    Fact: From Portland, Maine

2. ELIZA SOUTHWICK, b. March 21, 1793; m. SAMUEL PHILBRICK.
3. JACOB SOUTHWICK, b. October 24, 1795; d. February 07, 1851; m. MARY WAYNE.

    More about MARY WAYNE:
    Fact: From Vasselboro, Maine

4. DR EDWARD SOUTHWICK, b. August 30, 1798; d. November 05, 1840; m. (1) MARGARET TAPPAN; m. (2) MARY SNELL.

    More about DR EDWARD SOUTHWICK:
    Fact 1: physician
    Fact 2: Lived in Augusta, Maine

5. ABIGAIL SOUTHWICK, b. June 30, 1800; d. October 01, 1801.
6. PHILIP SOUTHWICK, b. March 19, 1802; d. September 28, 1806.
7. PHILIP SOUTHWICK, b. July 13, 1808; d. February 15, 1873; m. AMELIA DEXTER.

84. JOSIAH5 SOUTHWICK *(JOHN4, DANIEL3, DANIEL2, LAWRENCE1)* was born July 17, 1742. He married ELIZABETH SOUTHWICK in at Quaker Meeting, Salem, Massachusetts. She died February 15, 1818.

More about JOSIAH SOUTHWICK:
Fact: tanner
Religion: Quaker

Children of JOSIAH SOUTHWICK and ELIZABETH SOUTHWICK are:

1. JOHN6 SOUTHWICK, b. March 09, 1768; d. May 24, 1833; m. REBECCA ALLEY.

    More about JOHN SOUTHWICK:
    Fact: Schoolmaster

2. DANIEL SOUTHWICK, b. March 12, 1769; d. January 30, 1770.

3. PHEBE SOUTHWICK, b. March 01, 1770; m. WILLIAM COBB, December 27, 1791.

    More about WILLIAM COBB:
    Fact: From Portland, Maine

4. HANNAH SOUTHWICK, b. November 09, 1771; m. ABIJAH PURINGTON.

    More about ABIJAH PURINGTON:
    Fact: From Salem, MA

5. DANIEL SOUTHWICK, b. December 31, 1773; d. July 27, 1779, Portland, Maine.
6. ELIZABETH SOUTHWICK, b. August 10, 1775; d. August 28, 1777.
7. CASSANDRA SOUTHWICK, b. July 10, 1777; d. August 13, 1777.
8. ELIZABETH SOUTHWICK, b. December 05, 1778; d. August 12, 1825, Windham, Maine; m. EBENEZER ALLEN.
9. CASSANDRA SOUTHWICK, b. March 02, 1781; m. STEPHEN NICHOLS, October 29, 1812.

    More about STEPHEN NICHOLS:
    Fact 1: From Salem, MA
    Fact 2: Blacksmith

85. ELIZABETH5 SOUTHWICK *(DANIEL4, DANIEL3, DANIEL2, LAWRENCE1)* was born March 29, 1746. She married JEREMIAH WILKINSON December 04, 1777.

> **More about JEREMIAH WILKINSON:**
> Fact: From Cumberland, RI

Children of ELIZABETH SOUTHWICK and JEREMIAH WILKINSON are:

1. DANIEL6 WILKINSON, b. 1778; m. UNKNOWN ALDRICH.
2. JAMES WILKINSON, b. 1780; m. UNKNOWN ALDRICH.
3. JUDITH WILKINSON, b. 1782; m. LOUIS WALCOTT.
4. LYDIA WILKINSON, b. 1784.

    More about LYDIA WILKINSON:
    Fact: unmarried

86. HANNAH5 SOUTHWICK *(DANIEL4, DANIEL3, DANIEL2, LAWRENCE1)* was born March 19, 1749/50. She married JESSE DARLING January 04, 1771 in Smithfield, Rhode Island.

> **More about JESSE DARLING:**

Fact: From Gloucester, MA

Children of HANNAH SOUTHWICK and JESSE DARLING are:
1. ELMA6 DARLING, b. 1772, Mendon, Massachusetts.

    More about ELMA DARLING:
    Fact: Unmarried

2. JAMES DARLING, b. 1773, Mendon, Massachusetts; d. April 04, 1804.

    More about JAMES DARLING:
    Fact: Unmarried

3. RUTH DARLING, b. December 03, 1783, Mendon, Massachusetts; d. November 03, 1858, Boston, Massachusetts; m. JAMES SOUTHWICK.

87. RUTH5 SOUTHWICK *(DANIEL4, DANIEL3, DANIEL2, LAWRENCE1)* was born March 20, 1755, and died June 10, 1813. She married BENEDICT REMINGTON October 05, 1780, son of JOHN REMINGTON and MARY.

1. HANNAH6 REMINGTON, b. November 06, 1782; m. WILLIAM ALDRICH.

    More about WILLIAM ALDRICH:
    Fact: From Blackstone, MA

2. BENEDICT REMINGTON, b. July 26, 1799; d. 1861; m. MARY CARTHCART.

    More about BENEDICT REMINGTON:
    Fact: Lived in Northbridge, MA

3. DANIEL REMINGTON, b. March 21, 1786; m. PATIENCE MOULTON.

    More about DANIEL REMINGTON:
    Fact: Lived in Smithfield, RI

4. JOHN REMINGTON, b. August 23, 1793; d. 1862; m. ANNA REMINGTON.
5. MARY REMINGTON, b. April 08, 1791; m. LEWIS WARFIELD.

88. JONATHAN5 SOUTHWICK *(JONATHAN4, DANIEL3, DANIEL2, LAWRENCE1)* was born July 10, 1736. He married JUDITH MUSSEY November 01, 1759, daughter of THOMAS MUSSEY.

More about JONATHAN SOUTHWICK:
Fact 1: Farmer

Fact 2: Later moved to White Hall, NY
Fact 3: Moved to Hoosick Falls, NY

Children of JONATHAN SOUTHWICK and JUDITH MUSSEY are:
1. NATHAN6 SOUTHWICK, b. 1760; d. March 11, 1806; m. HANNAH MCWATERS.

    More about NATHAN SOUTHWICK:
    Fact: Brick mason

2. AARON SOUTHWICK, b. 1763.

    More about AARON SOUTHWICK:
    Fact: Went to sea and was not heard from again.

3. ELIJAH SOUTHWICK, b. November 06, 1768; d. Oneida Lake Village, Madison County, NY; m. ELIZABETH BENTLEY.

    More about ELIZABETH BENTLEY:
    Fact: From Point Judith

4. HULDAH SOUTHWICK, b. 1770; m. SAMUEL COTTRELL.

89. **JOHN5 SOUTHWICK** *(JONATHAN4, DANIEL3, DANIEL2, LAWRENCE1)* was born September 06, 1744, and died January 23, 1831. He married CHLOE A BARTLETT, daughter of JOSEPH BARTLETT. She was born October 04, 1749, and died April 25, 1817.

    More about JOHN SOUTHWICK:
    Fact 1: Farmer
    Fact 2: Lived at Uxbridge, MA

Children of JOHN SOUTHWICK and CHLOE BARTLETT are:
1. LUCY6 SOUTHWICK, b. April 22, 1767; d. December 17, 1805; m. DAVID GREEN, December 05, 1787.

    More about DAVID GREEN:
    Fact: From Smithfield, RI

2. EBER SOUTHWICK, b. November 27, 1768; d. November 15, 1856; m. MARY CASS.

    More about MARY CASS:
    Fact: From Smithfield, RI

3. PHILADELPHIA SOUTHWICK, b. April 05, 1770; d. September 09, 1845; m. PASCHAL COOK.

More about PASCHAL COOK:
Fact: From Mendon, MA

4. JOHN SOUTHWICK, b. August 29, 1771; d. January 23, 1831; m. ANN CALLUM.

More about ANN CALLUM:
Fact: From Mendon, MA

5. ENOCH SOUTHWICK, b. June 07, 1776; m. WAIT ARNOLD.

More about WAIT ARNOLD:
Fact: From Leicester, MA

6. AMASA SOUTHWICK, b. March 05, 1778; m. ALICE CHACE.

More about ALICE CHACE:
Fact: From Newport, RI

7. CHLOE SOUTHWICK, b. December 14, 1779; d. November 18, 1869; m. JOEL ALDRICH.

More about JOEL ALDRICH:
Fact: From Uxbridge, MA

8. WAIT SOUTHWICK, b. January 10, 1782; d. June 13, 1841; m. SAVAL ALDRICH.

More about SAVAL ALDRICH:
Fact: From Uxbridge, MA

9. GEORGE SOUTHWICK, b. February 28, 1784; m. SALLY DANIELS.

More about GEORGE SOUTHWICK:
Religion: Quaker

More about SALLY DANIELS:
Fact: From Mendon, MA

10. LAVINIA SOUTHWICK, b. January 26, 1786; m. ELLIS ALBEE.

More about ELLIS ALBEE:
Fact: From Uxbridge, MA

11. DANIEL SOUTHWICK, b. January 11, 1791; d. April 29, 1871; m. HANNAH SMITH.

More about HANNAH SMITH:
Fact: From Mendon, MA

90. **ESTHER5 SOUTHWICK** *(JONATHAN4, DANIEL3, DANIEL2, LAWRENCE1)* was born 1748 in Mendon, Massachusetts. She married JAMES BUXTON 1773.

More about ESTHER SOUTHWICK:
Date born 2: June 26, 1665, Salem, Massachusetts

Children of ESTHER SOUTHWICK and JAMES BUXTON are:
1. RUTH6 BUXTON, b. 1776; m. WHIPPLE MANN.
2. RUFUS BUXTON, b. September 15, 1778; m. JUDITH BUXTON, September 18, 1802.
3. HANNAH BUXTON, b. 1780; m. (1) JOSEPH ELLIOTT; m. (2) JOHN CRAMPTON.
4. CHARITY BUXTON, b. 1782; m. PELATHIA GOLDTHWAIT.
5. ELIZABETH BUXTON, b. 1784; m. ELLIS ALBEE.
6. OTIS BUXTON, b. 1786; m. SALOMA BUXTON.
7. DAVID BUXTON, b. 1788; m. PHILADELPHIA DARLING.

91. **GEORGE5 SOUTHWICK** *(JONATHAN4, DANIEL3, DANIEL2, LAWRENCE1)* was born February 08, 1753 in Smithfield, Rhode Island, and died October 12, 1825 in Collins, Erie County, NY {area now North Collins}. He married LYDIA SARGENT February 05, 1778, daughter of RICHARD SARGENT. She was born July 09, 1757 in Smithfield, Rhode Island, and died July 27, 1845 in Collins, Erie County, NY {area now North Collins}.

More about GEORGE SOUTHWICK:
Fact: 1810, brought family to area which would become North Collins

Children of GEORGE SOUTHWICK and LYDIA SARGENT are:
1. JOB6 SOUTHWICK, b. February 12, 1796, Queensbury, Washington County, NY; d. 1882; m. SOPHIA SMITH, December 07, 1815, Tubtown, Collins, Erie County, NY; d. before 1883.

More about JOB SOUTHWICK:
Fact 1: 1883, Lived in North-East corner of Brant, NY
Fact 2: From Buffalo followed lake to mouth of Cattaraugus Creek, then cut across reservation to Lawtons
Fact 3: took 28 days to arrive via ox cart
Fact 4: Was 15 years old when moved to Collins
Fact 5: March 1811, Came to Collins: area now known as North Collins

Fact 6: 1816, Alternate wedding year
Fact 7: 1826, Moved from North Collins to Brant, NY
Political 1: Highway Commissioner: town of Evans
Political 2: Supervisor: town of Brant

2. JONATHAN SOUTHWICK, b. August 15, 1786; d. February 23, 1852; m. MARTHA IRISH, September 1809; b. February 03, 1791; d. February 23, 1852.

More about JONATHAN SOUTHWICK:
Fact 1: March 1811, Came to Collins: area now known as North Collins
Fact 2: Farmer
Fact 3: Moved to Farmington, Ontario County, NY
Fact 4: Nurseryman

3. GRACE SOUTHWICK, d. Aurora, Erie County, NY; m. JOHN BRAGG.

More about GRACE SOUTHWICK:
Fact: oldest Female in family

4. GEORGE SOUTHWICK, b. September 1810, North Collins, Erie County, NY; d. February 23, 1852, Meadville, Pennsylvania; m. JANE BOWSON, August 1809.

More about GEORGE SOUTHWICK:
Fact 1: Settled first in Collins, NY
Fact 2: Moved from Collins to Meadville, PA
Fact 3: 1780, Alternate birth year
Fact 4: 1812, Came to Collins {area now known as North Collins}

More about JANE BOWSON:
Fact: Bowron alternate last name

5. ROYAL SOUTHWICK, b. 1782; d. April 03, 1857, Wales, Erie County, NY; m. CHRISTINA LANGDON, October 1809; d. 1872.

More about ROYAL SOUTHWICK:
Fact 1: Settled first in Collins, NY [now known as North Collins]
Fact 2: disowned by Quakers for marrying outside of religion
Fact 3: Moved from Collins to Wales, NY
Religion: Quaker

More about CHRISTINA LANGDON:
Fact: From Aurora, NY

6. LYDIA S SOUTHWICK, b. September 10, 1784; d. July 18, 1872, Iowa; m. HUGH MCMILLEN, January 1807; d. Bef. 1883, North Collins, Erie County, NY.

More about LYDIA S SOUTHWICK:
Fact: All descendants were in Southern California in 1940

More about HUGH MCMILLEN:
Fact: From Adolphtown, Upper Canada

7. JONATHAN SOUTHWICK, d. before 1883, North Collins, Erie County, NY; m. MARTHA IRISH; d. before 1883, North Collins, Erie County, NY.
8. ENOS SOUTHWICK, b. 1788; d. March 05, 1875, Gowanda, NY; m. (1) PAULINE BARKER; d. before 1883, Gowanda, NY; m. (2) PAULINE BARKER, July 10, 1810; d. Bef. 1883, Gowanda, NY.

More about ENOS SOUTHWICK:
Fact 1: Lived in Gowanda, NY
Fact 2: 1810, Lived in Collins [area now North Collins]
Religion: Quaker

More about PAULINE BARKER:
Fact 1: First name may be Pamelia
Fact 2: From Gowanda, NY

9. HANNAH SOUTHWICK, b. March 12, 1790; d. April 20, 1876, Illinois; m. LEVI WOODWARD, March 1812; b. 1788, Warren County, NY; d. 1876, 'Woodward Hollow', Concord, Erie County, NY.

More about HANNAH SOUTHWICK:
Fact: This would be the first wedding in North Collins

More about LEVI WOODWARD:
Fact 1: 1811, Came to Collins {area now known as North Collins}
Fact 2: 1849, Moved to area in town known as Woodward Hollow

10. PHEBE SOUTHWICK, b. February 20, 1798; d. December 29, 1878; m. SAMUEL SOUTHWICK, 1843; b. 1775.

More about PHEBE SOUTHWICK:
Fact: Settled in Western, NY

11. JANE SOUTHWICK, b. 1778; m. JOHN BRAGG, January 1804.

More about JOHN BRAGG:
Fact: From Glenn Falls, NY

92. **JACOB5 SOUTHWICK** *(JONATHAN4, DANIEL3, DANIEL2, LAWRENCE1)* was born June 04, 1751, and died August 19, 1833. He married SARAH FOWLER June 04, 1778. She was born October 20, 1753, and died July 28, 1829.

Children of JACOB SOUTHWICK and SARAH FOWLER are:
1. MARY ANN6 SOUTHWICK, b. July 30, 1779; d. 1869; m. SIMEON BUCKLAND.
2. DANIEL SOUTHWICK, b. December 10, 1780.

   More about DANIEL SOUTHWICK:
   Fact: Married

3. EZRA SOUTHWICK, b. April 14, 1782; d. 1854; m. JUDITH WHITE.
4. ESTHER SOUTHWICK, b. December 25, 1783; d. July 07, 1858; m. AMASA EDDY.
5. ISAAC SOUTHWICK, b. May 01, 1785; d. 1872; m. TABITHA ROBERTS.
6. JONATHAN SOUTHWICK, b. January 06, 1789.

   More about JONATHAN SOUTHWICK:
   Fact 1: Twin to David
   Fact 2: Went away and was never heard from again

7. DAVID SOUTHWICK, b. January 06, 1789; m. LUCRETIA LARKIN.

   More about DAVID SOUTHWICK:
   Fact: Twin to Jonathan

8. JONATHAN SOUTHWICK, b. June 19, 1786; d. November 08, 1788.
9. OLIVE SOUTHWICK, b. October 20, 1787; d. 1870; m. MARTIN DAVIS.
10. HANNAH SOUTHWICK, b. May 29, 1791; d. July 04, 1810.
11. SARAH SOUTHWICK, b. January 17, 1793; d. May 22, 1860; m. ZEBULON SPRAGUE, April 07, 1842.

    More about ZEBULON SPRAGUE:
    Fact: From Northbridge, MA

12. PHEBE SOUTHWICK, b. July 09, 1794; d. June 10, 1880; m. JOEL MARSH.

    More about PHEBE SOUTHWICK:
    Fact: No children

    More about JOEL MARSH:

Fact: From Northbridge, MA

13. LUCY SOUTHWICK, b. May 09, 1797.

93. **ENOCH5 SOUTHWICK** *(JONATHAN4, DANIEL3, DANIEL2, LAWRENCE1)* was born April 04, 1753. He married MARY SWETT 1778. She was born May 11, 1758.

    More about ENOCH SOUTHWICK:
    Fact: 1811, Moved from Vermont to Holland Purchase [area now known as Colden, NY]

Children of ENOCH SOUTHWICK and MARY SWETT are:
1. CYNTHIA6 SOUTHWICK, b. June 17, 1779; m. JOHN BOWLES.

   More about CYNTHIA SOUTHWICK:
   Fact: Settled in Richmond, Cheshire County, VT

2. NANCY SOUTHWICK, b. August 18, 1780; m. HOSEA EDDY.

   More about NANCY SOUTHWICK:
   Fact: No children

3. BETSEY SOUTHWICK, b. February 20, 1782; d. October 07, 1851; m. GEORGE HARKNESS, Richmond, Vermont.
4. ABIGAIL SOUTHWICK, b. March 02, 1784; m. UNKNOWN.

   More about ABIGAIL SOUTHWICK:
   Fact 1: No children
   Fact 2: Moved to Hamburg, NY

5. JESSE SOUTHWICK, b. September 14, 1785.

   More about JESSE SOUTHWICK:
   Fact 1: Married
   Fact 2: Settled in Colden, NY

6. STEPHEN SOUTHWICK, b. February 02, 1788.

   More about STEPHEN SOUTHWICK:
   Fact 1: Settled in Collins, NY
   Fact 2: Married
   Fact 3: No children

7. HANNAH SOUTHWICK, b. August 29, 1789; m. DAVID BEATTY.

   More about HANNAH SOUTHWICK:

Fact: Had 2 children

8. MARY SOUTHWICK, b. September 20, 1791; m. WILLIAM KESTER.
9. AMEY SOUTHWICK, b. July 26, 1793; d. December 08, 1793.
10. ELIZABETH SOUTHWICK, b. March 24, 1795.
11. ENOCH SOUTHWICK, b. March 12, 1797; m. MARY.

   More about ENOCH SOUTHWICK:
   Fact 1: Moved from Berlin, MA to Richmond, VT
   Fact 2: Moved from Richmond, VT to Erie County, NY

   More about HULDAH SOUTHWICK:
   Fact: Had 2 children

12. WATSON SOUTHWICK, b. 1801; d. 1819.

94. ZACHEUS5 SOUTHWICK *(JONATHAN4, DANIEL3, DANIEL2, LAWRENCE1)* was born September 04, 1760, and died June 04, 1845. He married LAVINIA SAYLES January 04, 1787, daughter of THOMAS SAYLES and MARY. She was born September 05, 1760.

Children of ZACHEUS SOUTHWICK and LAVINIA SAYLES are:
1. HANNAH6 SOUTHWICK, b. December 23, 1787.

   More about HANNAH SOUTHWICK:
   Fact: Unmarried

2. DANN SOUTHWICK, b. September 19, 1789; m. MARTHA CUTLER.

   More about DANN SOUTHWICK:
   Fact: Had no children

3. WILLIS SOUTHWICK, b. June 23, 1791; m. SYLVIA ALBEE, November 28, 1816.
4. JAMES SOUTHWICK, b. June 23, 1793; m. DESDEMONA COOK, May 24, 1812.

   More about JAMES SOUTHWICK:
   Fact: About May 1818, Moved from Uxbridge, MA to Salem, MA

5. EDITH SOUTHWICK, b. May 03, 1798.

   More about EDITH SOUTHWICK:
   Fact: unmarried

95. **JOSEPH5 OSBORN** *(JOSEPH4 OSBORNE, ELEANOR3 SOUTHWICK, DANIEL2, LAWRENCE1)* was born August 06, 1726 in Salem, Massachusetts, and died July 09, 1804. He married MARY PROCTOR January 06, 1756. She was born December 13, 1733, and died January 06, 1791.

> **More about MARY PROCTOR:**
> Fact: Descendant of John Proctor: Witchcraft Martyr

Children of JOSEPH OSBORN and MARY PROCTOR are:
1. JOSEPH6 OSBORN, b. January 05, 1757; d. August 27, 1829; m. (1) MARY SHILLABAR; m. (2) JUDITH FRANCIS.
2. SYLVESTER OSBORN, b. November 10, 1758; d. October 02, 1845; m. (1) SUSANNAH SOUTHWICK; m. (2) ELIZABETH POOLE; m. (3) L W SANDERS.

> **More about L W SANDERS:**
> Fact: L W Sanders was a widow at time of marriage to Sylvester

3. RACHEL OSBORN, b. January 31, 1761; d. December 27, 1813; m. JONATHAN HOWARD; b. August 10, 1783; d. March 22, 1826.
4. JONATHAN OSBORN, b. August 30, 1763; d. July 29, 1833; m. SUSANNAH SMITH.
5. JOHN OSBORN, b. November 03, 1765, Danvers, Massacchusetts; m. LYDIA SOUTHWICK, March 22, 1785; b. November 01, 1766; d. January 07, 1834.

> **More about JOHN OSBORN:**
> Fact: Area where born: Salem - before 1752; Danvers - 1855: S Danvers - 1868: now Peabody

> **More about LYDIA SOUTHWICK:**
> Fact: 1881, Lived in Peabody, MA

6. DANIEL OSBORN, b. September 10, 1768; d. February 11, 1826; m. MEHITABLE PROCTOR.
7. AMOS OSBORN, b. April 02, 1773; d. June 21, 1836; m. NANCY FOWLER.
8. MARY OSBORN, b. August 14, 1779.

Generation No. 6

96. JESSE6 SOUTHWICK *(JESSE5, JONATHAN4, SAMUEL3, JOHN2, LAWRENCE1)* was born 1758 in New Lebanon, Massachusetts, and died September 1826. He married NANCY MOORE about 1793.

Children of JESSE SOUTHWICK and NANCY MOORE are:
1. ORPHA7 SOUTHWICK, b. 1794, New York; d. April 1827; m. ABRAHAM PEASE, 1808.
2. . ELECTA SOUTHWICK, b. April 1796; d. August 1818.
3. EUNICE SOUTHWICK, b. 1798; d. October 1819; m. PATRICK LYNCH, 1818.
4. ADELINE SOUTHWICK, b. 1800; d. October 1845; m. FORTUNATUS BERRY, August 1818.

   More about FORTUNATUS BERRY:
   Fact 1: tanner
   Fact 2: Moved to Wisconsin

5. LUCINDA SOUTHWICK, b. 1801; d. July 1869; m. WILLIAM HAWS, October 1824; b. 1800.

   More about LUCINDA SOUTHWICK:
   Fact: Moved to Magnolia, Putnam County, Illinois

6. WILLIAM SOUTHWICK, b. February 09, 1805, New York; m. LOVICA PROCTOR, September 1833, Sangamon County, Illinois.
7. JAMES LAWRENCE SOUTHWICK, b. July 1812; d. February 1867; m. LOVICY TRUMBO, 1834; d. 1875.
8. PAULINE SOUTHWICK, b. 1814; d. June 1867; m. UNKNOWN FIELDS.

97. SAMUEL6 SOUTHWICK *(JESSE5, JONATHAN4, SAMUEL3, JOHN2, LAWRENCE1)* was born 1768. He married HANNAH.

Children of SAMUEL SOUTHWICK and HANNAH are:
1. LUCIUS7 SOUTHWICK.
2. ELVY SOUTHWICK.

98. DAVID6 SOUTHWICK *(JESSE5, JONATHAN4, SAMUEL3, JOHN2, LAWRENCE1)* was born 1770, and died June 1843. He married EUNICE DEMING 1801. She died 1836.

More about EUNICE DEMING:
Fact 1: From Pittsfield, MA
Fact 2: 1802, Alternate wedding year

Children of DAVID SOUTHWICK and EUNICE DEMING are:
1. JESSE7 SOUTHWICK, b. 1802; d. 1807, Fatal Injury.
2. DAVID SOUTHWICK, b. 1804; m. (1) AURELIA HYDE, April 1830; m. (2) CATHERINE COOPER, 1852.

   More about DAVID SOUTHWICK:
   Fact: Settled in Junius, Seneca County, NY

3. MARIA SOUTHWICK, b. 1806; d. 1861; m. DANIEL S KENDIG.

   More about DANIEL S KENDIG:
   Fact: From Waterloo, NY

4. ORIN SOUTHWICK, b. 1808; m. LAURA A HEWES.

   More about ORIN SOUTHWICK:
   Fact: Farmer
   Political 1: 1850, elected Assemblyman, NY
   Political 2: 9 Years Supervisor of Junius

   More about LAURA A HEWES:
   Fact: From Junius, NY

5. LARISSA SOUTHWICK, b. 1810; m. DR AMHERST CHILD.

   More about DR AMHERST CHILD:
   Fact 1: From Waterloo, NY
   Fact 2: physician

6. ADIN DEMING SOUTHWICK, b. 1813; m. (1) SUSAN HUNT; m. (2) MARGARET HUNT.

   More about ADIN DEMING SOUTHWICK:
   Fact: Lived in Junius, NY

99. **MARY6 SOUTHWICK** *(BENJAMIN JR5, BENJAMIN4, SAMUEL3, JOHN2, LAWRENCE1)* was born 1754. She married (1) JOHN HEMENWAY about 1783. She married (2) DR RETIRE TRASK about 1790 in New Salem, Massachusetts.

    More about MARY SOUTHWICK:
    Baptism: December 13, 1763, New Salem

Fact: Moved to Rochester, VT after 2nd marriage

Child of MARY SOUTHWICK and JOHN HEMENWAY is:
1. POLLY7 HEMENWAY, b. 1784; m. NATHANIEL BROWN.

    More about NATHANIEL BROWN:
    Fact: From Rochester, VT

Children of MARY SOUTHWICK and RETIRE TRASK are:
2. BENJAMIN7 TRASK, b. 1791; d. 1832.

    More about BENJAMIN TRASK:
    Fact 1: Married in Montreal, Canada
    Fact 2: had one child

3. JOHN TRASK, b. August 07, 1793; m. MARY WINSLOW, 1816.

    More about JOHN TRASK:
    Fact 1: had 13 children
    Fact 2: 5 children died in infancy

    More about MARY WINSLOW:
    Fact: From Barnard, VT

4. DR EZRA TRASK, b. July 1795; m. ABIGAIL GILBERT.

    More about DR EZRA TRASK:
    Fact 1: Physician
    Fact 2: had 4 children

    More about ABIGAIL GILBERT:
    Fact: From Sharon, VT

5. SOPHIA TRASK, b. 1797; m. AUSTIN MOOREHOUSE.

    More about SOPHIA TRASK:
    Fact: Had 8 children

100. RACHEAL6 SOUTHWICK *(BENJAMIN JR5, BENJAMIN4, SAMUEL3, JOHN2, LAWRENCE1)* was born July 1768, and died June 12, 1842. She married NATHANIEL RUST July 08, 1793. He was born July 08, 1773, and died October 10, 1843 in Rochester, Vermont.

   More about RACHEAL SOUTHWICK:
   Baptism: September 16, 1770, Congregational Church of New Salem, MA

Children of RACHEAL SOUTHWICK and NATHANIEL RUST are:
1. SALLY7 RUST, b. about 1796; d. 1856, Carthage, NY; m. SOLON WOOLEGE.
2. HORACE RUST, b. 1798, Rochester, Vermont; d. March 1879, Cambria, Wisconsin; m. ROXANNA MILLS.
3. ALMON RUST, b. 1800, Rochester, Vermont; d. 1872, Rochester, Vermont; m. SARAH MORSE.

More about ALMON RUST:
Fact: No children

4. ASA RUST, b. 1806, Rochester, Vermont; d. 1873, Dennison, Iowa; m. MINERVA SEGU.
5. HANNAH RUST, b. January 16, 1808; m. ORSON PERKINS.
6. GEHIAL RUST, b. 1810, Rochester, Vermont; d. Illinois.

More about GEHIAL RUST:
Fact 1: Married in Illinois
Fact 2: One child

101. **SIMEON6 SOUTHWICK** *(SIMEON5, BENJAMIN4, SAMUEL3, JOHN2, LAWRENCE1)* was born about 1763, and died May 1805. He married PATTIE NEWHALL 1793, daughter of THOMAS NEWHALL. She was born July 21, 1773.

Children of SIMEON SOUTHWICK and PATTIE NEWHALL are:
1. SIMEON7 SOUTHWICK, b. November 28, 1794; d. about 1805.

   More about SIMEON SOUTHWICK:
   Fact: Died at age 11

2. EBENEZER SOUTHWICK, b. 1796; d. March 02, 1805.
3. PATTY SOUTHWICK, b. April 20, 1798; d. about 1805.

   More about PATTY SOUTHWICK:
   Fact: Died at age 7

4. ANNA SOUTHWICK, b. August 08, 1800; d. about 1805.

   More about ANNA SOUTHWICK:
   Fact: Died at age 5

v. DANIEL H SOUTHWICK, b. February 20, 1802; d. about 1805.

   More about DANIEL SOUTHWICK:
   Fact: Died at age 3

5. DORCAS SOUTHWICK, b. November 06, 1804; d. about 1805.

> **More about DORCAS SOUTHWICK:**
> Fact: Died at age 9 months

102. **JONATHAN6 SOUTHWICK** *(SAMUEL5, DAVID4, SAMUEL3, JOHN2, LAWRENCE1)* was born August 22, 1772, and died August 18, 1863 in died at son Masa's Home in St Hilaire, Canada. He married (1) MARY BAKER. He married (2) SARAH BRANCH February 02, 1797, daughter of MASA BRANCH and THANKFUL. She died April 14, 1814.

> **More about MARY BAKER:**
> Fact: Mary was a widow when she married Jonathan

Child of JONATHAN SOUTHWICK and SARAH BRANCH is:
1. MASA BRANCH7 SOUTHWICK.

> **More about MASA BRANCH SOUTHWICK:**
> Fact: Moved to St Hilaire, Canada

103. **JOHN FLOOD6 SOUTHWICK** *(JOHN5, JOHN4, JOHN3, JOHN2, LAWRENCE1)* He married UNKNOWN.

> **More about JOHN FLOOD SOUTHWICK:**
> Baptism: June 05, 1768

Children of JOHN SOUTHWICK and UNKNOWN are:
1. JONATHAN SLADE7 SOUTHWICK.
2. ISRAEL SOUTHWICK.
3. JOHN SOUTHWICK.
4. ELLIS SOUTHWICK.

104. **STEPHEN6 SOUTHWICK** *(WILLIAM5, JOHN4, JOHN3, JOHN2, LAWRENCE1)* was born December 27, 1759. He married (1) PRUDENCE SOUTHWICK February 24, 1785, daughter of JOHN SOUTHWICK and ELIZABETH WILSON. She died before 1795. He married (2) HANNAH ROPES April 14, 1795.

> **More about PRUDENCE SOUTHWICK:**
> Baptism: May 25, 1766

> **More about HANNAH ROPES:**
> Fact: Widow when married Stephen

Children of STEPHEN SOUTHWICK and HANNAH ROPES are:

1. NANCY7 SOUTHWICK, b. April 13, 1797; m. UNKNOWN CHAPMAN.
2. DANIEL SOUTHWICK, b. March 11, 1800; m. ESTHER FOWLER.
3. MARY SOUTHWICK, b. June 16, 1802; m. SAMUEL GILMAN.
4. REBECCA SOUTHWICK, b. October 16, 1804; m. AMOS MANSFIELD.

More about AMOS MANSFIELD:
Fact: From Saugus

5. ELIPHALET SOUTHWICK, b. August 16, 1808; d. 1855; m. HANNAH.

More about HANNAH:
Fact: Hannah was a widow when she married Eliphalet

105. **WILLIAM6 SOUTHWICK** *(WILLIAM5, JOHN4, JOHN3, JOHN2, LAWRENCE1)* was born May 17, 1754, and died September 11, 1828. He married LUCY KILBURN February 04, 1778.

More about LUCY KILBURN:
Fact: From Rowley, MA

Children of WILLIAM SOUTHWICK and LUCY KILBURN are:
1. LUCY7 SOUTHWICK, b. October 17, 1778.
2. WILLIAM SOUTHWICK, b. November 03, 1780; d. December 30, 1787.
3. JEDEDIAH KILLBURN SOUTHWICK, b. June 06, 1783.
4. HANNAH PLATTS SOUTHWICK, b. July 20, 1785.
5. WILLIAM SOUTHWICK, b. July 30, 1787; d. January 15, 1825; m. BETSEY FOSTER, 1809.
6. SALLY SOUTHWICK, b. November 08, 1790; d. July 27, 1812.
7. JAMES CHAPMAN SOUTHWICK, b. November 20, 1793; d. November 14, 1841; m. ELIZA SOUTHWICK.
8. ELIPHALET SOUTHWICK, b. September 21, 1795; d. April 20, 1796.
9. ELIPHALET SOUTHWICK, b. May 04, 1797.

106. **JAMES6 SOUTHWICK** *(WILLIAM5, JOHN4, JOHN3, JOHN2, LAWRENCE1)* was born October 12, 1768. He married PERSIS PEABODY September 24, 1796.

Children of JAMES SOUTHWICK and PERSIS PEABODY are:
1. JAMES7 SOUTHWICK, b. May 30, 1797.
2. OLIVER SOUTHWICK, b. May 27, 1799.
3. FANNY SOUTHWICK, b. June 15, 1801.
4. CHARLES SOUTHWICK, b. July 14, 1803.
5. PERSIS SOUTHWICK, b. July 09, 1805.

6. SALLY SOUTHWICK, b. March 29, 1807.
7. JOHN SOUTHWICK, b. June 03, 1811.
8. TAMISON SOUTHWICK, b. March 30, 1813.

107. **HANNAH6 SOUTHWICK** *(JOSEPH5, JOHN4, JOHN3, JOHN2, LAWRENCE1)* was born November 16, 1756, and died May 17, 1806. She married ROBERT STONE May 08, 1782.

Children of HANNAH SOUTHWICK and ROBERT STONE are:
1. JOSEPH7 STONE, b. July 07, 1786.
2. ROBERT STONE, b. August 22, 1788.
3. WILLIAM STONE, b. April 01, 1790; d. December 29, 1835.
4. NATHANIEL HOLT STONE, b. October 31, 1793; d. February 02, 1838.
5. JONATHAN STONE, b. April 1797; d. May 1797.

108. **ELIZABETH6 SOUTHWICK** *(JOSEPH5, JOHN4, JOHN3, JOHN2, LAWRENCE1)* was born August 21, 1759, and died January 25, 1844. She married RICHARD SMITH June 07, 1785. He was born 1756, and died April 15, 1788.

Child of ELIZABETH SOUTHWICK and RICHARD SMITH is:
1. RICHARD7 SMITH, b. March 05, 1786.

109. **GEORGE JR6 SOUTHWICK** *(GEORGE5, JOHN4, JOHN3, JOHN2, LAWRENCE1)* He married BETSEY ASHTON.

   More about GEORGE JR SOUTHWICK:
   Baptism: November 09, 1761

Children of GEORGE SOUTHWICK and BETSEY ASHTON are:
1. JONATHAN STITCHELL7 SOUTHWICK, b. February 03, 1783.

   More about JONATHAN SOUTHWICK
   Fact: Died young

2. JOSEPH ASHTON SOUTHWICK, b. November 05, 1784; d. August 01, 1785.
3. GEORGE JR SOUTHWICK, b. July 14, 1786; m. KEZIAH PERKINS, June 22, 1808.

   More about KEZIAH PERKINS:
   Fact: Keziah was a widow when she married Joseph

4. JOSEPH A SOUTHWICK, b. December 24, 1788; m. KEZIAH PERKINS.

5. BETSEY SOUTHWICK, b. April 03, 1791; m. UNKNOWN PICKERING.
6. ABIGAIL SOUTHWICK, b. December 04, 1793; d. October 16, 1794.
7. MARY SMITH SOUTHWICK, b. September 15, 1796; m. UNKNOWN WILSON.

More about MARY SMITH SOUTHWICK:
Fact: No children

1. PLATTS SOUTHWICK, b. April 09, 1798; m. ELIZA TWISS, March 13, 1823; b. April 27, 1806.
2. ABIGAIL SOUTHWICK, b. 1801; m. CHARLES BRUCE, November 15, 1822.

110. **FRANCIS6 SOUTHWICK** (GEORGE5, JOHN4, JOHN3, JOHN2, LAWRENCE1) was born April 08, 1764. He married HANNAH MITCHELL February 1784. She was born 1767 in Lynnfield, Massachusetts.

More about FRANCIS SOUTHWICK:
Baptism: April 08, 1764

More about HANNAH MITCHELL:
Fact: widow when married Francis

Children of FRANCIS SOUTHWICK and HANNAH MITCHELL are:
1. REBECCA7 SOUTHWICK, b. December 25, 1786.
2. FRANCIS JR SOUTHWICK, b. November 03, 1788.

More about FRANCIS JR SOUTHWICK:
Fact: Went to Canada and was never heard from again.

3. JAMES SOUTHWICK, b. January 03, 1790; d. September 15, 1791.
4. HANNAH SOUTHWICK, b. September 13, 1792.
5. JAMES SOUTHWICK, b. April 03, 1795; m. ANN DOWNING.

More about JAMES SOUTHWICK:
Fact 1: Moved to Dover, NH
Fact 2: Had 3 children

6. ASA SOUTHWICK, b. 1797.

More about ASA SOUTHWICK:
Fact: Unmarried

111. MERCY6 SOUTHWICK *(GEORGE5, JOHN4, JOHN3, JOHN2, LAWRENCE1)* She married JOSEPH BROWN.

> **More about MERCY SOUTHWICK:**
> Baptism: March 19, 1769

Children of MERCY SOUTHWICK and JOSEPH BROWN are:
1. BETSEY7 BROWN.
2. JOHN BROWN.
3. DANIEL BROWN.
4. JOSEPH JR BROWN.
5. GEORGE BROWN.
6. SALLY BROWN.
7. REBECCA BROWN.
8. MERCY BROWN.

112. **NATHAN6 SOUTHWICK** *(GEORGE5, JOHN4, JOHN3, JOHN2, LAWRENCE1)* died July 20, 1836. He married MOLLY MOULTON February 11, 1795.

> **More about NATHAN SOUTHWICK:**
> Baptism: September 08, 1771

Children of NATHAN SOUTHWICK and MOLLY MOULTON are:
1. NANCY7 SOUTHWICK, b. June 07, 1797.
2. SARAH SOUTHWICK, b. March 24, 1799; d. May 09, 1825; m. JOHN ABORN.
3. LUCINDA SOUTHWICK, b. March 19, 1801; m. WILLIAM ABORN.

   More about LUCINDA SOUTHWICK:
   Fact: Had one child that died young

4. NATHAN JR SOUTHWICK, b. March 24, 1803; d. May 30, 1817.
5. JONATHAN S SOUTHWICK, b. May 10, 1805.
6. MARY SOUTHWICK, b. July 19, 1809.
7. EBEN MOULTON SOUTHWICK, b. July 29, 1811; m. ABIGAIL LOCKE.

   More about EBEN MOULTON SOUTHWICK:
   Fact: Had 3 children

8. GEORGE SOUTHWICK, b. May 17, 1813; m. ABIGAIL TAYLOR.
9. WILLIAM F SOUTHWICK, b. June 05, 1815; m. CLARISSA SWEETSTER, May 24, 1843.
10. ELIZABETH MOULTON SOUTHWICK, b. April 04, 1820; m. ALBION LAW.

More about ELIZABETH MOULTON SOUTHWICK:
Fact: No children

113. **REBECCA6 SOUTHWICK** *(GEORGE5, JOHN4, JOHN3, JOHN2, LAWRENCE1)* She married JAMES RADDIN.

> **More about REBECCA SOUTHWICK:**
> Baptism: March 13, 1774

Children of REBECCA SOUTHWICK and JAMES RADDIN are:
1. ALBERT7 RADDIN.
2. HENRIETTA RADDIN.

> **More about HENRIETTA RADDIN:**
> Fact: Twin to Marietta

1. MARIETTA RADDIN.

> **More about MARIETTA RADDIN:**
> Fact: Twin to Henrietta

114. **JOSEPH6 SOUTHWICK** *(BENJAMIN5, BENJAMIN4, JOHN3, JOHN2, LAWRENCE1)* was born 1738, and died March 23, 1813. He married HANNAH HUNT 1760.

> **More about JOSEPH SOUTHWICK:**
> Fact: Farmer

Children of JOSEPH SOUTHWICK and HANNAH HUNT are:
1. JOHN7 SOUTHWICK, b. 1761; d. December 11, 1833; m. (1) HANNAH CASS; m. (2) RHOENA TRASK; b. about 1784; d. 1868.
2. JACOB SOUTHWICK, b. 1763; d. March 03, 1842; m. SARAH DARLING.
3. PHILADELPHIA SOUTHWICK, b. 1765; m. NATHAN CASS.

> **More about PHILADELPHIA SOUTHWICK:**
> Fact: Moved west

4. KEZIAH SOUTHWICK, b. 1767; m. THADEUS PRENTISS, September 27, 1795.
5. SETH SOUTHWICK, b. January 27, 1768; d. October 16, 1835; m. (1) ALPHA WALDRON; m. (2) LUCINDA STAPLES, February 16, 1794.

> **More about LUCINDA STAPLES:**
> Fact: From Mendon, MA

6. HANNAH SOUTHWICK, b. March 20, 1770; d. February 23, 1835; m. SAMUEL HARKNESS, May 15, 1788.

More about SAMUEL HARKNESS:
Fact: From Blackstone, MA

7. MARION SOUTHWICK, b. 1772; d. September 14, 1790; m. SAMUEL PRENTISS.

More about SAMUEL PRENTISS:
Fact: From Mendon, MA

8. BENJAMIN SOUTHWICK, b. March 09, 1777; d. June 06, 1836; m. (1) AGNES SMITH; b. October 23, 1780; d. May 31, 1812; m. (2) LYDIA COATS; m. (3) UNKNOWN BATCHELLER; m. (4) ELIZA WILSON.

More about BENJAMIN SOUTHWICK:
Fact: No children

More about AGNES SMITH:
Fact: From Smithfield, RI

9. RHODA SOUTHWICK, b. May 24, 1780; d. May 25, 1848; m. AHAB SMITH, June 27, 1799.

More about AHAB SMITH:
Fact: From Smithfield, RI

115. **SOLOMON6 SOUTHWICK** *(JOSIAH5, JOSIAH4, JOSIAH JR.3, JOSIAH2, LAWRENCE1)* was born 1738. He married RACHEAL ZELLEY.

Children of SOLOMON SOUTHWICK and RACHEAL ZELLEY are:
1. HANNAH7 SOUTHWICK, b. 1774.
2. ELIZABETH SOUTHWICK, b. 1776.
3. JAMES SOUTHWICK, b. 1784; m. (1) SARAH MICK; m. (2) SARAH CARR.
4. DEBORAH SOUTHWICK, b. 1780.

116. **WILLIAM6 SOUTHWICK** *(JAMES5, JOSIAH4, JOSIAH JR.3, JOSIAH2, LAWRENCE1)* was born 1742. He married ELIZABETH ALLEN about 1772.

Children of WILLIAM SOUTHWICK and ELIZABETH ALLEN are:
1. MARY7 SOUTHWICK, b. November 01, 1773.
2. DOROTHY SOUTHWICK, b. February 17, 1776.
3. LYDIA SOUTHWICK, b. August 25, 1778; m. PHILIP HALZEL.
4. ABRAHAM SOUTHWICK.

More about ABRAHAM SOUTHWICK:
Fact: Died in infancy

5. RACHEAL SOUTHWICK, b. April 09, 1781; m. ELIJAH GASKILL.
6. ALLEN SOUTHWICK, b. September 10, 1783; m. BEULAH GRANT.
7. PRISCILLA SOUTHWICK, b. September 18, 1786; m. SAMUEL GOLDY.

More about PRISCILLA SOUTHWICK:
Fact 1: Had one child
Fact 2: Second wife of Samuel

8. SAMUEL SOUTHWICK, b. May 19, 1787; d. January 21, 1789.
9. WILLIAM SOUTHWICK, b. September 10, 1791; d. September 15, 1791.
10. JEMIMA SOUTHWICK, b. September 10, 1791; m. GERSHOM JOBES.

More about JEMIMA SOUTHWICK:
Fact: Twin to William

11. WILLIAM SOUTHWICK, b. September 14, 1794; m. ELIZA VANDERGRIFF.

117. **SILAS6 SOUTHWICK** *(JOHN5, JOSEPH4, SOLOMON3, JOSIAH2, LAWRENCE1)* was born 1780, and died October 03, 1864. He married HANNAH HEATH. She was born 1772, and died September 13, 1856.

More about HANNAH HEATH:
Fact: Hannah was a widow when she married Silas.

Children of SILAS SOUTHWICK and HANNAH HEATH are:

1. BENJAMIN7 SOUTHWICK, b. 1803; d. October 28, 1854; m. SARAH ANN MOORE.

More about BENJAMIN SOUTHWICK:
Fact: Moved west

2. JOHN SOUTHWICK, b. 1805; m. ELEANOR COOK, June 07, 1826.

More about ELEANOR COOK:
Fact: From Tiverton

3. MARY ANN SOUTHWICK, b. 1807; m. HENRY GLADDING, December 12, 1824.

More about HENRY GLADDING:
Fact: From Newport, RI

118. **JOSIAH6 SOUTHWICK** *(JOSEPH5, JOSEPH4, SOLOMON3, JOSIAH2, LAWRENCE1)* was born 1769. He married MARY CONGDON in Maine.

> **More about JOSIAH SOUTHWICK:**
> Fact: Moved to Maine

Children of JOSIAH SOUTHWICK and MARY CONGDON are:
1. SILENCE7 SOUTHWICK.

   > **More about SILENCE SOUTHWICK:**
   > Fact: Moved to NY

2. ELIZA SOUTHWICK.

   > **More about ELIZA SOUTHWICK:**
   > Fact: Moved to NY

119. **JOSEPH6 SOUTHWICK** *(JONATHAN5, JOSEPH4, SOLOMON3, JOSIAH2, LAWRENCE1)* was born December 18, 1782, and died December 25, 1861. He married SARAH HERSWELL. She was born 1788, and died June 03, 1818.

> **More about JOSEPH SOUTHWICK:**
> Military service 1: War of 1812
> Military service 2: He was with Com. Perry on Lake Erie

Children of JOSEPH SOUTHWICK and SARAH HERSWELL are:
1. CHARLES K7 SOUTHWICK, b. 1804; d. 1833; m. SARAH.
2. HENRY SOUTHWICK, b. 1806.
3. JOHN SOUTHWICK, b. 1808.
4. LYDIA A SOUTHWICK, b. 1815; d. 1833.
5. MARY JANE SOUTHWICK, d. March 19, 1842.

120. **STEPHEN6 SOUTHWICK** *(JOSIAH5, JOSEPH4, SOLOMON3, JOSIAH2, LAWRENCE1)* was born October 17, 1783, and died September 13, 1853. He married LYDIA BACKUS. She was born November 04, 1789, and died February 02, 1860.

> **More about LYDIA BACKUS:**
> Fact: Last name may be spelled Baccus

Children of STEPHEN SOUTHWICK and LYDIA BACKUS are:
1. REBECCA7 SOUTHWICK, b. 1809; m. ABRAHAM PECKMAN.

   > **More about ABRAHAM PECKMAN:**
   > Fact: From Middletown, RI

2. JOSIAH SOUTHWICK, b. 1812; d. 1875; m. (1) PHEBE PLACE; d. August 14, 1842; m. (2) MARY.

   More about MARY:
   Fact: Mary was a widow when she married Josiah.

3. ADELINE SOUTHWICK, b. July 28, 1817.
4. MATILDA SOUTHWICK, b. September 28, 1821; d. 1825.

121. HENRY COLLINS JR6 SOUTHWICK *(HENRY COLLINS5, SOLOMON4, SOLOMON3, JOSIAH2, LAWRENCE1)* was born December 28, 1806. He married MARY PARKINSON, daughter of JOHN PARKINSON and AGNES MCCALLISTER. She was born June 14, 1808, and died March 20, 1879.

   More about MARY PARKINSON:
   Fact: From Mayfield, Fulton County, NY

Children of HENRY SOUTHWICK and MARY PARKINSON are:
1. HENRY COLLINS JR7 SOUTHWICK, b. June 03, 1827, Albany, NY; m. MARGARET JULIA FRASER, April 08, 1850.

   More about MARGARET JULIA FRASER:
   Fact: From Albany, NY

2. JOHN TELFAIR SOUTHWICK, b. June 28, 1829, Albany, NY.

   More about JOHN TELFAIR SOUTHWICK:
   Fact 1: Unmarried
   Fact 2: Lived in Albany, NY

3. AGNES ANN SOUTHWICK, b. September 22, 1831, Albany, NY; m. FRANKLIN W MEECH, May 06, 1858.

   More about AGNES ANN SOUTHWICK:
   Fact: Moved to Rockford, Illinois

4. FRANCIS MCGUIGAN SOUTHWICK, b. September 28, 1833, Albany, NY; d. February 23, 1838.
5. EDWIN SOUTHWICK, b. January 17, 1836, Albany, NY; m. MARGARET RICKFORD, September 11, 1874.

   More about EDWIN SOUTHWICK:
   Fact: Moved to Council Bluff, Illinois

6. BENJAMIN WHITEHOUSE SOUTHWICK, b. August 07, 1838, Albany, NY; m. ROSE ANN HENSHAW, March 16, 1874.

   More about BENJAMIN WHITEHOUSE SOUTHWICK:
   Fact: Moved to NYC

7. JAMES MCALLISTER SOUTHWICK, b. September 05, 1841; d. April 05, 1862, Warwick Court House, Virginia.

   More about JAMES MCALLISTER SOUTHWICK:
   Fact: Unmarried
   Military service 1: Soldier - Civil War
   Military service 2: 93rd regiment NY State Volunteers
   Military service 3: Killed in Action
   Military service 4: Lieutenant

8. FRANK SOUTHWICK, b. April 11, 1844; d. Albany, NY.

   More about FRANK SOUTHWICK:
   Fact: Unmarried

9. MARY WOOL SOUTHWICK, b. July 15, 1846; m. WOLCOTT H PITKIN.

   More about MARY WOOL SOUTHWICK:
   Fact: Lived in Albany, NY

10. GEORGE COOK SOUTHWICK, b. May 24, 1850; d. November 09, 1853, Albany, NY.
11. JANE GILLISPE SOUTHWICK, b. July 20, 1852, Albany, NY; m. JOHN S HASTINGS, March 17, 1873.

    More about JANE GILLISPE SOUTHWICK:
    Fact: Lived in Brooklyn, NY

122. HENRY COLLINS6 SOUTHWICK *(SOLOMON5, SOLOMON4, SOLOMON3, JOSIAH2, LAWRENCE1)* was born July 05, 1808, and died January 30, 1866. He married JULIA CATHERINE BUEL, daughter of JESSE BUEL. She was born December 20, 1816.

   More about JULIA CATHERINE BUEL:
   Fact: From Albany, NY

Children of HENRY SOUTHWICK and JULIA BUEL are:
1. SUSAN BUEL7 SOUTHWICK, b. August 04, 1843; m. GEORGE CARY BRIGGS, November 10, 1865.
2. FRANCIS BARBER SOUTHWICK, b. August 03, 1845.
3. GILBERT DAVIDSON SOUTHWICK, b. July 04, 1847; d. January 27, 1852.

4. JULIA SOUTHWICK, b. February 08, 1851; d. February 02, 1852.
5. HOWARD SOUTHWICK, b. December 14, 1852.
6. ANN GARDNER SOUTHWICK, b. July 20, 1856.
7. ANNA PONSONBY SOUTHWICK, b. October 08, 1858.

123. SARAH SHERMAN6 SOUTHWICK *(WILMARTH5, SOLOMON4, SOLOMON3, JOSIAH2, LAWRENCE1)* was born April 12, 1812 in Plymouth, Massachusetts. She married WILLIAM GREENE FRY May 07, 1829 in Albany, New York. He was born in Albany, NY.

Children of SARAH SOUTHWICK and WILLIAM FRY are:
1. JOSEPH BOWLER7 FRY, b. March 27, 1830; m. MARY V B UTTER, April 27, 1852, Albany, new York.
2. ROBERT MAXWELL FRY, b. September 07, 1832; m. JULIA A, April 09, 1874, St Louis.

    More about JULIA A:
    Fact: Julia A was a widow when she married Robert.

3. MARY ANN FRY, b. January 10, 1835; m. CHARLES A EDWARDS, December 06, 1858, Albany, new York.
4. HELEN M FRY, b. September 30, 1837; m. JOHN E SIMMONS, May 17, 1860, Albany, new York.
5. SOLOMON SOUTHWICK FRY, b. June 03, 1841; d. October 22, 1844.
6. VIRGINIA FRY, b. January 10, 1844; d. January 14, 1846.

124. ELIZABETH6 SOUTHWICK *(EDWARD5, LAWRENCE4, LAWRENCE3, DANIEL2, LAWRENCE1)* was born 1790. She married MOSES CHILSON 1812 in Danby, Rutland County, Vermont, son of ISRAEL CHILSON and MARY SOUTHWICK. He was born 1792 in Hoosick, New York.

    More about ELIZABETH SOUTHWICK:
    Fact: June 26, 1806, Moved from Mendon, MA to Danby, VT

Children of ELIZABETH SOUTHWICK and MOSES CHILSON are:
1. EDWARD7 CHILSON.

    More about EDWARD CHILSON:
    Fact: 1880, Lived at Wallingford, VT

2. ANSON CHILSON, b. August 06, 1812, Danby, Rutland County, Vermont.
3. MARTIN CHILSON, b. March 1814.
4. SELA CHILSON, b. 1816; m. WALLACE C DANA.
5. INFANT CHILSON.

More about INFANT CHILSON:
Fact: Died in infancy

6. MARY CHILSON, b. June 21, 1819, Wallingford, Rutland County, Vermont; m. THOMAS DANA, December 29, 1817.
7. EMER CHILSON.
8. MARSHALL CHILSON.
9. EZRA CHILSON.
10. JUDSON CHILSON.

125. **HANNAH6 SOUTHWICK** *(EDWARD5, LAWRENCE4, LAWRENCE3, DANIEL2, LAWRENCE1)* was born October 03, 1773, and died September 16, 1862. She married (1) ANTHONY COMSTOCK 1787. He died 1808. She married (2) SAMUEL GASKILL 1843. He died 1847.

More about HANNAH SOUTHWICK:
Fact: Lived in Smithfield, RI when married to Comstock

Children of HANNAH SOUTHWICK and SAMUEL GASKILL are:
1. WILLIAM7 GASKILL, b. 1790.
2. PHEBE GASKILL, b. 1792.
3. . HANNAH GASKILL, b. 1794.
4. ANTHONY GASKILL, b. 1795; d. 1819, drowned.
5. MARTHA GASKILL, b. 1797.
6. EZRA GASKILL, b. 1799.
7. OLIVE GASKILL, b. 1800.
8. ELIZA GASKILL, b. 1802.

126. **DAVID6 SOUTHWICK** *(EDWARD5, LAWRENCE4, LAWRENCE3, DANIEL2, LAWRENCE1)* was born February 04, 1777 in Rhode Island, and died 1850. He married MARY SHERMAN March 01, 1804, daughter of SETH SHERMAN and MARY. She was born November 15, 1783.

More about DAVID SOUTHWICK:
Fact 1: Farmer
Fact 2: About 1805, Moved to Danby, Vermont
Religion: Quaker

Children of DAVID SOUTHWICK and MARY SHERMAN are:
1. ELIZA7 SOUTHWICK, b. October 15, 1804; d. 1869, Bolton, NY; m. FRANKLIN FRENCH.

More about ELIZA SOUTHWICK:
Fact: Lived at Mount Holly, Vermont

2. JUDITH SOUTHWICK, b. July 11, 1806; d. Chester, Vermont.
3. DAVID SHERMAN SOUTHWICK, b. December 07, 1807; d. June 03, 1853; m. (1) SUSAN M GARFIELD; m. (2) WIDOW MUDGE.
4. MARIA SOUTHWICK, b. September 09, 1810, Mount Holly, Vermont; d. November 1847, Fort Ann, NY; m. REV PELEG FULLER.
5. ABIGAIL SOUTHWICK, b. February 25, 1812; m. (1) ELIJAH D TARBELL; m. (2) ALPHEUS ATWOOD.

More about ABIGAIL SOUTHWICK:
Fact: Lived at Chester, VT

6. EDWARD SETH SOUTHWICK, b. October 03, 1814; m. LUCY R FULLER, August 31, 1847.

More about EDWARD SETH SOUTHWICK:
Fact 1: Lived at Rutland, VT
Fact 2: carpenter & joiner

7. ALBERT AUSTIN SOUTHWICK, b. October 29, 1816; d. June 17, 1874, Chester, NY; m. HANNAH FISH.
8. SYLVIA SOUTHWICK, b. November 18, 1819; d. September 23, 1845; m. REV HUBBARD CRANE, Andover, Vermont.
9. MARSHALL SILVESTER SOUTHWICK, b. November 26, 1822; m. CALISTER HATCH.
10. HANNAH L SOUTHWICK, b. May 08, 1825.

127. EZRA6 SOUTHWICK (EDWARD5, LAWRENCE4, LAWRENCE3, DANIEL2, LAWRENCE1) was born July 25, 1782, and died September 25, 1845 in Collins, Erie County, NY. He married DEBORAH SMITH.

More about EZRA SOUTHWICK:
Fact 1: June 26, 1806, Moved from Mendon, MA to Danby, VT
Fact 2: Farmer
Fact 3: Moved from Mount Holly to Danby Vermont
Fact 4: Shoemaker
Fact 5: Family traveled to Buffalo via the Erie Canal.

Children of EZRA SOUTHWICK and DEBORAH SMITH are:
1. ASA7 SOUTHWICK, b. November 22, 1807, Danby, Rutland County, Vermont; m. MARY HOPKINS.

More about ASA SOUTHWICK:
Fact: Moved to Rantoul, Illinois

2. ABRAHAM LAPHAM SOUTHWICK, b. August 04, 1809; m. UNKNOWN SMITH.

   More about ABRAHAM LAPHAM SOUTHWICK:
   Fact: Moved to Collins, NY

3. ALFRED SOUTHWICK, b. 1811; m. LYDIA FANCHER.

   More about ALFRED SOUTHWICK:
   Fact 1: No children
   Fact 2: Lived at Ellsworth, Kansas

4. HANNAH SOUTHWICK, b. 1813; m. ALFRED LAPHAM; d. about 1870, Champaign City, Illinois.
5. PHEBE SOUTHWICK, b. 1814, Mount Holly, Vermont; m. ELI RICE.

   More about PHEBE SOUTHWICK:
   Fact: Lived at Creston, Ogle County, Illinois

6. ELIZABETH SOUTHWICK, b. 1816, Danby, Rutland County, Vermont; d. 1854, Livonia, Wayne County, Michigan; m. DANIEL HALLECK.
7. JANE SOUTHWICK, b. 1817, Pawlet, Vermont; m. WILLARD TAYES.

   More about JANE SOUTHWICK:
   Fact: Lived on Bowen Avenue, Chicago, Illinois

8. LAURA B SOUTHWICK, b. 1825, Manchester, Vermont; d. about 1858, Livonia, Wayne County, Michigan; m. CHARLES BACKUS.

128. **EZRA6 SOUTHWICK** *(JOSEPH5, LAWRENCE4, LAWRENCE3, DANIEL2, LAWRENCE1)* was born February 22, 1780, and died April 19, 1847. He married (1) CHLOE TAFT. He married (2) SUSAN TAFT. He married (3) NANCY TURTLOTTE.

Children of EZRA SOUTHWICK and CHLOE TAFT are:
1. DUTY7 SOUTHWICK, b. November 01, 1803; d. 1803.
2. RUTH SOUTHWICK, b. July 28, 1805; d. May 31, 1865; m. JOHN E BAXTER.
3. FENNER SOUTHWICK, b. January 09, 1807.
4. SUSAN SOUTHWICK, b. February 10, 1810; d. July 22, 1843; m. SILAS COMSTOCK, May 01, 1842.
5. DUTY SOUTHWICK, b. 1812; m. SALLY PAINE, January 20, 1833.
6. JOHN C BAXTER SOUTHWICK, b. 1814; m. RUTH SOUTHWICK, September 09, 1836.

7. GEORGE E BAXTER SOUTHWICK, b. 1816; m. RUTH SMITH, May 12, 1840.

129. SARAH6 SOUTHWICK *(JOSEPH5, LAWRENCE4, LAWRENCE3, DANIEL2, LAWRENCE1)* was born July 02, 1781, and died January 01, 1867. She married GERSHOM KEITH. He was born 1783, and died October 1841.

Children of SARAH SOUTHWICK and GERSHOM KEITH are:
1. ELMIRA7 KEITH, b. August 09, 1804.

   More about ELMIRA KEITH:
   Fact: Died young

2. LYDIA KEITH, b. October 17, 1805; d. 1878; m. NAHUM MOWRY.
3. DUTY KEITH, b. April 03, 1808; m. PHEBE JEFFERSON.
4. GERSHOM KEITH, b. December 06, 1809; d. December 16, 1879; m. MARY ANN HOWARD, June 06, 1830.
5. LUKE S KEITH, b. February 28, 1812; d. July 24, 1879; m. LOUISA BALLOU.

   More about LOUISA BALLOU:
   Fact: From Burrillville, RI

6. SIMON KEITH, b. September 04, 1815; m. (1) ESTHER COOK; m. (2) SUSAN BALL.

   More about SUSAN BALL:
   Fact: From East Douglas

7. COLLINS KEITH, b. February 04, 1818; m. (1) LETTICE MCKAY; m. (2) HARRIET HOWARD; m. (3) PHEBE WHIPPLE; m. (4) MARY E MOORE.
8. SARAH E KEITH, b. July 31, 1821.

   More about SARAH E KEITH:
   Fact: Died young

9. MARY ELIZA KEITH, b. December 04, 1813; m. (1) EATHAM A ALBEE; m. (2) STEPHEN LOUGEE.

130. MOSES6 SOUTHWICK *(JOSEPH5, LAWRENCE4, LAWRENCE3, DANIEL2, LAWRENCE1)* was born May 06, 1783, and died October 04, 1828. He married SARAH PULSIFER December 08, 1804. She was born May 25, 1786 in Douglas, Massachusetts, and died August 19, 1859.

More about MOSES SOUTHWICK:

Fact 1: Farmer
Fact 2: Blacksmith
Fact 3: Millwright

Children of MOSES SOUTHWICK and SARAH PULSIFER are:

1. LUCY7 SOUTHWICK, b. July 07, 1805; d. July 16, 1852; m. LEONARD LOUGEE.
2. LOVELL PULSIFER SOUTHWICK, b. December 07, 1806; m. (1) PHOEBE LOUGEE, December 13, 1830; m. (2) LUCINDA THAYER, April 04, 1854.

   More about LOVELL PULSIFER SOUTHWICK:
   Fact 1: Millwright
   Fact 2: Carpenter

3. MARY SOUTHWICK, b. October 08, 1811; m. CHANDLER WALKER.
4. ELSIE SOUTHWICK, b. July 11, 1816; d. December 10, 1855; m. SMITH SHERMAN.
5. LUKE SOUTHWICK, b. December 02, 1823; m. SARAH THAYER.
6. MOSES B SOUTHWICK, b. December 07, 1827; m. PERSIS A THOMPSON.

131. **JOSEPH6 SOUTHWICK** *(JOSEPH5, LAWRENCE4, LAWRENCE3, DANIEL2, LAWRENCE1)* was born March 02, 1793, and died August 08, 1860. He married MIRANDA LAPHAM. She was born September 05, 1800, and died November 01, 1879.

Children of JOSEPH SOUTHWICK and MIRANDA LAPHAM are:

1. JULIA CHAPIN7 SOUTHWICK, b. October 06, 1823; d. February 06, 1869.

   More about JULIA CHAPIN SOUTHWICK:
   Fact: Unmarried

2. WILLIAM LAPHAM SOUTHWICK, b. May 17, 1827; d. February 02, 1867, Paralysis of the Brain; m. MARY E CLARK.

   More about WILLIAM LAPHAM SOUTHWICK:
   Fact: Lawyer

3. CHLOE SOUTHWICK.

   More about CHLOE SOUTHWICK:
   Fact: Died in infancy

4. SUSAN SOUTHWICK.

More about SUSAN SOUTHWICK:
Fact: Died in infancy

132. **ARNOLD6 SOUTHWICK** *(JOSEPH5, LAWRENCE4, LAWRENCE3, DANIEL2, LAWRENCE1)* was born February 14, 1798, and died November 15, 1869 in Paralysis of the Kidneys: Uxbridge, Massachusetts. He married PATIENCE LAPHAM March 08, 1827; daughter of WILLIAM LAPHAM and SUSAN BALLOU. She was born January 30, 1803 in Burrillville, Rhode Island.

More about ARNOLD SOUTHWICK:
Fact: Mechanic

Children of ARNOLD SOUTHWICK and PATIENCE LAPHAM are:
1. AMANDA JANE7 SOUTHWICK, b. April 08, 1828.

    More about AMANDA JANE SOUTHWICK:
    Fact: Lived at Millville, MA

2. CLOVIS LAPHAM SOUTHWICK, b. December 19, 1829; m. JULIA A HENETT, July 26, 1855.

    More about CLOVIS LAPHAM SOUTHWICK:
    Fact: Plater of scythes

3. ELIZABETH ALICE SOUTHWICK, b. July 24, 1833; d. March 11, 1834.
4. EMILY FRANK SOUTHWICK, b. May 09, 1840; d. April 28, 1877.

133. **AMASA6 SOUTHWICK** *(NATHANIEL5, LAWRENCE4, LAWRENCE3, DANIEL2, LAWRENCE1)* was born November 13, 1778, and died March 27, 1867. He married POLLY RICHARDSON. She was born November 29, 1780, and died December 21, 1868.

Children of AMASA SOUTHWICK and POLLY RICHARDSON are:
1. EDWARD7 SOUTHWICK, b. May 31, 1812; d. May 07, 1867; m. ANNA H EARL, June 03, 1847.

    More about ANNA H EARL:
    Fact: From Worcester, MA

2. ELIZABETH SOUTHWICK, b. January 27, 1814.

    More about ELIZABETH SOUTHWICK:
    Fact: Unmarried

3. THOMAS SOUTHWICK, b. April 28, 1816.
4. NATHAN SOUTHWICK, b. January 30, 1818.

134. ELISHA6 SOUTHWICK *(LAWRENCE5, DANIEL4, LAWRENCE3, DANIEL2, LAWRENCE1)* was born February 17, 1757, and died 1841. He married MARGARET MOSHER August 16, 1777. She was born August 16, 1758.

Children of ELISHA SOUTHWICK and MARGARET MOSHER are:
1. WAITY7 SOUTHWICK, b. February 14, 1778; m. MOSES GIBBINGS.
2. DANIEL SOUTHWICK, b. September 26, 1784; d. 1869; m. FRANCES PAINE, Troy, NY.
3. CYNTHIA SOUTHWICK, b. December 01, 1786; d. February 24, 1863.
4. SOPHRONIA SOUTHWICK, b. December 01, 1791.
5. PHEBE M SOUTHWICK, b. September 16, 1793; m. UNKNOWN HUSSEY, Union Springs, Cayuga County, NY.

135. RUTH6 SOUTHWICK *(LAWRENCE5, DANIEL4, LAWRENCE3, DANIEL2, LAWRENCE1)* was born March 04, 1763, and died March 17, 1851 in Grafton, Massachusetts. She married DAVID FARNUM December 02, 1781 in Uxbridge, Massachusetts. He was born September 29, 1753, and died February 29, 1844 in Grafton, Massachusetts.

More about DAVID FARNUM:
Fact: Farmer

Children of RUTH SOUTHWICK and DAVID FARNUM are:
1. HANNAH7 FARNUM, b. December 22, 1782; d. May 29, 1860; m. HUMPHREY TAYLOR, 1829.

   More about HANNAH FARNUM:
   Fact: Lived in Grafton, MA

2. DANIEL FARNUM, b. November 22, 1784; d. December 10, 1879, Grafton, Massachusetts.

136. EDWARD6 SOUTHWICK *(LAWRENCE5, DANIEL4, LAWRENCE3, DANIEL2, LAWRENCE1)* was born November 02, 1767, and died December 13, 1847. He married CATHERINE WILKINSON 1802. She was born July 25, 1772, and died February 13, 1813.

More about CATHERINE WILKINSON:
Fact: From Duchess County, NY

Children of EDWARD SOUTHWICK and CATHERINE WILKINSON are:
1. HANNAH7 SOUTHWICK, b. May 06, 1803; d. January 08, 1877; m. DR LESTER JEWETT, December 11, 1822; d. December 23, 1863.
2. JOHN W SOUTHWICK, b. March 15, 1805; d. 1813.

3. RUTH SOUTHWICK, b. April 09, 1806; d. August 10, 1874; m. WILLIAM TODD, October 01, 1840.

More about RUTH SOUTHWICK:
Fact: No children

4. ROBERT SOUTHWICK, b. March 04, 1808; d. March 08, 1808.
5. GILBERT W SOUTHWICK, b. July 26, 1810; m. CYNTHIA C GREELY.
6. EDWARD JR SOUTHWICK, b. August 10, 1812; d. November 26, 1857; m. LUCINDA SMITH, January 1846.

137. **JESSE6 SOUTHWICK** *(LAWRENCE5, DANIEL4, LAWRENCE3, DANIEL2, LAWRENCE1)* was born December 05, 1772, and died 1832. He married CHARLOTTE MARSH 1794 in Dorset, Vermont. She died 1856.

Children of JESSE SOUTHWICK and CHARLOTTE MARSH are:
1. CLARISSA7 SOUTHWICK, b. 1798; d. 1876.

More about CLARISSA SOUTHWICK:
Fact: Unmarried

2. MARIA SOUTHWICK, b. 1801; m. NORMAN JEWEL, 1827.
3. JOHNSON M SOUTHWICK, b. 1803; m. ANN CASTLE, 1830.
4. HANNAH SOUTHWICK, b. 1805; m. ELIAS J MERSHON, 1826.
5. HAMILTON SOUTHWICK, b. October 03, 1806; m. MARTHA SHERWOOD, January 1838, Monroe, Michigan.

More about HAMILTON SOUTHWICK:
Fact 1: Lived at Monroe, Michigan
Fact 2: Lived at Danville, NY
Fact 3: Lived at Rochester, NY

6. BENJAMIN SOUTHWICK, b. October 03, 1806; m. ELIZA RIGGS, 1836.
7. DORCAS SOUTHWICK, b. 1810; d. 1856; m. THERON TAYTON, 1828.
8. GEORGE W SOUTHWICK, b. 1812; d. 1870; m. UNKNOWN BOUTWELL, 1844.
9. JANE ANN SOUTHWICK, b. 1818; d. 1844; m. WILLIAM 2ND STUDDIFORD, 1839.
10. WILLIAM H SOUTHWICK, b. 1820; m. MARY FROST, 1845.

138. **CHADE6 SOUTHWICK** *(LAWRENCE5, DANIEL4, LAWRENCE3, DANIEL2, LAWRENCE1)* was born October 01, 1774, and died March 16, 1841 in Palmyra, Wayne County, NY. He married (1) CHLOE GIDDINS. She was born August 02, 1773, and died August 04, 1823 in Walcott, Wayne County, NY. He married (2) MARGARET JENNINGS.

More about CHADE SOUTHWICK:
Fact: Tanner & Currier at Union Springs, NY

Children of CHADE SOUTHWICK and CHLOE GIDDINS are:
1. HANNAH7 SOUTHWICK, b. August 12, 1798; d. April 24, 1816, Ottumwa, Wisconsin.
2. ELIZA SOUTHWICK, b. October 21, 1800.
3. JAMES SOUTHWICK, b. September 13, 1802; d. July 28, 1803, Manchester, Vermont.
4. WILLIAM HENRY SOUTHWICK, b. February 10, 1815, Manchester, Vermont; d. February 06, 1879; m. HENRIETTA A CHAPMAN, June 23, 1840.

More about WILLIAM HENRY SOUTHWICK:
Fact: Lived at Palmyra, Wayne County, NY

139. **THOMAS MUSSEY6 SOUTHWICK** *(GEORGE5, DANIEL4, LAWRENCE3, DANIEL2, LAWRENCE1)* was born March 17, 1778 in Uxbridge, Massachusetts. He married MATILDA CAREY.

Children of THOMAS SOUTHWICK and MATILDA CAREY are:
1. GEORGE WILLIAM7 SOUTHWICK, m. UNKNOWN QUAKENBOS.

More about UNKNOWN QUAKENBOS:
Fact: From New York

2. JULIA SOUTHWICK, m. UNKNOWN PRIOR.

140. **DANIEL6 SOUTHWICK** *(GEORGE5, DANIEL4, LAWRENCE3, DANIEL2, LAWRENCE1)* was born May 28, 1780 in Uxbridge, Massachusetts, and died June 13, 1817. He married LUCINA THAYER 1803.

Child of DANIEL SOUTHWICK and LUCINA THAYER is:
1. BENJAMIN T7 SOUTHWICK, b. October 1804; m. MARY ANN WILBUR, December 1825.

141. **RUTH6 SOUTHWICK** *(GEORGE5, DANIEL4, LAWRENCE3, DANIEL2, LAWRENCE1)* was born November 28, 1782 in Uxbridge, Massachusetts, and died November 29, 1861. She married ASAHAL ALDRICH February 08, 1817.

Children of RUTH SOUTHWICK and ASAHAL ALDRICH are:

1. CYNTHIA M7 ALDRICH, b. November 28, 1818, Uxbridge, Massachusetts.

   More about CYNTHIA M ALDRICH:
   Fact: Unmarried

2. DANIEL WHEELOCK ALDRICH, b. August 28, 1822, Uxbridge, Massachusetts; m. SUSAN THAYER.

   More about DANIEL WHEELOCK ALDRICH:
   Fact: No children

3. WILLIAM WILLIS ALDRICH, b. December 18, 1825, Uxbridge, Massachusetts; d. August 09, 1828.

142. **ELIZABETH6 SOUTHWICK** *(GEORGE5, DANIEL4, LAWRENCE3, DANIEL2, LAWRENCE1)* was born October 02, 1785 in Uxbridge, Massachusetts, and died October 24, 1872. She married NATHANIEL DAY. He was born October 09, 1783 in Uxbridge, Massachusetts, and died May 1860.

   More about NATHANIEL DAY:
   Fact: From Uxbridge, MA

Children of ELIZABETH SOUTHWICK and NATHANIEL DAY are:
1. RUTH E7 DAY, b. October 09, 1814; m. C SHAW.
2. DAVID L DAY, b. January 29, 1822.

143. **GEORGE6 SOUTHWICK** *(GEORGE5, DANIEL4, LAWRENCE3, DANIEL2, LAWRENCE1)* was born January 11, 1789 in Uxbridge, Massachusetts. He married BETSEY CHILSON 1820.

Children of GEORGE SOUTHWICK and BETSEY CHILSON are:
1. SARAH N7 SOUTHWICK, b. July 20, 1824; m. THOMAS ALDRICH, August 15, 1841.
2. GEORGE W SOUTHWICK, b. May 13, 1826.
3. JAMES LAWRENCE SOUTHWICK, b. 1828.

   More about JAMES LAWRENCE SOUTHWICK:
   Fact: Lived in Philadelphia, PA

4. ELOISA SOUTHWICK, b. September 21, 1830; m. HIRAM WHITNEY, October 18, 1851.

   More about ELOISA SOUTHWICK:
   Fact 1: Lived in Bellingham, MA

Fact 2: No children

144. **JUDITH6 SOUTHWICK** *(GEORGE5, DANIEL4, LAWRENCE3, DANIEL2, LAWRENCE1)* was born July 21, 1791 in Uxbridge, Massachusetts. She married OTIS ALDRICH.

Child of JUDITH SOUTHWICK and OTIS ALDRICH is:
1. GEORGE SOUTHWICK7 ALDRICH.

145. **LYDIA6 SOUTHWICK** *(GEORGE5, DANIEL4, LAWRENCE3, DANIEL2, LAWRENCE1)* was born January 01, 1800 in Uxbridge, Massachusetts, and died November 30, 1828 in Lee, NY. She married DANIEL MORSE December 1822.

Children of LYDIA SOUTHWICK and DANIEL MORSE are:
1. HARRIET ELIZABETH7 MORSE, b. January 05, 1824; d. July 31, 1871; m. EDWIN JENKS.
2. LYDIA ANN MORSE, b. February 19, 1828; d. January 13, 1829.

146. **NATHAN6 SOUTHWICK** *(JONATHAN5, JONATHAN4, DANIEL3, DANIEL2, LAWRENCE1)* was born 1760, and died March 11, 1806. He married HANNAH MCWATERS.

More about NATHAN SOUTHWICK:
Fact: Brick mason

Children of NATHAN SOUTHWICK and HANNAH MCWATERS are:
1. HOSEA7 SOUTHWICK, b. October 04, 1798; d. March 02, 1876; m. ANNA HATCH, February 06, 1817.
2. DEWEY SOUTHWICK, b. December 12, 1799; m. DORCAS BIGALOW, 1822.
3. JOHN WESLEY SOUTHWICK, b. 1802; m. (1) HULDAH WELLS; m. (2) ESTHER CHAPMAN, January 08, 1823.
4. JOHN HANNAH SOUTHWICK, b. 1802; d. 1865.

   More about JOHN HANNAH SOUTHWICK:
   Fact: Twin to John Wesley

5. AMANDA SOUTHWICK, b. May 04, 1804, Whitehall, Washington County, NY; d. July 29, 1850.
6. NATHAN SOUTHWICK, b. May 22, 1806; d. March 29, 1866; m. SUSAN GUY, April 1828.

   More about NATHAN SOUTHWICK:
   Fact 1: bricklayer

Fact 2: Moved from RI to Hoosick Falls, then Whitehall, NY

147. **ROYAL6 SOUTHWICK** *(LAWRENCE5, DANIEL4, LAWRENCE3, DANIEL2, LAWRENCE1)* was born December 06, 1760. He married PHEBE FARNUM.

Generation No 7

148. PHEBE7 SOUTHWICK *(JOB6, GEORGE5, JONATHAN4, DANIEL3, DANIEL2, LAWRENCE1)* was born 1817. She married WALTER KIMBALL.

> **More about PHEBE SOUTHWICK:**
> Fact: 1883, Lived in Brant, NY
>
> **More about WALTER KIMBALL:**
> Fact: From Brant, NY

Child of PHEBE SOUTHWICK and WALTER KIMBALL is:
    1. UNKNOWN8 KIMBALL.

149. PRISCILLA7 SOUTHWICK *(JOB6, GEORGE5, JONATHAN4, DANIEL3, DANIEL2, LAWRENCE1)* was born 1825, and died 1855. She married THOMAS BRUNELL.

Child of PRISCILLA SOUTHWICK and THOMAS BRUNELL is:
    1. ALICE8 BRUNELL.

150. JOSIAH H7 SOUTHWICK *(JOB6, GEORGE5, JONATHAN4, DANIEL3, DANIEL2, LAWRENCE1)* was born 1828. He married HULDAH ANN HAWLEY.

> **More about JOSIAH H SOUTHWICK:**
> Fact: 1883, Lived in Evans, NY

Child of JOSIAH SOUTHWICK and HULDAH HAWLEY is:
    1. LILLIAN8 SOUTHWICK.

151. SOPHIA7 SOUTHWICK *(JOB6, GEORGE5, JONATHAN4, DANIEL3, DANIEL2, LAWRENCE1)* was born 1835. She married STEPHEN LANDON.

> **More about STEPHEN LANDON:**
> Fact: From Evans, NY

Child of SOPHIA SOUTHWICK and STEPHEN LANDON is:
    1. HARMON S8 LANDON.

152. JOB JR.7 SOUTHWICK *(JOB6, GEORGE5, JONATHAN4, DANIEL3, DANIEL2, LAWRENCE1)* was born 1837. He married PHEBE A SMITH.

> **More about JOB JR. SOUTHWICK:**

Education: Westfield Academy
Fact: 1883, Lived in Brant, NY
Political 1: Deputy Clerk under Remington
Political 2: 1881, Elected 5th District Assemblyman

Children of JOB SOUTHWICK and PHEBE SMITH are:
1. GRACE8 SOUTHWICK, b. November 1863; m. HARRISON PARKER.

More about GRACE SOUTHWICK:
Fact: 1941, Lived in North Collins, NY

2. GEORGIANNA SOUTHWICK, b. June 1867; d. before 1941.
3. LYNN SOUTHWICK, b. October 1875; m. EMMA CREGOR.

More about LYNN SOUTHWICK:
Fact: 1941, Operator of Erie Railroad at Blasdell, NY

153. **PHOEBE7 MCMILLEN** *(LYDIA S6 SOUTHWICK, GEORGE5, JONATHAN4, DANIEL3, DANIEL2, LAWRENCE1)* died 1883. She married DANIEL ALLEN 1853. He was born 1820, and died 1885.

More about PHOEBE MCMILLEN:
Fact: Youngest daughter

More about DANIEL ALLEN:
Fact 1: Worked in Whaling Industry from New Bedford, MA
Fact 2: Moved from California to Collins {are now known as North Collins}
Fact 3: Wounds received in Battle of Fair Oaks crippled him for life
Fact 4: 1849, Crossed country to California
Military service 1: Soldier - Civil War
Military service 2: 64th NY Volunteers
Military service 3: Participated in Battle of Fait Oaks where he was wounded 3 times
Military service 4: WIA {Wounded in Action}
Political 1: Bet. 1865 - 1870, Supervisor North Collins, NY
Political 2: Bet. 1872 - 1881, North Collins Superintendent of the Poor

Children of PHOEBE MCMILLEN and DANIEL ALLEN are:
1. DANIEL WILLIAMS8 ALLEN, b. March 09, 1856, North Collins, Erie County, NY.
2. IDA ALLEN, b. 1854; m. M J BUNDY.

More about IDA ALLEN:
Fact: 1906, Lived in Angela[?]

154. **CLARINDA7 SOUTHWICK** *(ENOS6, GEORGE5, JONATHAN4, DANIEL3, DANIEL2, LAWRENCE1)* She married THOMAS S HIBBARD. He died 1881 in North Collins, Erie County, NY.

Child of CLARINDA SOUTHWICK and THOMAS HIBBARD is:
1. ENOS S8 HIBBARD, b. April 24, 1841, Collins, Erie County, NY.

155. **ISAAC7 WOODWARD** *(HANNAH6 SOUTHWICK, GEORGE5, JONATHAN4, DANIEL3, DANIEL2, LAWRENCE1)* was born September 19, 1816 in Collins, Erie County, NY {area now North Collins}. He married EMELINE MOREHOUSE 1840. She was born 1820 in Warren County, NY.

> **More about ISAAC WOODWARD:**
> Fact: 1842, Moved to Woodward Hollow
> Political 1: 1842, Appointed Postmaster at Woodward Hollow under Franklin Pierce
> Political 2: 2 Terms Justice of the Peace
> Political 3: Concord Town Assessor

Children of ISAAC WOODWARD and EMELINE MOREHOUSE are:
1. WILLIAM8 WOODWARD.

> **More about WILLIAM WOODWARD:**
> Fact: 1883, Lived in Dakota Territory
> Military service: Soldier - Civil War

2. JENNIE M WOODWARD.
3. FRED WOODWARD.

> **More about FRED WOODWARD:**
> Military service: Soldier - Civil War

4. WARNER WOODWARD.

> **More about WARNER WOODWARD:**
> Military service: Soldier - Civil War

5. PHILO WOODWARD.

> **More about PHILO WOODWARD:**
> Military service: Soldier - Civil War

6. JOSIAH WOODWARD.

> **More about JOSIAH WOODWARD:**
> Military service: Soldier - Civil War

7. MELISSA M WOODWARD.
8. HENRY FATHY WOODWARD.

> **More about HENRY FATHY WOODWARD:**

Military service: Soldier - Civil War

9. FLORENCE M FOREST MATTHEWS WOODWARD.

More about FLORENCE M FOREST MATTHEWS WOODWARD:
Fact: 1883, Lived in Collins

156. **TRUMAN7 SMITH** *(SYLVIA6 SOUTHWICK, ISSAC5, LAWRENCE4, LAWRENCE3, DANIEL2, LAWRENCE1)* was born 1825. He married (1) LYDIA COMSTOCK. He married (2) MARY BACHUS. She died before 1869 in Minnesota.

More about TRUMAN SMITH:
Fact 1: Moved to St Paul, Minnesota
Fact 2: Member of Minnesota Agriculture & Horticultural Societies

Child of TRUMAN SMITH and MARY BACHUS is:
1. MARY8 SMITH.

Generation No. 8

157. UNKNOWN8 KIMBALL *(PHEBE7 SOUTHWICK, JOB6, GEORGE5, JONATHAN4, DANIEL3, DANIEL2, LAWRENCE1)* She married ULRICH BAKER.

Children of UNKNOWN KIMBALL and ULRICH BAKER are:
PHOEBE9 BAKER, m. CHARLES TANNER.

More about PHOEBE BAKER:
Fact: 1941, Lived on Mile Block Road in North Collins

MAMIE BAKER.
WALTER BAKER, d. before 1941; m. JESSIE.

More about JESSIE:
Fact: 1941, Lived in North Collins, NY

158. ALICE8 BRUNELL *(PRISCILLA7 SOUTHWICK, JOB6, GEORGE5, JONATHAN4, DANIEL3, DANIEL2, LAWRENCE1)* She married HERMAN WIGHTMAN.

More about HERMAN WIGHTMAN:
Fact: Twin to Heman

Children of ALICE BRUNELL and HERMAN WIGHTMAN are:
LAVERNE9 WIGHTMAN, m. MARY BELLE RANSOM.

More about LAVERNE WIGHTMAN:
Fact: 1941, well known businessman in Lawtons, NY

ORSON WIGHTMAN.

159. HARMON S8 LANDON *(SOPHIA7 SOUTHWICK, JOB6, GEORGE5, JONATHAN4, DANIEL3, DANIEL2, LAWRENCE1)* He married EMMA HUSON.

Children of HARMON LANDON and EMMA HUSON are:
1. WETSON9 LANDON.

More about WETSON LANDON:
Fact: 1941, Editor of Angola Record

2. ROSE LANDON, m. REV REXFORD RAYMOND.

160. **GEORGIANNA8 SOUTHWICK** *(JOB JR.7, JOB6, GEORGE5, JONATHAN4, DANIEL3, DANIEL2, LAWRENCE1)* was born June 1867, and died before 1941. She married GEORGE H BURGOTT. He died before 1941.

Children of GEORGIANNA SOUTHWICK and GEORGE BURGOTT are:
1. BLANCHE9 BURGOTT, d. January 1918.
2. LAWRENCE BURGOTT, m. MADGE BRAUN.

More about LAWRENCE BURGOTT:
Fact: 1941, Station Agent for Erie Railroad at Newark, NJ

161. **DANIEL WILLIAMS8 ALLEN** *(PHOEBE7 MCMILLEN, LYDIA S6 SOUTHWICK, GEORGE5, JONATHAN4, DANIEL3, DANIEL2, LAWRENCE1)* was born March 09, 1856 in North Collins, Erie County, NY. He married ANNA M MOORE July 10, 1879, daughter of GEORGE MOORE and CATHERINE BROWN.

More about DANIEL WILLIAMS ALLEN:
Education 1: North Collins District Schools
Education 2: Conneaut, Ohio High School
Education 3: Griffith Institute, Springville, NY
Education 4: Hamburg, NY High School
Education 5: 1877, Graduated Medical Department University of Buffalo, NY
Education 6: 1879, Graduated Albany Law School
Fact 1: Bet. 1877 - 1878, Principal Hamburg High School
Fact 2: Member of: Masonic Lodge Fraternal Lodge #625 Hamburg, NY
Fact 3: Member of: Society of Natural Sciences
Fact 4: responsible for inauguration of Hamburg Railway
Fact 5: Specialized in Real Estate & Corporation Law
Fact 6: Bet. 1877 - 1885, engaged in oil business
Fact 7: 1879, Opened law practice in Buffalo, NY
Fact 8: 1895, Undertook building of Hamburg Railway
Fact 9: 1896, Completed Hamburg Railway
Religion: Universalist Church of the Messiah

Children of DANIEL ALLEN and ANNA MOORE are:
1. CARRIE LOUISA9 ALLEN.

    More about CARRIE LOUISA ALLEN:
    Fact: Teacher of Science: Wellesley

2. ANNA ALLEN.

    More about ANNA ALLEN:
    Fact: 1906, Student at Cornell

3. ARTHUR A ALLEN.

    More about ARTHUR A ALLEN:

Fact: 1906, Student at Cornell

4. CATHERINE ALLEN.

   More about CATHERINE ALLEN:
   Fact: 1906, Student at Cornell

5. WILLIAM D ALLEN.

More about WILLIAM D ALLEN:
Education: 1906, Graduated Cornell University
Fact: Engineer

6. HOWARD ALLEN.

   More about HOWARD ALLEN:
   Fact: 1906, Student at Lafayette High School

162. **ENOS S8 HIBBARD** (CLARINDA7 SOUTHWICK, ENOS6, GEORGE5, JONATHAN4, DANIEL3, DANIEL2, LAWRENCE1) was born April 24, 1841 in Collins, Erie County, NY. He married H JOSEPHINE HALL 1867. She was born August 14, 1846.

   More about ENOS S HIBBARD:
   Fact: Area of birth now North Collins, NY
   Military service 1: September 24, 1861, enlisted: Co D, 10th NY Cavalry
   Military service 2: Commissary Sergeant of his Company
   Military service 3: Participated in battles: Final Surrender: Appomattox Court House
   Military service 4: Participated in battles: Gettysburg, Sheridan's Raid, Upperville & Cold Harbor,
   Military service 5: Participated in battles: Spotsylvania Court House, Mine explosion at Petersburg
   Military service 6: Participated in battles: Travillion Station, Lees Mills, Boynton Plank Road
   Military service 7: Soldier - Civil War
   Military service 8: June 09, 1863, First Battle took part in: Brandy's Station
   Military service 9: July 01, 1865, mustered Out: Washington DC
   Political 1: republican
   Political 2: Secretary of Republican Committee

   More about H JOSEPHINE HALL:
   Fact: From Rochester, NY

Children of ENOS HIBBARD and H HALL are:
   1. HOYT R9 HIBBARD, b. March 30, 1871, North Collins, Erie County, NY.
   2. HOWARD G HIBBARD, b. March 19, 1873, North Collins, Erie County, NY.

3. IRENE HIBBARD, b. April 04, 1875, North Collins, Erie County, NY.
4. CLARINDA HIBBARD, b. July 03, 1876, North Collins, Erie County, NY.
5. FRED L HIBBARD, b. October 21, 1878, North Collins, Erie County, NY.
6. EDGAR H HIBBARD, b. September 11, 1880, North Collins, Erie County, NY.

163. **LILLIAN8 SOUTHWICK** *(JOSIAH H7, JOB6, GEORGE5, JONATHAN4, DANIEL3, DANIEL2, LAWRENCE1)* She married HERBERT I BURNHAM, son of UNKNOWN BURNHAM and UNKNOWN TUCKER.

Children of LILLIAN SOUTHWICK and HERBERT BURNHAM are:
1. HARRY9 BURNHAM.
2. WALLACE BURNHAM.

   More about WALLACE BURNHAM:
   Fact: 1941, Lived on farm near Rochester, NY

3. GERTRUDE BURNHAM, d. before 1941.
4. LAWRENCE BURNHAM, d. about 1937, Automobile Accident.

Generation No. 9

164. MAMIE9 BAKER *(UNKNOWN8 KIMBALL, PHEBE7 SOUTHWICK, JOB6, GEORGE5, JONATHAN4, DANIEL3, DANIEL2, LAWRENCE1)* She married WILBER TANNER. He died about 1939.

Children of MAMIE BAKER and WILBER TANNER are:
    1. BERNICE10 TANNER, m. MORRIS HORTON.

       More about BERNICE TANNER:
       Fact: 1941, Lived in Eden, NY

    2. BEATRICE TANNER, m. HARMON TAYLOR.

       More about BEATRICE TANNER:
       Fact: 1941, Lived in Lawtons, NY

    3. WILMA TANNER.
    4. BLANCHE TANNER, d. about 1938; m. WILSON CRENNELL.

165. ORSON9 WIGHTMAN *(ALICE8 BRUNELL, PRISCILLA7 SOUTHWICK, JOB6, GEORGE5, JONATHAN4, DANIEL3, DANIEL2, LAWRENCE1)*

Child of ORSON WIGHTMAN is:
    WALTER10 WIGHTMAN.

       More about WALTER WIGHTMAN:
       Fact: 1941, North Collins Banker

166. HARRY9 BURNHAM *(LILLIAN8 SOUTHWICK, JOSIAH H7, JOB6, GEORGE5, JONATHAN4, DANIEL3, DANIEL2, LAWRENCE1)* He married ALICE TAFT.

Children of HARRY BURNHAM and ALICE TAFT are:
    1. LILLIAN10 BURNHAM.
    2. REXFORD BURNHAM.

167. GERTRUDE9 BURNHAM *(LILLIAN8 SOUTHWICK, JOSIAH H7, JOB6, GEORGE5, JONATHAN4, DANIEL3, DANIEL2, LAWRENCE1)* died before 1941. She married MARTIN TAFT.

    More about MARTIN TAFT:
    Fact: 1941, Lived on Milestrip Road, Brant

Children of GERTRUDE BURNHAM and MARTIN TAFT are:
1. LEROY10 TAFT.
2. VERN TAFT.

168. **LAWRENCE9 BURNHAM** *(LILLIAN8 SOUTHWICK, JOSIAH H7, JOB6, GEORGE5, JONATHAN4, DANIEL3, DANIEL2,LAWRENCE1)* died about 1937 in Automobile Accident. He married UNKNOWN.

Children of LAWRENCE BURNHAM and UNKNOWN are:
1. DOROTHY10 BURNHAM.
2. LUCILLE BURNHAM.

Descendants of Benjamin Albee

Descendants of Benjamin Albee

Generation No. 1

1. BENJAMIN1 ALBEE was born 1771 in Connecticut River, Vermont, and died December 30, 1858 in Concord, Erie County, NY. He married ABIGAIL THOMPSON. She was born about 1775 in Massachusetts, and died November 1861.

> **More about BENJAMIN ALBEE:**
> Fact: March 1811, Moved from Danby, VT to Collins, NY
> Military service: soldier: War of 1812

> **More about ABIGAIL THOMPSON:**
> Census: July 29, 1850, Collins, Erie County, New York

Children of BENJAMIN ALBEE and ABIGAIL THOMPSON are:

1. JEHIAL2 ALBEE7,8, b. Danby, Rutland County, Vermont; d. before 1883, Collins, Erie County, NY.

   > **More about JEHIAL ALBEE:**
   > Fact: Drove ox team to NY.
   > Military service: soldier: War of 1812

2. ADOLPHUS ALBEE, b. Danby, Rutland County, Vermont; d. before 1883, Indiana.
3. BENJAMIN ALBEE, b. 1798, Danby, Rutland County, Vermont; d. March 22, 1889, Collins, Erie County, NY.
4. HOWARD ALBEE, b. Danby, Rutland County, Vermont; d. before 1883, Michigan.
5. ENOCH ALBEE, b. Danby, Rutland County, Vermont; d. Wisconsin.
6. RACHEL ALBEE, b. Danby, Rutland County, Vermont.
7. CLARISSA ALBEE b. Danby, Rutland County, Vermont; m. UNKNOWN WRIGHT.

   > **More about CLARISSA ALBEE:**
   > Fact: 1883 Lived in Avon, NY.

8. DIANTHA ALBEE, b. Danby, Rutland County, Vermont.

Generation No. 2

2. ADOLPHUS2 ALBEE *(BENJAMIN1)* was born in Danby, Rutland County, Vermont, and died before 1883 in Indiana. He married POLLY KING, daughter of NATHAN KING and MARY VIOL.

> More about ADOLPHUS ALBEE:
> Fact: Drove ox team to NY

Child of ADOLPHUS ALBEE and POLLY KING is:
1. RHODA3 ALBEE.

3. BENJAMIN2 ALBEE *(BENJAMIN1)* was born 1798 in Danby, Rutland County, Vermont, and died March 22, 1889 in Collins, Erie County, NY. He married RHODA WHEELER. She was born about 1802 in Vermont.

> More about BENJAMIN ALBEE:
> Education: Attended a log school house in Collins Center.
> Fact: 1883, had family of 8 children

> More about RHODA WHEELER:
> Fact: 1850, listed in census as Ruby.

Children of BENJAMIN ALBEE and RHODA WHEELER are:
1. JOHN C3 ALBEE, b. October 1821, Collins, Erie County, New York; m. JEANETTE52, about 187852; b. May 1829, Indiana.
2. HENRY ALBEE52, b. about 1826, Collins, Erie County, New York.
3. EMILY ALBEE52, b. about 1828, Collins, Erie County, New York.
4. ADOLPHUS ALBEE52, b. about 1829, Collins, Erie County, New York.
5. HORACE ALBEE52, b. about 1831, Collins, Erie County, New York.
6. ENOCH ALBEE52, b. about 1833, Collins, Erie County, New York.
7. FANNY ALBEE52, b. about 1835, Collins, Erie County, New York.
8. ALLEN ALBEE52, b. about 1837, Collins, Erie County, New York.

4. HOWARD2 ALBEE *(BENJAMIN1)* was born in Danby, Rutland County, Vermont, and died before 1883 in Michigan. He married VICENA FAY. She was born 1808 in Geneseo, Livingston County, NY, and died January 18, 1886 in Albee Township, Saginaw County, Michigan.

> More About VICENA FAY:
> Fact: 1870, Census list her as Bianca.

Children of HOWARD ALBEE and VICENA FAY are:
1. HOWARD JODSON3 ALBEE, b. July 24, 1824, Geneseo, Livingston County, NY; d. May 11, 1902, Albee Township, Saginaw County, Michigan.
2. THEODORE BENJAMIN ALBEE, b. June 05, 1828, Collins, Erie County, New York; d. June 25, 1864, Shelbyville, Shelby County, Indiana.
3. JEANETTE ALBEE, b. May 28, 1830, Collins, Erie County, New York.
4. MARIETTE ALBEE, b. May 28, 1830, Collins, Erie County, New York.
5. WILLIAM CLINTON ALBEE, b. March 29, 1833, Collins, Erie County, New York; d. March 09, 1878, Albee Township, Saginaw County, Michigan.
6. CORYDON FAY ALBEE, b. October 11, 1835, Collins, Erie County, New York.
7. HENRIETTA ALBEE, b. February 14, 1840, Collins, Erie County, New York; d. October 15, 1847, Collins, Erie County, New York.
8. NAPOLEAN BONAPARTE ALBEE, b. November 16, 1845, Collins, Erie County, New York; d. October 07, 1849.

5. **ENOCH2 ALBEE** *(BENJAMIN1)* was born in Danby, Rutland County, Vermont, and died in Wisconsin. He married ALMIRA HAZARD. She was born about 1807 in New York.

Children of ENOCH ALBEE and ALMIRA HAZARD are:
1. PERRY3 ALBEE, b. March 18, 1847, Collins, Erie County, New York; d. February 16, 1914.
2. EZRA ALBEE, b. about 1833, Collins, Erie County, New York.
3. JANE ALBEE60, b. about 1836, Collins, Erie County, New York.
4. SUSAN ALBEE, b. about 1844, Collins, Erie County, New York.
5. BYRON ALBEE, b. about 1846, Collins, Erie County, New York.

6. **RACHEL2 ALBEE** *(BENJAMIN1)* was born in Danby, Rutland County, Vermont. She married HENRY PALMERTON November 28, 1816 in Collins, Erie County, NY. He was born 1794 in Eastern New York State, and died September 09, 1870 in Collins, Erie County, NY.

    More about RACHEL ALBEE:
    Fact: 1883 Lived in Collins, Erie County, NY.

    More about HENRY PALMERTON:
    Burial: Collins Center cemetery, town of Collins, Erie County, NY.
    Fact: about 1811, Came to Collins, NY.
    Military service: soldier: War of 1812.

Children of RACHEL ALBEE and HENRY PALMERTON are:
1. SARAH E3 PALMERTON, b. March 14, 1829, Collins, Erie County, NY; m. JAMES F BEVERLY, July 1879, Collins, Erie County, NY.
2. JULIA ANN PALMERTON, b. January 15, 1819, Collins, Erie County, NY; m. MEDAD TOWILEGAR.

> **More about JULIA ANN PALMERTON:**
> Fact: 1883 Lived in Angola, Erie County, NY.

3. WARREN A PALMERTON, b. December 04, 1820, Collins, Erie County, NY; d. September 25, 1822, Collins, Erie County, NY.
4. ALBERT T PALMERTON, b. February 17, 1833, Collins, Erie County, NY; d. November 19, 1852, Collins, Erie County, NY.
5. DAVID AKINS, b. September 18, 1822; d. 1876, Collins, Erie County, NY.

> **More about DAVID AKINS:**
> Adoption: By the Henry Palmerton Family.

7. **DIANTHA2 ALBEE** *(BENJAMIN1)* was born in Danby, Rutland County, Vermont. She married ISAAC HUNT 1831 in New York, son of DANIEL HUNT and MERCY. He was born June 14, 1808 in Pittstown, Rensselaer County, NY.

> **More about DIANTHA ALBEE:**
> Fact: 1883 Lived in Collins, Erie County, NY.

> **More about ISAAC HUNT:**
> Fact: Bound to Smith Bartlett at the age of 17.

Children of DIANTHA ALBEE and ISAAC HUNT are:
1. WARREN P3 HUNT, b. March 23, 1832, Collins, Erie County, NY.

> **More about WARREN P HUNT:**
> Fact: 1883 Lived in Idaho.

2. CLARISSA HUNT, b. June 02, 1836, Collins, Erie County, NY; m. REED CLARK; b. about 1834, Collins, Erie County, NY.

> **More about CLARISSA HUNT:**
> Fact: 1883 Lived in Collins, Erie County, NY.

> **More about REED CLARK:**
> Fact: 1883 Lived in Collins.
> Military service: Soldier: Civil War.

3. BENJAMIN F HUNT, b. May 18, 1850, Collins, Erie County, NY.

Generation No. 3

8. RHODA3 ALBEE *(ADOLPHUS2, BENJAMIN1)*. She married PHILANDER PIERCE January 10, 1841, son of CHARLES PIERCE and BETSY. He was born August 31, 1818 in Hamburg, Erie County, NY.

> **More about PHILANDER PIERCE:**
> Fact: 1836 Came to Collins, NY.

Children of RHODA ALBEE and PHILANDER PIERCE are:

1. LYMAN4 PIERCE, b. January 22, 1842, Collins, Erie County, NY; d. Collins, Erie County, NY.

   > **More about LYMAN PIERCE:**
   > Fact: Died Young.

2. MYRON PIERCE, b. October 26, 1842, Collins, Erie County, NY; m. ABBIE FORD.

   > **More about MYRON PIERCE:**
   > Fact: 1883, owned farm formerly owned by his father.

3. ABIGAIL PIERCE, b. April 11, 1847, Collins, Erie County, NY.
4. ALICE PIERCE, b. December 01, 1853; m. MILTON B SHERMAN.

   > **More about ALICE PIERCE:**
   > Adoption: she was adopted by the Pierce family.
   > Fact: 1883 Lived in Collins Center, Erie County, NY.

9. WILLIAM CLINTON3 ALBEE *(HOWARD2, BENJAMIN1)* was born March 29, 1833 in Collins, Erie County, New York, and died March 09, 1878 in Albee Township, Saginaw County, Michigan. He married PHEBE. She was born about 1836 in Michigan.

> **More about WILLIAM CLINTON ALBEE:**
> Fact: Albee Township, Michigan was named for him.

Children of WILLIAM ALBEE and PHEBE are:

1. THEODORE4 ALBEE, b. about 1858, Albee, Saginaw County, Michigan.
2. CORDONI ALBEE, b. about 1868, Albee, Saginaw County,

10. **BENJAMIN F3 HUNT** *(DIANTHA2 ALBEE, BENJAMIN1)* was born May 18, 1850 in Collins, Erie County, NY. He married FLORENCE CANFIELD 1872. She was born February 1850 in Concord, Erie County, NY.

>**More about BENJAMIN F HUNT:**
>Fact: 1883, Lived with his father in Collins, NY.

Children of BENJAMIN HUNT and FLORENCE CANFIELD are:
1. IRA B4 HUNT, b. 1874, Collins, Erie County, NY.
2. CORRIDAN F HUNT, b. 1877, Collins, Erie County, NY; d. September 1881, Collins, Erie County, NY.
3. CORIDAN F HUNT, b. 1877, Collins, Erie County, NY; d. September 1881, Collins, Erie County, NY.

Generation No. 4

11. **ABIGAIL4 PIERCE** *(RHODA3 ALBEE, ADOLPHUS2, BENJAMIN1)* was born April 11, 1847 in Collins, Erie County, NY. She married LUZERNE CLARK. He was born about 1845 in Collins, Erie County, NY.

>**More about ABIGAIL PIERCE:**
>Fact: 1883 Lived in Collins, Erie County, NY.
>
>**More about LUZERNE CLARK:**
>Fact: 1883 Lived in Collins.
>Military service: Soldier: Civil War.

Child of ABIGAIL PIERCE and LUZERNE CLARK is:
1. EUNICE5 CLARK, b. about 1869, Collins, Erie County, NY.

Descendants of John Allen

Descendants of John Allen

Generation No. 1

1. **JOHN1 ALLEN**

    More about JOHN ALLEN:
    Fact: From Rhode Island

Children of JOHN ALLEN are:
   1. ZOETH2 ALLEN, b. about 1759; d. September 14, 1848, Collins, Erie County, NY.
   2. PRINCE ALLEN.
   3. JOHN JR. ALLEN, b. about 1761; d. 1852.
   4. JUDE ALLEN, d. Genesee County, NY; m. PHEBE BENSON.

       More about JUDE ALLEN:
       Fact: Settled in Genesee County, NY

   5. ISAAC ALLEN, m. SYLVIA STAPLES.

Generation No. 2

2. ZOETH2 ALLEN *(JOHN1)* was born about 1759, and died September 14, 1848 in Collins, Erie County, NY. He married JANE HARPER. She died October 05, 1822 in Collins, Erie County, NY.

> **More about ZOETH ALLEN:**
> Burial: Pine Grove Cemetery, Gowanda, town of Collins, Erie County, NY.
> Fact: 1820, Moved from Danby, VT to Collins, NY.
> Military service: Revolutionary War Soldier.
> Political: Selectmen of Danby 9 years.
>
> **More about JANE HARPER:**
> Burial: Pine Grove Cemetery, Gowanda, town of Collins, Erie County, NY.

Children of ZOETH ALLEN and JANE HARPER are:
1. SARAH3 ALLEN, b. May 16, 1796, Danby, Rutland County, Vermont; d. August 09, 1861, Collins, Erie County, NY.
2. ISAAC ALLEN, b. August 26, 1793, Danby, Rutland County, Vermont.
3. JOSHUA ALLEN.
4. SYLVIA ALLEN18, m. PETER WHITE.

> **More about SYLVIA ALLEN:**
> Fact: Moved to the Holland Purchase, NY.

5. JANE ALLEN.

3. PRINCE2 ALLEN *(JOHN1)* He married UNKNOWN BROWN, daughter of DANIEL BROWN.

Children of PRINCE ALLEN and UNKNOWN BROWN are:
1. ABIGAIL3 ALLEN.
2. DANIEL ALLEN.
3. IRA ALLEN, m. REBECCA CALKINS.
4. PRUSSIA ALLEN.
5. JOSEPH ALLEN, d. Lincoln, Vermont.
6. LAURA ALLEN.

4. JOHN JR.2 ALLEN *(JOHN1)* was born about 1761, and died 1852. He married SALLY BROWN. She was born about 1780, and died 1851.

More about JOHN JR. ALLEN:
Fact: 1815, Moved to Pawlet, Vermont

Children of JOHN ALLEN and SALLY BROWN are:
1. NATHAN3 ALLEN, b. about 1791; d. 1863.
2. ELISHA ALLEN.

Generation No. 3

5. SARAH3 ALLEN *(ZOETH2, JOHN1)* was born May 16, 1796 in Danby, Rutland County, Vermont and died August 09, 1861 in Collins, Erie County, NY. She married SMITH BARTLETT January 01, 1815 in Danby, Rutland County, Vermont, son of ABNER BARTLETT. He was born April 11, 1790 in Cumberland, Rhode Island, and died September 12, 1859 in Collins, Erie County, NY.

> **More about SARAH ALLEN:**
> Burial: Bartlett Family Cemetery, Quaker Street, Collins, Erie County, NY.
>
> **More about SMITH BARTLETT:**
> Burial: Bartlett Family Cemetery, Quaker Street, Collins, Erie County, NY.
> Fact: 30 Years as tanner & Shoemaker in Collins, NY.
> Military service: War of 1812.

Children of SARAH ALLEN and SMITH BARTLETT are:

1. ZOETH ALLEN4 BARTLETT, b. April 23, 1816, Collins, Erie County, NY; d. September 27, 1874, Collins, Erie County, NY.
2. MARY BARTLETT, b. January 14, 1817, Collins, Erie County, NY; d. January 05, 1899.
3. JANE BARTLETT32, b. November 09, 1819, Collins, Erie County, NY; d. 1857, Evans, Erie County, NY; m. GEORGE LAWTON, January 18, 1838.

    > **More about JANE BARTLETT:**
    > Fact: 1837, Alternate Marriage Year.

4. SETH F BARTLETT, b. January 04, 1822, Collins, Erie County, NY; d. 1912.
5. JOHN SMITH BARTLETT, b. September 14, 1825, Collins, Erie County, NY; d. May 02, 1917, Pasadena, Los Angeles County, California.
6. SILVA BARTLETT32, b. January 29, 1828, Collins, Erie County, NY; d. 1830.

    > **More about SILVA BARTLETT:**
    > Burial: Bartlett Family Cemetery, Quaker Street, Collins, Erie County, NY.
    > Fact: Died young.

7. RICHARD BARTLETT, b. November 28, 1829, Collins, Erie County, NY; d. 1909, Pontiac, Oakland County, Michigan.
8. SYLVIA 2ND BARTLETT, b. May 07, 1832, Collins, Erie County, NY; d. March 04, 1935.
9. . SARAH BARTLETT, b. September 24, 1834, Collins, Erie County, NY; d. May 11, 1866, Michigan.
10. ANN O BARTLETT, b. October 26, 1837, Collins, Erie County, NY; d. March 1913.

6. **ISAAC3 ALLEN** *(ZOETH2, JOHN1)* was born August 26, 1793 in Danby, Rutland County, Vermont. He married LYDIA BARTLETT April 15, 1815, daughter of ABNER BARTLETT. She was born June 25, 1793 in Cumberland, Rhode Island.

> **More about ISAAC ALLEN:**
> Fact: June 1815, Came to Collins, NY VIA FOOT.

Children of ISAAC ALLEN and LYDIA BARTLETT are:
1. DANIEL4 ALLEN, b. April 28, 1817, Collins, Erie County, NY.
2. . MARY ELLEN ALLEN, b. April 11, 1819, Collins, Erie County, NY.
3. DRUCILLA C ALLEN, b. June 18, 1821, Collins, Erie County, NY.
4. JANE ALLEN, b. March 13, 1814, Collins, Erie County, NY; d. about 1816, Collins, Erie County, NY.
5. JOSHUA ALLEN, b. March 10, 1826, Collins, Erie County, NY.

7. **JOSEPH3 ALLEN** *(PRINCE2, JOHN1)* died in Lincoln, Vermont. He married LAURA BARRETT, daughter of ALEXANDER BARRETT. She died 1858.

> **More about JOSEPH ALLEN:**
> Fact: Inherited homestead of his father

Children of JOSEPH ALLEN and LAURA BARRETT are:
1. ALEXANDER4 ALLEN, m. UNKNOWN DEKALB.

> **More about ALEXANDER ALLEN:**
> Fact: Moved to the West
>
> **More about UNKNOWN DEKALB:**
> Fact: From Granville, NY

2. CATHERINE ALLEN.
3. ISAAC ALLEN.
4. MELISSA ALLEN, m. FRANK BURNHAM.

> **More about MELISSA ALLEN:**

Fact: Moved to Canada

5. HANNAH ALLEN.
6. WILLIAM ALLEN, m. UNKNOWN TRACEY.

   More about WILLIAM ALLEN:
   Fact: Moved to Ohio

7. SAMANTHA ALLEN.
8. ELIAKIM ALLEN.

8. NATHAN3 ALLEN *(JOHN JR.2, JOHN1)* was born about 1791, and died 1863. He married JULIA LEFFINGWELL.

   More about NATHAN ALLEN:
   Fact: Settled in Pawlet, Vermont
   Religion: Methodist

   More about JULIA LEFFINGWELL:
   Fact: From Middletown

Children of NATHAN ALLEN and JULIA LEFFINGWELL are:
1. JOHN4 ALLEN.
2. CHARLES ALLEN.
3. ISAAC ALLEN.
4. HENRY ALLEN.
5. SARAH ALLEN.
6. LUCY ALLEN.
7. ELISHA ALLEN, b. about 1794; d. 1856.

Generation No. 4

9. ZOETH ALLEN4 BARTLETT *(SARAH3 ALLEN, ZOETH2, JOHN1)* was born April 23, 1816 in Collins, Erie County, NY, and died September 27, 1874 in Collins, Erie County, NY. He married RUTH WHITE 1838 in Collins, Erie County, NY. She was born 1820 in New York, and died 1898 in Collins, Erie County, NY.

> More about ZOETH ALLEN BARTLETT:
> Burial: Bartlett Family Cemetery, Quaker Street, Collins, Erie County, NY.
>
> More about RUTH WHITE:
> Burial: Bartlett Family Cemetery, Quaker Street, Collins, Erie County, NY.

Children of ZOETH BARTLETT and RUTH WHITE are:
1. CYNTHIA5 BARTLETT, b. November 25, 1838, New York.
2. JERUSHA V BARTLETT, b. about 1840, New York; d. 1867, Collins, Erie County, NY.

    > More about JERUSHA V BARTLETT:
    > Burial: Bartlett Family Cemetery, Quaker Street, Collins, Erie County, NY.

3. MILLARD FILLMORE BARTLETT32, b. 1849, New York.
4. ELWIN A BARTLETT, b. August 01, 1854, New York; d. 1922; m. FLORENCE J32, about 1877; b. October 1858, New York.
5.

10. MARY4 BARTLETT *(SARAH3 ALLEN, ZOETH2, JOHN12* was born January 14, 1817 in Collins, Erie County, NY, and died January 05, 1899. She married JOHN G PRATT January 28, 1835. He was born August 02, 1813 in Macedon, New York, and died March 20, 1869 in Collins, Erie County, NY.

> More about MARY BARTLETT:
> Fact: Lived in North Collins, NY.
>
> More about JOHN G PRATT:
> Fact: about 1825, Came to Collins, NY.

Child of MARY BARTLETT and JOHN PRATT is:
1. SMITH B5 PRATT, b. June 06, 1844, North Collins, Erie County, NY; m. MARY FOSTER32, 1868.

11. **SETH F4 BARTLETT** *(SARAH3 ALLEN, ZOETH2, JOHN1)* was born January 04, 1822 in Collins, Erie County, NY, and died 1912. He married (1) MARIETTA JANE O'BRIEN March 17, 1847. She was born April 01, 1827 in Collins, Erie County, NY, and died June 20, 1847 in Collins, Erie County, NY. He married (2) AURILLA PEASLEY 1849 in Collins, Erie County, NY. She was born December 1829 in New York, and died 1911.

> **More about SETH F BARTLETT:**
> Burial: Bartlett Family Cemetery, Quaker Street, Collins, Erie County, NY.
>
> **More about AURILLA PEASLEY:**
> Burial: Bartlett Family Cemetery, Quaker Street, Collins, Erie County, NY.

Child of SETH BARTLETT and MARIETTA O'BRIEN is:

1. ALICE5 BARTLETT, b. about 1863.

Children of SETH BARTLETT and AURILLA PEASLEY are:

2. JULIA A5 BARTLETT, b. August 30, 1850, New York; d. October 31, 1930; m. (1) NATHAN PIERCE; b. February 12, 1843, Collins, Erie County, NY; d. January 22, 1907; m. (2) NATHAN PIERCE; b. February 12, 1843; d. January 28, 1907.

   > **More about JULIA A BARTLETT:**
   > Burial: Bartlett Family Cemetery, Quaker Street, Collins, Erie County, NY.
   >
   > **More about NATHAN PIERCE:**
   > Burial: Bartlett Family Cemetery, Quaker Street, Collins, Erie County, NY.

3. ALICE B BARTLETT, b. August 02, 1862, New York; d. 1936; m. JOHN G HEIM, about 1884; b. April 1852, New York; d. 1931.

11. **JOHN SMITH4 BARTLETT** *(SARAH3 ALLEN, ZOETH2, JOHN1)* was born September 14, 1825 in Collins, Erie County, NY, and died May 02, 1917 in Pasadena, Los Angeles County, California. He married MARY KELLEY April 10, 1851. She was born 1825 in Vermont, and died 1922.

> **More about JOHN SMITH BARTLETT:**
> Fact: Was a banker in Gowanda, NY.

Children of JOHN BARTLETT and MARY KELLEY are:

1. JENNIE L5 BARTLETT, b. August 15, 1852, New York; d. 1877.
2. MELVIN BARTLETT, b. April 15, 1854; d. 1860.
3. FLORENCE MAY BARTLETT, b. 1859, Wisconsin; d. 1878.
4. LOUIS E BARTLETT, b. September 02, 1862, Wisconsin; d. July 29, 1954, Alameda, California; m. EVA R, about 1898; b. October 1873, Kansas.

> **More about LOUIS E BARTLETT:**
> Biography: Obituary: Gowanda News August 26, 1954.
> Burial: August 22, 1954, Bartlett Cemetery, Quaker Street, Collins, Erie County, NY.
> Fact: 1920, Listed in 2 Census reports one has his name being Louisa A.
>
> **More about EVA R:**
> Fact: 1920, List her name as Louisa A, same as Husband.

5. HORACE BARTLETT, b. 1863; d. 1934.
6. CLARA BARTLETT, b. October 1864, Wisconsin; d. 1935; m. HORACE K HALE, about 1896, California; b. April 1862, New York.

13. RICHARD4 BARTLETT *(SARAH3 ALLEN, ZOETH2, JOHN1)* was born November 28, 1829 in Collins, Erie County, NY, and died 1909 in Pontiac, Oakland County, Michigan. He married PHOEBE L SMITH 1851 in Collins, Erie County, NY. She was born March 08, 1832 in Collins, Erie County, New York, and died between 1910 & 1920 in Pontiac, Oakland County, Michigan.

> **More about RICHARD BARTLETT:**
> Fact: May 1865, moved to Oakland County, Michigan.
> Political: Republican.
>
> **More about PHOEBE L SMITH:**
> Fact: 1878 lived in Pontiac, Michigan.

Children of RICHARD BARTLETT and PHOEBE SMITH are:
1. CHARLES S5 BARTLETT, b. about 1849, Collins, Erie County, NY; d. July 25, 1917, Pontiac, Oakland County, Michigan; m. (1) CARRIE B OSMUN, 1881, Michigan; b. May 1862, New York; m. (2) HELENA CAITLIN, February 25, 1917, Michigan; b. March 24, 1862, Persia, Cattaraugus County, New York; d. April 25, 1939, Pontiac, Elizabeth Lake, Oakland, Michigan.
2. SMITH AUGUSTUS BARTLETT, b. May 16, 1860, New York; m. LOUISE D CARR, 1883, Pontiac, Oakland County, Michigan; b. May 1864, Germany.
3. AUGUSTA M BARTLETT, b. about 1850, Collins, Erie County, NY.

4. CHARLES BARTLETT, b. May 21, 1856, Collins, Erie County, NY.

14. SYLVIA 2ND4 BARTLETT *(SARAH3 ALLEN, ZOETH2, JOHN1)* was born May 07, 1832 in Collins, Erie County, NY, and died March 04, 1935. She married ELIJAH WILLETT.

> **More about SYLVIA 2ND BARTLETT:**
> Fact: May 02, 1832, alternate birth date.

Children of SYLVIA BARTLETT and ELIJAH WILLETT are:
1. PAUL H5 WILLETT, b. July 02, 1872.
2. PRINCE A WILLETT, b. May 1864.
3. ROBERT FAYETTE WILLETT, b. September 30, 1859.

15. SARAH4 BARTLETT *(SARAH3 ALLEN, ZOETH2, JOHN1)* was born September 24, 1834 in Collins, Erie County, NY, and died May 11, 1866 in Michigan. She married ANDREW JACKSON ALLEN 1854.

> **More about SARAH BARTLETT:**
> Fact: 1866, alternate death year.

Children of SARAH BARTLETT and ANDREW ALLEN are:
1. GEORGE PRINCE5 ALLEN, b. December 09, 1854.
2. CELLIA ALLEN, b. 1863, Michigan.
3. MARY HESTER ALLEN, b. September 14, 1858, Pompeii, Gratiot County, Michigan.
4. BARTLETT ALLEN, b. May 11, 1866, Pompeii, Gratiot County, Michigan.
5. ZOETH ALLEN, b. December 28, 1856, Pompeii, Gratiot County, Michigan.

16. ANN O4 BARTLETT *(SARAH3 ALLEN, ZOETH2, JOHN1)* was born October 26, 1837 in Collins, Erie County, NY, and died March 1913. She married GEORGE W TAYLOR 1864. He was born March 27, 1832 in Essex, Essex County, New York.

Children of ANN BARTLETT and GEORGE TAYLOR are:
1. JOSEPH B5 TAYLOR, b. April 16, 1865, Collins, Erie County, NY; m. MATTIE E; b. about 1879, New York.
2. MARION B TAYLOR, b. March 27, 1867, Collins, Erie County, NY.
3. BENJAMIN GRANT TAYLOR, b. December 27, 1872, Collins, Erie County, NY.

17. DANIEL4 ALLEN *(ISAAC3, ZOETH2, JOHN1)* was born April 28, 1817 in Collins, Erie County, NY. He married ELEANOR WELLS.

Children of DANIEL ALLEN and ELEANOR WELLS are:
1. SARAH JANE5 ALLEN, b. Collins, Erie County, NY.

    More about SARAH JANE ALLEN:
    Fact: Died at 14 years of age.

2. WALTER W ALLEN.
3. ALICE ALLEN, d. April 1881.
4. LEONARD D ALLEN.

    More about LEONARD D ALLEN:
    Fact: Moved to Michigan.

18. **MARY ELLEN4 ALLEN** *(ISAAC3, ZOETH2, JOHN1)* was born April 11, 1819 in Collins, Erie County, NY. She married BENJAMIN P WELLS. He was born about 1815.

Children of MARY ALLEN and BENJAMIN WELLS are:
1. ISAAC A5 WELLS, b. about 1840.
2. ARESTENE C WELLS, b. about 1842.
3. MARY JOSEPHINE WELLS, b. about 1844.

19. **DRUCILLA C4 ALLEN** *(ISAAC3, ZOETH2, JOHN1)* was born June 18, 1821 in Collins, Erie County, NY. She married REVEREND IRA STODDARD.

More about DRUCILLA C ALLEN:
Fact: Worked as missionary in Assam India.

More about REVEREND IRA STODDARD:
Fact: worked as missionary in Assam India.

Children of DRUCILLA ALLEN and IRA STODDARD are:
1. BERTHA5 STODDARD, b. India.
2. ELLA STODDARD, b. India.
3. IRA JOY STODDARD, b. India.

20. **JOSHUA4 ALLEN** *(ISAAC3, ZOETH2, JOHN1)* was born March 10, 1826 in Collins, Erie County, NY. He married EMELINE ETSLER. She was born November 01, 1830 in Liberty, Frederick County, Maryland.

More about JOSHUA ALLEN:
Education: Select School, Gowanda, NY.

Children of JOSHUA ALLEN and EMELINE ETSLER are:
1. CHARLES E5 ALLEN.
2. MYRON H ALLEN.
3. R HARPER ALLEN.
4. EVA ALLEN.
5. CLARA M ALLEN.

21. **CATHERINE4 ALLEN** *(JOSEPH3, PRINCE2, JOHN1)* She married EDSON VALENTINE. He died in California.

> **More about EDSON VALENTINE:**
> Fact: from Tinmouth, Vermont

Children of CATHERINE ALLEN and EDSON VALENTINE are:
1. MELISSA5 VALENTINE, m. JOHN GOODSPEED.
2. JOSEPH VALENTINE.

22. **ELISHA4 ALLEN** *(NATHAN3, JOHN JR.2, JOHN1)* was born about 1794, and died 1856. He married ANNIS STAFFORD.

> **More about ELISHA ALLEN:**
> Fact: Settled in Pawlet, Vermont.
> Political: 4 years member of legislature.

Children of ELISHA ALLEN and ANNIS STAFFORD are:
1. HORACE5 ALLEN.
2. MERRITT ALLEN.

Descendants of Abner Bartlett

Descendants of Abner Bartlett

Generation No. 1

1. **ABNER1 BARTLETT** was born in England, and died 1801 in of Smallpox in Danby, Rutland County, Vermont. He married DRUSCILLA SMITH 1798.

More about ABNER BARTLETT:
Fact: Settled 1st in Danby.

Child of ABNER BARTLETT and DRUSCILLA SMITH is:
1. SMITH2 BARTLETT, b. Danby, Rutland County, Vermont; d. 1859, Collins, Erie County, NY.

Generation No. 2

2. **SMITH2 BARTLETT** *(ABNER1)* was born in Danby, Rutland County, Vermont, and died 1859 in Collins, Erie County, NY. He married SARAH ALLEN.

> **More about SMITH BARTLETT:**
> Fact: 1812, Moved to Collins, NY.
> Religion: Quaker.

Children of SMITH BARTLETT and SARAH ALLEN are:
1. SETH F BARTLETT, b. January 04, 1822, Collins, Erie County, NY.
2. ALLEN BARTLETT.
3. ANN O BARTLETT.

Generation No. 3

3. **SETH F BARTLETT** *(SMITH2, ABNER1)* was born January 04, 1822 in Collins, Erie County, NY. He married (1) AURILLA PEASLEY. He married (2) MARGARETTA O'BRIEN 1855 in Collins, Erie County, NY. She died about 1856 in Collins, Erie County, NY.

Children of SETH BARTLETT and AURILLA PEASLEY are:
1. JULIA4 BARTLETT, m. UNKNOWN PIERCE.
2. ALICE BARTLETT, m. UNKNOWN HEIM.
3. ALTON BARTLETT, d. Collins, Erie County, NY.

>**More about ALTON BARTLETT:**
>Fact: Died at 7 yrs old.

4. **ALLEN3 BARTLETT** *(SMITH2, ABNER1)*.

Child of ALLEN BARTLETT is:
1. CYNTHIA4 BARTLETT, b. November 1838, New York; d. between1920 - 1930.

5. **ANN O3 BARTLETT** *(SMITH2, ABNER1)*. She married GEORGE W TAYLOR.

>**More about GEORGE W TAYLOR:**
>Fact: Moved to Bartlett Homestead in Collins.

Children of ANN BARTLETT and GEORGE TAYLOR are:
1. JOSEPH B4 TAYLOR.
2. MARION TAYLOR.
3. BENJAMIN GRANT TAYLOR.

Generation No. 4

6. CYNTHIA4 BARTLETT *(ALLEN3, SMITH2, ABNER1)* was born November 1838 in New York, and died between 1920 - 1930. She married NORMAN COOK 1857. He was born July 18, 1829 in Collins, Erie County, NY, and died 1889 in California.

>   **More about NORMAN COOK:**
>   Fact: About 1837, moved to Concord, NY.

Children of CYNTHIA BARTLETT and NORMAN COOK are:

1. CLARA5 COOK, b. about 1873, Collins, Erie County, NY.
2. HELEN COOK.

>   **More about HELEN COOK:**
>   Fact: Died at age 3.

7. JOSEPH B TAYLOR *(ANN O3 BARTLETT, SMITH2, ABNER1)*.

Child of JOSEPH B TAYLOR is:

1. HARMON5 TAYLOR.

>   **More about HARMON TAYLOR:**
>   Fact: Lived on Bartlett Homestead in Taylor's Hollow.

Descendants of Enoch Conger

Descendants of Enoch Conger

Generation No. 1

1. ENOCH¹ CONGER¹ was born February 02, 1758¹, and died December 05, 1826¹. He married (1) RUTH IRISH¹, daughter of DAVID IRISH. She was born October 18, 1759 in Danby, Rutland County, Vermont¹. He married (2) HANNAH KELLEY.

More about ENOCH CONGER:
Fact: 1774, Moved to Danby, Vermont
Religion: Quaker¹

More about RUTH IRISH:
Fact: 1st wife of Enoch

Children of ENOCH CONGER and HANNAH KELLEY are:
- 2. i. **DAVID² CONGER**, b. July 17, 1779, Vermont; d. February 14, 1824, Collins, Erie County, NY.
- 3. ii. **HIRAM CONGER**, b. about 1794; d. 1852, Danby, Rutland County, Vermont.
- iii. **LYDIA CONGER**, m. ROBERT BAKER.

    More about LYDIA CONGER:
    Fact: Moved to Easton, NY

- 4. iv. **NOAH CONGER**.

Generation No. 2

2. DAVID² CONGER *(ENOCH¹)¹* was born July 17, 1779 in Vermont¹, and died February 14, 1824 in Collins, Erie County, NY¹. He married RACHEL WILBER¹ in Danby, Rutland County, Vermont¹, daughter of ISAAC WILBER. She was born about 1780 in Danby, Rutland County, Vermont¹.

More about DAVID CONGER:
Burial: Wilcox Cemetery, North Collins, Erie County, NY¹
Fact: Moved from Danby, VT to Collins, NY

Children of DAVID CONGER and RACHEL WILBER are:

    i. **SALLY³ CONGER**, b. 1804, Danby, Rutland County, Vermont; m. PETER WHITE.

    More about SALLY CONGER:
    Fact: Moved to California

    More about PETER WHITE:
    Fact: May be Stephen White

    ii. **NOEL CONGER**, b. June 30, 1802, Danby, Rutland County, Vermont; m. (1) BETSEY SHERMAN; m. (2) SUSAN OGDEN.

    More about NOEL CONGER:
    Fact: 1883, Lived in North Collins, NY

5.   iii. **ABRAM FORD CONGER**, b. October 25, 1811, Danby, Rutland County, Vermont; d. January 20, 1887, North Collins. Erie County, NY.

    iv. **MARION CONGER**, b. 1801, Danby, Rutland County, Vermont; d. 1880, Minnesota; m. JAMES RAY.

    v. **MOSES CONGER**, b. 1806, Danby, Rutland County, Vermont; d. about 1818, North Collins, Erie County, NY.

    More about MOSES CONGER:
    Fact: Died at age 12

    vi. **ANN CONGER**, b. 1808, Danby, Rutland County, Vermont; m. ANSIL FORD.

    More about ANN CONGER:
    Fact: Moved to Michigan

vii. **GEORGE CONGER**, b. 1810, Danby, Rutland County, Vermont; m. ELIZA HOAG.

More about GEORGE CONGER:
Fact: 1883, Lived in Michigan

6. viii. **STEPHEN CONGER**, b. January 28, 1814, Tinmouth, Rutland County, Vermont; d. January 25, 1877, North Collins, Erie County, NY.

3. HIRAM² CONGER *(ENOCH¹)* was born about 1794, and died 1852 in Danby, Rutland County, Vermont. He married (1) ANNA BARRETT, daughter of ALEXANDER BARRETT. He married (2) THEDA.

More about THEDA:
Fact: was a widow when she married Hiram

Children of HIRAM CONGER and ANNA BARRETT are:
    i. **PAULINA³ CONGER**, m. GIDEON TABER.
    ii. **LAURA ANN CONGER**.
    iii. **ANNA CONGER**.
    iv. **SOPHRONIA CONGER**, m. NICHOLAS COOK.

    More about NICHOLAS COOK:
    Fact: From Wallingford, Vermont

4. NOAH² CONGER *(ENOCH¹)* He married (2) HANNAH GRIFFITH, daughter of DAVID GRIFFITH.

More about NOAH CONGER:
Fact: Quaker Preacher

Child of NOAH CONGER is:
7. i. **ANSON G³ CONGER**, b. October 26, 1812, Danby, Rutland County, Vermont; d. February 12, 1880, Collins, Erie County, NY.

Children of NOAH CONGER and HANNAH GRIFFITH are:
8. ii. **ALMOND D³ CONGER**, b. January 12, 1815, Danby, Rutland County, Vermont.
    iii. **ENOCH CONGER**.
    iv. **DAVID CONGER**.
    v. **RUTH CONGER**.
    vi. **LYDIA CONGER**.
    vii. **ALLEN CONGER**, m. UNKNOWN GORTON.

More about ALLEN CONGER:
Fact: 1869, Moved west

Generation No. 3

5. ABRAM FORD[3] CONGER *(DAVID[2], ENOCH[1])*[1] was born October 25, 1811 in Danby, Rutland County, Vermont[1], and died January 20, 1887 in North Collins, Erie County, NY[1]. He married ANNA HUNT[1] June 1830[1]. She was born about March 1812 in New York[1], and died April 19, 1895 in North Collins, Erie County, NY[1].

More about ABRAM FORD CONGER:
Burial: Wilcox Cemetery, North Collins, Erie County, NY[1]
Fact: 1883, lived in North Collins, NY

More about ANNA HUNT:
Burial: Wilcox Cemetery, North Collins Erie County, NY

Children of ABRAM CONGER and ANNA HUNT are:

    i. **EMILY[4] CONGER[1]**, b. about 1833, Collins, Erie County, NY[1]; m. LYMAN CLARK[1]; b. November 16, 1816, Gloucester, Providence County, Rhode Island[1].

    More about EMILY CONGER:
    Fact: 1883, Lived at Princeton, Green Lake County, Wisconsin

9.   ii. **MARY JANE CONGER**, b. about 1838, Collins, Erie County, NY.
10. iii. **GEORGE D CONGER**, b. December 10, 1842, Collins, Erie County, NY; d. October 26, 1908, At his home in Springville, town of Concord, Erie County, NY.
    iv. **FIDELIA CONGER[1]**, b. about 1846, Collins, Erie County, NY[1]; d. before. 1883[1]; m. JOHN GOODELL[1].
11.   v. **ABRAM FORD CONGER**, b. March 1850, Collins, Erie County, NY; d. 1911.

6. STEPHEN[3] CONGER *(DAVID[2], ENOCH[1])* was born January 28, 1814 in Tinmouth, Rutland County, Vermont, and died January 25, 1877 in North Collins, Erie County, NY. He married FIDELIA EATON 1834. She was born February 25, 1813 in Springville, Concord, Erie County, NY.

Children of STEPHEN CONGER and FIDELIA EATON are:

    i. **STEPHEN W[4] CONGER**, b. March 12, 1847, North Collins, Erie County, NY; m. MARY E LANDON, 1866.
    ii. **RACHEL CONGER**, b. June 24, 1838, North Collins, Erie County, NY.

iii. **PORTIA CONGER**, b. September 08, 1850, North Collins, Erie County, NY.

7. ANSON G³ CONGER *(NOAH², ENOCH¹)* was born October 26, 1812 in Danby, Rutland County, Vermont, and died February 12, 1880 in Collins, Erie County, NY. He married PORTIA WHITE September 1845, daughter of ISAAC WHITE.

More about ANSON G CONGER:
Fact: Taught school in Vermont
Political: Bet. 1859 - 1860, Collins Supervisor
Religion: Quaker

Children of ANSON CONGER and PORTIA WHITE are:
12.   i. **ELLA PORTIA⁴ CONGER**, b. 1853.
    ii. **J ANSON CONGER**, b. about 1862, Collins, Erie County, NY; d. 1864, Collins, Erie County, NY.
13.   iii. **EMMA M CONGER**, b. 1857, Collins, Erie County, NY.

8. ALMOND D³ CONGER *(NOAH², ENOCH¹)* was born January 12, 1815 in Danby, Rutland County, Vermont. He married SOPHRONIA POTTER April 21, 1839 in Collins, Erie County, NY by James Parkinson, Esq., daughter of PETER POTTER.

More about ALMOND D CONGER:
Fact: 1869, Lived in Collins, NY
Political: 21 Years Assessor in Collins

More about SOPHRONIA POTTER:
Fact: From Collins, NY

Children of ALMOND CONGER and SOPHRONIA POTTER are:
14.   i. **NOAH⁴ CONGER**, b. April 26, 1841, Collins, Erie County, NY; d. April 27, 1873, Collins, Erie County, NY.
    ii. **HANNAH M CONGER**, b. August 31, 1844, Collins, Erie County, NY.
    iii. **LYDIA E CONGER**, b. November 07, 1847, Collins, Erie County, NY; d. July 08, 1868.
    iv. **ANDREW W CONGER**, b. June 05, 1850, Collins, Erie County, NY; m. FLORENCE CLARK.

      More about ANDREW W CONGER:
      Fact: 1883, Lived in Collins, NY

    v. **ALBERT E CONGER**, b. October 24, 1857, Collins, Erie County, NY.
    vi. **JESSIE M CONGER**, b. December 15, 1859, Collins, Erie County, NY; m. RUSSELL F BRYANT.

More about JESSIE M CONGER:
Fact: 1883, Lived in Springville, NY

Generation No. 4

9. MARY JANE⁴ CONGER (ABRAM FORD³, DAVID², ENOCH¹)¹ was born Abt. 1838 in Collins, Erie County, NY¹. She married CHARLES BARTHOLOMEW¹.

More about MARY JANE CONGER:
Fact: 1883, Lived in North Collins, NY¹

Children of MARY CONGER and CHARLES BARTHOLOMEW are:
  i. **MELVERN HILL⁵ BARTHOLOMEW¹**, b. July 01, 1862, North Collins, Erie County, NY¹.

  More about MELVERN HILL BARTHOLOMEW:
  Fact: Born on same day as Battle of Malvern Hill

  ii. **FLORENCE BARTHOLOMEW¹**.

  More about FLORENCE BARTHOLOMEW:
  Fact: Died at age 2

  iii. **EMMA BARTHOLOMEW¹**.

10. GEORGE D⁴ CONGER (ABRAM FORD³, DAVID², ENOCH¹)¹ was born December 10, 1842 in Collins, Erie County, NY¹, and died October 26, 1908 in At his home in Springville, town of Concord, Erie County, NY¹. He married DIANTHA SAMPSON¹ February 16, 1865¹.

More about GEORGE D CONGER:
Fact: 1863, Moved to Springville, NY became dealer in carriages
Military service: August 08, 1861, enlisted: Co A NY Volunteers

Child of GEORGE CONGER and DIANTHA SAMPSON is:
  i. **CORA MAY⁵ CONGER¹**, b. August 10, 1869, Concord, Erie County, NY¹.

11. ABRAM FORD⁴ CONGER (ABRAM FORD³, DAVID², ENOCH¹)¹ was born March 1850 in Collins, Erie County, NY¹, and died 1911¹. He married ROSETTA H about 1870¹. She was born April 1852 in New York¹, and died 1913¹.

More about ABRAM FORD CONGER:
Burial: North Collins Cemetery, North Collins, Erie County, NY

More about ROSETTA H:

Burial: North Collins Cemetery, North Collins, Erie County, NY

Child of ABRAM CONGER and ROSETTA H is:
  i. **CLARENCE[5] CONGER[1]**, b. August 1871, North Collins, Erie County, NY[1]; m. BEULAH[1], about 1894[1]; b. March 1872, New York[1].

12. ELLA PORTIA[4] CONGER *(ANSON G[3], NOAH[2], ENOCH[1])* was born 1853. She married CHARLES WATERHOUSE GOODYEAR March 23, 1876. He was born October 15, 1846 in Cortland, Cortland County, NY.

More about ELLA PORTIA CONGER:
Fact: From Collins Center, Erie County, NY

More about CHARLES WATERHOUSE GOODYEAR:
Fact: 1883, Lived in Buffalo, NY
Political: Bet. April 01, 1875 - October 01, 1877, Erie County District attorney
Religion: First Presbyterian

Children of ELLA CONGER and CHARLES GOODYEAR are:
  i. **ANSON CONGER[5] GOODYEAR**, b. June 20, 1877.
  ii. **ESTHER GOODYEAR**, b. May 20, 1881.
  iii. **CHARLES W JR GOODYEAR**.
  iv. **BRADLEY ANSON CONGER GOODYEAR**.

13. EMMA M[4] CONGER *(ANSON G[3], NOAH[2], ENOCH[1])* was born 1857 in Collins, Erie County, NY. She married CHARLES W LAPHAM 1880.

More about CHARLES W LAPHAM:
Fact: From Chicago, Illinois

Child of EMMA CONGER and CHARLES LAPHAM is:
  i. **ANSON G[5] LAPHAM**, b. July 14, 1881.

14. NOAH[4] CONGER *(ALMOND D[3], NOAH[2], ENOCH[1])* was born April 26, 1841 in Collins, Erie County, NY, and died April 27, 1873 in Collins, Erie County, NY. He married MARY ANN HEATH May 08, 1864.

More about MARY ANN HEATH:
Fact: From Collins, NY

Children of NOAH CONGER and MARY HEATH are:
  i. **WILLIE H[5] CONGER**, b. August 30, 1866, Collins, Erie County, NY; d. April 11, 1870, Collins, Erie County, NY.
  ii. **ADA CONGER**, b. May 04, 1871, Collins, Erie County, NY; d. July 27, 1875, Collins, Erie County, NY.
  iii. **ALMON N CONGER**, b. March 27, 1873, Collins, Erie County, NY.

Generation No. 5

7. CLARENCE[5] CONGER *(ABRAM FORD[4], ABRAM FORD[3], DAVID[2], ENOCH[1])*[1] was born August 1871 in North Collins, Erie County, NY[1]. He married BEULAH[1] about 1894[1]. She was born March 1872 in New York[1].

Children of CLARENCE CONGER and BEULAH are:
    i. **EUNICE R[6] CONGER[1]**, b. February 1896, New York[1].
    ii. **ELIZABETH CONGER[1]**, b. May 1900, New York[1].

Descendants of Sylvanus Cook

Descendants of Sylvanus Cook

Generation No. 1

1. SYLVANUS¹ COOK was born January 14, 1795 in Richmond, Massachusetts, and died April 19, 1885 in Collins, Erie County, NY. He married NANCY PHILLIPS daughter of CHAD PHILLIPS and SARAH WELLER. She was born December 06, 1796 in Danby, Rutland County, Vermont, and died December 16, 1873 in Collins, Erie County, NY.

More about SYLVANUS COOK:
Burial: Shaw Cemetery, Collins, Erie County, NY
Fact: Moved with family from MA to Danby, VT
Military service: Colonel

More about NANCY PHILLIPS:
Burial: Shaw Cemetery, Collins, Erie County, NY

Children of SYLVANUS COOK and NANCY PHILLIPS are:
- i. **ARTHUR² COOK.**
- 2. ii. **HIRAM COOK**, b. September 28, 1834, New York; d. December 22, 1920.
- 3. iii. **SALLY COOK**, b. 1819; d. 1909.
- iv. **CHAUNCEY COOK**, b. about 1841, Collins, Erie County, NY.
- 4. v. **SYLVANUS B COOK**, b. about 1831, Collins, Erie County, NY.
- vi. **ALONZO COOK**, b. about 1837, Collins, Erie County, NY.

Generation No. 2

2. HIRAM[2] COOK *(SYLVANUS[1])* was born September 28, 1834 in New York, and died December 22, 1920. He married (1) EMILY. She was born Abt. 1844 in New York. He married (2) MELISSA A. BATES Bet. 1850 - 1860 in Collins, Erie County, NY. She was born November 08, 1835 in Collins, Erie County, New York, and died November 28, 1871 in Collins, Erie County, New York.

More about HIRAM COOK:
Burial: Shaw Cemetery, Foster Road, town of Collins, Erie County, NY

More about MELISSA A. BATES:
Burial: November 1871, Shaw Cemetery

Children of HIRAM COOK and EMILY are:
  i. **ETHEL[3] COOK**, b. about 1878, Collins, Erie County, NY.
  ii. **UNNAMED COOK**, b. about June 1880, Collins, Erie County, NY.

3. SALLY[2] COOK *(SYLVANUS[1])* was born 1819, and died 1909. She married ANDREW PHILLIPS. He was born 1820, and died 1905.

More about SALLY COOK:
Burial: Shaw Cemetery, Collins, Erie County, NY

More about ANDREW PHILLIPS:
Burial: Shaw Cemetery, Collins, Erie County, NY

Children of SALLY COOK and ANDREW PHILLIPS are:
  i. **EMMA L[3] PHILLIPS**, b. September 07, 1860, Collins, Erie County, NY; d. March 25, 1881, Collins, Erie County, NY.

   More about EMMA L PHILLIPS:
   Burial: Shaw Cemetery, Collins, Erie County, NY

  ii. **SETH PHILLIPS**, b. about 1845, Collins, Erie County, NY.
  iii. **JUSTUS PHILLIPS**, b. about 1852, Collins, Erie County, NY.

4. SYLVANUS B[2] COOK *(SYLVANUS[1])* as born about 1831 in Collins, Erie County, NY. He married RHODA[129]. She was born about 1832 in New York.

Child of SYLVANUS COOK and RHODA is:
  i. **LUCETTA[3] COOK**, b. about 1852, Collins, Erie County, NY.

Descendants of Samuel Wildbore

Descendants of Samuel Wildbore

Generation No. 1

1. SAMUEL¹ WILDBORE was born about 1590 in Braintree, Essex County, England¹, and died September 29, 1656 in Boston, Massachusetts. He married ANN BRADFORD in England, daughter of THOMAS BRADFORD. She was born in England.

More about SAMUEL WILDBORE:
Fact: Bef. 1633, Came to America
Political: 1634, Boston, Ma Assessor of taxes

More about ANN BRADFORD:
Fact: December 1633, Admitted to Church in Boston, MA

Child of SAMUEL WILDBORE and ANN BRADFORD is:
2.   i. **WILLIAM² WILBER**, b. May 21, 1630, Little Compton, Rhode Island; d. April 15, 1710, Tiverton, Newport County, Rhode Island.

Generation No. 2

2. WILLIAM² WILBER *(SAMUEL¹ WILDBORE)* was born May 21, 1630 in Little Compton, Rhode Island, and died April 15, 1710 in Tiverton, Newport County, Rhode Island. He married MARTHA HOLMES⁷ 1653 in Newport County, Rhode Island.

More about WILLIAM WILBER:
Fact: Not mentioned in his father's will

Child of WILLIAM WILBER and MARTHA HOLMES is:
3.   i. **BENJAMIN³ WILBER**, b. 1670, Tiverton, Newport County, Rhode Island; d. 1729, Portsmouth, Rhode Island.

Generation No. 3

3. BENJAMIN[3] WILBER *(WILLIAM[2], SAMUEL[1] WILDBORE)* was born 1670 in Tiverton, Newport County, Rhode Island, and died 1729 in Portsmouth, Rhode Island. He married ELIZABETH HEAD[1] November 02, 1710 in Rhode Island[1]. She was born about 1690 in Rhode Island[1], and died 1734.

Child of BENJAMIN WILBER and ELIZABETH HEAD is:
4.   i.   **GEORGE[4] WILBER**, b. September 23, 1718, Portsmouth, Rhode Island; d. 1777.

Generation No. 4

4. GEORGE[4] WILBER *(BENJAMIN[3], WILLIAM[2], SAMUEL[1] WILDBORE[1])* was born September 23, 1718 in Portsmouth, Rhode Island, and died 1777. He married DEBORAH RANDALL about 1747 in Little Compton, Newport County, Rhode Island. She was born September 24, 1721 in Gloucester, Essex County, Massachusetts.

Child of GEORGE WILBER and DEBORAH RANDALL is:
    i.   **ISAAC[5] WILBER**[2,3], b. December 24, 1748; d. July 27, 1835; m. (1) ELIZABETH BAGDLEY; b. December 05, 1758[3]; d. August 13, 1848; m. (2) ELIZABETH BAGDLEY; b. December 05, 1758[3]; d. August 13, 1848.

Generation No. 5

1. ISAAC⁵ WILBER *(GEORGE⁴, BENJAMIN³, WILLIAM², SAMUEL¹ WILDBORE)* was born December 24, 1748, and died July 27, 1835. He married (1) ELIZABETH BAGDLEY. She was born December 05, 1758², and died August 13, 1848. He married (2) ELIZABETH BAGDLEY. She was born December 05, 1758, and died August 13, 1848.

Child of ISAAC WILBER and ELIZABETH BAGDLEY is:
2.   i. **STEPHEN⁶ WILBER**, b. July 27, 1777; d. August 21, 1862, Collins, Erie County, NY.

Generation No. 6

2. STEPHEN⁶ WILBER *(ISAAC⁵, GEORGE⁴, BENJAMIN³, WILLIAM², SAMUEL¹ WILDBORE)* was born July 27, 1777, and died August 21, 1862 in Collins, Erie County, NY. He married MARY KING October 16, 1800 in Danby, Rutland County, Vermont. She was born March 06, 1782, and died October 1866 in Collins, Erie County, NY.

More about STEPHEN WILBER:
Burial: Collins Center Cemetery, Collins Center, Erie County, New York
Fact: May 1810, Came from Danby, Vermont to Scipio, NY

More about MARY KING:
Burial: Collins Center Cemetery, town of Collins, Erie County, NY
Fact: 1868, Alternate death year

Children of STEPHEN WILBER and MARY KING are:

- 3. i. **DAVID⁷ WILBER**, b. December 16, 1800, Danby, Rutland County, Vermont.
- 4. ii. **JOHN WILBER**, b. September 27, 1802, North Hero Island, Lake Champlain, Vermont; d. 1888, Collins, Erie County, NY.
- iii. **PAULINA WILBER⁶**, b. June 20, 1804, Danby, Rutland County, Vermont; d. 1875; m. ROBERT ARNOLD⁶.
- iv. **ALMA WILBER**, b. April 26, 1806, Danby, Rutland County, Vermont; m. THOMPKINS WHITE⁶.
- v. **GEORGE R WILBER**, b. August 07, 1808, Danby, Rutland County, Vermont; d. 1867, Wayne County, Michigan⁶; m. JANE LAPHAM⁶.
- 5. vi. **ELIZABETH WILBER**, b. September 25, 1810, Danby, Rutland County, Vermont; d. March 08, 1882, Collins, Erie County, NY.
- vii. **JAMES WILBER⁶**, b. January 25, 1813, Collins, Erie County, NY⁶; d. February 1815, Collins, Erie County, NY⁶.
- viii. **JOB WILBER**, b. January 18, 1815, Collins, Erie County, NY; d. Bef. 1883.
- ix. **DANIEL WILBER⁶**, b. April 12, 1817, Collins, Erie County, NY⁶; d. October 1826, Collins, Erie County, NY⁶.
- 6. x. **JOSHUA WILBER**, b. June 19, 1819, Collins, Erie County, NY.
- 7. xi. **STEPHEN WILBER**, b. July 14, 1821, Collins, Erie County, NY.
- xii. **MARY WILBER**, b. July 10, 1820, Collins, Erie County, NY; d. October 22, 1868.
- xiii. **ALMA WILBER⁶**, b. April 25, 1806, Danby, Rutland County, vermont⁶; m. THOMPKINS WHITE⁶.

8.   xiv. **JOB WILBER**, b. January 15, 1815, Collins, Erie County, NY; d. before 1883.
       xv. **MARY WILBER**, b. June 10, 1820, Collins, Erie County, NY; d. October 22, 1868; m. CHARLES STEWART; b. about 1824, New York.

Generation No. 7

3. DAVID⁷ WILBER *(STEPHEN⁶, ISAAC⁵, GEORGE⁴, BENJAMIN³, WILLIAM², SAMUEL¹ WILDBORE)* was born December 16, 1800 in Danby, Rutland County, Vermont. He married POLLY H RUSSELL. She was born 1808.

Children of DAVID WILBER and POLLY RUSSELL are:

    i. **DANIEL⁸ WILBER**, b. May 31, 1830; d. 1910; m. (1) UNKNOWN HAZARD; m. (2) UNKNOWN HAZZARD.

    More about DANIEL WILBER:
    Burial: Collins Center Cemetery, Collins Center, Erie County, New York
    Fact: 1883, Lived in Collins, NY

    ii. **LUCY R WILBER**, b. May 22, 1835; m. THOMAS RUSSELL.

    More about LUCY R WILBER:
    Fact: 1883, Lived in Farmington, Oakland County, Michigan

    iii. **ROBERT A WILBER**, b. July 12, 1844; m. EUNICE ALLEN, September 04, 1866.

    More about ROBERT A WILBER:
    Fact: 1883, Lived in Collins, NY
    Military service: Soldier: Civil War

4. JOHN⁷ WILBER *(STEPHEN⁶, ISAAC⁵, GEORGE⁴, BENJAMIN³, WILLIAM², SAMUEL¹ WILDBORE)* was born September 27, 1802 in North Hero Island, Lake Champlain, Vermont, and died 1888 in Collins, Erie County, NY. He married CHRISTINA STRANG 1826 in Collins, Erie County, NY; daughter of JOHN STRANG. She was born about 1810 in New York.

More about JOHN WILBER:
Burial: Collins Center Cemetery, Collins Center, Erie County, New York
Fact: 1811, Came to Collins with his parents

More about CHRISTINA STRANG:
Fact: ancestors fled from France due to Religious persecution

Children of JOHN WILBER and CHRISTINA STRANG are:
9.   i. **EMILY⁸ WILBER**, b. November 24, 1827, Collins, Erie County, NY.
10.   ii. **MARY E WILBER**, b. April 18, 1839; Collins, Erie County, NY.

11.   iii. **ALBERT WILBER**, b. February 28, 1832, Collins, Erie County, NY; d. 1927.
12.   iv. **JAMES WILBER**, b. February 20, 1835, Collins, Erie County, NY.
13.   v. **PAULINA WILBER**, b. August 16, 1840, Collins, Erie County, NY; d. 1879, Collins, Erie County, NY.
     vi. **EUGENE WILBER**, b. January 24, 1844, Collins, Erie County, NY; m. MARY BARRY.

More about EUGENE WILBER:
Fact: 1883, Lived in Collins, NY

14.   vii. **M EUGENE WILBER**, b. January 24, 1844, Collins, Erie County, NY.

5. ELIZABETH[7] WILBER *(STEPHEN[6], ISAAC[5], GEORGE[4], BENJAMIN[3], WILLIAM[2], SAMUEL[1] WILDBORE)* was born September 25, 1810 in Danby, Rutland County, Vermont, and died March 08, 1882 in Collins, Erie County, NY. She married (1) STUKLEY HUDSON. She married (2) STUCKLEY HUDSON March 08, 1832 in Collins, Erie County, NY. He was born March 21, 1812 in Chenango County, NY, and died February 09, 1868 in Collins, Erie County, NY.

More about ELIZABETH WILBER:
Burial: Mount Pleasant Cemetery, Collins, Erie County, NY
Fact: 1883, Lived in Collins Center, NY

More about STUCKLEY HUDSON:
Burial: Mount Pleasant Cemetery, Collins, Erie County, NY

Child of ELIZABETH WILBER and STUCKLEY HUDSON is:
15.   i. **STEPHEN WILBER[8] HUDSON**, b. May 23, 1834, Collins, Erie County, NY; d. November 03, 1866, Collins, Erie County, NY.

6. JOSHUA[7] WILBER *(STEPHEN[6], ISAAC[5], GEORGE[4], BENJAMIN[3], WILLIAM[2], SAMUEL[1] WILDBORE)* was born June 19, 1819 in Collins, Erie County, NY. He married CLARINDA. She was born about 1820 in New York.

More about JOSHUA WILBER:
Fact: 1883, Lived in Dayton, Cattaraugus County, NY

Children of JOSHUA WILBER and CLARINDA are:
    i. **GEORGE[8] WILBER[18]**, b. about 1841, Collins, Erie County, NY.
    ii. **ELLEN WILBER[18]**, b. about 1845, Michigan.
    iii. **DANIEL WILBER[18]**, b. about 1848, Illinois.
    iv. **IMMOGENE WILBER[18]**, b. about April 1850, New York.

7. STEPHEN⁷ WILBER *(STEPHEN⁶, ISAAC⁵, GEORGE⁴, BENJAMIN³, WILLIAM², SAMUEL¹ WILDBORE)* was born July 14, 1821 in Collins, Erie County, NY. He married ANN. She was born about 1828 in New York.

More about STEPHEN WILBER:
Fact: 1883, Lived in Northwest Michigan

More about ANN:
Fact: May be Amy

Child of STEPHEN WILBER and ANN is:
    i. **ALICE⁸ WILBER**[18], b. about 1849, Collins, Erie County, NY[18].

8. JOB⁷ WILBER *(STEPHEN⁶, ISAAC⁵, GEORGE⁴, BENJAMIN³, WILLIAM², SAMUEL¹ WILDBORE)* was born January 15, 1815 in Collins, Erie County, NY, and died before 1883. He married DEBORA JANE KNIGHT. She was born June 01, 1817 in Otsego County, NY.

Child of JOB WILBER and DEBORA KNIGHT is:
    i. **CHAUNCEY⁸ WILBER**[18], b. about 1838, Collins, Erie County, NY.

Generation No. 8

9. EMILY[8] WILBER *(JOHN[7], STEPHEN[6], ISAAC[5], GEORGE[4], BENJAMIN[3], WILLIAM[2], SAMUEL[1] WILDBORE)* was born November 24, 1827 in Collins, Erie County, NY. She married WILLIAM T POPPLE. He was born January 04, 1822 in Ontario, Orleans County, NY.

More about EMILY WILBER:
Fact: 1883, Lived in Collins, NY

More about WILLIAM T POPPLE:
Fact: Tanner & Currier

Children of EMILY WILBER and WILLIAM POPPLE are:
     i. **WALLACE L[9] POPPLE[18]**, b. about 1849, New York.
     ii. **CHARLES L POPPLE[18]**.

10. MARY E[8] WILBER *(JOHN[7], STEPHEN[6], ISAAC[5], GEORGE[4], BENJAMIN[3], WILLIAM[2], SAMUEL[1] WILDBORE)* was born April 18, 1839 in Collins, Erie County, NY. She married WILLIAM C POTTER 1853. He was born 1828 in Collins, Erie County, NY.

More about MARY E WILBER:
Fact: 1883, Lived in Waupaca County, Wisconsin

More about WILLIAM C POTTER:
Fact: Admitted to bar
Military service: Served in Army

Children of MARY WILBER and WILLIAM POTTER are:
     i. **HERBERT W[9] POTTER[18]**.
     ii. **CATHERINE POTTER[18]**.

11. ALBERT[8] WILBER *(JOHN[7], STEPHEN[6], ISAAC[5], GEORGE[4], BENJAMIN[3], WILLIAM[2], SAMUEL[1] WILDBORE)* was born February 28, 1832 in Collins, Erie County, NY, and died 1927. He married RUTH BARTLETT. She was born Abt. 1836 in Vermont.

More about ALBERT WILBER:
Burial: Collins Center Cemetery, town of Collins, Erie County, NY
Fact: 1883, Lived in Collins, NY

Child of ALBERT WILBER and RUTH BARTLETT is:
  i. **WILLIS E[9] WILBER**, b. about 1857, Collins, Erie County, NY.

12. **JAMES[8] WILBER** *(JOHN[7], STEPHEN[6], ISAAC[5], GEORGE[4], BENJAMIN[3], WILLIAM[2], SAMUEL[1] WILDBORE)* was born February 20, 1835 in Collins, Erie County, NY. He married LYDIA CHASE 1857 in Collins, Erie County, NY. She died October 06, 1896 in Collins, Erie County, NY.

More about JAMES WILBER:
Education: Collins, Erie County, NY
Fact: 1883, Lived in Collins, NY

Children of JAMES WILBER and LYDIA CHASE are:
  i. **JOHN C[9] WILBER**.
  ii. **WARD J WILBER**.
  iii. **JENNIE WILBER**, m. UNKNOWN KAMERRER.
  iv. **GRETCHEN WILBER**.

13. **PAULINA[8] WILBER** *(JOHN[7], STEPHEN[6], ISAAC[5], GEORGE[4], BENJAMIN[3], WILLIAM[2], SAMUEL[1] WILDBORE)* was born August 16, 1840 in Collins, Erie County, NY, and died 1879 in Collins, Erie County, NY. She married (1) ALBERT BRUCE. He was born 1840 in Collins, Erie County, NY, and died 1868 in Collins, Erie County, NY. She married (2) JOHN P JOHNSON. She married (3) FRANK P JOHNSON.

More about ALBERT BRUCE:
Burial: Collins Center Cemetery, town of Collins, Erie County, NY

Child of PAULINA WILBER and ALBERT BRUCE is:
  i. **FRED[9] BRUCE**.

14. **M EUGENE[8] WILBER** *(JOHN[7], STEPHEN[6], ISAAC[5], GEORGE[4], BENJAMIN[3], WILLIAM[2], SAMUEL[1] WILDBORE[8]* was born January 24, 1844 in Collins, Erie County, NY. He married MARY BARRY 1867.

More about M EUGENE WILBER:
Education: Gowanda Academy
Fact: 1883, Lived in Collins, NY

Children of M WILBER and MARY BARRY are:
  i. **FRANK[9] WILBER[18]**.
  ii. **HENRY WILBER[18]**.
  iii. **PAULINE C WILBER[18]**.

15. STEPHEN WILBER⁸ HUDSON *(ELIZABETH⁷ WILBER, STEPHEN⁶, ISAAC⁵, GEORGE⁴, BENJAMIN³, WILLIAM², SAMUEL¹ WILDBORE)* was born May 23, 1834 in Collins, Erie County, NY, and died November 03, 1866 in Collins, Erie County, NY. He married CHARLOTTE BLAIR about 1856 in Collins, Erie County, NY. She was born about 1838 in Ashtabula, Ashtabula County, Ohio, and died September 11, 1857 in Collins, Erie County, NY.

More about STEPHEN WILBER HUDSON:
Burial: Mount Pleasant Cemetery, Collins, Erie County, NY

More about CHARLOTTE BLAIR:
Burial: Mount Pleasant Cemetery, Collins, Erie County, NY

Child of STEPHEN HUDSON and CHARLOTTE BLAIR is:

i. **GRACE⁹ HUDSON**, b. March 11, 1859, Collins, Erie County, NY; d. June 02, 1948, Collins, Erie County, NY; m. HERBERT A REYNOLDS, 1878, Collins, Erie County, NY; b. December 21, 1852, Collins, Erie County, NY; d. August 17, 1921, Collins, Erie County, NY.

More about GRACE HUDSON:
Fact: about 1830, Moved to Sardinia to Scrabble Hill Collins

Descendants of Abram Lapham

Descendants of Abram Lapham

Generation No. 1

1. **ABRAM1 LAPHAM**

>**More about ABRAM LAPHAM:**
>Fact: 1809 came to Collins from Genesee County

Children of ABRAM LAPHAM are:
    1. STEPHEN2 LAPHAM, m. MARGARET ROBINSON, Genesee County, New York.

>**More about STEPHEN LAPHAM:**
>Fact: 1810 came to Collins

    2. JOHN LAPHAM.
    3. DANIEL LAPHAM.
    4. SAVERY LAPHAM.
    5. IRA LAPHAM.

Descendants of Luke Sr. Crandall

Descendants of Luke Sr. Crandall

Generation No. 1

1. LUKE SR¹ CRANDALL died in Collins, Erie County, NY.

More about LUKE SR CRANDALL:
Fact: 1815 Came to Collins from Vermont
Military service: Soldier: Revolutionary War

Children of LUKE SR CRANDALL are:
    i. **DARIUS² CRANDALL**, d. Collins, Erie County, NY.

        More about DARIUS CRANDALL:
        Fact: 1815 Came to Collins from Vermont

2.   ii. **WILLIAM CRANDALL**, b. 1795, Danby, Rutland County, Vermont; d. 1861, Collins, Erie County, NY.
    iii. **PHILANDER CRANDALL**, d. Collins, Erie County, NY.

        More about PHILANDER CRANDALL:
        Fact: 1815 Came to Collins from Vermont

    iv. **LUKE JR CRANDALL**, d. Illinois.

        More about LUKE JR CRANDALL:
        Fact: about 1811, Came to Collins from Vermont
        Military service: Soldier: War of 1812

Generation No. 2

2. WILLIAM² CRANDALL *(LUKE SR¹)* was born 1795 in Danby, Rutland County, Vermont, and died 1861 in Collins, Erie County, NY. He married BETSEY HARRINGTON. She was born in Vermont, and died 1855 in Collins, Erie County, NY.

More about WILLIAM CRANDALL:
Fact: 1815 Came to Collins from Vermont

More about BETSEY HARRINGTON:
Fact: 1856, Alternate death date

Children of WILLIAM CRANDALL and BETSEY HARRINGTON are:

  i. **WATSON³ CRANDALL.**

   More about WATSON CRANDALL:
   Fact: 1883, Lived in Missouri
   Military service: Soldier: Civil War

  ii. **JAMES CRANDALL.**

   More about JAMES CRANDALL:
   Fact: 1883, Lived in Missouri

  iii. **DELOS CRANDALL.**

   More about DELOS CRANDALL:
   Fact: 1883, Lived in Missouri

  iv. **JEFFERSON CRANDALL.**

   More about JEFFERSON CRANDALL:
   Fact: 1883, Lived in Collins, Erie County, NY

  v. **PHILANDER CRANDALL.**

   More about PHILANDER CRANDALL:
   Fact: 1883, Lived in Stuban County, NY

  vi. **RACHEL CRANDALL.**

> **More about RACHEL CRANDALL:**
> Fact: 1883, Lived in Wisconsin

vii. **PHOEBE CRANDALL.**

> **More about PHOEBE CRANDALL:**
> Fact: 1883, Lived in Illinois

viii. **SOPHIA CRANDALL.**

> **More about SOPHIA CRANDALL:**
> Fact: 1883, Lived in North Collins

3. ix. **OLIVE CRANDALL.**

Generation No. 3

3. OLIVE³ CRANDALL *(WILLIAM², LUKE SR¹)* She married HIRAM STAGE.

More about OLIVE CRANDALL:
Fact: 1883, Lived in Collins Center, Erie County, NY

More about HIRAM STAGE:
Fact: Had 3 sons all lived in Buffalo, NY
Military service: Soldier: Civil War

Child of OLIVE CRANDALL and HIRAM STAGE is:
  i. **FLORA⁴ STAGE**, m. UNKNOWN COOPER.

   More about FLORA STAGE:
   Fact: 1883, Lived in Concord, Erie County, NY

BIBLIOGRAPHY

BIBLIOGRAPHY

- Abbott, J. S. C. (1903). *Christopher Columbus*. New York: University society.
- Abler, T. S. (2007). *Cornplanter: chief warrior of the Allegany Senecas*. The Iroquois and their neighbors. Syracuse, N.Y.: Syracuse University Press.
- Adams, C. K. (1892). *Christopher Columbus: his life and his work*. Makers of America. New York: Dodd, Mead and company.
- *Albany Advertiser;* (1816), various weather related articles.
- Albee, R. S. (1920). *Albee family records*. Washington, D.C.: [R.S. Albee].
- Alnorca. (May 17, 1934). *An Old Homestead East of Collins Center*. Collins Historical Department.
- Alnorca. (1930). *The Neighborhood of the Little Red School House*. Collins Historical Department.
- American Philosophical Society. (1957). *Proceedings of the American Philosophical Society held at Philadelphia for promoting useful knowledge. Cumulative index [to] volumes 76-100, 1936-1956.* Philadelphia: The Society.
- Anderson, J. J., & Flick, A. C. (1902). *A short history of the state of New York*. New York: Maynard, Merrill.
- Armstrong, J., & Roth, R. (2006). *The American story: 100 true tales from American history / by Jennifer Armstrong ; illustrated by Roger Roth*. New York: A. A. Knopf.
- Axelrod, A. (2000). *The complete idiot's guide to the American Revolution*. Indianapolis, IN: Alpha Books.
- Barber, J. W., & Howe, H. (1841). *Historical collections of the state of New York: containing a general collection of the most interesting facts, traditions, biographical sketches, anecdotes, &c. relating to its history and antiquities, with geographical descriptions of every township in the state; illustrated by 230 engravings*. New York: S. Tuttle.
- Beverley, R., & Wright, L. B. (1947). *The history and present state of Virginia*. Chapel Hill: Published for the Institute of Early American History and Culture at Williamsburg, Va., by the University of North Carolina Press.
- Biddle, R. (1915). *A memoir of Sebastian Cabot*. Philadelphia: Carey and Lea.
- *Biographical record: this volume contains Biographical sketches of leading citizens of Oakland County Michigan*. (2002). Salem, Mass: Higginson Book Co.
- Blacksnake, Williams, B., & Abler, T. S. (1989). *Chainbreaker: the Revolutionary War memoirs of Governor Blacksnake as told to*

- *Benjamin Williams. American Indian lives.* Lincoln: University of Nebraska Press.
- Ancestry.com; on-line data base. *Border Crossings from Canada to U.S.: 1895 – 1956.*
- Bonnie, M. P., & Cutter, W. R. (1969). *Index of Genealogical and family history of northern New York, compiled under the supervision of William Richard Cutter.* Lubbock, Tex: M.P. Bonnie.
- Buffalo Evening News; articles, various issues.
- Buffalo Evening News; Obituaries, various issues.
- Briggs, E. (1883). *History of the original town of Concord: being the present towns of Concord, Collins, N. Collins, and Sardinia, Erie County, New York.* Rochester, N.Y.: Union and Advertiser Co.'s Print.
- Brodhead, J. R. (1853). *History of the state of New York.* New York: Harper & Brothers.
- Brown, Nora, & Wood, Carlotta (February 21, 1935) *By the Old Mill Stream.* Collins Historical Department.
- Brown, Nora, & Wood, Carlotta (August 26, 1937) *History of Scrabble Hill.* Collins Historical Department.
- Caller, J. M., & Ober, M. A. (1881). *Genealogy of the descendants of Lawrence and Cassandra Southwick of Salem, Mass.: the original emigrants, and the ancestors of the families who have since borne his name.* [S.l: s.n.].
- Caswell, H. S. C. (1892). *Our life among the Iroquois Indians.* Boston: Congressional Sunday-school and Pub. society.
- Cheney, A. P. (1884). *A Review of the first fourteen years of the Historical, Natural History and Library Society of South Natick, Mass.: with the field-day proceedings of 1881-1882-1883.* South Natick, Mass: Printed for the Society.
- Clarke, G. K. (1912). *History of Needham, Massachusetts, 1711-1913.* Clarke, G. K. (1900). *Epitaphs from graveyards in Wellesley (formerly West Needham.), North Natwick and Saint Mary's churchyard in Newton Lower Falls, Massachusetts; with genealogical and biographical notes.*
- Cambridge, Ma: University Press.
- Colket, M. B. (1975). *Founders of early American families: emigrants from Europe, 1607-1657.* Cleveland: General Court of the Order of Founders and Patriots of America.
- Columbus, C., Markham, C. R., & Toscanelli, P. d. P. (1893). *The journal of Christopher Columbus (during his first voyage, 1492-93) and documents relating to the voyages of John Cabot and Gaspar Corte Real.* Works issued by the Hakluyt Society, no. LXXXVI. London: Printed for the Hakluyt Society.
- Craig, N. B. (1851). *The history of Pittsburgh with a brief notice of its facilities of communication, and other advantages for commercial*

and manufacturing purposes ; with two maps. Pittsburgh: J.H. Mellor.
- Crane, E. B. (1907). *Historic homes and institutions and genealogical and personal memoirs of Worcester county, Massachusetts*. New York: Lewis Pub. Co.
- Crockett, W. H. (1921). *Vermont, the Green mountain state, Vol. 1-4*. New York: The Century history company, Inc.
- Cullum, G. W. (1980). *Campaigns of the War of 1812-15, against Great Britain, sketched and criticized with brief biographies of the American engineers*. New York: J. Miller.
- Cutter, W. R. (1908). *Historic homes and places and genealogical and personal memoirs relating to the families of Middlesex County, Massachusetts*. New York: Lewis historical Pub. Co.
- Cutter, W. R. (1995). *Genealogical and personal memoirs relating to the families of Boston and eastern Massachusetts*. Baltimore, Md: Reprinted for Clearfield Co. by Genealogical Pub. Co.
- CUTTER, W. R. (1995). *Genealogical and personal memoirs relating to the families of Boston and eastern Massachusetts*. Baltimore, Md, Reprinted for Clearfield Co. by Genealogical Pub. Co.
- Dodd. Jordan: Massachusetts Marriages, 1633-1850
- Dunlap, W. (1970). *History of the New Netherlands, Province of New York, and State of New York, to the adoption of the Federal Constitution*. Burt Franklin research & source works series, 538. New York: B. Franklin.
- Edinburgh: Privately printed. (1887) *Two rare tracts relating to the state of New York, 1609-15; viz: Champlain's expeditions to northern and western New York (1632) A letter from a gentleman of the city of New York concerning the late revolution (1698)*.
- Field, E. (1902). *State of Rhode Island and Providence Plantations at the end of the century: a history*. Boston: Mason Pub. Co.
- Fleming, T. J. (2006). *Everybody's revolution: a new look at the people who won America's freedom*. New York: Scholastic Nonfiction.
- Florida Death Index: 1877 – 1998.
- French, J. H., & Place, F. (1860). *Gazetteer of the State of New York: embracing a comprehensive view of the geography, geology, and general history of the State, and a complete history and description of every county, city, town, village, and locality. With full tables of statistics*. Syracuse, N.Y.: R.P. Smith.
- Hale Collection: Headstone at the "Old Ashford Cemetery" at Ashford, CT., Located back of Church.
- Hallahan, W. H. (2000). *The day the American Revolution began: 19 April 1775*. New York: William Morrow.

- Harris, A. (1872). *A biographical history of Lancaster County ... being a history of early settlers and eminent men of the county; as also much other unpublished historical information, chiefly of a local character.* Lancaster, Pa: E. Barr & Co.
- Higgins, R. (1996). *The Niagara frontier: its place in U.S. and Canadian history.* North American heritage series. Kitchener, Ont: Upney Editions.
- Hill, D. G. (1998). *The record of births, marriages and deaths and intentions of marriage in the town of Dedham, volumes 1 & 2, 1635-1845, with an appendix containing records of marriages before 1800, returned from other towns under the statute of 1857.* [Boston, Mass: New England Historic Genealogical Society.
- Hodgson, G. (2006). *A great & godly adventure: the Pilgrims & the myth of the first Thanksgiving.* New York: Public Affairs.
- Hopkins, T. (1903). *The Kelloggs in the Old World and the New.* San Francisco, Calif: Sunset Press and Photo Engraving Co.
- Ingersoll, C. J. (1845). *Historical sketch of the second war between the United States of America, and Great Britain: declared by Act of Congress, the 18th of June, 1812, and concluded by peace, the 15th of February, 1815.* Philadelphia: Lea and Blanchard.
- Irving, W. (1973). *The life and voyages of Christopher Columbus, to which are added those of his companions.* [New York: AMS Press].
- Jackson, J. N., Burtniak, J., & Stein, G. P. (2003). *The mighty Niagara: one river, two frontiers.* Amherst, N.Y.: Prometheus Books.
- Janney, S. M. (1861). *History of the religious Society of Friends from its rise to the year 1828.* Philadelphia: T.E. Zell.
- Jennings, F. (1984). *The ambiguous Iroquois empire: the Covenant Chain confederation of Indian tribes with English colonies from its beginnings to the Lancaster Treaty of 1744.* New York: Norton.
- Johnson, C. (1876). *Centennial history of Erie County, New York: being its annals from the earliest recorded events to the hundredth year of American independence.* Buffalo, N.Y.: Print. House of Matthews & Warren.
- Johnson, E. (1881). *Legends, traditions and laws, of the Iroquois, or Six nations, and history of the Tuscarora Indians.* Lockport, N.Y.: Union Printing and Pub. Co.
- JSTOR (Organization). (1995). *JSTOR.* New York, N.Y.: JSTOR. http://www.jstor.org/.
- Kelsey, R. W. (1917). *Friends and the Indians, 1655-1917.* Philadelphia: Associated Executive Committee of Friends on Indian Affairs.
- Kimm, S. C. (1900). *The Iroquois: a history of the Six nations of New York.* Middleburgh: N.Y., Press of P.W. Danforth.

- Latter Day Saints Genealogical Library. Various microfilms from worldwide genealogy project, preserving worldwide genealogical records.
- Lee, G. C., & Thorpe, F. N. (1903). *The History of North America*. Philadelphia: Printed for subscribers only by G. Barrie & Sons.
- Lossing, B. J. (1968). *The Empire State; a compendious history of the Commonwealth of New York*. Hartford: American Pub. Co.
- Lossing, B. J., Lossing, B. J., & Lossing, B. J. (1869). *Lives of celebrated Americans: comprising biographies of three hundred and forty eminent persons*. Hartford [Conn.]: Belknap.
- Lynn (Mass.). 1905. *Vital records of Lynn, Massachusetts, to the end of the year 1849*. Salem, Mass: Essex Institute.
- Martin, J. P., Roop, C., Roop, P., Kubinyi, L., & Martin, J. P. (2001). *The diary of Joseph Plumb Martin, a Revolutionary War soldier*. New York: Benchmark Books.
- McGee, T. D. (1855). *The Catholic history of North America. Five discourses. To which are added two discourses on the relations of Ireland and America*. Boston: P. Donahoe
- McKnight, W. J. (1905). *A pioneer outline history of northwestern Pennsylvania*. Philadelphia: Printed by J.B. Lippincott Co.
- McLaughlin, A. C., & Hart, A. B. (1914). *Cyclopedia of American government*. New York: D. Appleton and Co.
- Medway (Mass. : Town). (1905). *Vital records of Medway, Massachusetts, to the year 1850*. Boston: Pub. by the New-England historic genealogical Society, at the charge of the Eddy town-record fund.
- *Memorial and family history of Erie County, New York*. (1906). New York: Genealogical Publ. Co.
- New England Historic Genealogical Society. (1874). *The New England historical and genealogical register*. Boston: New England Historic Genealogical Society.
- Norton, A. T. (1879). *History of Sullivan's campaign against the Iroquois; being a full account of that epoch of the revolution*. Lima, N.Y.: A.T. Norton.
- Olson, J. E., & Bourne, E. G. (1906). *The Northmen, Columbus, and Cabot, 985-1503. Original narratives of early American history*. New York: Charles Scribner's Sons.
- Osgood, C. S., & Batchelder, H. M. (1879). *Historical sketch of Salem, 1626-1879*. Salem: Essex Institute.
- Pestana, C. G. (1991). *Quakers and Baptists in colonial Massachusetts*. Cambridge [England]: Cambridge University Press.
- Randall, S. S. (1870). *History of the state of New York, for the use of common schools, academies, normal and high schools, and other seminaries of instruction*. New York: J.B. Ford and Co.

- Roberts, E. H. (1887). ... *New York: the planting and the growth of the Empire state.* ... Boston and New York: Houghton, Mifflin and company.
- Roosevelt, T. (1987). *The naval War of 1812, or, The history of the United States Navy during the last war with Great Britain: to which is appended an account of the Battle of New Orleans.* Classics of naval literature. Annapolis, Md: Naval Institute Press
- Rutherford, M. L. (1907). *The South in history and literature; a handbook of southern authors, from the settlement of Jamestown, 1607, to living writers.* [Atlanta, Ga: Franklin-Turner Co.
- Salem, Mass: Essex Antiquarian. *The Essex Antiquarian.* (1903).
- Schouler, J. (1896). *Historical briefs.* New York: Dodd, Mead.
- Sherman, R., & Seldon, P. (1997). *The complete idiot's guide to classical music.* New York, NY: Alpha Books.
- Severance, F. H. (1903). *Old trails on the Niagara frontier.* Cleveland: Burrows Bros
- Shillinglaw, J. J. (1850). *A narrative of Arctic discovery, from the earliest period to the present time. With the details of the measures adopted by Her Majesty's government for the relief of the expedition under Sir John Franklin.* London: W. Shoberl.
- Smith, G. (1862). *History of Delaware County, Pennsylvania, from the discovery of the territory included within its limit to the present time, with a notice of the geology of the county, and catalogues of its minerals, plants, quadrupeds, and birds, written under the direction and appointment of the Delaware County Institute of Science.* Philadelphia: Printed by H.B. Ashmead.
- Snowden, J. R. (1867). *The Cornplanter memorial: an historical sketch of Gy-ant-wa-chia -- the Cornplanter, and of the six nations of Indians.* Harrisburg, Pa: Singerly & Myers, State Printers.
- Social Security Death Index. On-line.
- Stearns, E. S., Whitcher, W. F., & Parker, E. E. (1908). *Genealogical and family history of the state of New Hampshire: a record of the achievements of her people in the making of a commonwealth and the founding of a nation.* New York, Chicago: Lewis Pub. Co.
- Stone, W. L. (1841). *Life and times of Red-Jacket, or Sa-go-ye-wat-ha being the sequel to the history of the Six Nations.* New York: Wiley and Putnam.
- Stone, W. L., & Stone, W. L. (1865). *The life and times of Sir William Johnson, bart.* Albany: J. Munsell.
- Sullivan, J., Williams, E. M., Conklin, E. P., & Fitzpatrick, B. (1927). *History of New York State, 1523-1927.* New York: Lewis Historical Pub. Co.
- The Dedham Historical Society. *The Dedham Historical Register, Old Burial Ground, Dedham, Norfolk County, Massachusetts.*

- Turner, O. (1852). *History of the pioneer settlement of Phelps & Gorham's purchase, and Morris' reserve.* Rochester: W. Alling
- Turner, O. (1849). *Pioneer history of the Holland purchase of western New York: embracing some account of the ancient remains ... and a history of pioneer settlement under the auspices of the Holland company; including reminiscences of the war of 1812; the origin, progress and completion of the Erie canal, etc., etc., etc.* Buffalo: Jewett, Thomas & Co. [etc.].
- *United Stated Federal Census.* Various years, States, Counties and Towns.
- Van Rensselaer, S., & Armstrong, J. (1836). *A narrative of the affair of Queenstown; in the war of 1812. With a review of the strictures on that event, in a book entitled, "Notices of the war of 1812.".* New-York: Leavitt, Lord & Co.
- *United States War Center.* Located online at: http://www.cwc.lsu.edu/other/stats/warcost.htm
- Van Rensselaer, S. (1909). *History of the city of New York in the seventeenth century.* New York: The Macmillan Company.
- Weare, G. E. (1897). *Cabot's discovery of North America.* London: John Macqueen.
- Weller, E. (1941). *North Collins remembers: a comprehensive history of North Collins and vicinity.* Gowanda, N.Y.: Niagara Frontier Pub. Co.
- White, T. C. (1898). *Our county and its people; a descriptive work on Erie County, New York.* [Boston]: Boston history Co.
- White, T. (1902). *Our wonderful progress: the world's triumphant knowledge and works, a vast treasury and compendium of the achievements of man and the works of nature.* [S.l: s.n.].
- Williams, J. C. (1869). *The history and map of Danby, Vermont.* Rutland, Vt: Printed by McLean & Robbins.
- Wimer, J. (1841). *Events in Indian history: beginning with an account of the origin of the American Indians, and early settlements in North America, and embracing concise biographies of the principal chiefs and head-sachems of the different Indian tribes, with narratives and captivities ... also an appendix containing the statistics of the population of the U. States, and an Indian vocabulary; illustrated with eight fine engravings.* Lancaster [Pa.]: G. Hills.
- Winsor, J. (1891). *Christopher Columbus and how he received and imparted the spirit of discovery.* Boston: Houghton, Mifflin & Co.
- Winsor, J. (1884). *Narrative and critical history of America.* Boston: Houghton, Mifflin and Co.

- Winthrop, J., & Hosmer, J. K. (1908). *Winthrop's journal, "History of New England," 1630-1649.* Original narratives of early American history. New York: C. Scribner's Sons.
- Wooster, M. (1991). *Somewhere to go on Sunday: a guide to natural treasures in western New York & southern Ontario.* Buffalo, N.Y.: Prometheus Books.
- Young, A. W. (1875). *History of Chautauqua County, New York: from its first settlement to the present time ; with numerous biographical and family sketches.* Buffalo, N.Y.: Printing house of Matthews & Warren.

ABOUT THE AUTHOR

LINDA [NUNWEILER] MUNRO would be born six weeks prior to her scheduled birth after her mother suffered a slip and fall incident. Complications from the fall combined with dysphagia and cancer left a devastating prognosis for the infant, general practitioners and specialists agreed that the tiny infant would never see her first birthday. ....

Having been a *sickly* child, Linda would learn to read at an extremely young age; her mind always questioning, then seeking answers. ...

Linda Munro began her freelance writing career as an author of short romance stories. After several years, as a means of expanding her writing knowledge, she moved into freelance reporting for local weekly newspapers where she fell in love with non-fiction writing. After all, she states; *"Fact is by far more interesting than fiction!"*

At the age of thirty-six, she would place her writing career on hold in order to pursue a college education; earning a Bachelor's of Science in the field of history and communications. Shortly after completing her course of study, an injury, combined with life-long physical problems, would dramatically change her life.

Spiraling physically, emotionally and financially out of control, Munro would grasp for normalcy by utilizing her three great loves; reading, history and her grandchildren; slowly bringing herself back into a new form of normalcy. Mixing two long-term goals; updating the history of the once magnificent town which has been her home for more than half a century and leaving her grandchildren with at least a glimpse of both the Town of Collins and the America that she grew up in, for indeed it was *a different world.*

Knowing that God left her here for a reason, it would take some time for her to figure out just what that reason was to be. *"It may have taken a lot of years, but I have always known in my heart that the Town of Collins and the people who lived here were an interesting special crew. I finally have realized that sharing what I have learned about the town and her people is what I was put on earth to complete."*

www.ingramcontent.com/pod-product-compliance
Lightning Source LLC
Chambersburg PA
CBHW051625230426
43669CB00013B/2187